TOWARDS A CHRISTIAN PHILOSOPHY

STUDIES IN PHILOSOPHY
AND THE HISTORY OF PHILOSOPHY

General editor: Jude P. Dougherty

**Studies in Philosophy
and the History of Philosophy**   **Volume 21**

Towards a Christian Philosophy

by Joseph Owens, C.Ss.R.

THE CATHOLIC UNIVERSITY OF AMERICA PRESS
Washington, D.C.

Library of Congress Cataloging-in-Publication Data

Owens, Joseph.
    Towards a Christian philosophy / by Joseph Owens.
        p.   cm.—(Studies in philosophy and the history of
    philosophy ; v. 21)
        Bibliography: p.
        Includes indexes.
        1. Christianity—Philosophy.   2. Catholic Church and philosophy.
    3. Thomists.   I. Title.   II. Series.
    B21.S78   vol. 21
    [BR100]
    100 s—dc20
    [190]   89-10008
    ISBN 0-8132-0708-8 (alk. paper)

Contents

Non tento, domine, penetrare altitudinem tuam, quia nullatenus comparo illi intellectum meum; sed desidero aliquatenus intelligere veritatem tuam, quam credit et amat cor meum.

St. Anselm, *Proslogion* 1
(ed. Schmitt, *Op. Om.* 1, 100.15–18)

I am not attempting, Lord, to penetrate your sublimity, for to no degree do I match my understanding with it; but I do long to understand to some degree your truth, which my heart believes and loves.

Acknowledgments

The author gratefully acknowledges the permission of the original publisher to reprint in this volume the works listed below.

1. "The Christian Philosophy of the *Aeterni Patris*," *Revista de Filosofia* 13 (1980), 229–46.

2. "Need Philosophy Hold That Nature Is Something Complete?" in *Essays Honoring Allan B. Wolter*, ed. William A. Frank and Girard J. Etzkorn (Bonaventure, N.Y.: Franciscan Institute, 1985), 221–44.

3. "The Notion of Catholic Philosophy," *Antigonish Review* 1 (197?), 112–40.

4. "The Distinguishing Feature in Catholic Philosophy," in *The Papin Gedenkschrift: Dimensions in the Human Religious Quest—Essays in Memory of Joseph Papin*. Edited by Joseph Armenti, Univ. Microfilms Int., Michigan (Vols. I–IV); 1986–1989.

5. "Scholasticism—Then and Now," *Proceedings of the American Catholic Philosophical Association*, 1966, 1–12.

6. "Confronto fra la Coscienza Cristiana e la Retta Ragione Aristotelica," in *La Coscienza Morale Oggi: Omaggio al Prof. Domenico Capone*. Editiones Academiae Alphonsianae Roma (Rome: Accademia Alfonsiana, 1987), 109–143.

7. "God in Philosophy Today," in *God, Man and Philosophy: A Symposium*, ed. Carl W. Grindel (New York: St. John's University, 1971), 41–51.

8. "This Truth Sublime," in *Speaking of God: Essays on Belief and Unbelief*, ed. Denis Dirscherl, S.J. (Milwaukee: Bruce, 1967), 128–58.

9. "Aquinas—Darkness of Ignorance in the Most Refined Notion of God," in *Bonaventure and Aquinas: Enduring Philosophers*, edited and with an introduction by Robert W. Shahan and Francis J. Kovach (Norman, Okla.: University of Oklahoma Press, 1976), 69–86.

10. "'Cause of Necessity' in Aquinas' *Tertia Via*," *Mediaeval Studies* 33 (1971), 21–45.

11. "The Special Characteristic of the Scotistic Proof that God Exists," *Analecta Gregoriana* 67 (1954), 311–27.

12. "Soul as Agent in Aquinas," *New Scholasticism* 48 (1974), 40–72.

13. "Aquinas on the Inseparability of Soul from Existence," *New Scholasticism* 61 (1987), 249–70.

Preface

The present volume collects and reprints thirteen previously published papers that bear on a unitary topic aptly designated as "Christian philosophy." The first six of the papers deal with the nature of the topic itself. The remaining seven illustrate it at work in instantiations that may be regarded as typical. The papers retain their original titles, except that the titles in Spanish and Italian are now in English, and those of the second and fifth papers have been changed for adaptation to the new surroundings.

The rationale of the project emerges from the traditional conception of western philosophy. Philosophy, in Cicero's phrasing, was knowledge of "things human and divine" and of their controlling causes. Against the background of Jewish, Christian, and Islamic belief, the "things human and divine" were open to both theological and philosophical study. They constituted a universe known in its natural aspects through characteristically human cognition, and in its divine dimension through supernatural revelation. Anyone facing the world in this composite setting will be doing violence to his or her thought in attempting to philosophize as though an explanation of the one integrated world could be rounded out successfully apart from persistent attention to its supernatural elevation. A world penetrated through and through by the supernatural cannot be understood satisfactorily when the naturally knowable aspects are regarded as making it a complete and finished object. The supernatural dimension, in its turn, is not exempt from the naturally knowable categorizations of existence, being, action, quality, relation, and the like. It invites philosophical study under those facets.

This situation gives rise to a discipline radically and drastically different from sacred theology. It calls for a procedure in which the reasoning is based solely on naturally knowable premises. Any recourse to divinely revealed premises to initiate or to support the reasoning is most strictly forbidden it. It functions entirely on the philosophical level all the while it is dealing with aspects that are believed. The setting for the present volume is explicitly Christian. But the thematic tenets should hold proportionally for Islamic or Jewish philosophy, and may be extended to other religious backgrounds.

In this tenor an "Introduction" to the collection examines historically and doctrinally the intricate problem of Christian philosophy. At the end, an "Epilogue" seeks to cull from the papers both motives and methods for continued pursuit of the enterprise, in projecting the papers as work towards a viable Christian philosophy. Permission from the respective editors to reprint the papers is gratefully acknowledged.

J.O.

TOWARDS A CHRISTIAN PHILOSOPHY

Introduction

I

"Christian philosophy" is an expression that has been in use since the time of St Augustine,[1] with widely varying senses. By the last half of the nineteenth century it could stand in Catholic circles for a type of the rational discourse contradistinguished on the one hand from sacred theology and on the other hand from the mathematical, natural, life, linguistic, and historical sciences. That systematic way of locating the generic "philosophy" was quite in accord with the already current division of the academic disciplines. With "philosophy" so taken as the noun, the adjective "Christian" envisaged a notably distinct type or species of the general pursuit.

Very broadly, "Christian philosophy" was in this way regarded as philosophy that was proper to Christian life and tradition.[2] In that

1. "Obsecro te, non sit honestior philosophia Gentium, quam nostra Christiana, quae una est vera philosophia, quandoquidem studium vel amor sapientiae significatur hoc nomine." *Contra Julianum pelagianum* 4.14.72; PL 44, 774. On the pre-history of the notion back to Tatian in the second century A.D., see Maurice Nédoncelle, *Is There a Christian Philosophy?* trans. Illtyd Trethowan (New York: Hawthorn Books, 1960), pp. 30–40. For a survey of its senses that have philosophic interest, see Nédoncelle, pp. 44–81; 100–114. It has also been used to mean the monastic life, infra, chap. 1, n. 4. Coverage of nineteenth-century Catholic writers who have produced what is now considered to be Christian philosophy may be found in *Christliche Philosophie im katholischen Denken des 19. und 20. Jahrhunderts*, ed. Emerich Coreth et al. (Graz: Verlag Styria, 1987–88), with a history (1, 29–45) of the concept "Christian philosophy" by Heinrich M. Schmidinger, and a defense by Coreth of the stand that "Christliche Philosophie ist eine geschichtliche *Wirklichkeit*" (p. 23). A collection of instances of Christian philosophy in the present century may be found in *Christliche Philosophie in Deutschland 1920 bis 1945*, ed. Paul Wolff (Regensburg: Josef Habbel, 1949).

   Duilio Bonifazi, *Filosofia e cristianesimo* (Rome: Università Lateranense, 1968), p. 11, n. 14, claimed that Augustine took the expression "Christian philosophy" from Lactantius, *De opificio Dei* 20.1. There the critical text, ed. Michel Perrin, *Lactance: L'ouvrage du Dieu créateur* (Paris: Editions du Cerf, 1974), p. 214.5–6, reads only "uerae philosophiae doctrinam." The notion may be the same, but the adjective "Christian" is not used. By the same reasoning it would go back through Tatian to Justin. Augustine is still the first known to have called the philosophy "Christian." For a brief overview of objective histories of Christian philosophy, see Nédoncelle, p. 85.

2. Cf. ". . . the study of philosophy which shall respond most fitly to the excellence of true faith, and at the same time be consonant with the dignity of human science." Leo XIII, *Aeterni Patris* 1; in *The Papal Encyclicals*, ed. Mary Claudia Carlen (Wilmington,

1

perspective it could be contrasted with the materialistic, skeptical, Greek, Islamic, and other types of philosophy that lay outside the specifically Christian heritage. Also, though from another angle, it could be polemically faced with types of thinking like ontologism and fideism, types that had originated inside the Catholic orbit yet by way of allegedly heretical interpretations of the Christian spirit and teachings. But from whatever angle one cares to approach it, "Christian philosophy" had come to signify in the nineteenth-century context a characteristically Christian method of thinking that met fully the standards of genuine philosophical procedure, in the way "philosophy" had by that time been accepted as a distinctive area in western academic pursuits. Such was at least the notion projected by its advocates. Yet whether there actually was or could be a reality corresponding to that notion has been brought under lively debate.

At first hearing, in earlier Christian circles, there could hardly have been anything strange about the union of the notion "Christian" with "philosophy" in the one phrase "Christian philosophy." Etymologically the term "philosophy" meant "love of wisdom." Beyond doubt Christian thought was devoted to wisdom with thoroughness and depth. In its sacred books and in its traditions it extolled wisdom. It urged the love and pursuit of that highly prized virtue. Christian doctrine, in fact, presented itself as the quintessence of wisdom, far superior to any kinds of wisdom developed or inherited outside its pale. In regard to the validity of naturally grounded reasoning, the Catholic teaching on original sin left human nature wounded yet, albeit with difficulty, able to function on its own proper level. Love of wisdom on the human plane could still be encouraged, and the results of its activity could always be appreciated and put to full use. Christian practice had no hesitation in spoiling the Egyptians of their cultural artifacts for its own advantage, or in snatching up the sword of Goliath for its own self-defense.[3] It drew abundantly on the wealth of Greek and Islamic philosophical thinking, and upon the Roman experience in legal structures. It had modesty enough to look upon itself not only as absorbing but also as profiting by the best that flowed into it from pagan or Islamic philosophical founts. In fact, it could feel quite at home in the intellectual language of the non-Christian writers, and in the logic

NC: McGrath Publishing Company, 1981), 2, 17b. "But the natural helps . . . are neither to be despised nor neglected, chief among which is evidently the right use of philosophy." Ibid., 2; 2, 18a.

3. *Aet. Patr.* 4; 2, 18b. 7; 2, 20a. See text from Augustine, supra, n. 1, for the connection from the start with the etymological signification of the word "philosophy."

with which they drew their conclusions. Facing other ways of thinking in the nineteenth and twentieth centuries, it did not feel the least embarrassment in speaking of its own philosophy, in the general meaning of its pursuit and development of the wisdom built up with pagan and Islamic and Jewish aid. It could readily employ the phrase "our philosophy"[4] for its own heritage of rational thinking in the departmental area that had come to be accepted as characteristically philosophical engagement.

Not even the clearcut Scholastic distinctions worked out in the medieval listings of the sciences could affect this attitude. In them the incisive division between philosophy and sacred theology stemmed from radical difference between their respective starting points. The starting points of sacred theology were divinely revealed truths that either were utterly inaccessible to a human mind unaided by faith, or, if they were in some way naturally accessible to it, were in point of fact presented on divine authority. In either case they were accepted on faith, without requirement of intrinsic evidence. On the other hand, the starting points of philosophy were naturally attained, open to ultimate scrutiny by reason, and accepted on the ground of their intrinsically manifest truth.[5] The disciplines that proceeded respectively from these two sets of starting points sprang from very different roots, and were in consequence radically distinct procedures.

True, theology throughout its reasoning made ample use of naturally known principles and logical structures. But in so doing it elevated them to its own procedural level, changing them for the moment into the wine of theology.[6] Through predication, the terms of the naturally known propositions became identified with those of the revealed premises in a union of cognitional existence, when the lower type of proposition was subsumed under the higher. The naturally known premises were in this way absorbed into the strict unity of the

4. *Aet. Patr.* 30; 2, 26a. So "our Christian . . . philosophy" in the text from Augustine, supra, n. 1. Cf. "Our traditional philosophy . . . ," Pius XII, *Humani generis* 32; ed. Carlen, *The Papal Encyclicals,* 4, 180b. In the latter encyclical it is referred to as "our perennial philosophy" (ibid.), and is taken up again in the following paragraph as "Christian philosophy" (33; 4, 181a).

5. ". . . each being allotted to its own proper place and derived from its own proper principles." *Aet. Patr.* 6; 2, 19b. "Philosophy should make use of its own method, principles and arguments." Ibid., 8; 2, 20a.

6. "So those who use the works of the philosophers in sacred doctrine, by bringing them into the service of faith, do not mix water with wine, but rather change water into wine." Aquinas, *In Boeth. de trin.* 2.3.ad 5m; trans. Armand Maurer, *Faith, Reason and Theology* (Toronto: Pontifical Institute of Mediaeval Studies, 1987), p. 50. The scriptural background of the metaphor was indicated by Aquinas, ibid., arg. 5, p. 46. On its use by Bonaventure, see Maurer, p. xv, n. 24.

one theological procedure. No preliminary objection to their harmonious functioning with revealed starting points in the higher discipline made itself felt. There was no clash. The God of the Scriptures was the ultimate source of all truth, both of revealed truth and of truth naturally attainable. Nothing but reciprocal help in drawing conclusions need be expected from the close association and cooperation of the revealed and the naturally acquired premises in the procedure of the sacred science. In the contrasted philosophical reasoning, all the terms not only originated on the strictly natural level, but remained on it throughout.

From this medieval viewpoint, one can readily deduce, the notion "Christian" meant something extrinsic and accidental to purely philosophical reasoning. The considerations it denoted pertained intrinsically to revealed religion or to sacred theology. They were outside the content of unaided natural reason. They were only accidentally connected with philosophy, for they arose from the accidentally connected historical fact of divine revelation. Philosophy had existed in Greece centuries before the advent of Christianity. Christianity on its part had existed among ordinary people without a developed philosophy. From the viewpoint of precisively abstracted essence neither of them involved the other. In a word, Christianity was something both accidental to and extrinsic to philosophy.

Yet even against the sharply etched medieval background the neo-scholastics of the middle and late nineteenth century had in the main no qualms in regarding as Christian philosophy the enterprise they were pursuing in their philosophical manuals, articles, and monographs. The pioneer coverage by Gaetano Sanseverino, widely used in Catholic seminaries and colleges during the last half of the nineteenth century, was entitled *Elements of Christian Philosophy*.[7] The expressly philosophical program urged by Pope Leo XIII's encyclical *Aeterni Patris* (1879) was from within a year of its publication officially designated as a call for the restoration of Christian philosophy. Likewise, early in the twentieth century Norbert Del Prado could publish a highly and deliberately controversial monograph on the fundamental truth for Christian philosophy, without really noticeable consciousness on his part or on the part of his adversaries that the very notion of Christian philosophy could be called into question.[8] Under the cir-

7. Gaetano Sanseverino, *Elementa philosophiae christianae cum antiqua et nova comparatae*, 2nd ed. (Naples: Biblioteca Catholica Scriptorum, 1873).

8. Norbert Del Prado, *De veritate fundamentali philosophiae christianae* (Fribourg: Consociatio Sancti Pauli, 1911). On exceptions in which the notion of "Christian philosophy" had been questioned, see infra, n. 17.

cumstances of the time a specifically Christian philosophy could hardly appear to these thinkers and to their readers as other than an entirely normal development in Christianity's encounter with intellectual problems throughout the long course of its evangelizing history, without any need either to flaunt or to defend the designation. No matter how closely the Neoscholastic philosophical writers kept their eyes fixed on what they themselves accepted through supernatural faith, they enjoyed complete and unquestioned confidence in the authentically philosophic tenor of the work in which they were engaged. In their own view it was genuinely on the philosophical level, in the technical meaning the term "philosophy" had taken on in the academic circles of their day. They explicitly meant to restrict all their operative premises to the plane of naturally attainable knowledge. Moreover, they distinguished their own work sharply from that of the theologians. Conversely, the professional theologians of their day, quite as the theologians of the present time, would not class the work of those writers as theology. Definitely the writers themselves were convinced that they were doing philosophy in the sense in which philosophy had been precisely distinguished from theology in the medieval classifications of the sciences.

Historically understandable, then, was the neoscholastic complacency in regard to an established and secure status for Christian philosophy. From the viewpoint of those writers it enjoyed a centuries-old background in undisturbed possession of the heritage to which it laid claim. But this ingrained complacency was dealt an arousing jolt in three lectures given in 1928 at Brussels by the prominent French historian of philosophy Emile Bréhier. The substance of these lectures was published later under a title asking *if* there is a Christian philosophy.[9] In their published form, Bréhier (p. 133) prefaced his remarks with a warning against the tendency to define "Christian" and "philosophy" at the beginning of the discussion. As an expert in dealing with the history of philosophy, he was well aware that the concept should be given its determining lines only at the end of the study. But he was just as well aware that in practice the topic of Christian philosophy was regularly approached with an already set concept of what it had to be. The result was that each investigator either found or did not find in historical reality the concept formed in advance. The ver-

9. Émile Bréhier, "Y a-t-il une philosophie chrétienne?" *Revue de métaphysique et de morale* 38 (1931), 133–62. The question had been asked in exactly the same words in English, "Is There a Christian philosophy?" by W. R. Matthews, *Studies in Christian Philosophy* (London: Macmillan and Co., 1921) as a chapter heading pp. 1–35, with the answer that "religion and philosophy . . . are indissolubly united" (p. 35).

dict was predetermined. In consequence, the question was answered in the affirmative or in the negative on the basis of conformity or disagreement with the writer's preconceived notion of what Christian philosophy should be.

In spite of his own warning, however, Bréhier himself was no exception to the observation he had made. For him there were in this context only two ways of conceiving what a Christian philosophy could mean. Replying expressly to Étienne Gilson, he explained that he meant his question to bear on historical reality. He was asking if in historical fact there is a Christian philosophy.[10] In one conception, Christian philosophy would mean what a religious magisterium accepts. It would claim to be a philosophical domain under the surveillance of the magisterium, without precise philosophical delineation, and arbitrary in character. In that sense, Bréhier asserted, Christian philosophy does exist historically, but it has no interest whatever for a philosopher. The other conception mentioned by Bréhier would be that Christianity has been the starting point of positive philosophical inspiration. In that case Christian philosophy would have interest for philosophers if it had ever existed. But so conceived it does not exist.[11] Bréhier's reply then goes on to show that the alleged examples, the various Augustinianisms, stem philosophically from sources other than Christian revelation. The conclusion, accordingly, is that Christianity involves only a story of mysteries that can be known solely by revelation, while philosophy means "the clear and distinct awareness of the reason which is in things and in the universe."[12]

For Bréhier, then, the two elements in Christian philosophy, taken as a notion, were contradictorily opposed to each other. Philosophy is based upon what is intrinsically evident, Christianity on what is authoritatively revealed without intrinsic evidence. The one, therefore, annuls the other. Instead of specifying philosophy, the characterization of "Christian" would destroy the generic philosophical nature. Consequently the notion "Christian" cannot be a specifying differentia of philosophy. The nature expressed by the one term would set aside

10. É. Bréhier, "La notion de philosophie chrétienne," *Bulletin de la Société française de Philosophie* 31 (1931), 49.

11. Bréhier, *Bulletin,* pp. 49–52. His more detailed discussion of the various Augustinianisms and other alleged instances of Christian philosophy is given in his longer article (supra, n. 9), pp. 134–62. In Christian philosophy in his first sense he notes "une absence de limite précise, et dans sa censure, un manque de suite" (*Bulletin,* p. 50), making it appear something entirely arbitrary.

12. ". . . la conscience claire et distincte de la raison qui est dans les choses et dans l'univers." Bréhier, *Bulletin,* p. 52. Cf.: "Either we know something or else we believe it: when knowledge supervenes, belief has no longer a place. Philosophy and Christianity can no more mix, if I may so put it, than oil and vinegar." Nédoncelle, p. 55.

the nature expressed by the other. Later, in Heidegger's much-quoted simile, Christian philosophy would be on a par with wooden iron.[13] What is iron by nature cannot be wooden. In a more familiar comparison, a plane figure cannot be square and circular in the same perspective. The introduction of the least circularity would prevent it from being geometrically a square. In similar fashion the least dependence upon divine revelation would keep a reasoning process from being genuinely philosophical. Another illustration might be seen in the way Christian evangelism has been alleged to repel the tyranny of Aristotelian structural rigidity.[14] From the contrasted side of philosophy, a more recent simile could be that an authentic philosophical organism would inevitably reject any implant of Christian specification. In becoming based even at any one point upon a specifically Christian truth, the reasoning would cease to be genuinely philosophical. A blackout of naturally accessible evidence in any one of the propositions would inevitably nullify the cogency of the intended rational discourse, which is a chain no stronger than its weakest link. No mixture of the two—that is, of the intrinsically evident and the not intrinsically evident—can be permitted in a philosophy. It would mean both being and not being something in exactly the same context and at the same time. The contradiction was that rudimentarily glaring. "Christian" and "philosophy" could not fuse in a way that would constitute a unitary specific nature. A combination of the two would be at best an attempt at an amalgam that would at once show itself to be impossible.

To return to Bréhier himself, one may note that, in the way his view was advanced, a philosophy had to remain entirely uninfluenced by supernatural revelation. "Christian" meant mystery, "philosophy" meant clear and distinct perception. Bréhier remained impervious to Gilson's insistence that revealed doctrine *never* plays the role of a proof or a principle for deduction in Christian philosophy as it is found in historical fact.[15] Bréhier had left himself only one option, namely the ultra-fideistic conception that Christian philosophy denotes what a religious magisterium accepts. On that point Gilson's reply was courteous yet fully as concise as Bréhier's assertion. The Christian philos-

---

13. ". . . ein hölzernes Eisen und ein Misverständnis." Martin Heidegger, *Einführung in die Metaphysik* (Tübingen: Max Niemeyer, 1953), p. 6.

14. So Ortega y Gasset. See text infra, chap. 3, n. 10.

15. "Jamais le dogme n'y joue le rôle d'un principe de la déduction; jamais il n'y est invoqué non plus à titre de preuve; . . . la philosophie, prise en elle-même, n'est justiciable que de la raison." Étienne Gilson, "La notion de philosophie chrétienne," in *Bulletin de la Société française de Philosophie* 31 (1931), 42. See also pp. 39 and 49 for the same assertion.

ophy that Bréhier claimed to be the only kind that had ever existed historically had never existed in fact. On the other hand, the type that Bréhier claimed had never existed, did in fact exist.

This situation poses queries. Two capable historians of philosophy look at the same historical facts and interpret them in ways that directly contradict each other. The deepseated cleavage between the two interpretations needs to be studied and explained. One may ask if it lies merely in the nature of the present problem of Christian philosophy. Or does it indicate a more profound difference in the way each of the interpreters conceives philosophy itself? As regards the nature of Christian philosophy, Bréhier seems clearly enough to identify it with revealed doctrine, insofar as its content is what the religious magisterium accepts. That would allegedly make it a species of the philosophy of religion. It would be restricted to a particular area, like a branch of philosophy. The Neoscholastics, on the contrary, regarded it as a general philosophy that extended its coverage to all topics of philosophical interest. That is the range that the encyclical *Aeterni Patris* seemed to view for the philosophy it was promoting. Also, Bréhier's other supposed conception of Christian philosophy, namely, that of a hypothetical philosophy that would have its starting point in divine revelation, would seem to have as its content what is virtually contained in revealed truth. Again the content would be a restricted area, revelation, so not that of a general philosophy. The question of the range of Christian philosophy is accordingly involved in the present problem, along with the possibility that the problem is being approached from two radically different conceptions of philosophical procedure itself.

Be that as it may, Bréhier's attack set off a long debate that flared up brilliantly in the years immediately following the publication of his provocative article. The debate has continued ever since to excite intermittent attention and interest, though in restricted circles. At least the endurance of the attention given it testifies that as a topic of discussion and of pursuit "Christian philosophy" is a label that seems here to stay. No common consensus on its nature has so far emerged. In fact, one may ask if either side in the long dispute about it has really come to grips with the other, or even if sufficient sensitivity to the issues involved on each side has been exhibited or really felt by the respective opponents. At the height of the debate the stakes were high, and the reactions quick and spirited. In that charged atmosphere arguments were advanced with heat, pained patience, and unrelenting insistence. Often, too, a kind of blindness to the adversaries' conception of philosophy seemed to hinder communication.

With those opposed to the notion of Christian philosophy, the purity of philosophical thinking was paramount. Thoroughgoing freedom from injection of superstition and from interference by religious authority had to be safeguarded. Ghosts from happenings in the past were easily conjured up. Numerous Catholic philosophers in due course espoused the Bréhier side, anxious to show openly and pointedly to their colleagues that their own religious belief was not in any way harming their philosophical acumen. They claimed to be doing philosophy in the same way as anybody else. They prided themselves on speaking the language of their non-Catholic colleagues. They wanted to make sure of an even footing for participation in philosophical associations and conferences and dialogue, and for publication in philosophical journals. They were profoundly anxious to avoid a ghetto, and keenly interested in bringing about a common philosophical forum for all people engaged in the profession, with unimpeded access to employment in secular philosophical departments. Even some fallout from the theologians' turmoil about the right to dissent in face of authoritative ecclesiastical pronouncements made itself felt. This latter, however, was very slight, for on the part of the proponents of Christian philosophy there was no real question of making any one Catholic philosophy obligatory and exclusive, in the sense of one philosophy just as there is one God and one faith. Yet painful memories lingered from the efforts to impose authoritatively the twenty-four Thomistic theses as the model for Catholic academic teaching in philosophy.[16] Ecclesiastical interference was still dreaded by many. Separation of philosophy and religious belief seemed, like the American separation of church and state, to be in order. As with the Catholic candidate for the U.S. presidency in 1928, open and emphatic avowal that they recognized no ecclesiastical right to dictation in secular matters was the suggested policy. Catholic interests, from their viewpoint, would be best served by basing philosophy frankly on sound scholarly norms common to all. They wished to make clear that authority was not interfering in philosophy. They tended to be pained by any suggestion that they would be unable to keep their religious beliefs from clouding their professional judgment, or from marring their integrity by either help or hindrance in their strictly professional work. These philosophers were Catholics who claimed that they were doing their work in exactly the same way as they would if they had not been Catholics. They were indeed Catholic

16. For a survey of this problem, see Thomas J. A. Hartley, *Thomistic Revival and the Modernist Era* (Toronto: Institute of Christian Thought, 1971).

philosophers in the sense of Catholics doing philosophy. But they were
not doing Catholic philosophy. In their view there was no such thing.

How far that attitude actually conformed to the reality of the time
might be subjected to careful and critical examination. But does the
attitude as it stands come at all to grips with the problem? Looked at
from the other side of the dispute it seemed to lack objective bearing.
Étienne Gilson, already ranking with Bréhier among the leading historians of philosophy, needed only to glance back at the continual flow
of Christian philosophy through preceding ages. With rhetorical surprise that corresponded to the consternation of his adversaries at the
thought of injecting religious beliefs into philosophy, he could ask
pointedly how any believer could do philosophy as though having
never heard of the Christian teachings.[17] No matter how philosophy
in the abstract might leave out of consideration the specific differentiating trait brought about by the philosopher's Christian engagement,
the actual pursuit of the discipline had in fact to take place according
to the concrete circumstances of the philosopher's own life. The influence of the extrinsic and accidental factors has, as a matter of historical
observation, intrinsically affected the very core of the philosophizing.

17. Étienne Gilson, *The Spirit of Mediaeval Philosophy*, trans. A. H. C. Downes (New
York: Charles Scribner's Sons, 1940), p. 5. Cf.: "This fact makes it hard for me to
understand how a Christian can ever philosophize as if he were not a Christian." *The
Philosopher and Theology* (New York: Random House, 1962), p. 9. In the original debate,
Gilson had stated his own position concisely. Christian philosophies are those whose
existence cannot be historically explained without taking account of the Christian religion: "S'il y a eu des philosophies, c'est-à-dire des systèmes de vérités rationnelles, dont
l'existence ne saurait historiquement s'expliquer sans tenir compte de l'existence du
christianisme, ces philosophies doivent porter le nom de philosophies chrétiennes."
Gilson, *Bulletin*, p. 48. Gilson was nevertheless well aware that certain "neo-thomistes"
(p. 38) accepted the rationalist way of posing the problem, and that other Neoscholastic
and Catholic writers took a different stand from his. He called attention (pp. 42–43)
to Constant Sierp's "Avant-propos" in the French translation of Kleutgen's widely used
manual *La philosophie scolastique exposée et defendue par le R. P. Kleutgen* (Paris: Gaume
Frères et J. Duprey), 1, viii, where that work was introduced as meant to justify "l'emploi
de la philosophie socratique dans la théologie chrétienne." The reason was that there
was basically no Christian philosophy. There was only a true philosophy that was in
accord with Christian faith and of which Christians made use. In America a similar
stand had been taken by Brownson, for whom there was a Christian use of philosophy
but no Christian philosophy nor possibility of one. See Armand Maurer, "Orestes A.
Brownson" in Coreth's *Christliche Philosophie* (see supra, n. 1), 1, 732–33. *Aeterni Patris*
had indeed described what it was promoting as "the right use of philosophy" (text supra,
n. 2), but what it meant was the philosophy itself in actual exercise. Though the question
of Christian philosophy is wider than the point immediately at issue between Gilson
and Bréhier, the lines of the debate have remained pretty well as they were drawn up
in that original exchange, centering on whether Christian belief could bring about the
specification of a philosophy without entering into the philosophy's probative discourse.
Histories of the debate are listed in Mark D. Jordan, "The Terms of the Debate over
'Christian Philosophy,'" *Communio* (Notre Dame, IN), 12 (1985), 293, n. 1. Articles on
its problem from 1928 to 1955 are given in chronological order in Luigi Bogliolo, *Il
problema della filosofia cristiana* (Brescia: Morcelliana, 1959), pp. 276–81.

Such was Gilson's maturely considered stand. For him the faith of the Christian believer had brought about a distinctive type of philosophical thinking found nowhere else.

Somewhat similarly, Jacques Maritain brought in the distinction between the *nature* of philosophy and the *state* in which philosophy now is actually found. These two viewpoints were meant to correspond, in their own way, respectively to the order of specification and the order of exercise. Philosophy is always something done here and now by a person who is meant for a supernatural destiny. Since philosophy is now done in a *Christian state*, religious belief does occasion an intrinsic difference in the intellectual discourse. It is in the concrete order, therefore, that the problem of Christian philosophy is to be assessed. In that order, items of religious belief exercise influence on the intrinsic constitution of the philosophical achievement, though without making revealed truth the basis of any philosophical reasoning. Their effect turns out to be intrinsic to the philosophy, even though the originating factors themselves range above the philosophical orbit. Their influence becomes sufficient to account for the specific differentiation in Christian philosophy.[18]

18. Jacques Maritain, "La notion de philosophie chrétienne," in *Bulletin de la Société française de Philosophie* 31 (1931), 59–72, and *An Essay on Christian Philosophy*, trans. Edward H. Flannery (New York: Philosophical Library, 1955), pp. 11–31. The latter, published originally in French in 1933, resulted from an expansion of Maritain's contribution to the original Bréhier discussion and was given in lecture form at Louvain later in the same year as the debate (1931). Maritain (*Bulletin*, p. 67; *Essay*, p. 30) adopts a perspective in which the relationship between philosophy and Christianity "is not an accidental one; it results from the very nature of philosophy, from its natural longing to know its proper objects as well as possible, as also from the very nature of the Christian doctrine and life, and from the inner and outer bolstering which they afford reason" (*Essay*, p. 30). From that viewpoint it is of course natural and intrinsic for philosophy to pursue its course in elucidating Christian tenets on its own level, and it is likewise natural and intrinsic to Christianity to seek whatever help it needs to clarify its message. But in the perspective in which a philosopher does not have to be a Christian and a Christian does not have to be a philosopher, the relationship of the two in Christian philosophy has to be regarded as accidental. This comes out more clearly in Maritain's *Science and Wisdom*, trans. Bernard Wall (London: Centenary Press, 1940), pp. viii; 92–100. Cf.: "[P]hilosophy is as affected by this christian state as intimately as nature is affected by the state of grace" (p. 97); and "Is grace in turn not rooted in the soul *per modum naturae*, so that it makes of man truly a new man? All this is accidental to the human essence taken in itself, but it is not accidental with regard to the earthly existence and conditions of life of mankind" (pp. 98–99). But already in the *Essay* Maritain had written: "This regimen directly involves functions higher than philosophy; . . . I should like for the moment to outline briefly what to my mind are the chief components of this *Christian state* of philosophy" (*Essay*, p. 18). Yet "no reasoning issuing from faith finds its way into its inner fabric" (p. 15) when it is taken "simply as a philosophy" (ibid.).

The question of state touches a point of deep disagreement between Maritain and Gilson. Maritain's lively appreciation of the supernatural prompted him to stress the internal working of grace in a Christian's philosophizing, while Gilson insisted that

Under the unpretentious styling of "*obiter dicta* on a distinction made by Jacques Maritain," a paper by Ralph McInerny aimed to supplement Maritain's suggestions by emphasizing the requirement of "appropriate moral orientation" in the Christian philosopher.[19] Christianity, in proclaiming "the common supernatural goal of human persons" (p. 73), can in that way exercise the intrinsic influence necessary for the specification of a philosophy. That goal, in spite of the fact that it is common, leads "to a far greater differentiation among us than to sober sameness" (p. 70). Here one meets a considered attempt to explain how something accidental to the internal constitution of a philosophy can occasion intrinsic differentiation in its essence. McInerny, appealing to Plato, means that "appropriate moral orientation" can be understood in a setting that "lifts the moral from mere modal status to a substantive feature of philosophizing" (p. 67). "Substantive" is here understood as denoting a feature that belongs to the essence of the philosophizing, in distinction from what would be accidental to that intellectual activity. The jump from external association to substantive differentiation is obviously the crucial consideration in the problem at issue. McInerny (p. 69) shows convincingly that, not only for Christian philosophy but correspondingly for all philosophies, some initial dependence on external guidance is required to set the philosophy afoot. It thereby accounts for the philosophy's differentiation. "Viewed in this light," he concludes, "the situation of the Catholic is like anyone else's" (p. 69).

Whether or not one accepts the moral influence as the cause of specific differentiation in the case of Christian philosophy, McInerny's (p. 69) observation—that for all philosophies the determining of the starting points has been radically influenced by external environment—is important. It shows that the question of the differentiating factor in Christian philosophy is at least on a par with the problems of differentiation by external factors that have to be faced in any other philosophy. In every case the differentiating "starting point" (p. 69) is dependent on external teaching and guidance. The dependence of Christian philosophy on the "existential situation" is not to be viewed as "anomalous and in need of apology" (p. 70). In the general sense

---

human nature as nature is not changed by difference in state. On their final exchange over this issue, see infra, chap. 2, nn. 12–13. But already at the time (1935) of writing *Science and Wisdom* Maritain was thinking in terms of the way man was "wounded *in naturalibus*" by "the sin of Adam" (p. 98). Well enough known was Maritain's attitude that as a layman he could bring religious language more freely into a discussion than could clerics, who had a certain decorum to observe.

19. Ralph McInerny, "Reflections on Christian Philosophy," in *One Hundred Years of Thomism,* ed. Victor B. Brezik (Houston: Center for Thomistic Studies, 1981), p. 67.

of being influenced by extrinsic and accidental factors in selecting the starting points for philosophizing, the person doing Christian philosophy is no different from anybody else in the way of approaching the work and specifying thought. How a goal *common* to all can serve in specifying a particular type of philosophy needs more careful consideration. But McInerny's distinctive contribution to the debate is the framework for a role to be played by moral orientation in the problem of Christian philosophy.

That seems to be as far as the effort to show how something extrinsic and accidental can cause the intrinsic specification has been in fact carried, up to the present, in the dispute. One might insist, however, on this—the Christian philosophy tradition claims that, far from destroying the nature of philosophy, the Christian factor is a positive help on the properly philosophical plane. It enables philosophy to attain the best of philosophical results. Hence the keen philosophical interest in the role that the Christian specification plays. Its proponents have been deeply and devotedly concerned with promoting the beneficial effect that Christianity should exercise on contemporary culture. Accordingly, the religious leaven was an all-pervading factor in their general thinking. It was anything but a matter of indifference in their pursuit of philosophy, and the fact that the bread was leavened did not at all make it cease to be bread. They experienced personally its stimulating philosophical influence. Their lively feelings of course did not have the implication that every philosopher would have to become a Christian in order to do his or her best work. But they did mean that Christian philosophy should be conspicuous enough to serve as a "friendly star"[20] for all comers by pointing out possibilities and directions for philosophic engagement. The defenders of Christian philosophy already mentioned were well-established writers, and did not have to fear rejection as philosophers on account of their preference for it. Their situation in this respect was different from that of graduates from Neoscholastic schools, who wondered whether traces of a disliked philosophical vocabulary and a too-narrow range of philosophical interests might be held against them in applications for employment, or for space in philosophical journals. These oppo-

---

20. *Aet. Patr.* 9; 2, 20b. Conspicuous publicity in the past has in point of fact tended to be adverse. Gilson did have some ground for claiming: "He who carelessly announces his intention to philosophize as a Christian is sure to find himself excluded from the society of philosophers." *The Philosopher and Theology*, p. 8. Maritain, in connection with the opposition to be expected, could draw attention to a suggestion that the Scholastic mentality is on the level of childhood from eight to eleven years of age. See *An Essay on Christian Philosophy*, p. 25. In the original debate (*Bulletin*, p. 66) Maritain had deftly commended a touch of childhood vigor here.

nents were concerned with showing definitely that their philosophy was in no way influenced by their religious faith.

In point of fact, neither the arguments for Christian philosophy nor the enthusiasm of its proponents seemed to make much impression on those opposed to it. Fernand Van Steenberghen, one of the early participants in the Bréhier debate, could after some fifty years maintain without change or nuance his original stand against the notion of Christian philosophy.[21] Catholic writers on the Bréhier side were indeed concerned with furthering Christian influence in contemporary culture. But for them that influence was hindered rather than advanced by the repellent notion of a specifically Christian philosophy. On the other side, Gilson and Maritain continued to defend the notion without any wavering whatever before what seemed to their opponents the airtight case presented by Bréhier's argument in its original setting. The sensitive reactions on both sides could hardly help but dull an adequate appreciation of the other's reasoning. The respective conditioning of each side seemed to forestall any real empathy.

The general problematic of the dispute about the notion of Christian philosophy, though, emerges in fairly clear outline from the foregoing considerations. The notions "Christian" and "philosophy" (in its current sense) are undoubtedly accidental and extrinsic to each other. One can be a Christian without being a philosopher, and a philosopher without being a Christian, quite as in Aristotle's (*Metaph.* 5.7.1017a10–13) example of housebuilder and musician accidentally united in the same person. Likewise, philosophy can be extrinsic to Christianity, as it was in Plato and Aristotle, and Christianity can be extrinsic to professional philosophy, as it is in practicing Christians who are not philosophers. The accidental and extrinsic relation of Christianity to philosophy is beyond challenge. But that is hardly in question here. The question is whether the two are compatible with each other in the one notion of Christian philosophy, in a way that allows "Christian" the role of the philosophy's specifying differentia.

A specific differentia, of course, has to be intrinsic to the thing it

---

21. "[J]e pense que la révélation chrétienne a exercé et continue d'exercer une influence profonde sur le philosophe chrétien. Mais cette influence ne peut dénaturer le travail philosophique s'il est accompli correctement et, dès lors, elle ne peut avoir comme résultat de constituer des philosophies spécifiquement chrétiennes." Fernand Van Steenberghen, "Étienne Gilson et l'Université de Louvain," *Revue philosophique de Louvain* 85 (1987), 12. The same alleged "denaturing" of philosophy and the ingrained prospect of a philosophical ghetto still functioned as a strong deterrent in Van Steenberghen's 1987 stand. In "Philosophie et christianisme. Épilogue d'un débat ancien," *Revue philosophique de Louvain* 86 (1988), 180–91, Van Steenberghen pleads (p. 191) for the banishment of the expression "Christian philosophy" from our vocabulary.

specifies. It pertains to the thing's formal nature. In consequence its causality is formal and internal. But, like any other element in the thing, it has its own extrinsic causes. In traditional terminology, these causes are final, exemplar, and efficient. In any of those three orders the specific differentiation of a thing can come from something extrinsic and accidental to the thing itself. The specific characteristics that differentiate a summer cottage from any other type of house are caused respectively by the purpose of summer relaxation, the blueprint of the architect, and the work of the carpenter or mason. It would be idle to contend that the intrinsic differentiation is not brought about by those external causes, each functioning in its own way. Correspondingly, when philosophy is looked upon in its exercise as an activity produced by a person, the external factors of purpose, model, and agent may work together harmoniously to bring about a specifically distinct type of philosophical procedure. The fact that they are external and accidental gives no ground for incompatibility. The extrinsic and accidental teaching or guidance can in its own way determine the intrinsically distinct type of philosophy in which a person molds his thought. Christian considerations can in this way bring about an intrinsic differentiation in a philosophy.

How the external factors of belief contribute to the specific differentiation of Christian philosophy requires close examination. But a general view of the problematic suffices to show that the external and accidental relation of Christianity to philosophy does not pose an a priori objection to the notion of Christian philosophy, provided that philosophy is taken as an activity of human persons. That is the way the defenders of Christian philosophy contend it has to be viewed in this context. As brought into being through the activity of a person, any philosophy is dependent upon extrinsic and accidental causes for its intrinsic and essential specification. The problematic has shown that there is nothing strange or exceptional about opting for this way of taking philosophy. "Summer" and "cottage" are external and accidental in relation to each other, yet summering can be the cause of the intrinsic specification of the house by way of both purpose and architectural design. This approach allows a coherent meaning to the concept of Christian philosophy. One will still have to show that in their respective approaches the two sides in the debate are thinking in terms of radically different conceptions of philosophy, conceptions that inevitably blind each other to the force of the opposing arguments. Further, one will likewise have to justify this pluralistic view of the situation. But for the moment, at least in the pluralistic atmosphere of today's philosophical world, one is not barred from entering the lists by the a priori objection that Christian philosophy is a contradiction in terms. Though so in one approach, it may not be so in another.

Against the background of the Bréhier debate, therefore, the first step today towards building up a Christian philosophy has had to be the assurance that the very notion of it is not at all self-contradictory. The self-contradiction, the Bréhier debate has made clear, would lie in the injection of premises not intrinsically evident to unaided human reason. These would be rejected by any healthy philosophical bloodstream. Unaffected by Bréhier's argument would be a Christian philosophy based *entirely*—and this cannot be emphasized too strongly— upon premises naturally available at least in principle to human reason. Bréhier himself seemed blind to this conception of Christian philosophy, even when it was brought forcefully to his attention by Gilson.[22] Bréhier saw only his own two alternative conceptions of Christian philosophy and remained impervious to this third alternative. Here one can well follow Bréhier's advice about examining the historical reality in thoroughgoing fashion prior to forming one's definite concept of what Christian philosophy is. One will find the occasional attempts of some individuals at mixing revealed premises into what they advance as their notions of Christian philosophy.[23] How these can bypass the a priori roadblock of internal contradiction is a problem each has to face. But the mainstream of the historical reality, as the foregoing survey has shown, carefully distinguishes philosophy from theology, and strictly limits Christian philosophy to reasoning based entirely on premises available at least in principle to unaided natural reason. It is solely towards this mainstream conception of Christian philosophy that the ensuing study proposes to work.

That, then, is the first step. The second will be to ascertain what Christian philosophy is about. What is its object, or, if you wish, what is the subject matter with which it deals? Already in the foregoing survey there has been occasion to broach the question whether it is a general philosophy treating of all things human and divine, or whether it is a particular branch of philosophy bearing on a restricted area only. This point will have to be decided by inquiry into the range of Christian philosophy as an historical reality. If it is a particular branch of philosophy, its specification will straightway be determined by its object, just as cosmology for instance is specified by the cosmos or psychology by the soul. If, however, it should present itself in fact

---

22. Text supra, n. 15. See Bréhier's reply, *Bulletin de la Société française de Philosophie* 31 (1931), 49.

23. See instances discussed in Nédoncelle, pp. 102–105.

as a general philosophy, its manner of specification will demand further inquiry and perhaps occasion more difficulty. But this inquiry, one may readily see, is a necessary step in the effort towards building an acceptable Christian philosophy. Upon its results will depend in large part one's view of how Christian philosophy is specified.

II

The Bréhier debate has indicated effectively that for one conception of philosophizing the notion of Christian philosophy is self-destructive. For another conception, it has shown on the contrary that the notion is normal and gives promise of a fruitful enterprise. In order to weigh the respective merits of the two approaches, one needs first of all to make sure that the arguments on both sides are really bearing upon the same topic, regardless of the radical differences in their final judgments about it. Unless the two sides are talking about the same thing, there is not much point in an effort to assess the worth of their opposed conclusions in regard to what is assumed to be an identical subject. What, then, is the subject matter upon which Christian philosophy bears?

The answer to this question, as has just been noted, is to be sought in the way Christian philosophy has been carried on in actual historical reality. With what range of subject matter has it in fact been concerned? If one looks at Christian philosophy as factually pursued in the course of the centuries, one sees immediately that the subject matter upon which it bears is not limited to any particular domain that would constitute its object, in the way mathematics is limited to the quantitative, philosophy of nature to the sensible world, ethics to human conduct, and philosophies of law, art, religion, sport and the like to the respective activities upon which they bear. Christian philosophy, on the contrary, has in practice been regularly understood as a philosophy of general inquiry. In the neoscholastic context this is evident through a mere glance at the manuals used. Its objective sweep extended to all things, human and divine, in accord with Cicero's (*De Officiis* 2.2.5) definition. In the patristic, medieval, and contemporary contexts, close scrutiny will show that it is accorded the same general range, at least in the mainstream of its proponents.

Christian philosophy, in consequence, is not to be distinguished from other philosophies in the way metaphysics, logic, philosophy of nature, philosophy of religion, and so on are distinguished from one another. Its specific differentiation is to be conceived on the model of the distinction of one general philosophy from other general philosophies. It is the way the philosophy of Berkeley is distinguished from materialism, Kantianism from phenomenalism, pragmatism from idealism, Greek philosophy from medieval philosophy, German philosophy from Russian philosophy. All these and many other general philosophies are distinguished from one another by the way they approach their subject matter, each from its own viewpoint.

The projection of Christian philosophy as a general philosophy eliminates at once the possibility of distinguishing it from other philosophies on the basis of different objective areas upon which each would bear. This means that Christian philosophy cannot be regarded as a particular branch of the general enterprise. It is not a branch. It is a whole tree. It is not to be differentiated from other philosophies in the way the philosophy of being and the philosophy of nature and the philosophy of art are distinguished from one another. Even metaphysics, as the philosophy of being, and logic, as the philosophy of reasoning processes, are particular branches of philosophy from this viewpoint.[24] Thematically both these disciplines have strictly limited objects, namely, being and reasoning processes. These aspects give them a certain entrance into all things and into all thought. But as far as specific differentiation of disciplines is concerned, metaphysics and logic are each characterized by a limited object. As a thematic object specifying a branch of philosophy, being is a different objective aspect from nature or conduct, and logical relation is different from other aspects. In that way all the particular branches of philosophy are distinguished from one another by the limits of their objects. But for general philosophies the object is the same for all. It covers the totality of philosophical topics. The distinction of one general philosophy from another cannot arise therefore from the objective side. It has to come from the personal dispositions of the respective philosophers. From the viewpoint of objective range, every general philosophy is meant, each in its own way, to cover the whole philosophical domain.

In all general philosophies, then, the source of the specification is to be looked for in the personal conditioning and approach of their respective proponents. That habituation gives rise in each case to a distinctive manner of dealing with the same general subject matter of philosophical inquiry. As a general philosophy, Christian philosophy is far from being an exception. Indeed, some very definite influence from the personal side is obviously required for bringing all "things

24. See Aquinas, *In Boeth. de trin.* 5.1.ad 6. Cf. "[L]ogic and metaphysics . . . both are universal sciences and in a sense treat of the same subject." Ibid., 6.1.ad 1; trans. A. Maurer, *Thomas Aquinas: The Division and Methods of the Sciences*, 4th ed. (Toronto: Pontifical Institute of Mediaeval Studies, 1986), p. 64.

human and divine" into the relation with Christianity demanded for a general philosophy. When philosophy is regarded solely in precisive abstraction, no such relation becomes manifest through a study of the discipline's general subject matter. Christianity, as already noted, is accidental and external to philosophy. The relation springs, in consequence, from the approach of the philosopher. The specific differentiation will be comparable to the way Platonism, Aristotelianism, materialism, or idealism each involves a special order of approach for the treatment of the whole philosophical subject matter. In this way, as noted above,[25] Christian philosophy is not at all anomalous in being dependent on the external teaching and guidance that leads up to its pursuit.

The point at issue here may aptly be illustrated by the contrast between Christian philosophy and the philosophy of religion.[26] Philosophy of religion is now an established philosophical discipline, academically recognized as a legitimate and important branch of philosophy. It is distinguished clearly enough from the other branches of philosophy by the objective area upon which it bears. That area is religion as a human activity, distinct in itself from other human pursuits such as law, art, or sport. The area can be marked out clearly in virtue of that activity considered just in itself. It need not look to any subjective disposition on the part of the philosopher of religion to set up the study as a distinct philosophical discipline. Notably, it does not involve any religious tendencies on the part of the philosopher. Any philosopher, whether Christian or non-Christian, agnostic or atheist, can do philosophy of religion. The writer's motive may even be to show that religion is irrational or degrading, and therefore something that should be entirely abolished. No liking for religion, or desire to promote its practice, is necessarily present in the philosopher of religion. The general love for knowledge, signalized by Aristotle in the opening lines of the *Metaphysics* as the origin of all philosophical pursuit, need be the only purpose at work. That general motive could hardly be expected to *specify* a particular type of philosophy.

25. See McInerny, pp. 67–69 (supra, n. 19).
26. Cf.: "Il problema della filosofia cristiana non è il problema della filosofia del cristianesimo, se non forte indirettamente e in obliquo." Bogliolo, p. 8 (supra, n. 17). Nédoncelle (p. 93) summarizes Pierre Guérin's view as: "The 'philosophy of Christianity' would not have the drawbacks of a 'Christian philosophy.'" For Nédoncelle himself, Christian philosophy bears on "a region which is proper to itself, for it expresses that part of reality which corresponds to the thinking experience of a believer" (pp. 136–37). There is difficulty in seeing how this latter view does not bring Christian philosophy definitely under the philosophy of religion, posing an awkward problem about how it can be universal in scope.

With Christian philosophy, on the other hand, the situation is quite different. The work of those who have actually been engaged in its development floodlights a spirit of dedication to a cause. That spirit is visible enough to irritate opponents of the notion of Christian philosophy. It prompts them to look for something non-philosophical or antiphilosophical in its procedure, and conjures up an alleged introduction of premises not naturally evident that would belie an authentically philosophical treatment. So, while a philosophy of religion can be indifferent to or even bitterly opposed to promoting religious practice, the very notion of Christian philosophy tends to carry with it the aim of furthering Christian interests. This enthusiasm, the historical reality shows, is part of the personal habituation to which the specifying of Christian philosophy is to be attributed. It is implied in the insistence of Gilson and Maritain that here the specification is to be sought in the philosophy as actually exercised, and not in the notion of philosophy taken in abstraction from the person who is philosophizing. It lends weight to McInerny's stand that the source of the specification is to be sought in the final cause of the engagement, and thereby in the motivation of the Christian philosopher. But that motivation will have to be relevantly narrowed in order to specify here, for the "common supernatural goal of human persons"[27] is *general* for all human actions. In any case, these considerations make explicit the reason why philosophy as exercised in historical reality, and not philosophy merely in the abstract, is what has to be used as the framework in which the nature of Christian philosophy is assessed. Its nature as a general philosophy requires that the sources of specification be sought on the subjective side.

At the same time, the requirement of positive religious motivation for Christian philosophy cannot be so narrowed that it would demand formal membership in a Christian church, or the profession or practice of the particular church's public worship. Quite in accord with Tertullian's "anima naturaliter Christiana,"[28] writers without explicit

27. McInerny, p. 73. On the common supernatural goal, see infra, chap. 2, nn. 19–20.

28. "O testimonium animae naturaliter Christianae!" Tertullian, *Apologeticus* 17; PL, 1, 433a. On the prehistory of the expression, showing that *naturaliter* here has the philosophical sense of "by nature," see G. Quispel, "Anima naturaliter christiana," *Latomus* 10 (1951), 167–69. So in English, "O noble testimony of the soul by nature Christian!" in *The Ante-Nicene Fathers*, ed. Alexander Roberts and James Donaldson (Grand Rapids: Eerdmans, 1957), 3, 32a. But this does not mean that all philosophy is basically Christian, or suggest the formulation "si la philosophie n'est pas chrétienne par essence"—Pierre-Philippe Druet, in *Pour une philosophie chrétienne* (Paris: Lethielleux, 1983), p. 14. The *actual* union of the notions remains accidental, despite their adaptability to each other.

adherence to any Christian denomination have been motivated by keen interest in preserving Christian cultural and moral standards, and have made important contributions to Christian philosophical thought. In the same spirit, non-Christian philanthropists and religiously neutral benevolent organizations contribute to the activities of Christian churches. A basic appreciation of the work of Christianity, and a liking for what it means, suffice to provide the motivation required for doing Christian philosophy. In actual practice, though, much more than that is usually found. The noted "Christian" in this context is in consequence very flexible. But the least that is to be asked is concern for furthering Christian standards through philosophical exploration and development. Without that concern it is hard to see what would prompt a person to do philosophy with consistence from a Christian viewpoint.

The point at issue for the moment, however, is that the Christian philosophy outlined and promoted by *Aeterni Patris* and at issue in the Bréhier debate is in scope a general philosophy, even though heuristically it approaches its general subject matter from the viewpoint of special interests. It selects its leading topics of consideration on the basis of those interests. In that way it works out its own method and order of discussion, thereby marking its procedure as that of a distinct type of philosophizing. What enables it to make important contributions to philosophy is the way its distinctive interests bring to the fore significant points that are in principle naturally attainable but would be missed in other approaches to the philosophical territory. This makes room in practice for a special philosophical discipline, quite as an approach from language occasions linguistic analysis, and an approach from vivid existentials marks off the starting points for phenomenology, and an approach from economic crises results in development of Marxism or of liberation philosophy.[29]

29. Specification by reason of the selection of starting points on the basis of various interests distinguishes one general philosophy from another without infringing upon the philosophy's general scope. Each in this way is a special philosophical discipline even though the range of its object is general. This situation parallels the way in which, for Aquinas (see supra, n. 24), metaphysics and logic could each be a distinct science even though both have a general object. On the special interests of liberation thought in its selection of starting points, see Enrique Dussel, *Philosophy of Liberation*, trans. Aquilina Martinez and Christine Morkovsky (Maryknoll, NY: Orbis Books, 1985); Arthur F. McGovern, *Marxism: An American Christian Perspective* (Maryknoll, NY: Orbis Books, 1980); and Michael Novak, *Will It Liberate? Questions about Liberation Theology* (New York: Paulist Press, 1986). Also, in the only type of "Christian philosophy" that Bréhier saw in historical fact, the range was unlimited from his viewpoint, even though the subject matter was restricted in the narrowest possible way to the religious field. Allegedly the magisterium could accept arbitrarily any tenets it wishes, without possibility of philosophic control. See supra, n. 11.

The stand that the specific differentiation of Christian philosophy has to be sought in subjective factors, then, is not a defense ploy excogitated solely for this particular debate. It is something that follows necessarily from the exigencies of any general philosophy. The object, or subject matter, is the same for all. The differentiations arise from the personal approach. Just as Greek philosophy, Islamic philosophy, German philosophy, Russian philosophy are differentiated by the distinct ways in which each approaches and handles the general subject matter of philosophy, so Christian philosophy is to be regarded as dealing with the whole range of philosophical material through an approach that arises from the special habituation of its proponents. This way of distinguishing makes itself readily felt as one reads Greek, Islamic, British, or American philosophies. The primitive occasion of these distinctions is historical, or geographical, or based upon some other factor that lies outside strict philosophical engagement. Nevertheless its influence penetrates into the substantive nature of the philosophical activity itself. It can remain unshaken long after the external circumstances have disappeared or are no longer active. To be doing Greek philosophy today one does not have to be a Greek, let alone an ancient Greek. Yet Greek philosophy, for instance in Aristotelianism and Platonism, is still being actively developed in modern versions. The live Neoplatonic societies that have been flourishing in recent years have been prompted not so much by mere historical interest as by the enduring worth of characteristically Neoplatonic thought for philosophizing today. Similarly, German philosophy or Russian philosophy can be discerned in writers whose nationality or citizenship is neither German nor Russian. The fact of this type of differentiation is there to be seen. The present problem is to investigate in detail how it applies in the case of Christian philosophy.

These details of application have to be sought in factual historical reality. Both sides in the Bréhier dispute acknowledged that point. Neither side claimed to be dealing with something of its own invention. The one historical reality, as Bréhier saw it, was a merely fideistic acceptance of magisterial teachings and not a characteristically Christian development of Greek philosophy. As *Aeterni Patris* viewed it, and as Bréhier's opponents upheld it, Christian philosophy was a type of genuine philosophizing that had been developed in a theological matrix by patristic writers, been extended in wide-ranging fashion by the medieval theologians, and finally been separated as an academically distinct discipline by writers from the seventeenth century on. For neither side was Christian philosophy restricted to any particular philosophical area, as though it were a branch of philosophy. For its patristic originators, it was at liberty to deal with any philosophical difficulty encountered in their theological work; in its medieval developments it reached out into the minute details of logic, metaphysics, and philosophy of nature; and with *Aeterni Patris* it was called upon to face all the problems of modern philosophy. Everywhere it is marked clearly as a philosophy of general scope. Even with Bréhier, the hypothetical Christian philosophy that had in fact never existed bore on the entire Neoplatonic range, and the fideistic type, though limited to the particular area of magisterial pronouncements, was nevertheless acknowledged to be indefinite from the viewpoint of philosophical delineation. From whatever angle one views it, Christian philosophy as an historical reality has to be regarded as a general philosophy. It can of course treat of religion and even reflexively of itself, but only as particular items encountered in its general subject matter. It deals with them only as portions of its all-embracing thematic field.

As regards its own nature, then, Christian philosophy emerges, from its origins on, as a general philosophy that receives its specific differentiation from the personal dispositions of the thinkers who engage in it. That is what the historical reality brings out. Those are the contours to be envisaged in any effort today towards the building of an authentic Christian philosophy.

III

The first of the preceding introductory sections brought out how Christianity and a developed philosophy are both accidental and external to each other. They are accidental in the sense that the concept of neither of them necessarily involves the concept of the other. They are external insofar as each may exist outside the other, for in historical reality they have existed factually apart from each other. Then the second introductory section examined how Christian philosophy is a general philosophy and therefore receives its specification from the subjective dispositions of the persons who are doing the philosophizing.

Three preliminary questions, however, arise spontaneously from the foregoing considerations. They call for answers before the already existing body of Christian philosophy may be probed for assurance that it is genuinely philosophy and offers guarantee of a viable future towards which one's efforts may still be devoted. First, how does something accidental and external bring about the essential differentiation that is intrinsic to a philosophical discipline? Further, does specification through subjective disposition involve a radically pluralistic understanding of philosophy, to the extent that each side is rendered impervious to the probative force of the other's arguments? Third, how can a way of philosophizing that developed historically within sacred theology successfully cut the umbilical cord and carry on an independent life of its own?

The first of these three questions springs directly from the wording of Bréhier's objection. It asks how beliefs not intrinsically evident can play a role in the specification of a philosophical discipline. This is part of the more general problem of how factors extrinsic and accidental to philosophy can occasion an intrinsic specification within the discipline itself. Our own problem is how the specific differentiation of Christian philosophy can have its origin in a religious source and yet be intrinsic to a genuinely philosophical procedure. Authentically philosophical thought is based solely on what is both accessible, at least in principle, to unaided human cognition and, in fact, grasped by the natural power of human cognition in all the premises used in the philosophical reasoning. The reasoning cannot be grounded even to the slightest degree upon any religious authority. That stand, as has been noted above, is common to the Scholastic tradition on the distinction between philosophy and sacred theology and to Bréhier and others who reject the notion of Christian philosophy. From this particular viewpoint there can be no question of regarding philosophy as changed into the wine of theology. Philosophy has to remain philosophy. It has to defend itself without any theological support, and this more than ever in a context where its nature as philosophy is under discussion. The reasoned discourse has to remain strictly on the philosophical level.

But, on the other hand, can the strictly philosophical level ever be attained except by way of non-philosophical preparation? Descartes, as is well known,[30] had emphasized how the sense experience and the prejudices ingrained from earliest childhood exercised in fact a tremendous influence on a person's philosophical thinking. The stern intellectual asceticism of his *Meditations* was devised for counteracting that influence. With Aristotle, quite on the contrary, the cumulative experience of the past was the proper approach to successful philosophical reasoning. His approach to philosophy was dialectical, a process not on the strictly philosophical level. He displayed the clashing tenets of his predecessors in aporematic fashion, gave prominence to sayings of the poets and mythologists and drew copiously upon the legal experience enshrined in the constitutions of the Greek city states.

---

30. See Descartes, *Meditationes* 2–3; *Principia* 1.1–12.

All this constituted a dialectic that was carefully distinguished from the properly philosophical discourse. In Aristotle's view the exploratory dialectic "is the path to the principles of every inquiry" (*Topics* 1.2.101b3–4; Apostle-Gerson trans.). The dialectic did not furnish the principles themselves. Rather, it led the mind to center attention on those starting points already there in the things under scrutiny. The speculations of the Presocratics, for instance, were used to focus the mind's attention both on the contraries that were observable in nature and on the subject that was undergoing change in the sensible world. It was not the authority of the Presocratics that grounded Aristotle's acceptance of the doctrine of matter and form. It was what he saw in the real sensible world. The views of the Presocratics were indeed the path by which Aristotle and his hearers were led to focus their attention on the first principles of the philosophy of nature. But Aristotle was basing the philosophical inquiry upon those starting points themselves that were seen in the sensible world. He was not grounding it on the authority of any Presocratic thinkers. Traditional beliefs and even mythological indications were used to lead the mind in that way to the starting points or principles of genuine philosophy.

Those starting points, one cannot insist too strongly, were seen in the things themselves. They were not accepted on any authority, nor were they merely postulated as presuppositions. They were seen directly in what was before the mind's eye in reality itself. But it was the exploratory dialectic that had brought the mind to notice those starting points and to direct its focus upon them. The dialectic was the way to them, but the reality independent of the dialectic furnished them. In this way the dialectic, although the path to them, did not enter into the strictly philosophical procedure. The path ended before the paved road was trodden upon. Once the starting points were correctly isolated in the thing, it was they that initiated the properly philosophical reasoning. From them the authentic philosophy issued. One cannot emphasize too strongly that for Aristotle the path of dialectic merely led the mind to where the starting points might be found. But those starting points, it bears repeating, were found in the things themselves.

In a corresponding way the interests of Christian belief can bring the mind to see in things a number of philosophical starting points that otherwise might be missed. The revealed doctrine of creation in time led inquiring Christian minds to focus, for instance, on the problem of change without a subject that changed, on the notions of duration before and after time, on the beginning and ending of the temporal continuum in either a part or an indivisible, and on the extent of the power required for bridging the gap from nothing to being. Interest in the revealed doctrine of the Trinity, with three Persons the same in nature and in being, but really distinct from each other in relation, concentrated attention on what a real relation is and on how it does not increase the absolute being in a thing. The revealed doctrines of bodily resurrection and of Eucharistic presence led to closer looks at individuation and substance, and the problems these entailed. The belief in a supernatural destiny for mankind and the consequent reality of grace centered attention upon the naturally observable defects and frustrations of human nature and on the functioning of habituation as something really added to the nature itself. Concern about ecclesiastical infallibility could bring on inquiry into the obviously fallible performance of human reasoning and the difficult nature of semantics. In Aquinas, notably, the scriptural declaration that God's proper name is Being led to concentration on the being of observable things in a way that engendered a distinctive metaphysics of existence.

Faced with issues of this kind, the Christian thinker may be expected to concentrate on new starting points that are indeed found in the things observed, but which otherwise might have escaped notice. Those starting points were there in the things for all to see. But they could easily be passed unnoticed if the Christian faith did not draw special attention to them. Here the faith is not at all furnishing the starting points. Faith is merely guiding the mind to them in the role of a "friendly star."[31] It remains external to them, and the encounter of the one with the other is accidental to both. But solely on the starting points seen in the thing itself does the mind erect a philosophy. No support is given to the reasoning by the revealed doctrine. The procedure is philosophical through and through.

Yet it is a new type of philosophy. Its starting points have been reached in a noticeably special way. When these distinctive starting points come to play the dominant role in initiating the philosophical thinking, they thereby give rise to a characteristically new kind of philosophizing. In consequence, this type may rightly be called Christian, since general philosophies are distinguished from one another by the character of their respective starting points. The selection and

31. ". . . like a friendly star, shines down upon his path and points out to him the fair gate of truth beyond all danger of wandering." *Aet. Patr.* 9; 2, 20b. So in an approach from the viewpoint of specification by formal object, Umberto Degl'Innocenti, "Osservationi sulla filosofia cristiana," *Angelicum* 18 (1941), 357–78, rejected (pp. 364–66) a philosophy that is Christian *ex obiecto*, while allowing it *ex subiecto*: "La Rivelazione dunque non è soltanto norma negativa ma in un certo senzo anche positiva" (p. 369).

internal grouping of the starting points is always brought about by external influence, and here the external influence is Christian belief.

A way of thinking that claims to be a Christian philosophy in today's academic sense of philosophy should conform to this pattern. The philosopher will be guided to his starting points by Christian interests. Otherwise, the philosophy would have no clear title to the designation "Christian." But it will have to base its reasoning entirely upon those starting points as they are seen in the things themselves, starting points that are, at least in principle, naturally knowable and are, in fact, actually known on the strength of their natural evidence when they are functioning in this role. If the procedure brings anything else into its starting points, it is no longer genuine philosophy, as philosophy is technically taken today.

Any critique of work intended to be Christian philosophy should accordingly be made from this twofold viewpoint. Has the writer actually been led to his starting points in things by the promptings of Christian beliefs? Does his philosophizing then sprout from those naturally knowable starting points and keep the entire force of the demonstrative processes based on them alone? If he is basing them at all on the beliefs that led him to them, his reasoning is no longer functioning as philosophy. If it appeals to those beliefs for support at any stage or in any particular item, it is going outside its philosophical mandate. The reasoning must be grounded on the naturally known premises alone. Only thereby will its conclusions be genuinely philosophical. In this regard the critique of any proposed Christian philosophy should be incisive and severe, in order to remove possible misunderstanding. Clear expression of the way the reasoning is based solely on the naturally evident premises is continually required. The purity of the philosophical discourse has to be made apparent.

Close examination will show that the philosophy signalized and encouraged by *Aeterni Patris* did in fact come into being in the way just sketched.[32] Difficulties or problems arising from particular points in

---

32. The deep influence of Christian belief on western philosophical thinking can hardly be denied by Catholic critics of the existence or possibility of "Christian philosophy." Sierp (1, viii; supra, n. 17), while denying that there is any Christian philosophy, was in accord with the church fathers in promoting the use of true philosophy "pour élever à Dieu le temple de la science chrétienne." That implies strong influence in the order of final causality, and also in the distinguishing of the true from the false in philosophy itself. Nédoncelle (p. 57) would allow that "the Thomist philosophy is Christian, if by that one means that it came to birth in an atmosphere of Christian reflection, that it leads normally to Christ, and that, despite its internal autonomy, it must give way to the requirements of faith if there should seem to be conflict between the two." Van Steenberghen (p. 12; text supra, n. 21) could agree with Gilson that Christian

Christian belief and requiring philosophical explanation were in fact the *occasion* for the origin and development of Christian philosophy. But the philosophy so engendered was not at all taking its doctrinal origin in the Christian beliefs or arising from them in the sense of being built upon them. As philosophy it originated solely in the naturally known starting points and was developed from them alone. Its principles and conclusions all remain on the level of naturally evident knowledge. This enables it as a body of philosophy to meet the strictest standards for philosophical thinking, and to extend its range to anything of philosophical interest. It did indeed enter the circuit of philosophical thinking on the occasion of problems encountered by Christian belief. But once in the circuit, it has access to all the rational energy that may be required for illumination throughout the whole domain of a general philosophy. It can proceed from one philosophic topic to another, according to the ways interest is aroused.

These broad but sufficiently incisive reflections can be readily substantiated by the historical details. The Christian philosophy at issue did follow that pattern. In the patristic sources it stays for the most part quite close to the more immediate problems occasioned by Christian belief, although in Boethius is gives instances of spreading out into the wider fields pointed to by the Aristotelian treatises. In medieval times this extension of interest becomes strikingly evident. The commentaries on the *Sentences* of Peter Lombard start out from interests close to items of Christian belief, as drawn up systematically in Lombard's collection. But then they go on in uninhibited fashion to range over the whole relevant territory of metaphysics and logic, as well as over much in the domains of natural philosophy and ethics. Where the commentaries base their demonstrations even partly on revealed premises, the procedure has to be regarded as theological. But much intermittent reasoning contained in the procedure, if excerpted from the theological setting, could easily appear as philosophical. In Aquinas, for instance, the division and methods of the sciences are dealt with in a theological commentary on Boethius's *De trinitate*. Yet the epistemological sections can be isolated and used to-

---

revelation has exercised and continues to exercise a profound influence on the Christian philosopher. Nevertheless, these writers are unwilling to allow that the external and accidental Christian factors can function as cause of the philosophy's intrinsic specification. They seem unable to realize that any philosophy, insofar as it is a human activity, carries with it intrinsically a relation to those accidental circumstances that occasioned its specification. This relation is essential to it, though the factual terminus upon which the relation bears is accidental and is determined by historical circumstances. So Gilson (*Bulletin*, p. 39) could write: "Les deux ordres restent distincts, bien que la relation qui les unit soit intrinsèque."

day as a text for courses in philosophy. This gives rise to the problem how the same reasoning can in one context appear as philosophical, and in another as theological (thus bringing up the third preliminary question noted at the beginning of this section). The present point is merely that the reasoning in Christian philosophy has to be based solely on premises that are naturally evident, if it is to satisfy the notion signalized by *Aeterni Patris* and be able to offer its distinctive service to the faith.

These considerations suffice to show how, in the mainstream of Christian philosophy, there is no attempt at fusion of premises that are not naturally knowable with the premises that are evident to un-aided human cognition. Yet the specification "Christian," though coming from an accidental and external source, occasions an intrinsic differentiation in the philosophy. It does this through the selection it indicates for the philosophical starting points. Nevertheless, it is the character of the starting points so selected, namely the relevant interest they can have for Christian thought, that precisely accounts for the internal specification. This specification, as noted above (n. 19) in regard to McInerny, may rightly be called substantive, insofar as it enters into the essence of the philosophical *habitus* that is being exercised.

These considerations will apply likewise to the work of individuals who do Christian philosophy from time to time even though their general philosophical formation and interests are of a different kind. There is no contradiction in being an existentialist or a phenomenologist or a linguistic philosopher and in doing some work in Christian philosophy. Instances such as the case of Gabriel Marcel may readily be brought forward. Provided that in the particular piece of work the starting points of the reasoning are of the kind that give rise to Christian philosophy, there is no reason why the writer may not be said to be doing that type of philosophy in the particular undertaking. Likewise, writers in the field of general literature may be found included in listings of Christian philosophers. A recent survey, for instance, gives John Henry Newman, Orestes A. Brownson, and Friedrich von Hügel as representatives of Christian philosophy in the Catholic thought of the nineteenth and twentieth centuries.[33] The Society of Christian Philosophers, which meets regularly in connection with other philosophical associations, and which publishes as its journal *Faith and Philosophy* (1983–   ), has a membership with widely varying philosophical backgrounds.[34] All these ramifications have to be taken into

33. See Coreth, *Christliche Philosophie* 1, 698–749.
34. On its cover page *Faith and Philosophy* carefully distinguishes its field from that

consideration in a survey of the historical reality of Christian philosophy. They show the flexibility that has to be assigned to the notion, even when one is working towards the development of the mainstream type that, as just noted, flows from patristic sources through medieval Scholasticism into the program envisaged by *Aeterni Patris*.

The external and accidental character of the relation of Christianity to philosophy, however, does not at all preclude the carrying over of clearly fixed subdivisions that have their historical origin in the partitions of Christianity itself. One may speak of Catholic philosophy, of Protestant philosophy, of Lutheran philosophy, of Calvinistic philosophy, of Reformed epistemology. The subjective habituation characteristic of each Christian denomination or persuasion will prompt a corresponding selection of basic philosophical starting points, and these starting points in turn will give rise to different Christian philosophies, bearing family resemblances to one another on generic and specific levels. This will mean that the more specific Christian philosophies will differ from each other in correspondence to the denominations professed by their proponents, while generically all come under the one caption of Christian philosophy. But in each, the philosophic reasoning must have as its sole basis the naturally evident starting points that have been selected according to the lead given by the proponent's faith. To base the reasoning on the acceptance of any divinely revealed tenet would make the procedure theological.

As far as the present issue is concerned, these reflections reinforce the importance of viewing philosophy in the concrete. Philosophy is not to be gauged in precise detachment from the person who is doing the philosophizing. Philosophy is a human activity. As an activity, it is inherent as an accident in the substance of the one from whom it proceeds. Because the person is substantially human, his or her philosophizing has to be regarded as a human act. But because the person is accidentally a number of other things, the character of the philosophizing can be profoundly influenced by these. Because the individual happens to be a Christian, of whatever denomination, the approach to philosophy can be different and the starting points selected can readily give rise to a distinctive type of philosophizing. To abstract the notion "philosophy" from its particular instances precisively, and set it up as though it were a substance in its own right, may easily falsify the situation. Philosophy does not have any real existence in that substantial fashion. It exists in reality only as determined by

of philosophy of religion, which nevertheless is included in its general range. It has shown little interest in the expression "Christian philosophy" as denoting a distinct type of philosophy.

the relevant specifying and individuating characteristics of the person from whom the activity proceeds. In the case of Christian philosophy, Christian tendencies dominate and thereby occasion a substantive specification of the philosophy, a specification that calls for the distinctive title "Christian." Upon mature reflection there seems to be nothing more mysterious about specifically different philosophies proceeding from differently habituated persons than there is in the phenomenon of grand opera and hard rock issuing from radically different types of musical habituation.

In this context, accordingly, Gilson's explanation of Christian philosophy in terms of its selection of topics has solid footing. Similarly, Maritain's distinction of the nature and the state of a philosophy is at least in solidarity with the Aristotelian setting of substance and accident. Likewise, McInerny's observation, that from this angle the conditioning of Christian philosophy is quite parallel to the conditioning of all other philosophies, fits into the Aristotelian background. All philosophies are conditioned by the preceding dialectic that leads up to their starting points. Entrance to philosophy has to take place through a teacher. With Aristotle (*Metaph.* 2.1.993b11–19) that process can go back through long decades of preparation. Whether one likes it or not, there is teaching authority leading up to everyone's first selection of philosophical starting points. The starting points so selected differentiate the philosophy specifically, and in that sense allow the external and accidental circumstances to provide a geographical or historical or religious designation for it.

This necessity of conceiving philosophy as an activity being carried on by a human person is deeply embedded in the Aristotelian tradition. The more general principle was that an accident could not be thought of without involving the notion of a substance in which it inhered. The notion of philosophy involved the notion of a human person who was doing the philosophizing. That human person required special habituation in order to philosophize. In intellection one can of course universalize each of the notions and consider each apart from the other. In the terminology of Aquinas that expressed what was implicit in the Aristotelian text, one may abstract each of these notions either non-precisively or precisively.[35] Abstracted non-preci-

35. Aquinas, *De ente et essentia* 2.85–308; Leonine ed., *Opera Omnia* 43, 371–73. See trans. A. Maurer, *On Being and Essence*, 2nd ed. (Toronto: Pontifical Institute of Mediaeval Studies, 1968), 2.5–13; pp. 37–44. The viewpoint of "with precision" (*cum precisione—De ente* 2.126; 255; 278; 282; 290) and "without precision" (*non fiat precisio—De ente* 3.70; cf. *sine determinatione*, 2.211) is that of Aquinas himself. But the doctrine is present in Aristotle. The non-precisive type may be seen in the way Aristotle finds a

sively, the concept did not exclude anything that went with it in the original concretion. It continued to embrace all the rest, though "implicitly and indistinctly."[36] Abstracted precisively, however, it excluded all the rest. In precisive abstraction, philosophy is represented as something just in itself, that is, as though it were a substance. But when you take it to exist in that way, you are not dealing with it as it is in reality. You have cut it off from what it requires for real existence and activity. To deal with it as it actually is, you have to leave substance and habituation in it, though implicitly and indistinctly. Yet it is exactly that implicitness and indistinctness that the Bréhier approach rules out in demanding "clear and distinct awareness."[37]

The contrast at issue here is, accordingly, that of a philosophy based on clear and distinct ideas on the one hand, and on the other of a philosophy based upon real things known with what they contain implicitly and indistinctly. Descartes' far-reaching claim was that philosophy had to be based only upon clear and distinct ideas. Indistinctness was not to be allowed in their content. Ideas no longer had their origin in sensible things, and were not abstracted from them. They could be taken as standing before the mind just in themselves, each finely honed and rendered clearly distinct from the others. Descartes was well aware that people base their thinking upon sensible experience. The reason was that we are born infants, and grow up in a world of sensible activity. We likewise accumulate prejudices stemming from the faulty thinking of our predecessors. The prolonged Cartesian meditation was brought in to rid the mind of this ingrained habituation and make it accustom itself to ground its thoughts on clear and distinct ideas only. Descartes' model was the clearcut precision of mathematical ideas, in which a circle on the mathematical plane is circular to full perfection, regardless of the variable contours that sensible circles do in fact have. The result of this approach is that no considerations antecedent to the distinct clarification of ideas may be allowed to influence philosophy. The sensible experience in which one

---

universal notion to be identical severally with each of its instances at *Metaph.* 5.26.1023b30–32. The non-precisive type may be found at work in the way each accident has to be represented as a substance in order to be understood, at *Metaph.* 7.1.1028b1–2. The general scholastic tradition, however, failed to absorb this doctrine and tended to use abstraction and precision as synonyms. Accordingly, "precisive" is recognized but labeled "rare" by the *O.E.D.*, s.v. On substance in the notion of every accident, see Aristotle, *Metaph.* 7.1.1028a35–36; cf. *Anal. Post.* 1.6.74b6–9.

36. ". . . implicite continet eam et indistincte," *De ente* 2.297. Maurer translates this as, "contains it implicitly and indistinctly," 2.13; p. 44.

37. ". . . conscience claire et distincte"—Bréhier, *Bulletin*, p. 52; text supra, n. 12. Mark Jordan, p. 299, noted that the main parties in the dispute "do not agree about philosophy itself."

has grown up, and the traditional teaching one has received from others, have to be relentlessly disregarded. They cannot serve in Aristotelian fashion as a dialectic leading up to a vantage point from which one can see the starting points in the things under investigation. Rather, the mind has to look immediately and directly at its own ideas, and at nothing else. In an approach of this kind, there is obviously no possibility that anything external and accidental to the strictly philosophical thinking could give rise to a specifically differentiating characteristic within the philosophy itself.

In the Aristotelian approach, on the contrary, only external sensible things were immediately and directly present to human cognition. But in the actuality of the cognition, the knower and the thing known were identical, as far as the cognition was concerned. In knowing the external sensible thing, the knower was thereby immediately aware of himself or herself, but just concomitantly and in terms of sensible reality. The direct focus remained solely on the external thing itself. In this way external sensible things were epistemologically prior to ideas. Epistemologically the external things were more present to human cognition than were the concepts in which they were known. From the things, and from them alone, the concepts had to be derived. The things themselves were the bedrock upon which a philosophy was built.

From this Aristotelian viewpoint, the Cartesian philosophy is deliberately shutting out by mental asceticism the intrinsic bearing of human concepts upon their actual origin in real sensible things. Instead of being left in the non-precisive abstraction that would allow them still to contain implicitly and indistinctly the reality from which they were abstracted, they have been cut off precisively from their sensible origins. All that they were abstracted from is deliberately and firmly excluded. They are now put forward as clear and distinct ideas, and made the basis of all acceptable philosophizing. It is a basis, however, that can have existence solely in the mind. In the real world their content exists only in union with what they were abstracted from. Only when left in non-precisive abstraction, then, can the concepts express the real world and present the foundation required for correct philosophical thinking, according to the Aristotelian understanding of philosophy.

Such is the confrontation between the two radically different philosophical procedures. Applied to the present problem, it means that the Cartesian approach can take the notion of philosophy itself as a precisively abstracted essence and deal with it in isolation from all else. In that approach, nothing external or accidental is allowed entry into the problem of a philosophy's specification. Christianity is both external and accidental to philosophy, and therefore cannot initiate its specification. There can be no such thing as an authentic Christian philosophy. Any contribution of Christianity has to remain accidental and external to the philosophical thinking. Because it is based on faith, it is incompatible with philosophical procedure. In consequence it is to be firmly and perhaps not too politely denied entry at any of philosophy's checkpoints.

On the other side of the isolating wall, philosophy is seen as a human activity carried on in a real world. It is something actually dependent upon a human person as the substance in which it inheres, and upon that person's habituation for the source of its specification. These factors cannot be left out when its specification is being investigated. Against that background, no incompatibility between "Christian" and "philosophy" arises, for no distinctively Christian or otherwise non-evident premises are thereby introduced into the philosophical reasoning. The premises all come from things attainable by unaided human cognition. The external and accidental factors merely led the mind to see the specifying aspects in the essential reality itself. Christian philosophy is not something that was first planned out on the drawing board and then produced in reality. It developed spontaneously in the patristic and medieval writers. It was already there for epistemologists to recognize the external and accidental factors that shaped its course. There is no question of looking for something that follows necessarily from either Christianity or philosophy. The order of inquiry is exactly the opposite. From the concrete reality, the ultimate source of the intrinsic specification is traced to something that is external and accidental to philosophy's essential nature. What is there are the persons who are doing the philosophizing. The external circumstances may guide the particular person into becoming a phenomenologist, a linguistic analyst, a Thomist, a Scotist, a Marxist, or a liberation philosopher. They may similarly guide him or her to becoming a Christian philosopher.

The radical difference of approach, then, is not at all an ad hoc device thought up for a solution to the Bréhier problem. It is a straight historical explanation of the factual background of this debate about Christian philosophy. It shows why one side can look upon philosophy as an essence just in itself, like a Platonic idea or an Avicennian common nature, and therefore something to be studied like a mathematical circle in geometry, without any attention to the vagaries inevitably present in the visible drawing on the board. This approach will exclude the influence of anything accidental or external, such as sensible experience or teaching by others. It will prevent the force of the opponent's reasoning from being felt, for it would require the Christian factor to be something intrinsic to the philosophy if it is to bring about the specification. It can regard that factor only as blindly authoritative and as a pre-philosophical habituation. On either of those counts, it finds but a blatant self-contradiction when "Christian" is forced into a verbal union with the generic notion of philosophy. It has utterly no means of seeing that the generic notion of philosophy is merely a concept abstracted non-precisively from the activities of individual persons, quite as any other universal notion.

Those are the two approaches. For the present, the problem is not to settle which of them is correct. The objective for the moment is just to show that they are radically different ways of facing the Christian philosophy problem, and that the inability of each of the two sides to see the other's arguments hinges consequently upon that radical difference. But the situation does bring up the more general question of what permits philosophy to be carried on in such radically different ways. This is the question of philosophical pluralism, a question that now calls for careful investigation to the extent that it bears upon the present problem. The preceding overview of the Bréhier debate has shown how the controversy on Christian philosophy is grounded on a confrontation between two philosophically different conceptions of philosophy itself. They could hardly differ more radically. The same reasoning that is cogent and conclusive in the one appears to be sophistical and repellent in the other. From this angle, the question of philosophical pluralism becomes an integral consideration for the present study.

IV

The immediately preceding section has located in radical pluralism the inability of the two sides in the Christian philosophy debate to come to grips with each other. It thereby gives rise to a second preliminary question prior to any actual engagement in the enterprise. Is philosophy so pluralistic in its very nature that no two philosophies can agree with each other? Even a quick glance over the history of western philosophy will bring out the point of the question. Atomism, Platonism, Aristotelianism, Hegelianism, phenomenology, existentialism, structuralism—these are but a few of its manifold divisions. They can hardly be considered as successively improved varieties in the same substantially identical endeavor, in the way each new advance in modern physics absorbs the preceding stages and carries the accomplishments progressively to new heights. Is that the case in philosophy? No, except to a very limited extent. The successive philosophies continue to function each in its own independent way, clashing with one another and giving rise to the interminable controversies of which the Bréhier dispute is but one comparatively minor instance. Some philosophies, such as Cartesianism and linguistic analysis, have even made the express declaration that all the preceding efforts are to be effaced, quite as in the political philosophy of Plato's *Republic* (6.501A), where the former habituation was to be drastically broken by segregation of the children from their parents, and a fresh start made from a clean slate.

The obvious and widespread lack of agreement among philosophers tends to turn people away from philosophy itself, on the ground that nothing certain can be found in its teachings. Its sole occupation would seem to consist in continually regurgitating and chewing once again the same old cud. True, the philosophies can be grouped on the basis of family resemblances, as is perhaps most readily seen in the Christian philosophies of the middle ages.[38] In that way, some order is read into the wildly rambling array. But in the ultimate analysis each authentically new philosophy will be found radically different from the others. As with Aristotelianism and Cartesianism, the occasion for the variety will be found in each case to lie outside the realm proper to philosophy itself. It will lie in the training and habituation of the individual person who is doing the philosophizing. This can vary indefinitely, as do the individuals themselves.

Nevertheless, though the philosophies may differ as extensively as the physiognomies, the resemblances by which they may be grouped are just as noticeable. Historically, the starting points of philosophies in the broadest range will be found located either in things, or in human thought, or in language. The ancients located them in things. Even with Plato (*Parmenides* 132CD) the Ideas were objects existent in reality, as expressly contrasted with merely mental existence. In Augustine (*De magistro* 40.1; CSEL, 77, 49, 2–5) the things themselves were seen in their presence in the divine Word. From Descartes on, the tendency has been to start with the content of one's own cognition in its mental status, and with linguistic analysis in the present century the method has been to start from language. But these three areas

---

38. So "family resemblances," in Maurice De Wulf, *Scholasticism Old and New*, trans. P. Coffey (London: Longmans, Green and Co., 1909), p. 46. Also "family likenesses," De Wulf, *History of Medieval Philosophy*, 3rd ed., trans. P. Coffey (London: Longmans, Green and Co., 1909), p. 108. "Like the various members of a single family, each of the scholastics reveals his own individuality"—*History*, p. 109.

may all aim to open out on the same objects. Things are what one thinks and speaks about. Thought bears on things and is expressed in language. Speech aims to convey what is thought about things. The content is in that way common. So, in regard to the present topic, Christian philosophy was discussed as an object known to both sides, and the question about its nature as a general philosophy could be debated, even though one side is starting from the notion of philosophy as a clear and distinct essence, and the other side from the notion of it as a real activity. The content of the object under discussion is the same, even though on the one side it is understood against the background of Cartesian clear and distinct ideas, and on the other against a background that gives epistemological priority to external things while studying them in nonprecisive abstraction from their condition in reality. Because the content is in this way common, communication and dialogue are possible and fruitful. But the philosophical explanation in terms of causes will be radically different in each of the two respective approaches.

How deeply this cleavage in explanation goes may be seen by considering the two different ways in which the first principle of demonstration is viewed. In the Aristotelian approach, that maxim has traditionally been called the principle of contradiction. At first it meant that being contradicts nonbeing, and it was applied in a universe where being was taken in many ways, accidental as well as substantial. From the time of Sir William Hamilton on, there has been a tendency to call it the principle or law of non-contradiction, in the sense in which Leibniz called it the principle of essences.[39] The result

39. E.g. "Again, metaphysics, Christian or non-Christian, must have recourse to various criteria in measuring its approach to the truth; critical philosophy itself finds the principle of non-contradiction too slow and rudimentary a producer of concepts and must add the organizing power of ideas and their conformity with an experience which is both intellectual and moral at the same time." Nédoncelle, p. 147. Cf. ". . . the other great principle of our reasonings, viz., that of essences; that is, the principle of identity or of contradiction . . ." Leibniz, in *The Leibniz-Clarke Correspondence*, ed. H. G. Alexander (New York: Philosophical Library, 1956), p. 57. "As it enjoins the absence of contradiction as the indispensable condition of thought, it ought to be called, not the Law of Contradiction, but the Law of Non-contradiction, or of *non-repugnantia*." Sir William Hamilton, *Lectures on Metaphysics and Logic*, ed. Henry L. Mansel and John Veitch (New York: Sheldon and Company, 1883), 2, 58–59. The transformation of the notion of being throughout the Scholastic period in this direction is tellingly traced by Rolf Schönberger, *Die Transformation des klassischen Seinsbegriffs im Mittelalter* (Berlin: Walter de Gruyter, 1986). Schönberger sums up the result: "The schools of Scotism and Thomism converge thereby in the tendency to define being (*Seiendheit*) primarily through non-contradiction, that is, possibility, with existence on the other hand understood as pointing out factuality or presence" (p. 386; my translation). Against this deep historical background, the expressions "principle of contradiction" and "principle of non-contradiction" can hardly be regarded as innocent variants for the same metaphysical notion. The difference in what they represent is radical.

for the Bréhier side of the Christian philosophy debate has been that the question focuses upon the internal constitution of philosophy as an essence, an essence that would, as thoroughly rational, become self-contradictory if differentiated by the fideistic characterization of "Christian." Anything outside that clear and distinct essence, such as contingent circumstances of place and personal disposition, are phased out of the discussion about it.

In consequence, the Bréhier approach, when assessed from the opposite side of the dispute, is seen as viewing the nature of a philosophy solely in precisive abstraction from the philosophy's status in real existence. It sets the philosophy up as something just in itself, as though it were a substance instead of a predicamental accident, somewhat in the fashion of logical atomism. That approach effectively excludes the thinking person from the global notion of the philosophy. By the same token it excludes also the person's habituation and the philosophy's inevitable intrinsic relation to the definite accidental circumstances that occasioned the selection of the basic starting points. That selection specifies the philosophy intrinsically as linguistic, pragmatic, Marxist, Platonic, Islamic, or of whatever kind in question, and in this present case, Christian.

A philosophy, then, could not really be a philosophy without that intrinsic bearing on the external accidents. In its categorical being it is not a substance. Real status for it as substance is what the principle of contradiction, as the principle of being, fundamentally vetoes. Concerned first of all with a thing's categorical being, which here is a person's activity intrinsically related to external and accidental circumstances, the principle of contradiction cannot in reality allow the exclusion of the categorical accident's intrinsic dependencies. The principle of contradiction is a fighting maxim, holistic and dynamic in its coverage. In seemingly kaleidoscopic variation it matches exactly the multifold aspects of real being. It brings all of them simultaneously under its grasp, warding off vigorously whatever would exclude any of them. It demands imperiously that a philosophy be specified by the individual historical circumstances in which it was formed. It cannot tolerate in reality a philosophy whose specification is cut off from those external and accidental origins, even though the external factors vary incessantly and give rise in deeply pluralistic fashion to innumerable types of philosophies. With Christian philosophy, those external and accidental factors are revealed beliefs.

In its thoroughgoing sweep, of course, the principle of contradiction forbids internal incompatibility. It does not permit a philosophy's reasoning to be based on any fideistic premises, nor allow appeal to any non-evident tenets for support. By definition, philosophy is a type of naturally evident discourse. The principle requires that all historical aberrations and any hypothetical instances that use non-evident prin-. ciples be excluded pitilessly from the ambit of Christian philosophy. Yet its absolute and most profound bearing is to safeguard philoso-phy's status as a predicamental accident dependent upon historical circumstances for specification and development. Here the litmus test with the principle of contradiction does not show any red clash of internal incompatibility. Rather, it presents a clear blue that indicates first and foremost a dynamic yet firm and holistic base for the erection of a vigorous Christian philosophy. The principle of contradiction is not at all confined to a flat surface within an essence that is being regarded as a Cartesian clear and distinct idea. In far different fashion it breathes and struggles and rules throughout all the variations of lived reality.

Since even the most fundamental principle of reasoning is under-stood so differently by the opposed sides, it would seem that a radically pluralistic conception of philosophy is required for evaluating the de-bate on Christian philosophy and for appreciating the intransigence of the participants. The pluralistic conception need not involve any skepticism or any thoroughgoing type of relativism. It is relativistic only in the historical sense that each philosophy starts from its own set of principles and draws the conclusions that follow from them and correspond to them. It allows each philosophy to make an epistemo-logical evaluation of the truth or falsity in each of the others on the basis of firmly accepted starting points in that philosophy itself. This evaluation can be, and usually is, very dogmatic. In the Christian philosophy debate, the adherence to the Aristotelian background about the origin of human cognition in external sensible things results in what might seem at first hearing a ludicrously dogmatic stand, since it involves the conclusion that all the new philosophies from Descartes on are wrong from start to finish. They all locate their starting points either on cognition or in language, and thereby build upon a wrong basis.

That stand would be ludicrously dogmatic if it excluded commu-nication and dialogue, or if it left no possibility of change from one philosophy to another. But it does allow intercommunication and di-alogue, since the objects in all the philosophies have a content that is common. Nor does it rule out a radical passing over from one phi-losophy to a new one. True, once the starting points of a philosophy have been adopted, there is no strictly philosophical way open for change from that philosophy to one with another basis. The change cannot be made in virtue of the philosophy's own principles. Yet people do change from one philosophy to another. If the conclusions reached in the philosophical reasoning begin to appear unacceptable, the dissatisfaction can lead to a reassessing of the starting points and eventually to abandoning them for a new set. Russell, for instance, found while still a young man that he could no longer accept the idealistic tenet, learned from Bradley, that knowing a thing means changing it in some way.[40] Though students may usually be expected to retain the outlook prevalent in their graduate school, they sometimes abandon it and start out on a radically new path. So in the Christian philosophy debate it is possible, but none too likely, for someone to experience enough discomfort to cause a deeper look at the Cartesian starting points, with a gradual realization that, though physically nothing can be more close to the mind than the mind itself and its ideas, in cognition an external sensible thing can have epistemological priority. The fear of naïve realism will have to be overcome by study of the Aristotelian doctrine that form is the cause of being, and that when a form is received immaterially, it makes the cognitive agent be the external thing of which it is the form. The jolt given by this new study would be required for the nuclear quantum jump into another philosophical orbit. In practice, this is difficult. But it is possible, and its prospect gives meaning to communication and dialogue within the pluralistic understanding of philosophy.

For the moment, however, the pluralistic conception assures citizen rights for all philosophies in today's global village, and opens the way to profitable interchange of thought in the Christian philosophy debate. As a philosophy, Christian philosophy asks nothing more than a recognized place in an open forum. But it can be content with nothing less. From patristic times on it has striven to avoid a ghetto. Today's pluralistic mentality assures Christian philosophy an acknowledged place, and at the same time enables it to understand both the intransigence of its opponents and the benefit of dialoguing with them. By guiding each side down to the ultimate roots of its respective reasoning, and thereby showing how radical the difference between them is, the pluralistic understanding of philosophy offers the basic explanation why the two sides remain so far apart after the many decades of discussion. By the same token, the pluralistic mentality wards off any skepticism and, while acknowledging historical relativism, safeguards the adherence to firm and definitely established truths. Pluralistic

---

40. See Bertrand Russell, "Logical Atomism," in *Contemporary British Philosophy*, ed. J. H. Muirhead (London: George Allen & Unwin, 1924), 1, 360.

understanding allows each side to elucidate the other's content, even though each retains its own specific slant on whatever is brought under its gaze. The pluralism is in this way a carefully reasoned dogmatic conception.

All this is involved in a comprehensive understanding of the cleavage between the two sides in the Bréhier debate. The separating barrier is fully as deep and as high as the wall between Descartes and Aristotle, and like the temple veil, it will be shattered only by a catastrophic jolt. A pluralistic conception of philosophy brings out the reason why this is so.

V

The third preliminary question in regard to the nature of Christian philosophy concerns its identity with or distinction from sacred theology. Thematically the situation may be clear enough. Sacred theology has divinely revealed premises as its starting points. Christian philosophy, on the contrary, has only naturally knowable premises for that role. At least in principle, these latter are attainable by the unaided human mind. In contrast, the divinely revealed premises are accepted authoritatively, without intrinsic evidence being offered for their truth. But in each of the two disciplines the conclusions are drawn from the premises in accord with the regular norms of logic. Connatural affectivity to the supernatural by grace is of course an important and constant help to the theologian, especially when the conclusions are only probable or are in the area of moral matters. Yet the logical pattern of the discourse is parallel in the two cases, and the difference in starting points allows ample ground for distinguishing radically the one discipline from the other.

However, that is not the whole story. Sacred theology is continually using naturally known premises in the course of its reasoning. If it is dealing with the goodness of God, for instance, it can take as the divinely revealed premises the numerous scriptural assertions about the ways in which God is good. But to develop what those premises entail, say in a controversy with Manicheans, it uses naturally known truths. It reasons that goodness follows on being, that it functions as final cause of action and provides the motive for creation. It is thereby using naturally known premises and conclusions, and making them part of the theological discourse. Similarly, it can take as a premise the scriptural assertion that the name of God is being, and then, with naturally available premises, show that at the time of the scriptural assertion a name was meant to express the nature of the thing so

named, and that the nature of no other thing is being. All this is
theological discourse, though it is drawing upon both history and philosophy. But if the philosophical reasoning is detached from its theological setting, will it not look exactly the same? The starting points
could be found in the goodness and the being of sensible things, with
a demonstration concluding that goodness in its primary instance is
identical with God. What has happened is that in the theological discourse the implications of being and goodness have been predicated
of the supernaturally revealed God of the Scriptures. In that predication those naturally available notions are united with the revealed
God in one cognitional existence in the human mind, through predication that says the one is the other. The result is that the natural
premise is raised to the theological level through the identification of
its terms with the major term of the revealed premise. The discourse
is wholly theological, grounded in revealed premises about God. It
means that the Christian God is good, and not merely as in metaphysics that subsistent existence is good.

But the notions of being and goodness as found in secondary instances can also be taken as starting points. Through focal meaning,
each of those instances gives expression to the nature of the respective
primary instances, although in secondary fashion. The being and
goodness so known can serve as the starting points for philosophical
reasoning about what their natures imply. Instead of commencing
with divine revelations, the reasoning is from created things to the
first cause of everything created. In this case the reasoning starts on
and remains on the philosophical plane. But everything in Aquinas's
De ente et essentia may be found worked out in scattered fashion in his
commentary on the *Sentences* of Peter Lombard. Yet the *De ente* can
be used as a text in philosophy courses. The material is arranged in
philosophical order, but the reasoning is exactly the same. So much is
this so, that a recent work has endeavored to see a virtual correspondence of the philosophical order with the schematization followed in
the *Summa theologiae* on the nature and attributes of God. The con-
tention is that Aquinas would have written a philosophical treatise on
God and his attributes in exactly the same schematic order as that
followed in the *Summa theologiae*.[41]

But this "managing" of philosophy by theology has its dangers. Nuances already ingrained in the notions accepted through revelation

41. "Man kann daher annehmen, dass Thomas diese Ordnung auch dann einge-
halten hätte, wenn er eine rein philosophische Theologie geschrieben hätte." Leo J.
Elders, *Die Metaphysik des Thomas von Aquin in historischer Perspektive* (Salzburg-München:
Pustet, 1985–87), 2, 8.

can easily be carried over into those same notions as developed from their secondary instances. The notion of God as a father, founded upon the sharing of the divine nature through grace, could easily be read into the notion of the primary being that is attainable through reasoning from creatures. Similarly, other religious and theological notions could be insinuated unobtrusively into discourse based on naturally known premises.

In a strongly believing Christian the reaction of connaturality, moreover, may be so compelling that it spontaneously confers upon the naturally known aspects of the primary instance of being the reverence accorded to God as known through revelation. That attitude is laudable and meaningful enough in one's integral life as a Christian. But it can cause weakening in the close and detached attention required for the strictly philosophical cogency of the reasoning. It brings one face to face with Pascal's distracting charge that the God of the philosophers is not the God of Abraham and Isaac and Jacob.[42] One has to explain carefully that though the one and the same God is believed in by faith and is reached by metaphysical reasoning, the specifically Christian aspects are not attained by the philosophical discourse. Similarly, the current objections today that the cold notion of an Aristotelian prime mover cannot inspire religious devotion are beside the point. Those objections are based on the consideration that in the contemporary philosophy of religion God is studied first and foremost as the supreme object of worship, instead of metaphysically as the first cause of all other things. Likewise, people may speak of "biblical metaphysics," or claim to see in the naturally knowable imperfections of nature the way to establish the fallen state revealed in the doctrine of original sin. All those are instances of the tendency to read religious overtones into considerations that are claimed to be based solely upon what is naturally knowable.

Even more significant for the present questions, however, is that failure to understand correctly the relation of philosophy to theology can give rise to faulty notions in regard to their association with each other in Christian tradition. It can occasion the claim that the reasoning in the patristic and medieval authors is only theological, in the sense that it is not at all philosophical. On that account the thinking found in those authors has been denied any genuine philosophical

42. "Dieu d'Abraham, Dieu d'Isaac, Dieu de Jacob, non des philosophes et des savants." Blaise Pascal, *Le mémorial*. It is entirely true that the philosophical demonstration of God's existence and nature does not make God known as the biblical father of his people. To that extent Pascal is right. Yet one's own reasoning shows that "creator of heaven and earth" and "first efficient cause of all" coincide in the same being.

content. True, the sharp academic division into philosophy and theology did not make itself very sensitively felt in practice till the seventeenth century, after the systematic organization of philosophy by Bacon and Descartes. But before that time, a continued stream of philosophy had in fact kept emerging in commentaries on Aristotle and other ancient writers, as well as in discussions of Christian themes. Yet only with the sixteenth century did large scale philosophical works like Suarez's *Disputationes metaphysicae* come to be produced as separate undertakings to provide for the philosophical needs of theological engagement.[43] By mid-seventeenth century, Salmanticenses could refer regularly back to "our Complutenses" for an adequate and systematic coverage of philosophical problems encountered in the course of theological study.[44] In the eighteenth and nineteenth centuries philosophy became academically organized according to the Wolffian pattern. There was no longer any prima facie confusing of it with sacred theology. But against that Wolffian background, the undiscriminating patristic and medieval treatises could readily appear as theology only, and as in no way containing genuine philosophy.

For those on the Bréhier side of the debate about Christian philosophy, the objection was that the body of writings referred to by their opponents as Christian philosophy was in fact grounded ultimately upon premises accepted on faith without intrinsic evidence. That charge should range the alleged Christian philosophy under theology.[45] Their task was merely to show that what historically had passed

43. "Quemadmodum fieri nequit ut quis Theologus perfectus evadat, nisi firma prius metaphysicae jecerit fundamenta . . . Ita vero in hoc opere philosophum ago, ut semper tamen prae oculis habeam nostram philosophiam debere christianam esse, ac divinae Theologiae ministram." Suarez, *Disputationes metaphysicae*, in *Opera omnia* (Paris: Vivès, 1877), 25, Ad lectorem.

44. See Salmanticenses, *Cursus theologicus* 8.Prooemium no. 2 (Paris: Victor Palmé, 1878), 5, 2a. This was looked upon not just as a matter of agreement in doctrine, but rather "tamquam eumdem omnino laborem, idem opus, ibi incohatum, hic consummatum . . ." Ibid., no. 7 (p. 4b). Cf. ibid., 8.1.1.no. 13 (p. 12a); nos. 15 & 16 (p. 13); no. 27 (p. 18b); nos. 55 & 57 (p. 31).

45. The charge may be found recurring under different forms. E.g.: "I consider the idea of Christian philosophy, as an exercise of natural reasoning distinct from revealed theology, to be a self-destructive (indeed contradictory) notion." Peter Redpath, "Romance of Wisdom: The Friendship between Maritain and Saint Thomas Aquinas," in *Understanding Maritain: Philosopher and Friend*, ed. Deal W. Hudson and Matthew J. Mancini (Macon: Mercer University Press, 1987), p. 99. Cf. "The habitus that the Greeks called philosophy is, properly speaking, for a Christian the habitus of 'Scholastic theology.' Only as such a theology can it be analogously called a 'Christian philosophy.'" Redpath, p. 112. Rather, the notions of a wisdom developed from natural starting points and of one developed from revealed starting points need to be kept carefully distinguished from each other, even though natural wisdom is raised to a higher status when it is absorbed into sacred theology. The same difference in starting points militates

for Christian philosophy was doctrinally not philosophy at all. The attitude required nothing beyond the negative stance that, whatever it might be doctrinally, it certainly was not philosophy. The question of its positive academic status could be left to its advocates. The case against it as philosophy was that it introduced revealed premises into its reasoning processes. That would give it a mixed or even a hybrid character. On account of the Cartesian concept of philosophy as an essence just in itself, the opponents of Christian philosophy had no empathy for a philosophy based on naturally evident premises alone in the case where the Christian factor occasioned the selection of those starting points.

All this makes it strange at first to see how the positive classification of the medieval writings as entirely theological treatises came most strongly from the Gilson side of the Christian philosophy debate. Gilson insisted that what is contained in the medieval treatises is straightforward theology.[46] He thereby alienated many of his hitherto staunch supporters. Likewise, Anton Pegis warned tellingly against reading as philosophy what the medievals wrote as theology. This provoked a sharp reaction.[47] In neither Gilson nor Pegis was there any doubt about the genuine character of the traditional Christian philosophy. But according to their viewpoint, the medieval writings have to be read as theological in the original text. Only when read as sacred theology are those writings a proper guide towards developing one's own Christian philosophy.

What is to be made of this situation? Certainly much valuable philosophical reasoning is present in the patristic and medieval writers. Augustine and Aquinas are still read in respectable philosophic circles. Excerpted by itself and expressed in terminology from which the theological nuances have been eliminated, much of their thinking undoubtedly has all the appearances of philosophy. Further, a work like the *De principio individuationis*, classed among the doubtfully authentic

---

against the stand that "Biblical metaphysics and Christian metaphysics in outline are the same," Claude Tresmontant, *The Origins of Christian Philosophy*, trans. Mark Pontifex (New York: Hawthorne Books, 1963), p. 23.

46. "For theology to remain formally one as a science, all the natural knowledge it contains must be directed and subordinated to the point of view proper to the theologian, which is that of revelation." E. Gilson, *The Christian Philosophy of St. Thomas Aquinas* (New York: Random House, 1956), p. 10. Cf. Anton C. Pegis, "*Sub Ratione Dei*: A Reply to Professor Anderson," *The New Scholasticism* 39 (1965), 141–43. Gilson, *The Philosopher and Theology*, p. 100, in the context of water remaining water even in wine, could say about philosophy, "In a way it does lose its essence, and it profits by the change."

47. E.g., James F. Anderson, "Was St. Thomas a Philosopher?" *The New Scholasticism* 38 (1964), 435–44. Cf. Pegis, *Sub Ratione Dei*, pp. 141–57.

writings of Aquinas, surely has to be regarded as philosophy, while the *Summa totius logicae Aristotelis,* placed among the unauthentic works, is, like the logical works of the fourteenth and fifteenth centuries, to be viewed as definitely philosophical. Yet a case can be made that the authentic Aristotelian commentaries of Aquinas can be looked upon as coming under theology.[48] But taken just in themselves, as excerpted from their original theological setting, the philosophical passages in Aquinas undoubtedly exhibit genuinely philosophical thinking.

The situation is aptly illustrated by the comparison of philosophy, as the water, to theology as the wine. Wine is a liquid mixture, from which the water may be evaporated in distillation without change in its chemical nature. Both before and after the evaporation the chemical constitution of the water is the same. It remains a chemical compound of two parts of hydrogen to one of oxygen. If you are asked what is in the flask you say wine, the water being included in that content. Correspondingly, when you are asked what the content of Aquinas's *Summa theologiae* is, you say theology. When asked what has been evaporated from the wine, you say water. So when asked what the philosophical passages excerpted from the *Summa* are, you answer philosophy. The simile, like all similes, may limp in some respects. But in regard to the point immediately at issue, it illustrates the situation effectively. The philosophical reasoning remains exactly the same reasoning when viewed in the theological setting and when excerpted just by itself. Without internal change in its own sequence, it can be looked upon as either philosophy or theology. It is theology when in the *Summa* and is philosophy when excerpted. But this must be understood as leaving it always its philosophical character, parallel to the way water retains its chemical constitution of H_2O even in the wine. Though it is absorbed into the theological procedure, the philosophy remains itself, quite as does chemical or biological knowledge when incorporated into medical and industrial technology.

That is the situation in regard to patristic and medieval Christian philosophy. The probative force of the philosophical reasoning rests solely on naturally evident premises. Modern philosophic writers who

---

48. The limited and selective participation of theology in philosophy is discussed in my article "Aquinas as Aristotelian Commentator," in *St. Thomas Aquinas 1274–1974 Commemorative Studies* (Toronto: Pontifical Institute of Mediaeval Studies, 1974), pp. 213–38. Nothing prevents full agreement with the stand of John F. Wippel, *Metaphysical Themes in Thomas Aquinas* (Washington, DC: Catholic University of America Press, 1984), p. 26, that "the philosophical opuscula are surely philosophical works." But that does not infringe upon the claim that for their author they were included in a general theological intent. Cf. ibid., p. 17.

pursue a notion of Christian philosophy in which the reasoning is based partly on divinely revealed premises will have difficulty in meeting the Bréhier objection. They can hardly expect professional recognition as theologians, for they do not restrict their reasoning to what follows from scriptural texts and magisterial pronouncements. As engaged in a general philosophy, they may extend their work into topics with which the professional theologian has no concern, such as the relation of the natural sciences to metaphysics, or the behavior of nontheological words. As a result, their sphere of interest is in this way frankly philosophical, and not theological. But judged by philosophical standards, their procedure is necessarily faulty because of the intrusion of revealed premises.

The answer to the general question just posed is therefore clear. The same piece of reasoning can in fact be either philosophy or theology, depending on the perspective in which it is viewed. If, in the whole reasoning process, it continues in the elevated sense given it through the cognitional identity of its terms with the major term in the original theological premise, it remains theological in character throughout. If, on the contrary, the meaning of the basic premise for the excerpted passage is accepted on the evidence of naturally known instances—for example, the notion of being as it is known through finite existents—a genuinely philosophical reasoning process is begun and carried through. The premises then give rise solely to philosophy. Nevertheless, if the passage was originally worked out as philosophy, it may be elevated into sacred theology in virtue of the identity of a basic term with something known through revelation. For instance, the divine attributes may be explained as following cogently upon the subsistent being that is known through reasoning from the existence of sensible things. In that case, straight philosophy has been done. Or, the starting point may be the God known through scriptural revelation as "I am who am." In that event, the terms in all the ensuing premises enter into cognitional identity with the subject authoritatively accepted through faith and apart from intrinsic evidence. You are then doing sacred theology.

Because Christian philosophy is motivated by its inborn desire to further Christian interests, and because it is able in the above way to develop reasoning that can be absorbed into theology, it is always ready to be of service to the sacred science. It is not only proud to function as a handmaid to supernatural faith in the individual Christian, but also, while remaining essentially an independent discipline, it is happy to be of service to theology in whatever way it can. This is in full accord with the spirit in which *Aeterni Patris* saw theology thereby attaining a truly scientific status, with the use of philosophy regarded not just as a counsel but as a command.[49]

A final query may be prompted by the above observations. Even though Christian philosophy may claim to be erected only upon naturally accessible principles, does it not acknowledge subjection of its results to some kind of control by Christian authority? It may verbally claim to be answerable solely to the court of human reason.[50] But do not the preceding considerations seem to make it, like sacred theology, ultimately subject, in regard to its truth, to a magisterium based on revealed premises? Its decisive criterion of truth would in this way, as with theology, be based on what is known through divine revelation.

This query may be sharpened by asking how philosophy that dissents from authoritative Christian teaching can be called Christian philosophy. Philosophies such as those of Lamennais, Rosmini, and Gioberti are unhesitantly grouped under that title.[51] Except for disagreement with magisterial doctrine, they satisfactorily meet the requirements. They are prompted by Christian interests, they are dealing with Christian themes, and they are reasoning from naturally knowable principles. The same may be said of much of today's philosophical writing in opposition to traditional Christian sexual morality. The motive asserted is to serve Christianity and further its progress by bringing about change in its outdated traditional severity. In that regard on the theological plane, a church historian could remark that every heresiarch meant to help the church. But how can thinking opposed to authoritative Christian teaching be regarded as genuine Christian philosophy?

Theoretically, an easy answer is at hand. The above-mentioned instances are indeed Christian philosophy, but wrong Christian philosophy. Christian philosophy makes no special claim to infallibility. It can go wrong, just as can any other philosophy. The remedy is to reexamine both the evidence of its starting points and cogency with which its conclusions are drawn. The Christian philosopher as philosopher and as Christian knows that revealed and naturally attained truth cannot contradict each other. There is no question here of a double truth theory, with the two sides in mutual conflict. Responsibility as a philosopher is only to the naturally known starting points and the logical sequence of the reasoning. The authoritative red flag serves solely as a stop sign that alerts one to the presence of danger.

Practically, however, the situation is not that simple. It is hard to see

49. *Aet. Patr.* 7; 2, 20a.
50. See supra, nn. 15 and 22.
51. See Coreth, *Christliche Philosophie* 1, 7.

that the starting points of one's own philosophizing have been erroneous. Usually that requires a catastrophic jolt. Yet the highly prized "liberalism" that enthused Catholic intellectuals in Lamennais's day has in recent American politics (though not in theology or philosophy) become a pejorative term. Likewise, deteriorating morals can give people today second thoughts about the premissibility of freer sex. But even with these facts acknowledged, the *practical* arbiter for truth in religious matters would still be the authoritative decision of the magisterium. This is recognized by Christian philosophy itself. In actual practice, moreover, the decision will usually come to be made as a result of intricate theological reasoning, since the immediately obvious meaning of the Scriptures and of the creed is adhered to by both sides. Christian philosophy would in fact seem to be subordinated to theological interpretations and conclusions.

What these reflections show is that in practice the ultimate arbiter of truth for Christian philosophy lies outside the range of unaided natural reason. It is something accidental and external to the essence of philosophy in precisive abstraction. This should not be too hard to grasp where philosophical pluralism is taken seriously. In it, contradictory conclusions result from diverse starting points, with nothing left in the essence of philosophy so taken to give an unquestioned decision. The beginning and the end correspond to each other. For Christian belief all things are oriented to a supernatural end and guided by a special providence, with the magisterium having the final word in religious matters. But that is accidental and external to the philosophy taken in precisive abstraction. Consequently, neither at the beginning nor at the end does the Christian factor enter into the force of the philosophical reasoning. Both at the beginning and at the end the philosophy is marked as Christian by what is external to its intrinsic constitution. The start is from principles selected by Christian motivation, and the final result that is envisaged is meant to conform to Christian teaching. But to err is human. Wrong principles can be selected, and faulty inferences can be made.

Given that situation, a wrong Christian philosophy is an understandable possibility. The first appeal can be for reexamination before the tribunal of reason, with the clarification of misunderstandings. The next step throws the responsibility in drastic fashion upon the personal conscience of the philosopher. Just as in the case of dissenting theologians, the point may be reached at which no possibility of agreement can be seen. The theologians then have to choose between their theology and their faith. Likewise the critical moment may come for faith and philosophical reasoning. The struggle may be intense, and the drama to which it may give rise can be agonizing. The practical wisdom required will be at times superhuman, and the courage heroic. The Christian philosopher needs both the heart and the humility to face these odds. But one thing he or she does not have to doubt is that Christian philosophy starts from naturally knowable principles solely, and on their basis reaches cogently drawn conclusions without internal manipulation by outside factors. When error does occur, the correction is to be made in a strictly philosophical way, with gratitude to the "friendly star" that has pointed to the necessity of a reexamination of the previous reasoning.[52] The philosophical responsibility is always to the naturally known starting points. But the final Christian responsibility is to personal conscience, which on occasion in an individual may unfortunately be in direct conflict with Aristotelian right reason.

VI

More convincing than any theorizing about the nature of Christian philosophy, however, is one's actual engagement in it. Here, as so often elsewhere, the telling proof is in the product. The personal experience of working at Christian philosophy from the inside is by far the most apt way of coming to realize what it is and what it does. The following thirteen papers, published separately in a number of journals at different times and on various occasions over the last three and one-half decades, gather into a single volume some piecemeal encounters of this kind. Taken together, they cover many of the outstanding theoretical aspects of Christian philosophy in broad general fashion, with the practical area at least approached in one of them. So they may be fairly said to offer an experience of the philosophy from the inside.

True, this experience can hope at most to add but a small drop to the flood of Christian philosophy that wells up from the early church fathers and streams through the Christian middle ages down into our

---

52. "[T]he Catholic philosopher will know that he violates at once faith and the laws of reason if he accepts any conclusion which he understands to be opposed to revealed doctrine." *Aet. Patr.* 8; 2, 20a. The correction is to be made on the philosophic level. In theory this may be clear enough, but in practice it may be very complicated. In a carefully worded reply to Bréhier, Gilson (*Bulletin*, pp. 52–53) notes how there are many degrees of magisterial authority, and that the decisions are not always easy to align with philosophical statements: ". . . car l'ensemble des décisions ecclésiastiques, soit positives, soit négatives, ne constituerait en aucune façon un système de philosophie" (p. 53). But he acknowledges that the church always has the final word on whether a philosophical assertion is in agreement with Christian faith, though the occasions of definite clash are too minimal in number to have any noticeable effect on the pursuit of Christian philosophy.

own era. It is throughout those abundant waters that the deeply vibrating spirit of Christian philosophy is to be felt in all its dynamic fullness. Yet a quick survey of that almost forbiddingly extensive historical phenomenon from the outside may not explain overtly enough just how the philosophy functions as Christian. By and large, the Christian philosophy of the past was a stranger to any self-conscious attitude of showing clearly and in detail how the Christian factor leaves the philosophical reasoning unweakened by its relation to the faith. Even the writers of avowedly Christian philosophy in modern times, and the current promoters of Christian philosophy on the two American continents, are none too detailed in explaining how they eliminate all intrinsic influence of revealed doctrines in respect of their philosophical thinking. Their own special purposes have been definite and practical in regard to their chosen topics. They have comparatively little concern with the academic problem of the scholarly integrity of Christian philosophy itself. To investigate their writings from that reflexive viewpoint requires empathy and patience. It also demands considerable tact, if misunderstandings are to be avoided. And it quickly becomes boring.

There is some excuse, then, for falling back upon personal experience to illustrate how non-philosophical props can be deliberately avoided in working towards a Christian philosophy today. With this in mind, six of the ensuing papers explore the nature of Christian philosophy itself and are grouped under Part One. The remaining seven apply the philosophy to particular topics concerned with God and the spiritual soul. Accordingly, Part One deals with the general notion of Christian philosophy, Part Two with particular controversial themes.

The initial paper so listed discusses the program outlined in Pope Leo XIII's encyclical *Aeterni Patris*. That program aimed at the restoration of Christian philosophy, and the encyclical was in many respects its Magna Carta. The encyclical was a pastoral document. It was not an epistemological treatise. It did not occupy itself at all with the much later Bréhier problem whether the terms "Christian" and "philosophy" were notionally compatible. Rather, it took for granted from the centuries-long history of Christianity that philosophy was regularly used to support the faith, and that those "who to the study of philosophy unite obedience to the Christian faith, are philosophizing in the best possible way," for the faith "helps the understanding" and "adds greatly to its nobility, keenness, and stability."[53]

---

53. *Aet. Patr.* 9; 2, 20b. Cf.: "[S]o far is the super-added light of faith from extinguishing or lessening the power of the intelligence that it completes it rather, and by adding to its strength renders it capable of greater things." Ibid., 2; 2, 18a.

That was the situation. It was historically open for all to see. It showed that the two factors, namely philosophy and Christian faith, have in practice worked harmoniously together. Though not evincing any hesitation at all about philosophy's ability to function in this area without self-harm, the encyclical did not have the least occasion to invoke epistemological justification for the one composite notion "Christian philosophy." Nor did it manifest the slightest interest in regard to the pursuance of that defensive task.

Similarly *Aeterni Patris* felt no concern for the problem of philosophical pluralism. In its penetrating glance over ancient, medieval, and modern times it brought strongly into focus the role that philosophy had played in the spread of the Christian faith. It dwelt on the great need for it in the task of combatting many erroneous teachings of the last half of the nineteenth century. From its pastoral viewpoint the basic division of philosophy was into philosophy that accorded with the tenets of divine revelation and philosophy that was opposed to them. The first type was urgently required for the Christian enterprise. The second type was "a fruitful cause of the evils which now afflict, as well as those which threaten, us" (26; 2, 17b). In the pastoral setting this was the one basic philosophical pluralism, namely, the correct and the erroneous as viewed from the standpoint of divinely revealed truth. The good achieved by the first type was traced from ancient times through the middle ages into the renaissance period. That was the philosophy that had to be restored. It was a "patrimony" (14; 2, 22a and 24; 2, 24b) in which the old was to be continually strengthened and completed by the new (24; 2, 24b).

On the other side of the pastoral dividing line could be seen what the apostle Paul (Colossians 2.8) had called "philosophy and vain deceit" (1; 2, 18b). It taught errors in regard to the nature of God, the origin of the world, divine providence, the destiny of man, and numerous other sensitive Christian topics (10; 2, 21a). After the innovations of the sixteenth century, "systems of philosophy multiplied beyond measure, and conclusions differing and clashing one with another arose about those matters even which are the most important in human knowledge" (24; 2, 24b). This philosophy as a whole was looked upon as "a multiform system of this kind, which depends on the authority and choice of any professor, has a foundation open to change, and consequently gives us a philosophy not firm, and stable, and robust like that of old, but tottering and feeble" (24; 2, 24b).

Within the one "multiform system" (*ratio doctrinae*) on the erroneous side of the pastorally drawn division, this way of speaking indicates, a widespread pluralism is found. That pluralism was regarded as deleterious. But likewise in "the philosophers of old" (10; 2, 21a), and so within the ancient or "firm, and stable" philosophy, the presence of grave errors was recognized in regard to the most important of Christian topics. No express attention, however, was given by the encyclical to the fact that errors about the nature of God and the origin of the world were contained in the two most outstanding representatives of the "firm, and stable" tradition in pagan times, namely, Plato and Aristotle.[54] Moreover, in regard to the contemporary Thomism, *Aeterni Patris* insisted "that the doctrine of Thomas be drawn from its own fountains" and not from rivulets "which are said to flow thence, but in reality are gathered from strange and unwholesome streams" (31; 2, 26b). This was implicit recognition of the pluralism in the ancient philosophy and in the Thomism currently in vogue, not too different in principle from the pluralism seen in the "multiform system" of post-renaissance philosophy. On both sides of the pastoral dividing line, therefore, ample room may be found today for reading philosophical pluralism into the conceptions of *Aeterni Patris*. But the new approach is from the viewpoint of the later epistemological interests.

Yet the epistemological pluralism, though not excluded by the text of the encyclical, is something that has to be read into it from a later perspective. There is no explicit concern with pluralism in *Aeterni Patris* itself, outside the basic cleavage of true from false philosophy as judged by the standards of Christian faith. Rather, the overall impression on reading through the encyclical is that it has in mind a unitary philosophy persisting through the centuries somewhat after the fashion of a *philosophia perennis*, though that expression is nowhere used or even hinted at in its text. The immediate picture is that of what today might be called a monolithic structure, a philosophy gradually built through the course of the centuries and still capable of being strengthened and adorned by each new scientific discovery. Philosophical pluralism, where actually encountered in its effects, seems summarily dismissed as dissipating and destructive.

These views stemmed solely from a fundamental division of philos-

---

54. This is aptly illustrated by the way Aquinas, in *Commentary on the Metaphysics of Aristotle*, trans. John P. Rowan (Chicago: Henry Regnery, 1961), no. 2536; 2, 892, acknowledges that Aristotle considered the heavens to have souls and (no. 2496; p. 878) "firmly thought and believed that motion must be eternal and also time; otherwise he would not have based his plan of investigating immaterial substances on this conviction," and nevertheless himself goes on to assert that Aristotle's reasoning retains its demonstrative efficacy "even if the world were not eternal" (no. 2499; p. 879). Cf. Aquinas's commentary on Aristotle's *Physics*, *De physico auditu sive physicorum Aristotelis* (Naples: M. d'Aurio, 1953), p. 431 (no. 1991), where the same proof without the eternity of the world and its motion is declared to have "much greater" efficacy.

ophy into the correct and the erroneous, as judged by the measuring rod of Christian belief. They left untouched the epistemological problem—whether, on its own level, philosophy emerged from its starting points in pluralistic or unitary fashion. The views were expressed in terminology that without suspicion of any latent problem could refer to either side of the division as unitary or as multiple in character. It could speak of the erroneous side as one "multiple system" and of the currently existent Thomism as needing to free itself from the rivulets that were "gathered from strange and unwholesome streams." In a word, the language of *Aeternis Patris* remains wide open to pluralistic interpretation. But the problem surfaces only when the topic is brought to the fore through the exigencies of a debate like that initiated by Bréhier, even though pluralism is implicit in the role given by the encyclical itself to Augustine, Anselm, Albert, and Bonaventure.

In its own setting, however, *Aeterni Patris* is explicit beyond the least doubt in its assertions that the philosophy it promotes must conform unswervingly to the tenets of the Christian faith, and that this thinking in conformity with those tenets enhances philosophy itself. It extols the worth of philosophy in the ability to dispose people of intellectual accomplishments for the acceptance of the faith, and for defense of the faith against adversaries. But it correspondingly stresses the benefits of the faith for the pursuit of philosophy. The type of philosophy it envisages was almost immediately standardized as "Christian philosophy," and has gone under that designation in official documents ever since.

One possible prima facie objection might be raised. With appropriate reservations, the encyclical (4; 2, 18a–19a) dwells on philosophy as a preparation and prelude to Christianity. Does this allow the philosophy to be conceived as a way of thinking that holds any kind of essential priority to Christian belief? Hardly. Philosophy is here being considered in its possible relation to future reception of Christian faith in a particular individual. Any real relation in this case is something accidental. Chronologically the philosophy so related does antecede the particular individual's act of belief. The starting points of the philosophy were always naturally attainable, and in a particular case they could be those used by an individual to build up a philosophy prior to the acceptance of Christian faith. The one is external to the other. Even then the philosophy may nevertheless be called Christian, for it is regarded as focused upon the future reception of the religious belief for which it will prepare the way. It is Christian through its positive contribution to the evangelizing process. But here, as always, the two are accidental and external to each other.

On all the above accounts, then, *Aeterni Patris* outlines clearly the ways in which a philosophy may be called Christian. It does so, moreover, not on the strength of the opinions of private scholars, but in authoritative fashion as the view of the Catholic church. It proclaims in that way the notion of philosophy present in Christian thought down through the centuries and in possession of the field when the Bréhier debate occurred. A consideration of its contents should merit, in consequence, the initial niche in a collection of essays aiming at the development of an ongoing Christian philosophy today.

The second paper comes to grips with the problem of how there can be a proper place or scope or need for a specifically Christian philosophy. This touches a point of pride. A mind unaided by divine revelation tends to take for granted that the world immediately confronting people is something complete in itself, or at least, as with process philosophies, has within itself seeds or virtualities tending towards what is best for it. Approached with this presupposition, the natural world taken just in itself should normally be able to provide all the factors required for its explanation by the human intellect. The intellect should be sufficient for its self-imposed tasks. Were this actually so, the need for a distinctly Christian philosophy might not be so telling. Prolonged hard work on the part of the human intellect would be expected to reach all the basic tenets necessary for the entire philosophical enterprise. There would be no pressing need for even external guidance from Christian revelation.

In point of fact, however, there are important tenets essentially on the natural level that philosophy did not reach outside the approach from the viewpoint of Christian faith. One such tenet is that the existence of things is not originally grasped by the human mind through conceptualization but through a different and composing type of intellection technically called judgment. Another is that motion can originate instantaneously instead of in a part of time, a consideration that undermines the cogency of the arguments for a world without temporal beginning and reduces them to probability only. Further, some situations can be seen as facts, yet become difficult if not impossible to justify rationally on ordinarily accepted grounds. Such situations are, for example: the presence of so much evil and pain in the world; the supremacy of personal conscience in face of legal prescription; the inviolable respect for human life, yet the obligation to sacrifice in some circumstances one's own life or to inflict death on others. These phenomena fall into focus in a Christian philosophy, but elsewhere, though they may be recognized as facts, they seem to find no satisfactory philosophical explanation or defense.

A Christian approaching those philosophical problems against the background of religious beliefs has an attitude quite different from that of nonbelievers. Through faith there is constant awareness of a loving God who while unswervingly just in every way has the fondest regard of a parent towards all human beings, since they are meant to share the divine nature through grace. There is no amazement when God lets the sun shine and the rain fall on good and evil alike, since for the Christian God is the judge who will requite everything even to the extent of eternal reward or punishment in a state after bodily death. With Gilson one might well ask how anyone who accepted religious tenets like these could philosophize as though never having heard of them. What permeates all such considerations is the revealed doctrine that the whole material world has been created in order that human beings may attain the supernatural end of sharing through grace the eternal life and happiness of the triune God. This will mean that the world as known naturally through reason is something incomplete in itself. It is not a finished whole. In practice it can be adequately assessed only through reason working with faith. In it the philosopher is not king. This is the ground for the claim that philosophy can attain its greatest heights as philosophy only by working under guidance of the Christian faith.

With the thought of this naturally incomplete world, consequently, the guidance of faith emerges clearly enough as the condition for the best kind of philosophizing. Faith will not furnish any of the philosophical starting points. It will not add any probative force to the reasoning. But it does guide the Christian philosopher to see in the things themselves some crucial starting points that might otherwise have been missed. It will foster alertness in regard to the limits of what may be expected from the human mind. It will keep one from being scandalized when philosophy alone does not bring full conviction, or when pride of place is not found to go with the philosopher's calling. Not skepticism, but legitimate restraint, will be the result. Hence the second paper aims to show how the naturally knowable world leaves scope for the activity of a Christian philosophy. Approached by the Christian thinker in its incomplete status, the world confronting the human mind offers ample room for a type of genuine philosophy intrinsically differentiated from other types by reason of the extrinsic guidance occasioned by supernatural faith. The need for a characteristically Christian philosophy then becomes obvious to the believer.

The third and fourth papers deal respectively with the notions of Christian philosophy and Catholic philosophy as genus and as species. The extrinsic relation of each to its religious guiding star is reflected by the intrinsic differentiation in each of the respective philosophies. In the religious context by itself the adjective "Christian" is taken in ordinary use as generic in regard to Catholic, Lutheran, Calvinist, and the like. The philosophies developed under the external guidance of those religions correspond respectively in pattern. There need not be anything contentious about this grouping, even though at present it is not well received in philosophic circles. Christian philosophy can easily be taken as generic, Catholic or Protestant philosophies as more specific. The ecumenical banner may be displayed proudly and sincerely in both the generic and specific philosophical enterprises, as well as in the recognition of the worth in non-Christian philosophies. Nor does any epistemological difficulty arise in making the further distinctions. In all cases the starting points are in the naturally knowable things, or in common thought or language, with the specific guidance to them remaining external to the properly philosophical procedure.

The fifth paper gives a glance over the first forty years of the American Catholic Philosophical Association's attitude towards the philosophy it was founded to promote. At the time, important crossroads were being faced by organized Catholic philosophy. During those initial forty years, as may be readily verified, the sponsored philosophy had been viewed generally in monochromatic fashion, somewhat after the model of a *philosophia perennis*. That model was at times invoked, though later a moratorium was suggested from which the notion does not seem to have re-emerged. The association seems now, but in much more relaxed fashion, still to be groping for a theoretical understanding of its identity. For the present it seems content to acquiesce in a friendly pluralism.[55]

The sixth paper approaches the moral field. It confronts Christian conscience with the basic Aristotelian guide of human conduct, namely, right reason. In the present perspective this is not just another particular moral topic. It lies at the root of all moral actions, imparting to each its ultimate moral character in the practical sphere quite as

55. See the detailed review of Neo-Thomism in North America during the years 1926–86 by Gerald A. McCool, "The Tradition of St. Thomas in North America: At 50 Years," *The Modern Schoolman* 65 (1988), 185–206. The present situation is assessed from the viewpoint of "a less confident age, when Catholic colleges are struggling to define their identity" (p. 186) against the traditional background of "Christian philosophy" and "Catholic philosophy" (pp. 188–89). Even in the present pluralism, however, the force of McCool's comment holds as strongly as ever: "nothing did more to encourage cohesion, self-confidence and professionalism among teachers of philosophy in Catholic colleges than the foundation of the American Catholic Philosophical Association" (p. 191).

form gives each thing its character in the theoretical order. Traditionally, western moral philosophy in its major trends has viewed human
conduct as morally good when it is guided by mature right reason.[56]
Yet throughout the history of western thought, personalistic strains
have kept asserting the supremacy of individual conscience. The difference between the two tendencies can at times be startling. Both
history and ordinary experience furnish abundant examples of acts
contrary to right reason yet dictated by personal conscience. Religious
persecution and rebellion against legitimate authority provide notable
instances. Christian faith, for its part, looks upon human conduct on
earth as that of fond children in relation to a loving but just father.
That tenet remains extrinsic and accidental to philosophical discourse.
Yet as a "friendly star" it can point the way to intrinsic starting points
for moral philosophy, starting points that, though attainable by reason
through connatural attraction to the good, might easily be missed or
else realized in too weak a fashion to serve as effective starting points
for ethical reasoning. The ingrained respect for human life and its
procreation may, for instance, be present, yet without sufficient
strength for making the correct Christian decisions in regard to suicide, abortion, contraception, divorce, infanticide, hunger strikes,
tyrannicide, capital punishment, war, and other crucial problems
faced by today's civilization. Are these to be regulated by reason or
left to the individual conscience of each human person?

The Christian approach is from the viewpoint of ultimate destiny,
in regard to which human agents have immature status and need
divine grace. It will be prompted to look at motives of compassion
latent in profoundly human sentiments as encountered in actual life.
It will be sensitive to their appeal when harsher measures seem prescribed by reason. Here the morally correct middle point will remain,
as elsewhere, difficult to attain. But Christian philosophy will have at
least motives for always appreciating the innate human sense of compassion, and for always looking at both sides. It shows why neither
side can be ignored, and in general to what extent each is to influence
the decision. As this is an overall consideration pertaining to the specific differentia of Christian moral philosophy, the discussion of it
rightly belongs under Part One of the division for the present papers.
Conscience lies at the heart of the deepest differentiating feature in
Christian moral philosophy, rather than providing just an instance of
its range.

Part Two of the collection offers a few instances of Christian phi-

---

56. For a survey of the "right reason" tradition, see William K. Frankena, "The
Ethics of Right Reason," *The Monist* 66 (1983), 3–25.

losophy, understood in the way its notion has already been outlined, but now at work on some particular themes. The seventh paper is concerned with what is quite obviously its first and most important topic as Christian, namely God—God as recognized and discussed in the modern world. The eighth paper treats in detail of the most outstanding instance of a philosophical starting point naturally attainable but in fact isolated as such only when a scriptural text pointed to it. The ninth paper deals with the reverse side of that approach, namely, that we have no original concept of existence. If existence denotes the nature of God, the nature of God will then be inconceivable for the human mind. Nevertheless, because subsistent existence is infinite in perfection, it will allow all perfections to be predicated of it in the highest degree, fully justifying the positive theology as well as the negative. Unattainable through concepts, the divine nature is knowable by predication through judgment.

The tenth paper discusses the way the visible world leads philosophically to God, when the route is that of existence. This conforms to the scriptural declaration (Wisdom 13.1) that God is knowable through what is manifest in the universe. The eleventh looks at the same philosophical journey when attempted along the path of essence. That road may be cosmological, it may be ontological, or it may be phenomenological. Under the last heading could be ranged the moral argument, which proceeds from intense feelings of guilt or awe. In all these cases the starting point is an essential or accidental nature, as contradistinguished from existence. The paper analyzes what seems to be the most outstanding instance of this philosophical approach. In it the cosmological and the ontological arguments are combined, or, if you wish, the ontological argument is absorbed into and justified by the cosmological. It is the intensely interesting and influential demonstration of Duns Scotus. A number of other versions of the cosmological argument are far more widely known today, but there is none so profound and so instructive.

The two final papers concern the spiritual soul. The one probes the way the human soul is represented as a distinct agent in contrast to the body, even though the soul is physically a part of the body. The other paper examines the separability of the spiritual soul from matter. It shows that the perpetual existence of the human soul may be demonstrated metaphysically, but not its life after separation from the body. The latter item has to be left to faith and to theology. This is an excellent illustration of the way Christian philosophy can serve its limited yet important purpose without at all trying to substitute either for faith or for sacred theology.

PART ONE

THE NATURE OF
CHRISTIAN PHILOSOPHY

1

THE CHRISTIAN PHILOSOPHY OF
AETERNI PATRIS

I

Although the phrase "Christian philosophy" does not occur in the text of Leo XIII's encyclical letter *Aeterni Patris,* it was used by that pope himself as the document's title on the first anniversary of its publication.[1] This title, moreover, was specified on that occasion by the further notion of the "restoration" of Christian philosophy in Catholic schools.[2] Later, in the third decade of the present century, another papal document in quoting *Aeterni patris* emphasized that Pope Leo's great merit lay in his "having restored Christian philosophy."[3] The credentials of the later descriptive subtitle "On the Res-

1. See Leonard E. Boyle, "A Remembrance of Pope Leo XIII: The Encyclical *Aeterni Patris,*" in *One Hundred Years of Thomism,* ed. Victor B. Brezik (Houston: Center for Thomistic Studies, 1981), p. 21, n. 1. G. Van Riet, "Le titre de l'encyclique 'Aeterni Patris,'" *Revue philosophique de Louvain* 80 (1982), 35–63. Antonio Piolanti, *Il tomismo come filosofia cristiana nel pensiero de Leone XIII, Studi tomistici* 20 (Città del Vaticano: Pontificia Accademia di S. Tommaso, 1983), pp. 9–12; 100; 110. A bibliography on *Aeterni Patris* may be found in Piolanti, pp. 128–31, and an English translation of the encyclical in Brezik, pp. 173–97.

2. "... ab Encyclicis Litteris Nostris *De philosophia christiana ad mentem s. Thomae Aquinatis Doctoris Angelici in scholis catholicis instauranda,* quas superiore anno hoc ipso die publicavimus." Leo XIII, "De sancto Thoma Aquinate patrono coelesti studiorum optimorum cooptando" (*Cum hoc sit*), *Acta sanctae sedis* 13 (1880), 56. Similarly "... in Epistola Encyclica de *Philosophia christiana ad mentem Angelici Doctoris in scholis catholicis instauranda* pertractavimus ... ," in the Apostolic Letter *Quod iam inde,* May 9, 1985, text in Piolanti, pp. 109–11. The notion of "restoration" plays its part in the encyclical itself: "... praeclaram Thomae Aquinatis doctrinam restituere"—*Aeterni Patris, Acta S. Sedis* 12 (1879), p. 112.12–13; "... ab hac, quae Nobis est proposita, disciplinarum philosophicarum instauratione"—p. 113.20–21; "... auream sancti Thomae sapientiam restituatis"—p. 114.22. Cf. restoration of the human faculties (p. 110.30) and science (p. 104.35) by Christ. The encyclical, dated August 4, 1879, introduces its theme in its opening words, *Aeterni Patris,* with the meaning that the only-begotten Son of the eternal Father instituted a teaching authority on earth.

3. "Profecto ipsius Leonis magna laus est Philosophiam Christianam, excitato Doctoris Angelici amore cultuque, instaurasse." *De seminariis et de studiis clericorum, Acta apostolicae sedis* 14 (1922), 454.

toration of Christian Philosophy according to the Mind of St. Thomas Aquinas the Angelic Doctor" are accordingly solid enough. The import is that a Christian philosophy existed and flourished in former times. The aim of Pope Leo's encyclical was to restore the philosophy to its pristine vigor and to further its fruitful growth in the modern era.

The expression "Christian philosophy" had in fact been in use from quite early times, though with varying meanings. In the immediately preceding decades of the nineteenth century it had become familiar in the sense of the philosophy that was needed by the Catholic faith and that formed part of a required Catholic education and mentality. The phrase was well known in France through the title of the *Annales de philosophie chrétienne* (1830–1913), and in Italy through the widely used manual *Elementa philosophiae christianae* of Sanseverino.[4] Even earlier it had covered the type of philosophy advocated for Catholic seminarians and colleges.[5]

On one occasion *Aeterni Patris* itself did use the phraseology "Christian wisdom" to record the approbation showered upon Origen's skill at bringing into the defense of Christian teaching a number of tenets culled from pagan writers, as though snatching weapons from the enemy.[6] The notion projected was the Christian wisdom that could be served by philosophy. Christian wisdom was in this way differentiated from the human wisdom that was capable of ministering to it under the caption of "philosophy." The two were related as liege lady and handmaid. Set out vis-à-vis each other in that relation, they exhibited clearly enough the contrast meant. The use of the adjective "Chris-

---

4. Gaetano Sanseverino, *Elementa philosophiae christianae*, cum antiqua et nova comparatae (Naples: Typis Vincentii Manfredi, 1862). On another manual of the epoch with "philosophie chrétienne" in its title, by Louis de Poissy, see Antonio Piolanti, "Pio IX e la rinascita del tomismo," in *San Tommaso: Fonti e riflessi del suo pensiero, Studi tomistici* 1 (Città Nuova: Pontificia Accademia Romana di S. Tommaso d'Aquino. [1974]), pp. 366, n. 16; 367, n. 18. On the history of the term "Christian philosophy," see Maurice Nédoncelle, *Is There a Christian Philosophy?* trans. Illtyd Trethowan (New York: Hawthorn Books, 1960), pp. 30–99. On a traditional use of the notion "Christian philosophy" in the sense of monastic life, see J. Leclercq, "Pour l'histoire de l'expression 'philosophie chrétienne,'" *Mélanges de science religieuse* 9 (1952), 221–26.

5. See Jean-Baptiste Bouvier, *Institutiones philosophicae*, 13th ed. (Paris: Jouby, 1863), p. 2. It proposed to give "a truly Christian philosophy." Its first edition was in 1824. On its influence in France and francophone Canada, see Roland Houde, *Histoire et philosophie au Québec* (Three Rivers, Qué.: Editions du Bien Public, 1979), pp. 33; 99; 145, n. 26.

6. "[Q]uod plura ex ethnicorum placitis ingeniose decerpta, quasi erepta hostibus tela, in patrocinium christianae sapientiae et perniciem superstitionis singulari dexteritate retorserit. *Aet. Patr.*, p. 100.16–18. This is the notion of "Christian philosophy" understood according to the Greek etymology of "philosophy" as love of wisdom. Cf. Augustine, *Contra Julianum* 4.14.72; PL 44.774.

tian" for divinely revealed teaching did little more than renew the medieval etiquette of looking upon "philosophy" as something distinct from the doctrine that could be qualified as "sacred." In this use, consequently, "Christian" was envisaged as specifying a wisdom distinct from the whole range of "philosophy" rather than as distinguishing one type of philosophy from another.

Aeterni Patris (p. 103.21) also employed the term "Catholic philosopher," but only to warn the Catholic thinker that he violates the rights of both faith and reason if he embraces any conclusion understood to be incompatible with revealed doctrine. It reprimanded "Catholic philosophers" (p. 111.28) who set aside the heritage of ancient philosophy for more recent ways of thinking, instead of trying to increase and perfect the old by means of the new. In both instances the document was referring to Catholics whose ways of philosophizing differed sharply from its own program. In calling them "Catholic philosophers" it evidently had no intention of attributing to them a specifically Catholic philosophy. It regarded them patently as Catholics who had wrong philosophies, philosophies that even in today's categories cannot be brought under a characteristically Catholic designation in an entirely univocal fashion.

Further, the encyclical noted how Arnobius and Lactantius aimed to propagate the dogmas and precepts of "Catholic wisdom" (p. 106.14) without overturning philosophy in the fashion of the skeptics. Rather, they overcame the philosophers by using weapons taken partly from tenets held by the philosophers in their debating among themselves.[7] Again, the wisdom qualified by the religious term is set out in contrast to philosophy. "Catholic wisdom" was regarded as something different from philosophy, even though it respected the integrity and the worth of that human wisdom. No tendency towards specifying a distinct type of philosophy by the word "Catholic" is shown.

On reading *Aeterni Patris*, in fact, one soon becomes aware that the issue whether philosophy can be Christian and at the same time remain genuine philosophy aroused no interest or concern in the encounter with the problems of the day. The role that philosophy could play as handmaid to revealed truth was accepted as a fact. The designation "handmaid" in this regard goes back to Philo (*De congressu*

7. "[D]ogmata ac praecepta catholicae sapientiae persuadere hominibus strenue nituntur, non sic philosophiam evertentes, ut Academici solent, sed partim suis armis, partim vero ex philosophorum inter se concertatione sumptis eos revincentes." *Aet. Patr.*, p. 106.13–17. On the meaning, cf. Lactantius, *De opif. Dei*, 20.3; ed. Michel Perrin, *Lactance: L'ouvrage du Dieu créateur* (Paris: Editions du Cerf, 1974), 1, 216.12–13.

14.79–80), and had been transmitted and developed in Christian tradition.[8] The encyclical felt no need to justify its use. *Aeterni Patris* was concerned merely with outlining ways in which philosophy can be and should be of help to the faith and to the disciplines that go together to constitute a Christian education, and with the way philosophy itself can be helped reciprocally by Christian faith.

What, then, does *Aeterni Patris* understand by the philosophy so related to Christian revelation? The focus of the encyclical throughout is expressly on philosophy. Philosophy is its explicit topic. Its set purpose is to deal with the program of philosophical studies in Catholic education.[9] It has a clearly etched notion of the type of thought it envisages in the use of the term "philosophy." Without cavil it recognizes that philosophy has its own distinctive starting points and its own reasoning processes, as well as a preëminent status in regard to the humanistic and natural sciences.[10] It shows no tendency to absorb philosophy into theology. Rather, it keeps contrasting philosophy with theology and faith, sometimes as enemy, sometimes as friend. It looks upon philosophy as an enterprise that had been carried on with vigor before the advent of Christianity, and that later was developed and embellished and enriched in patristic, scholastic, and modern writings.[11] While speaking of philosophy as though it were a single enterprise pursued through the centuries, *Aeterni Patris* (pp. 102.3 and 102.8; 113.20) sees in it different disciplines or branches. The encyclical notes that the types of philosophy have multiplied excessively in modern times.[12] In regard to the philosophical thinking of Aquinas, which it champions decisively, it recognizes the existence of different interpretations and recommends the common understanding that has

---

8. "[I]n morem ancillae et pedissequae, famulari caelestibus doctrinis, easque alia ratione, Dei beneficio, attingere." *Aet. Patr.*, p. 103.13–15. As brought over from Philo into Christian tradition, the metaphor gradually took on the notion that use by revealed doctrine gave human wisdom full citizenship, though the interpretation varied. A sketch of its history may be found in my article "Reality and Metaphysics," *Review of Metaphysics* 25 (1972), 655–56, n. 28.

9. ". . . de ineunda philosophicorum studiorum ratione." *Aet. Patr.*, p. 98.15–16.

10. "[A]equum plane est, sua methodo, suisque principiis et argumentis uti philosophiam: non ita tamen, ut auctoritati divinae sese audacter subtrahere videatur." *Aet. Patr.*, p. 103.16–19. Cf. text in Franz Ehrle, *Zur Enzyklika "Aeterni Patris,"* ed. Franz Pelster (Rome: Edizioni di Storia e Letteratura, 1954), p. 22.32. See *Aet. Patr.*, p. 98.10–18, on the preëminence envisaged for philosophy by the encyclical. The "dignity" of the philosophical disciplines is continually stressed.

11. See *Aet. Patr.*, pp. 99–100; 107–108; 111–12.

12. "Adnitentibus enim Novatoribus saeculi XVI, placuit philosophari citra quempiam ad fidem respectum, petita dataque vicissim potestate quaelibet pro lubitu ingenioque excogitandi. Qua ex re pronum fuit, genera philosophiae plus aequo multiplicari, sententiasque diversas atque inter se pugnantes oriri etiam de iis rebus, quae sunt in humanis cognitionibus praecipuae." *Aet. Patr.*, p. 111.18–24.

been traditionally sanctioned by commentators.[13] But it looks askance at the efforts dating from the sixteenth century to develop philosophy without any regard for the faith, as though each of the two could proceed in utter independence of the other.[14] Nevertheless it keeps the religious adjective consistently on the side of revealed doctrine, as contrasted with philosophy.

By "philosophy," in consequence, the encyclical means what we today would call the whole philosophical enterprise. It sketches the history of philosophy only in the western tradition, but says nothing that would interfere with our present extension of interest to Persian, Hindu, and Chinese philosophies. What it has in mind is philosophy in general. It is concerned with "the right use of philosophy"[15] understood in this global fashion. In that use philosophy's own distinctive starting points and methods are guaranteed, yet the right to use them in total independence of divine revelation is not sanctioned. What is envisaged is a *philosophical genus* (p. 100.32) that opens a clear and facile way towards faith.

Can this particular use of philosophy in general be brought under what today is called Christian philosophy? That is a question that arose only after Émile Bréhier's attack in 1928 on the very notion of Christian philosophy.[16] To him it was a combination of incompatible terms. Half a century earlier, *Aeterni Patris* did not have that question to face. Fifty years afterwards, we ourselves do have to come to grips with it. From this angle the issue is not the particular use of philosophy in general. The issue is whether a specific type of philosophy is constituted by philosophy's relations to Christian faith as outlined in the encyclical. Do those relations give rise to a truly specific difference on the genuinely philosophical level, a differential that brings about a new species totally within the philosophical realm? Or do they destroy

13. "[U]t sapientia Thomae ex ipsis eius fontibus hauriatur, aut saltem ex iis rivis, quos ab ipso fonte deductos, adhuc integros et illimes decurrere certa et concors doctorum hominum sententia est: sed ab iis qui exinde fluxisse dicuntur, re autem alienis et non salubribus aquis creverunt, adolescentium animos arcendos curate." *Aet. Patr.*, p. 114.35–40. Consensus in a unitary interpretation, however, is not to be looked for today, and was hardly a fact even then.

14. See text supra, n. 12. Cf. *Aet. Patr.*, p. 103.18–19 (text supra, n. 10).

15. "rectum philosophiae usum"—*Aet. Patr.*, p. 99.5–6; "si rite a sapientibus usurpetur"—p. 99.19; "perpetuus et multiplex adhuc requiritur philosophiae usus"—p. 101.24–25. The type recommended is the use made of philosophy by Scholastics—pp. 108.8–9 and 16; 111.13; On the topic, cf. Étienne Gilson, *The Philosopher and Theology* (New York: Random House, 1962), pp. 189–93.

16. "[M]ais on ne peut pas plus parler d'une philosophie chrétienne que d'une mathématique chrétienne ou d'une physique chrétienne." Émile Bréhier, "Y a-t-il une philosophie chrétienne?" *Revue de Métaphysique et de Morale* 36 (1931), 162. See Nédoncelle, pp. 85–114.

the nature of truly philosophical thinking by contaminating its life-blood with alien and toxic ingredients? The answer has to be sought in a study of the ways in which philosophy and Christian teaching are found to be mutually related in the encyclical.

II

Aeterni Patris is clear enough in its explanation of the two facets of its single objective. On the one hand it presents the ways in which philosophy helps Christian faith. On the other hand it shows how Christian faith helps philosophy.

As regards the help given faith by philosophy, the first way noted is philosophy's ability to counteract on its own level the evils that have their origin in wrong philosophical notions. The actual and antici-pated evils of the day were regarded as springing from erroneous philosophy.[17] It was the task of philosophy itself to provide the com-mensurate remedy. St. Jerome was cited (p. 102.27–31) for the met-aphor of cutting off the head of the proud Goliath with his own sword. Further, the apologetic value of philosophy for positively upholding the faith against enemies was stressed (pp. 101; 104–105), for it makes manifest how the teachings of divine revelation are in agreement with the best of human reasoning. The catechetical value of philosophy in preparing adults for entrance into the Christian church was noted,[18] as was also its aid in organizing theology[19] and in forming a Christian mentality.[20]

Do any of these ways of aiding Christian faith infringe on the au-thentically philosophical character of the help used? It seems impos-sible to see how there is any infringement at all. Philosophy is being used for religious objectives quite as legitimately as it may be used for cultural, educational, or even political purposes, without detriment to its own intrinsic nature. Strictly viewed as handmaid, it does not

17. "[F]ecundam malorum causam, cum eorum que premunt, tum eorum quae pertimescimus, in eo consistere, quod prava de divinis humanisque rebus scita, e scholis philosophorum iampridem profecta, in omnes civitatis ordines irrepserint, communi plurimorum suffragio recepta." *Aet. Patr.*, p. 18.21–26. "[E]tiam ab humana scientia praesidium quaeratur." Ibid., p. 99.11–12.

18. "[I]ter ad veram fidem quodammodo sternere et munire valet, suorumque al-umnorum animos ad revelationem suscipiendam convenienter praeparare." *Aet. Patr.*, p. 99.20–22.

19. "ut sacra Theologia naturam, habitum, ingeniumque verae scientia suscipiat atque induat." *Aet. Patr.*, p. 101.25–26.

20. "Eam siquidem cognitionem et intelligentiam plenius et facilius certe illi conse-cuntur, qui cum integritate vitae fideique studio ingenium coniungunt philosophicis disciplinis expolitum." *Aet. Patr.*, pp. 101–102.

change in nature. If it did, the purpose would be defeated. The service as handmaid is in that way on a par with the use of chemistry and biology in medicine. In today's understanding of the relations of the sciences, there should not be any difficulty here.

The other relevant, and in contrast positive, question is whether this use in aid of Christian teaching adds a new specifying characteristic to philosophy in general. Does it justify the notion of "Christian philosophy" as a distinct species? The approach to the question is not easy, since the requirements for the notion of Christian philosophy vary significantly with the writers who discuss it.[21] One can but ask to which conceptions of Christian philosophy the use envisaged in *Aeterni Patris* for philosophy may actually be said to conform.

In that regard, the use upheld for it as handmaid does conform to one of the recognized interpretations of Christian philosophy. Choice of problems is the specifying characteristic in this conception.[22] Focus on the philosophical problems that are of interest and concern to Christian faith circumscribes a distinct approach. In that way it characterizes a new type of philosophy. One may compare it with law. Law in general is called into the service of corporations. The area thereby dealt with comes to specify a distinct type of law, corporate law. The specification is not by the nature of the commercial or social activities that call for its services, but by the kind of legal aspects they involve. The specification is within the legal sphere, even though the service is given to entities that are of a different order. The notion of philosophy in the service of Christian interests may readily be looked upon as specified in corresponding fashion. In this way new and specifically Christian philosophy has been engendered. There has been no detriment to its generically philosophic character. The designation "Christian" seems as fully legitimate as in the addition of any other extra-philosophic adjective to the noun "philosophy," as in American philosophy, Islamic philosophy, Hindu philosophy, Chinese philosophy.

Choice of problems, however, can hardly rank as more than a minimum requirement for the specification of Christian philosophy. It is a characteristic that stems from the aid rendered by philosophy to Christian faith. Does the other facet envisaged by *Aeterni Patris*, namely the help given by faith to philosophy, indicate closer and deeper specification?

21. See Nédoncelle, pp. 100–114.

22. "In the first place, and it is perhaps his most obvious trait, the Christian philosopher is one who effects a choice between philosophic problems." Étienne Gilson, *The Spirit of Mediaeval Philosophy*, trans. A. H. C. Downes (New York: Charles Scribner's Sons, 1940), p. 37.

The aid given by faith was introduced under the metaphor of light. For the encyclical the brightness of the divine truths, when present to the mind, far from detracting from the worth of human reason, adds to it the highest degree of excellence, acumen, and strength.[23] The metaphor of enlightenment was immediately explained in factual terms. It meant first the challenge and incentive struck by the mind's dedicated efforts in laying bare the falsity of opinions contrary to faith and in probing what is in accord with it. This incentive prompts human reason to activity that is elevated and extremely rewarding. Second, faith frees reason from habituated errors, protects it from falling into new ones, and makes it acquainted with wide-ranging items of knowledge. Third, instead of being hostile (inimica—p. 104.18) to reason, faith is a "friendly star" (sidus amicum—p. 104.21) that points out to it distinctly the harbor of truth.[24]

When fact is substituted for metaphor, then, the enlightenment given reason by faith consists first in incentive for reason to penetrate sublime heights, second in protection from error and endowment with helpful knowledge, and third in guidance to the port or haven of truth. How all this is done was not spelled out in detail, except partly in regard to protection against some errors such as polytheism, uncaused world, and fate. Human reason, led on by faith (fide praeeunte—p. 105.15), establishes the opposite truths.[25] Still more vaguely, the encyclical (pp. 106–107) noted how Augustine had dealt similarly with angels, soul, human mind, will and free choice, religion, beatitude, time, eternity, and the nature of bodies that are subject to change.

Even in these instances, however, Aeterni Patris does not explain how Christian faith can guide and enrich philosophy without contaminating it with non-philosophical content. Rather, the use made of philosophy by St. Thomas Aquinas is held up as the illustration and model of the way it is to be done. A close look at the use made of philosophy by Aquinas in the service of the faith, and at the manner in which revealed doctrine influences his genuinely philosophical thinking, should show in practice how faith functions as a light for stimulating

---

23. "[D]ivinarum veritatum splendor, animo exceptus, ipsam iuvat intelligentiam; cui non modo nihil de dignitate detrahit, sed nobilitatis, acuminis, firmitatis plurimum addit." Aet. Patr., p. 104.1–4. The encyclical insists repeatedly upon the dignity of human reason, preserved intact in its relations with the faith. It is against this background that the additions given it in its own order by faith are stressed.

24. "[N]on culpanda fides, veluti rationi et naturalibus veritatibus inimica, sed . . . inter multas ignorantiae causas et in mediis errorum fluctibus, sibi fide sanctissima illuxerit, quae, quasi sidus amicum, citra omnem errandi formidinem portum veritatis commonstrat." Aet. Patr., p. 104.17–22.

25. Aet. Patr., p. 105.8–20. Cf. p. 101.2–11.

and guiding purely human wisdom. The question will be whether the new light brings about an intrinsic specification in the philosophy it is illuminating, and whether the specification, though occasioned by a non-philosophical source, remains entirely philosophical in its nature.

III

In Aquinas (*ST* 1.1.5) the philosophical sciences have explicitly the role of handmaids to theology. In accord with this function the choice of themes in his philosophical thinking is in fact eminently Christian. God, spiritual soul, divine providence and activity in the world, and the other topics noted for Augustine by the *Aeterni Patris* (pp. 106–107) predominate and characterize the philosophical endeavor. On this criterion the use of philosophy in Aquinas may unhesitatingly be called Christian.

But does this use of philosophy on Christian themes by Aquinas affect intrinsically the philosophical nature of the thinking, at least in the way of the enlightenment signalized by the papal document? A highly visible test instance may be found in his doctrine of being. Being, for Aquinas, is originally grasped through the act of judgment. It consists in a composition. It has, in creatures, some of itself outside itself. It is the actuality of every form or nature. Yet it is no part of any finite nature. When it is subsistent, it is infinite and is the only pure actuality.

These tenets proclaim a metaphysics intrinsically different from any other metaphysics in the whole history of human thought. They show an intrinsic and thoroughly philosophical specification. Was that specification occasioned by Christian faith?

There is extreme difficulty in claiming that it could have come about otherwise. On reading Aquinas one realizes how deeply he was struck by the "truth sublime" (*CG* 1.22. Hanc autem) that the name of God is "being." This scriptural tenet, meditated upon by Aquinas from the time of his earliest writings, led him to see that existence, because it is the nature of God, has to be other than any created nature that partakes of it.[26] Nothing other than the concentration and challenge occasioned by this revealed conception of God seems able to account

---

26. See Thomas Aquinas, *Scriptum super libros Sententiarum Magistri Petri Lombardi*, 1.8.1.1; ed. P. Mandonnet (Paris: Lethielleux, 1929), I, 194–97. In this setting the Avicennian distinction between being and quiddity is introduced. So distinguished, being had to be known for Aquinas through a different intellectual activity from conceptualization; see *Sent.*, 1.19.5.1.ad 7m (I, 489–490) and 1.38.1.3.Solut. (I, 903–904). It presents itself not as a nature but as a synthesis in time, a synthesis that is other than any finite nature.

for the blossoming out of his thought into the doctrines that being is known through a different type of intellectual apprehension from the type by which natures are known, and that finite natures abstract from all being, and so on into the other tenets just listed. They are all recognizable facets of a distinctive type of metaphysics. All are in principle open to attainment by unaided human reason. Yet in point of fact they had never been so attained. The "friendly star" was the occasion and guide, but the seeing was entirely philosophical in nature.

Another instance is the way the revealed doctrine of the world's creation in time was the challenge and the guide towards the philosophical knowledge (*In Phys.* 8.2.2041–2045) that the production of things does not necessarily involve motion or require a preceding part of time. Likewise, the revealed doctrine that man was made to the image and likeness of God prompted and led Aquinas (*Sent.* 1.8.5.2.ad 5m; ed. Mandonnet, 1, 231) to see how the human soul could initiate motion and subsist in independence of the body, even though in Aristotelian fashion it was a bodily form. Not only as with Aristotle did it have activities above the material order, but it also could no more be separated from its being than from itself. It was not only a principle of motion but also an agent in its own right. Similarly, the tenet of the existence of the accidents in the Eucharist, apart from their natural substances, pointed the way (*ST* 3.77.1.ad 2m) to a new understanding of accidents as having a really distinct existence of their own. Further, man's natural desire for an infinite good could be upheld (*ST* 1–2.5.5) despite natural lack of capacity for attaining it.

These instances could be multiplied. What they show consistently is how the faith spurs the intellect on to consider more intently the philosophical topics that are of vital concern to Christian interests, and guides it in drawing from naturally knowable objects many conclusions that it would otherwise have failed to draw. The premises for the reasoning are in every case knowable to unaided human reason. The procedure is genuinely philosophical from start to finish. The specification given is therefore intrinsic to the philosophical order. But in point of fact it emerged only under the incentive and guidance of Christian faith. The fact that cultural and economic conditions bring about differentiations among philosophies is familiar enough to present-day knowledge. Philosophy has never developed in a vacuum. The fact is there. The problem is to show that these conditions are rather the occasions in which philosophy was spurred to produce intrinsically its own specific differentiae, even though the designation of the differentiae may stem from the external factors.

IV

In its own context, then, the question of the Christian philosophy in *Aeterni Patris* may be answered quite simply. The encyclical was vigorously interested in promoting the use of philosophy to serve the Christian faith. This required a choice of philosophical problems on the ground of their relation to revealed doctrines. It required also that the faith give incentive and guidance to genuinely philosophical procedures in the solution of those problems. These two criteria, namely, choice of problems on the one hand, and incentive and guidance to their philosophical solution on the other hand, are acceptable today for characterizing a philosophy as Christian. Yet the encyclical itself shows no interest either in asking whether a Christian philosophy is possible or in determining what is required to constitute that kind of thinking.[27] The concern of the document is solely with the use of philosophy in general for serving the interests of Christian faith as philosophy had actually done in past ages.

The question of what constitutes a Christian philosophy is accordingly not a question faced by *Aeterni Patris*. It is our question, not the question of the encyclical. We can gather an answer to that question by examining the contents of the document and drawing our own conclusions from them. The answer we have seen emerging is that the use of philosophy advocated by the encyclical may today be fairly called "Christian philosophy" in the two senses just noted. In those two ways it constitutes a distinct and genuine "type of philosophizing."[28]

On the other hand any notion of "Christian philosophy" that allows acceptance of either content or method from faith is incompatible with the spirit of the encyclical. In its extreme form this conception of Christian philosophy has been hostilely described by Nédoncelle as meaning that "philosophical reflection would be conducted with the categories of revelation themselves. . . . [I]t would be nourished by a

27. This does not at all mean that the document did not aim to promote what in its immediate background had been understood as Christian philosophy. Cf.: "This notion was nonetheless one of the most certain origins of *Aeterni Patris*. . . . The encyclical of 1879 had for one of its aims a clarification of the notion of Christian philosophy." Gilson, *The Philosopher and Theology*, pp. 176–77; cf. p. 180. What it does mean is that the document does not face formally the question later raised by Bréhier.

28. The expression *philosophandi genus* is used only once in the encyclical, in reference to the help given by philosophy in preparing the way to the faith: "Ecquis autem non videat, iter planum et facile per huiusmodi philosophandi genus ad fidem aperiri?" (p. 100.31–32). But the term *genus* indicates a distinct type of philosophy just as forcefully as *genera philosophiae* (p. 111.21–22; text supra, n. 12) means the different types of modern philosophy.

heavenly manna and derive from this its principles, its method and its soul."[29] But what *Aeterni Patris* (p. 103.17) understands as philosophy in the service of revealed doctrine is a discipline that has its own method, its own starting points, and its own reasoning processes. It arrives at its conclusions in a way other than that of faith (p. 103.14). In consequence it can receive neither method nor content from faith or from theology. Its content must be derived entirely from naturally accessible objects and, in the instance of Aquinas, from sensible things. It cannot allow even any mixing of a little theology into philosophy. The philosophy that can be of service to the faith has to be pure philosophy.

Christian philosophy, therefore, as envisaged by *Aeterni Patris*, remains altogether theology-free. As a philosophy it is specified only by naturally knowable aspects of the topics with which it deals, aspects that would have been missed if attention had not been called to them by Christian faith.[30] It could hardly be fair to attribute naively to Pope

29. Nédoncelle, p. 103. For *Aeterni Patris*, philosophy has its method and starting points (see supra, nn. 8 and 10). Theology likewise proceeds *ex propriis principiis* (*Aet. Patr.*, p. 101.30). For the encyclical, accordingly, philosophy does not "inherit" any content from revelation. Its entire content consists in starting points taken from naturally available things and in the conclusions drawn from them. Nédoncelle's conclusion is: "The conceptions of Christian philosophy which we have examined above are in fact for the most part forms of theology" (p. 111). In a theologian's perspective, that may well be true. In making use of philosophy, he changes it into the wine of theology. But that use does not affect its intrinsic nature as philosophy. In the colloidal metaphor it still remains water, even though absorbed in the wine. In the philosopher's perspective it continues to be genuine philosophy.

30. Aspects that are elaborated through phenomenological scrutiny or on the basis of connatural affectivity pose a complicated question. But for present purposes the answer is straightforward enough. To the extent these aspects are attained by knowledge that is communicable and that does not come by way of supernatural revelation, they may provide philosophical starting points. To the extent they are known through revelation or mystical intuition, they do not. *Aeterni Patris* does not seek a basis for its philosophical program in aspects such as holiness or awe or dread, even though it is well aware of the all-pervading order of grace as it recalls (p. 100.1–2) how things demanded by divine law are written on the hearts of men. Yet, in its adherence to the method seen (pp. 108–109) culminating in Aquinas, it could hardly allow these aspects to serve as premises for speculative conclusions. The moral argument, for instance, could at best be regarded only as an indication or "friendly star" pointing out a problem. It would not be serving as a proof for God's existence. In prescribing a clearcut and positive traditional program instead of encouraging Catholic thought to float with the currents of the age in a way regarded by some critics as introduced by Vatican II, *Aeterni Patris* may be viewed by such critics as unwittingly a great disaster for the church at the epoch. But the unguided immersion in the philosophical thought of its age was what the encyclical consciously and with set purpose strove to forestall.

The positive addition denoted by the adjective "Christian" is well expressed as: "[P]hilosophy *perceives* certain objects and *validly demonstrates* certain propositions, which in any other circumstances would to a greater or lesser extent elude it." Jacques Maritain, *An Essay on Christian Philosophy*, trans. Edward H. Flannery (New York: Philosophical Library, 1955), p. 30 (no. 12).

Leo the self-refuting project of calling upon theological content or theological method to offer *philosophic* support to the faith. In point of fact, the University of Louvain, upon whose activity the pope relied so heavily for implementing the program of the encyclical, distinguished philosophy so sharply from revelation that its tradition was adverse to the association of the term "Christian" with the specification of any genuinely philosophical endeavor. The background of this reluctance was quite obviously the clearcut differentiation of philosophy from theology that was prevalent in Neoscholastic theory at the time. Actually, there was no need to see any such deterrent. Even within the framework of that finely etched distinction, the encyclical of Pope Leo was able to assert steadfastly that "those who join the pursuit of philosophy with submission to Christian faith philosophize best of all."[31]

31. "Quapropter qui philosophiae studium cum obsequio fidei coniungunt, ii optime philosophantur." *Aet. Patr.*, pp. 103–104. *Aeterni Patris* was, of course, a pastoral document, written decidedly from a religious viewpoint. It is not a philosophical discussion. In its pastoral perspective, faith is what guides man to his supreme destiny. Contrary tendencies can mean only aberrations. From this standpoint, any philosophical conclusions contrary to the faith are likewise contrary to truth. They are unacceptable to believers, and open to destruction by philosophy itself in its service to revealed doctrine. To non-believers in their perhaps unconscious assumption that nature is in itself a finished whole, this attitude may seem deplorable. Yet it is upheld by the encyclical in the interests of truth itself, and as an aid to philosophy in philosophical work on the philosophical plane. The aid meant is in consequence not just negative guidance and protection. It is enthusiastically positive, adding to and deepening in its incidental role the content of the philosophical attainment. From the viewpoint of the encyclical, the *philosophical genus* envisaged cannot be dismissed as philosophy merely compatible with or at least not opposed to divine revelation. The instance it signalizes, namely the philosophical thinking of Aquinas, definitely sets aside the claim that Christian guidance leads to no positive addition in the philosophical reflection. Though for Bréhier, Thomism was a Christian philosophy in the sense that "[L]a foi exerce sa censure sur la philosophie, mais ne lui fournit aucune aide positive, aucune impulsion" ("Philosophie chrétienne?" p. 144), that entirely negative attitude is certainly not found in *Aeterni Patris*. Quite to the contrary, the encyclical means that the impulse and help given by faith bring philosophy to its highest peak.

2

IS NATURE SOMETHING COMPLETE?

I

In commenting on the way the opening question in the Prologue to Duns Scotus's *Ordinatio* is formulated, Fr. Allan Wolter noted that, while aiming to safeguard a place for theology among the then-recognized sciences, the discussion goes at once to a deeper basis upon which the issue ultimately rests.[1] Even a cursory glance at the text will confirm this judgment. Instead of merely outlining the difference between the object of sacred theology and the objects of the other sciences, Scotus immediately comes to grips with the fundamental query back of the epistemological consideration. His first concern bears directly on the reason why there is a problem in regard to a place for theology among the sciences.

According to the Aristotelian philosophic tradition in which Scotus was writing, the range of the human intellect is unlimited.[2] Nothing should lie outside the scope of its general competence. It should, therefore, be able to block off correctly the areas that call for scientific scrutiny. Anything concerning the intellect's own nature and abilities, including its admitted capacity for knowledge about the divine, should in principle come under its own vision. Yet philosophers have been able to hand down lists of sciences that seem to leave no place for a specific study dealing with the things that pertain to God.[3] Why is a

1. "Scotus does not ask simply: 'Do we need a supernatural theology?', for that is the real question at issue. But since the solution of the whole controversy between the philosophers and theologians hinges on the meaning of 'supernatural,' Scotus in view of his own ultimate position, formulates the question in such a way that it can be answered unambiguously." Allan Wolter, "Duns Scotus on the Necessity of Revealed Knowledge," *Franciscan Studies* 11 (1951), 234.

2. See Aristotle, *De anima* 3.4.429a18–22; 5.430a13–15. Cf. Scotus, *Ord.*, Prol., 1.1.1; ed. Vaticana, 1, 1.11–2.5. So: "The philosophers, on the contrary, believe that Aristotle's analysis of the nature of man is so complete that it must somehow include or embrace this so-called supernatural perfection or goal." Wolter, "Duns Scotus," p. 236.

3. See Scotus, *Ord.*, Prol., 1.1.8; 1, 6–14. On the divisions of the sciences in western

divinely inspired doctrine necessary, then, to ground characteristically theological science?

So faced, the problem is whether nature as something knowable to the unaided human intellect exhausts the objects of the science. The basic question is whether nature taken in that sense is something complete enough to manifest all its factual tendencies and requirements. True, today one might urge that the intellect can have some speculative knowledge of God on the supernatural level without formally worded revelation, somewhat as a confused but immediate knowledge of God has traditionally been allowed to it.[4] But even here the knowledge of the supernatural is based upon grace, not upon nature alone. The question continues to be whether nature just in itself points to the fullness of its own possible perfection. The philosophers answer in the affirmative, Scotus wrote, and the theologians in the negative.[5] To that extent, the division of opinion seemed clear-cut for the opening years of the fourteenth century.

Today, however, the situation may appear more fuzzy. There are modern theologians who either expressly or at least effectively deny the supernatural by rejecting the notion of grace as a real perfection beyond the order of nature. As *theologians* they would seem to hold what the above Scotistic text, in the framework of the present question, calls the *perfectionem naturae*. On the other hand, process philosophers can look upon nature as open to perpetual development, unable ever to attain ultimate perfection. As *philosophers* they would appear to deny the *perfectionem naturae* in the sense here understood. Nature remains always imperfect insofar as it is ever striving for and attaining further perfection, further development. In philosophy of that type, any ultimate and complete perfection for nature is rendered impossible.

Yet, in large part, Christian theologians still look upon their science as dealing with the object of a divine revelation contained in the sacred Scriptures and required for the eternal welfare of human beings. It is an object that nature itself does not include. In quite contrary vein, modern philosophers and scientists like to have full confidence in the self-sufficiency of the natural order. As a rule they are inclined to brook no interference in their own fields from anything above human reason and experience. They want to be left to their own resources in

---

tradition up to the last part of the thirteenth century, cf. Joseph Mariétan, *Problème de la classification des sciences d'Aristote à St. Thomas* (Paris: Alcan, 1901).

4. On this type of cognition through affectivity, see Rafael-Tomas Caldera, *Le jugement par inclination chez Saint Thomas d'Aquin* (Paris: Vrin, 1980), pp. 132–35.

5. "Et tenent philosophi perfectionem naturae, et negant perfectionem supernaturalem; theologi vero cognoscunt defectum naturae et necessitatem gratiae et perfectionem supernaturalem." *Ord.*, Prol. 1.1.5; 1, 4.14–17.

working out solutions to their problems on the basis of what is provided by nature and human decision, without distraction through the intrusion of alleged higher influence. The problem of the *perfectio naturae*, as seen by Scotus in the clash between the philosophers and his colleagues in theology, in this way continues to be a timely concern. And one may still ask what exactly is the basic issue at stake.

The basic issue would seem to be the worth of philosophy as a means of grasping reality. A person may make a sincere effort at learning philosophy, but give it up on finding that it does not give him the global apprehension of real events that he gets from literature and poetry and art. On the other hand, as Aristotle observed at the beginning of the *Metaphysics* (1.1.980a21–982a3), the human mind yearns to know things in terms of their highest causes, and knowledge through those causes is precisely what philosophy gives. Do important causes at work in the real world, then, elude philosophy's grasp? Are their effects nevertheless somehow registered in the sensitive reactions of art, literature, poetry, and myth, providing in this manner a global encounter with reality? Is philosophy, in virtue of its own procedure, missing something radical that is required for a rounded out picture of the natural world? That seems to be the issue involved.

II

First, though, a word about the correct rendition of the sentence quoted above (n. 5) from Duns Scotus is in order. The English translation "The philosophers insist on the perfection of nature"[6] does bring to the fore the main point involved. But do the emphasis and the bearing of the original phrasing come through satisfactorily? The Latin *perfectio*, formed on the perfect passive participle of the verb *facio* (make), implies the notion of something that has already been "made through" (*per*) to completion. It connotes a *factio* (making) that has been brought to the fullness indicated by the thing's own notion. In this perspective the thrust of Scotus's phrasing focuses on the aspect of completeness. The question is whether nature is something complete in itself. It is suggesting that nature requires addition from an order higher than itself to be completed even as a nature. Is nature, then, intrinsically incomplete, in the sense that in its deepest self it has an indispensable exigency for a completion that it itself somehow requires but cannot furnish or even make manifest to the unaided

---

6. Wolter, "Duns Scotus," p. 242. On the background, see Étienne Gilson, *Jean Duns Scot* (Paris: Vrin, 1952), pp. 1–14.

human intellect? In that setting the notion of incompleteness could refer either to nature taken in general, as the incompleteness of all nature looked upon as a single whole, or else to each particular instance of nature, as the incompleteness of the nature of each individual thing.

The incompleteness is obviously not something to be met by perfections from an essentially different Aristotelian category.[7] Any observable thing looks towards further perfection through its accidents and activities. A seed naturally tends to sprout, a duckling naturally seeks its watery habitat on emerging from the egg, human beings work continually to perfect themselves through the arts and sciences. All such perfecting will remain within the order of nature, for that is what the substance tends to by reason of its own positive appetencies. What is meant here, rather, is whether nature is complete within the scope of its combined substance and resultant powers or qualities or activities, so that without any endowment from a higher order it rounds itself out in orientation towards a definite and ultimate goal. Alternatively phrased, the question would be whether nature is meant for something above its own order, in such a way that to be completed even as a nature it requires addition from outside. In this case not only the power to attain its end, but even the articulation necessary to make manifest its own requirement of that end, would be lacking to it as a nature. The force of the Latin *perfectionem* in the sentence will accordingly bear upon the status of nature as a finished whole when nature is taken as just in itself and in virtue solely of the tendencies that arise in it aside from supernatural addition.

With these considerations in mind, might one not ask if the translation could be sharpened? If Scotus had been writing in present-day English, might he not be expected to have made the assertion read somewhat like "that nature is a finished whole"? The question would be pinpointed to the intrinsic incompleteness of nature in its entirety as presented to unaided human scrutiny, an incompleteness recognized by the theologian but evading the search of the philosopher. Or, if the incompleteness of each individual instance was meant, the wording could be, "The philosophers hold that a nature is a finished whole."

What, then, is the precise meaning of the term "nature" in this context? The Latin *natura*, formed from the participle *natus* (born), suggests "birth" as its typical point of reference. Vital in its overtones,

---

7. In this regard Aristotle's wording is careful. It is the substance itself that changes through the accidental perfections: "the substance remaining, but changing in its modifications" (*Metaph.* 1.3.983b9–10; Oxford trans.).

the Latin word focused on the world of becoming and change, the material world. In its accepted philosophical meanings, however, the term in medieval times followed the senses of the corresponding Greek *physis*, which etymologically signified both becoming and being, but which with Aristotle had found its basic technical meaning in "the source and cause of being moved and of being at rest."[8] In this way it referred first of all to the cause of change and stability in the material world. It corresponded in general to what in English is ordinarily called nature, namely, the dynamic visible and tangible universe that is studied by the cosmologist and physicist and chemist, manifesting itself most tellingly in the vital activity found in the particular subject matter of sciences like biology, botany, zoology, and genetics. The dynamism in the notion, as interpreted by Aristotle, centered on the purpose or end for which the activity was taking place, that is, on the final causality involved.

In accordance with its Greek etymology, however, nature likewise meant for Aristotle (*Metaph.* 5.4.1014b35–1015a11) the stable form or substance of things, as well as their matter. Moreover, on account of this meaning as substance, nature was regarded by him (1015a11–13) as denoting in a transferred sense any substance whatever. It thereby found application to the immaterial and unchangeable substances or forms, the final causes of all change that took place in the material world. What in that way continued to be emphasized in its meaning was the goal or purpose of generation, the stable form.

Nature had also come to be contrasted in Aristotle (*Metaph.* 6.1. 1025b18–24) with human choice as a source of activity. Further, it was set alongside the divine as cause of physical events (see *De Caelo* 1.4.271a33), a juxtaposition readily carried over into Christian literature for the contrast between nature and grace. Here "nature" for the Christian writers referred to the created universe with its inborn powers and drives, together with its corresponding activity under the divine conservation and concurrence. The perfections added gratui-

---

8. *Physics* 2.1.192b21–22; Oxford trans. On the use of the term in preceding Greek history, see Dowe Holwerda, *Commentatio de vocis quae est ΦΥΣΙΣ vi atque usus praesertim in graecitate Aristotele antiquiore* (Groningen: J. B. Wolters, 1955). With Scotus, theological knowledge of the states in which nature can be found may occasion some variation in his use of the term "natural." He can regard it as meaning what is in accord with a particular state of nature (*Ord.*, Prol., 1.1.37; 1, 21.13–16). He likewise concedes the claim (23; 1, 15.3–6) that man naturally desires God, a goal to be attained not naturally but supernaturally (32; 1, 19.6–11). Yet he denies that the possibility for this orientation is naturally knowable in the present state (28; 1, 17.4–14). For the history of the term "supernatural," see Henri de Lubac, *Surnaturel* (Paris: Aubier, 1946), pp. 325–428. Specifically, "'surnaturel' qualifie avant tout la fin dernière qui est aujourd'hui celle de l'homme et, par l'homme, de la création entière" (p. 421).

tously to nature in spiritual creatures for working out their super-natural destiny came under the notion of "grace." In this way the traditional contrast between the natural and the supernatural became definitely established. In the immediate background of Duns Scotus this was the framework in which grace and nature were understood by the theologians. It was the problematic in which he saw nature, recognized by theologians as incomplete, while appearing to the phi-losophers as a finished whole. It was a setting that required approach from the theological side, since one of the terms, grace, does not come under the purview of philosophy. There is no access to it from pure philosophical notions.

Finally, what is the bearing of the other noun in the sentence, the *philosophi*? Aristotle is regularly referred to by Scotus in the course of the discussion. Where Scotus mentions *philosophi* in the plural (1.1.18; 1, 13.1 and 1.1.41; 1, 25.3), the doctrines accredited to them are Peripatetic. What is meant by the term in this context is accordingly Aristotle with the pagan thinkers in the Peripatetic tradition, sages who approached their topics without express guidance from the Judeo-Christian revelation.[9] The "theologians" with whom they stood in contrast were the Christian, and perhaps also the Jewish and Mos-lem, writers who had developed their teaching on the basis of their own religious faith.

The theologians regarded finite spiritual beings, including man, as created by God to serve him and share forever the happiness of his heavenly kingdom in the eternal life that consisted in the beatific vision of the divine essence. That was the ultimate goal to which all creation was directed under divine purpose and providence. God had made all things for himself, with spiritual creatures meant to know and love and enjoy him directly, and the lower orders of creation meant to provide for the needs of man. The ultimate sublime destiny could be attained by spiritual creatures not through their natural powers but through God's supernatural gifts of grace. In this way the purpose of all nature was supernatural.

The philosophers, as understood in contrast to the theologians, looked to nature for the means of working out human happiness, *eudaimonia*. According to the Aristotelian teleology, the material world, animate as well as inanimate, provided the environment, shelter, cloth-ing, nourishment, and recreation that were required for the proper functioning of human intelligence. This was the goal of material

9. For explanation in terms of the situation at the universities of Paris and Oxford, and of the condemnation of 1277, see Wolter, "Duns Scotus," pp. 234–35, and Gilson, *Jean Duns Scot*, pp. 13–14.

things. All the sub-human levels were meant to administer to the needs of the human species. In that way they fulfilled the purpose of their existence in an ordered universe. To that they were directed by their natures, making possible in human beings the attainment of *eudaimonia* through intellectual contemplation.[10] It mattered little that countless plants and animals lived and died without contributing anything directly as individuals to human happiness. One has no reason today to object in the words of Gray's elegy:

> Full many a gem of purest ray serene
> The dark unfathomed caves of ocean bear;
> Full many a flower is born to blush unseen
> And waste its sweetness on the desert air.

The individual things of nature needed only to provide and perpetuate the environment in which human beings could contemplate. It was as species rather than as individuals that they attained their goal. Similarly, the theological orientation was not affected by the obstacles so many persons experience in their daily lives, often with the consequent impossibility of attaining happiness. For the dominant Greek tradition the form, the direction of the species as a whole, was what counted.

In that way the entire universe could, in the Aristotelian setting, be considered capable of achieving its ultimate destiny through its own powers, or at least of making manifest to human investigation what its supreme purpose is. Separate substances enjoyed the happiness of perpetual and unhindered contemplation. Human beings attained a corresponding happiness at intervals and for short periods during a complete lifetime on earth. The sub-human world fulfilled its purpose by providing for the needs of the human race. Within the human species itself, practical activity was a secondary way of happiness that brought about the conditions necessary for the contemplative life.[11] In that manner every nature, material as well as spiritual, had of its own power the intrinsic capacity for working out its own destiny. Nature, both as a whole and as it is present in individuals, was complete in its own powers.

This was the dominant philosophical (as contrasted with theological) conception at the end of the thirteenth century. It applied to nature both as a totality and as present in each individual. The gift of grace,

10. On the corresponding Christian teleology, see text cited supra, n. 8, from de Lubac, *Surnaturel*, p. 421.

11. Aristotle, *EN* 10.8.1178a9. Only one *eudaimonia* seems indicated, attainable in primary and secondary degrees.

known through theology, was located immediately in spiritual beings alone. But through humans it affected in mediate fashion the orientation of the lower orders of nature. In this panoramic spread, and with the three nouns understood in the way just discussed, the Latin sentence of Duns Scotus may be satisfactorily translated as, "The philosophers hold that nature is something complete."

III

There is another preliminary question that might be asked before proceeding to investigate the exact nature of the incompleteness attributed to nature by the Christian theologians. Scotus explicitly framed his own query in application to the state of fallen nature. This would suggest the further question about the reason why the philosophers fail to recognize the incompleteness. Is it because, as the theologian sees them, their intellects are darkened by the effects of original sin? Is it because the human mind cannot now function to the fullness of its natural capacity on account of a wound inflicted upon it? Or, on the other hand, is the deficiency present even in the fullness of the human intellect's natural powers? Is the intellect, just in itself and aside from any effects arising from the fallen state, unable to perceive that nature is something intrinsically incomplete?

This consideration has been brought to the fore by a present-century exchange of views. In an article published fifteen years ago, the late Jacques Maritain cited Thomas Aquinas for the stand that in the state of fallen nature a man is deficient in his ability to accomplish all that his nature equips him to do.[12] Though acknowledging that Aquinas himself did not apply this deficiency to the case of philosophical thinking, Maritain (pp. 5–8; 11) claimed that limitations in philosophy do, as a matter of fact, come under its range. Aside from any moral weakness, or weakness of will, the great philosophers are victims of an injured intelligence in the speculative order. Maritain (pp. 12–17) discussed at some length these wounds of the intellect in regard to the intuition of being, which is "the basic and primordial natural light of philosophic intelligence" (p. 15). "Adam had the intuition of being as a gift of nature. There is nothing more natural, in itself, than that intuition—the intelligence is made for it" (p. 14). The discussion of the topic led him to remark that his colleague Étienne

12. Maritain, "Réflexions sur la nature blessée et sur l'intuition de l'être," *Revue Thomiste* 68 (1968), 5–40. Cf. Aquinas, *ST* 1–2.109.2c. Maritain's article was reprinted in the posthumous *Approches sans entraves* (Paris: Fayard, 1973), pp. 249–91.

Gilson seemed fascinated by the intuition of being to the extent of denying any concept of it (pp. 18–20; cf. p. 34).

Scotus had faced the question of man's original knowledge of being. Avicenna, he wrote (*Ord.*, Prol. 1.1.24; 1.15.7.9 / 1.1.33; 1.19.12–20.5 / 1.1.92; 1.56.7–10), had known that being, in its full range of sensible and non-sensible being, is the object of the human intellect. But Avicenna knew this, Scotus maintained, not on philosophic grounds but from what he found in his Islamic religious belief, which he had mixed in with his philosophical reasoning. Aristotle, who did not have this revealed guidance, located the human intellect's object in the quiddity of sensible things. Only on the basis of reasoning from sensible quiddity, then, could one come to know the full extent of the notion of being.

Translated into Maritain's language, this would mean that, though Adam had the intuition of being, Aristotle knew the full extent of being only through an abstract concept taken from sensible quiddities. Comparisons here are hazardous, since Maritain was writing against the Thomistic background, in which quiddity is really other than being. That distinction does not interfere with Scotus's reasoning. But to translate in oversimplified fashion, sufficient for the moment, Adam had the intuition that grasped being in its whole range, while fallen man, as in Aristotle, had only a concept of it abstracted from the being of sensible things.

Gilson, for his part, reacted strongly. In one of the last of his articles published during his own lifetime, he departed from his previous attitude of not engaging in controversy with Maritain. Regretting the scandal that might be caused by the disagreement of two veteran proponents of Thomistic doctrine in their advanced age and on a crucial problem, he felt compelled to register deep objection to Maritain's stand on this issue. The nature of the human intellect, he insisted, could not be changed by the fall. If Adam had the intuition of being as described by Maritain, we have it too.[13]

Back of Gilson's (pp. 12–15) argument is Aristotle's (*De an.* 2.4. 415a16–22) tenet that every faculty is specified by its object. The specifying object of the human intellect is not being without any restriction, but the kind of being that is proportioned to an intellect bound to a body. To include supersensible being within its specifying scope would be, Gilson (p. 7) maintained, to give the human intellect a nature not specifically human. Seeing a difference between Duns

13. Étienne Gilson, "Propos sur l'être et sa notion," in *San Tommaso e il pensiero moderno*, ed. Antonio Piolanti (Città Nuova: Pontificia Accademia Romana di S. Tommaso d'Aquino, 1974), pp. 7–8.

Scotus on the condition of being, on the one hand, and Avicenna and Aquinas on the other, Gilson wrote: "The intellectual intuition of the *esse* as such would be that of something purely intelligible; in the philosophy of Thomas Aquinas, that intuition is denied us. . . . The rule is grounded in nature, therefore it does not tolerate any exception" (p. 16). The question of intuition or concept, Gilson insisted, is accordingly a matter of choosing between radically different philosophies of man.

The relevant point emerging from this exchange of views is that the problem has to be solved by reasoning from the natural capacities of the human intellect, and not from the state of fallen nature. Accidental hindrances arising from the fallen state, in which grace is regained by individuals in greatly varying degrees, need not confuse the issue. Rather, the decision will rest upon the way the human intellect naturally grasps being. If it has an intuition of the nature of being, and accordingly is specified by being in its entire range, it will be naturally oriented towards the primary instance of being, in which the nature of being is found. It will be able to attain its supreme goal naturally, and will thereby give tangible nature the character of a finished whole. The philosophers would have ample ground for regarding nature as something complete. But the theologians know that eternal life, the vision of the intellect's highest object face to face, is possible only through grace. They are in this way able to recognize that nature is incomplete. It requires the addition of grace for determinate orientation towards its factual goal.

Actually, even though Scotus is discussing the problem as it occurs in the state of fallen nature, he is arguing from the capacities of nature taken purely in itself. He is not basing his reasoning upon wounds that result from original sin. He can use the term "natural," moreover, to mean what is natural to a particular state, as in "natural, according to the state of fallen nature."[14] Grace, after all, has a nature of its own. From this viewpoint, one may speak of what is natural to man in his elevated state and say that, in the state of original justice, it was natural for man to be aware that he was meant for the vision of God. Able to contrast his natural with his supernatural capacities he would

---

14. *Ord.*, Prol., 1.1.37; 1, 21.15–16. Cf. "ex naturalibus" (13; p. 10.1–2) and "ex puris naturalibus" (41; p. 22.20). Henri de Lubac, *The Mystery of the Supernatural*, trans. Rosemary Sheed (London: Geoffrey Chapman, 1967), p. 278, speaks of "a less perfect state" for Scotus, where "natural reason might have been able to know more." That state is hard to identify, though it does not seem to be what Scotus means in saying "rectitudo in puris naturalibus, etiam sine gratia" (*Ord.*, 4.1.6.4; 16, 208a), or "Concedo ergo . . . quod de potentia absoluta posset Deus dimittere culpam originalem, non conferendo gratiam" (6; p. 209b).

naturally be aware of the incompleteness of his nature in the self-knowledge that went with the elevated state.

But in the present question, "natural" has to be taken, for clarity, in the sense of what pertains to nature as it is known by philosophy just in itself, without any addition from what is learned through divine revelation or through affective knowledge (supra, n. 4) based on grace. The problem is to see whether the human intellect, by its natural power, aside from the consideration of grace, can know that nature is something incomplete. In the hypothetical case of an affirmative answer, the further question would have to be faced why the philosophers, as a matter of fact, fail to recognize the incompleteness. Only then need the answer be sought in the effects of original sin; the theologian is thus left burdened with the task of explaining how the natural functioning of the intellect is impeded in the field of speculative thought. But the primary issue, as the exchange between Maritain and Gilson brings out, is centered upon the way the human intellect is specified by its object, being. The specification cannot be changed by the state in which nature happens to be found.

The question, therefore, is thrown squarely into the problem of being. Gilson's compulsive reaction to Maritain's stand can readily be appreciated in the light of this consideration. The issue is whether the extent of the human intellect's range over all being involves the ability to grasp the content of being in its highest and primary instance, or whether that intuition depends upon elevation to an order beyond its natural capacities, through grace. Even though framed, as with Scotus, in the state of fallen nature (the state in which the human intellect is now found), the question focuses on whether the human intellect in its natural powers alone is specified by the full range of being, including the primary being, God, or whether it is specified by the quiddities of material things and the kind of being that corresponds to them. Briefly, the problem is whether the intellect by its own natural power can intuit the primary instance of being, or at least know it equivalently through a universal concept.

The reasoning, then, centers wholly upon the powers of the intellect as they are known through philosophical investigation. The state in which human nature happens to be found does not affect the essentials of the inquiry. If the study does show that the intellect by its natural powers is able to recognize the intrinsic incompleteness of nature, the question of fallen state may be approached for the answer to the problem of why the philosophers remained ignorant of it. But for the moment, this item of state is helpful only in stressing the point that the solution rests ultimately upon the way the human intellect is specified.

IV

With these considerations in mind, the main question may now be encountered. In what does the deficiency of nature, as known to the theologian, consist?

There need not be anything too strange in the notion of incompleteness in regard to an observable nature. In at least two naturally knowable ways, any nature other than the divine has to be considered incomplete. First, as noted earlier (supra, n. 7), a substantial nature needs to be completed by its accidents and activities. It is a completion that takes place outside the category of substance. Second, any finite substance has to be completed within its own category by its individuation and its existence. A substance is something existing in itself and not in something else. But for this it requires individuation. With Duns Scotus, haecceity in unitive containment rounds the nature into completion. Without individuation, which does not come from the nature itself but is unitively contained in it, the nature could not exist in reality. To regard the nature as so existing without the haecceity would, in fact, involve a contradiction.[15] In Aquinas, as Gilson noted elsewhere,[16] no finite substance can be taken as something already complete, as though it were there waiting to receive its existence. As a nature it is not a complete recipient. Rather, the consideration of existence has to come first. As for Aquinas, only God is his existence, correspondingly with Scotus, only God is his haecceity. In all else, the one requires completion by the other. Any finite nature is in itself something incomplete.

But neither of these two types of incompleteness is at issue here. Dynamically, nature implies orientation towards a goal. That is its distinctive characteristic, when compared with what is signified by terms such as essence or quiddity. Is it incomplete also in this characteristic function? If incomplete in the two other respects, need one hesitate in looking for incompleteness in this further way? The ques-

15. To the objections that the specific nature understood in Socrates excludes division and is thereby individual ("Item, naturae specificae, quae intelligitur in Socrate sub hac differentia repugnat dividi . . . ; ergo est individua circumscripta illa differentia"—*Quaest. Metaph.* 7.13.19; ed. Vivès, 7, 419b) and that there does not seem to be any contradiction in separating the nature of man from the individual differentia in Socrates ("Non enim videtur contradictio, quod separatur, cum non includat illam"), Scotus noted (*Ord.* 20; p. 421b) that blackness is formally contradictory to a white stone by force of the whiteness ("lapidi albo formaliter repugnat nigredo per albedinem") and that from the side of the real thing nature and individual differentia are inseparable ("Si loquamur realiter, humanitas quae est in Socrate, non est humanitas quae est in Platone, et est realis differentia ex differentiis individualibus unitive contentis, inseparabilibus hinc inde").

16. Étienne Gilson, "Cajétan et l'existence," *Tijdschrift voor philosophie* 15 (1953), 274–76.

tion centers pointedly on incompleteness in human nature, since (supra, n. 10) sub-human things fulfill their destiny by ministering to human needs and bear upon the final goal only through man. But what exactly is the goal of human nature, as known to the philosophers? As Aristotle recalled at the beginning of the *Nicomachean Ethics* (1.4.1095a17–20), everybody places it in happiness. But different types of men locate their happiness, their ultimate goal, in different things. Some choose a life of sensual pleasure, others a life of power and prestige, others a life of contemplation (1.5.1095b14–1096a5). The goal in the concrete is not determined by nature, but is chosen by the individual. Human choice is, of course, rational in character, and reason shows that the function proper to man is the exercise of his highest faculty upon its highest object.[17] But what is that highest object?

Aristotle, with a metaphysics in which the degrees of truth coincided with those of being,[18] would seem compelled to locate the highest object in the primary instance of being. But for him that primary instance was separate substance, something finite and allowing a plurality of instances. How could the human intellect intuit separate substance so conceived? The Stagirite, with his accustomed philosophical caution, left this question unanswered, though his commentators have endeavored to supply appropriate responses. The picture Aristotle himself gave was that of an eternal succession of human beings able, in generation after generation, to keep contemplating—each individual for brief intervals at a time—the highest object of intellection, whatever it was. Could that kind of contemplation be considered complete and final as a goal? Action is something for individual things and is performed by individual agents. If no one individual could attain a unitary individual object in which the ultimate goal is located, and the continuance of individual acts of contemplation keeps going on without end, will not a philosophical suspicion arise that human nature, and thereby nature as a whole, is "endless"?[19]

17. Aristotle, *EN* 1.7.1097b24–1098a17; 10.7.1177a12–1178a8. Cf. *Metaph.* 1.2. 982a30–b2.

18. *Metaph.* 2.1.993b24–31; *EN* 1.6.1096a23–27. A critical discussion of these topics in Aristotle may be found in Karl Bärthlein, *Die Transzendentalienlehre der alten Ontologie* (Berlin: Walter de Gruyter, 1972), pp. 22–108.

19. See discussion by Anton C. Pegis, "Nature and Spirit: Some Reflections on the Problem of the End of Man," *Proceedings of the American Catholic Philosophical Association* 23 (1949) pp. 62–79, explaining the tenet that "man is endless by nature" (p. 73) as meaning, not that nature requires grace, but rather grace "calls into being spiritual creatures to receive it" (p. 79). See also Gerard Smith, "The Natural End of Man," ibid., pp. 47–61, for a philosophical treatment of the question whether man's end is "*de jure* only supernatural, or is it only *de facto* supernatural" (p. 49). For an introduction to the literature occasioned by de Lubac's *Surnaturel,* see Pegis, p. 62, n. 2.

In the theological context, this conception of nature as "endless" just in itself may quite readily emerge. Man has just one final destiny, in actual truth. It is the beatific vision, an end that is supernatural. It allows, compositively, no possibility of any other adequate end for human nature.[20] But if the reasoning is confined to the philosophical level, is not the incompleteness of nature, a tenet unknown to the philosophers, being presupposed in the argument? As far as the philosopher alone is concerned, could not human nature be meant ultimately for this unending succession of contemplative acts? It would be fulfilling itself perfectly in the eternally successive activity of different individuals. It would be meant for nothing more, and accordingly would be something complete in itself. Only when viewed theologically would a deficiency show.

It is true that the human intellect knows things under the most general aspect of being. It can grasp one object after another without cease. It can even conceive an infinite and eternal being as an object. Why then can it not know, philosophically, that it is meant for infinite being and that nothing else will satisfy its natural tendency? The argument seems clear, and to the point.

This way of thinking, nevertheless, is not immune from philosophical difficulty. In Aristotle's reasoning, no individual infinite being is attained. With Plotinus, a unique source is reached, above the distinctions of finite and infinite, but thereby also above the order of being. For Scotistic philosophy, a univocal concept of being admits the addition of the notion "infinite," but only by means of a leap from the finite.[21] In Aquinas a sensible thing's being is apprehended through judgment, and by causal demonstration leads to a positively infinite nature in God. (Even here no philosophically knowable means becomes apparent by which the finite human intellect could grasp in itself this positively infinite object. The unlimited range of the intellect's *concept* of being would be satisfied with the unendingly successive grasp of finite existents within its reach.) Finally, few modern philosophies will accept cogently demonstrative arguments for the existence of God in the sense of the creative Deity handed down in Judeo-Christian tradition. In fact, the extreme has even been reached of accepting the universe as a multiplicity of utterly unrelated things, something that

20. This is acceptable "provided also that we show intelligibly how God can never be under any obligation, any sort of requirement, to give himself to the being he has made, as is clear from the most elementary and basic Christian teaching, recalled in our own day in Pius XII's encyclical *Humani generis*." De Lubac, *Mystery*, p. 65.

21. Cf.: "il balzo fondamentale dal finito all'infinito, dall'essere diveniente all'Essere indiveniente è già compiuto." Efrem Bettoni, *L'ascesa a Dio in Duns Scoto* (Milan: Vita e Pensiero, 1953), p. 56.

would have appeared to Aristotle as a wretched tragedy.[22] Philosophically, therefore, the possession of the abstract notion of being does not guarantee that the human intellect is meant for the contemplation of a single primary and infinite instance of it. In fact, where an abstract concept is the ground, there is ample reason to reject all ontological reasoning to God's existence.

The philosopher, then, is left to judge the orientation of a nature from its activities as he knows them by his unaided intellect. He has no higher standard. From them he will reason to a commensurate ultimate end for the nature itself. He uses the same measure for both nature and end, with the result that the nature is adequate. It appears a finished whole. Only in the perspective of the theologian does the situation become different. The theologian, through his revealed sources, knows that an omnipotent and all-wise God, three in person while one in nature and being, has created all things for himself, placing man over the material universe and destining each human being for eternal happiness in the beatific vision of the divine essence. For this, God has provided human nature with elevation to a supernatural level through grace, which constitutes man a *viator* during life on earth[23] and culminates after death in the illumination required to behold the divine essence face to face. From this theological viewpoint human nature is seen to be capable of a goal far above any natural orientation. But that capacity is not known through a thing's nature.[24]

22. E.g.: "I think the universe is all spits and jumps, without unity, without continuity, without coherence or orderliness." Bertrand Russell, *The Scientific Outlook* (London: George Allen & Unwin, 1931), p. 98. Cf. Aristotle, *Metaph.* 12.10.1076a1–4.

23. On the history and meaning of the theological concept "wayfarer," see Gerhart B. Ladner, "*Homo Viator*: Medieval Ideas on Alienation and Order," *Speculum* 42 (1967), pp. 233–59.

24. On the natural inclination towards the beatific vision, or the natural desire to see God, see de Lubac, *Surnaturel*, pp. 431–38; 467–71; 475–94. For Duns Scotus the desire is natural, though not naturally known in the present state, and its object is not attainable by natural means: "[D]ico quod illa potentia habendi caritatem ut ipsa est dispositio respectu Dei in se sub propria ratione amandi, convenit naturae hominis secundum rationem specialem, non communem sibi et sensibilibus; et ideo non est illa potentialitas cognoscibilis pro statu isto de homine, sicut nec homo cognoscitur sub illa ratione sub qua eius est haec potentia. . . . concedo Deum esse finem naturalem hominis, sed non naturaliter adipiscendum sed supernaturaliter. Et hoc probat ratio sequens de desiderio naturali, quam concedo." *Ord.*, Prol., 1.1.32; 1, 18.19–19.11. Similarly Aquinas: "Quamvis enim homo naturaliter inclinetur in finem ultimum, non tamen potest naturaliter illum consequi, sed solum per gratiam, et hoc est propter eminentiam illius finis." *In Boeth. de Trin.* 6.4.ad 5m; ed. Decker, p. 229.9–12. "Sed quia homo ordinatur ad finem beatitudinis aeternae, quae excedit proportionem naturalis facultatis humanae," *ST* 1–2, 91, 4c. The two medieval theologians shift the bearing of the term "natural" (cf. supra, n. 8). It is "natural" in the present elevated state (a) to desire God, and (b) to be inclined towards God through the supernatural grace. In these two in-

For the theologian, in consequence, the ultimate goal of a man remains something chosen, but now chosen by God. In Aristotelian philosophy, each human person chose the concrete type of life in which he wanted to locate his own happiness. To that extent each may be seen basking in the unconquerable and unbowed defiance of William Ernest Henley's well-known lines:

> I am the master of my fate:
> I am the captain of my soul.
> (*I. M., R. T. Hamilton Bruce*)

But even in Aristotle, the choice was meant to be rational. Haphazardness was the last thing the Stagirite (*Metaph.* 12.10.1075a18–23) wanted to see associated with liberty. If a person acted according to his upbringing as a freeman, he would always make his choice rationally. He would choose and live the life of contemplation or of virtue. In both cases freedom is enhanced, not hindered, through the fact that it is directed by right reason.

Yet the incompleteness of nature, precisely as nature, does not lie in its requirement of human or divine choice to determine its ultimate end, but rather in its lack of capacity, as nature, to make manifest and to work out the destiny to which it is directed by divine decision. It has to be perfected by grace to have orientation to the goal for which it has been created. The potentiality for elevation through grace escapes the philosopher's investigation, therefore, and is known only to the theologian. The philosopher discovers no contradiction in the elevation of a created intellect to the beatific vision, as he could in the case of a non-cognitive faculty, yet he cannot show positively that it is possible. He does not know that there is a Trinity to be contemplated, nor that there are supernatural powers to equip the soul for that destiny. As with other revealed truths, the possibility cannot be positively demonstrated even though the arguments that aim to show a contradiction in it turn out to be inapplicable.

In this respect the incompleteness of nature is not like the incompleteness of a substance in regard to its existence. There would be a

---

stances, "natural" means what is characteristic of nature working through the superadded grace. But (c) in saying that this inclination is not naturally knowable and therefore unattainable by philosophy, "natural" is taken to mean what is proportioned to nature just in itself. Likewise, in the assertion that (d) capability of elevation belongs to spiritual nature but is not naturally knowable, "natural" refers to nature considered without grace. Finally, (e) the power to work out and attain the supernatural destiny is never called "natural," but is always attributed to grace, restricting "natural" in this area of operation to unaided nature. These uses of the term are established, and need to be respected in discussions on the topic.

contradiction in conceiving a substance as complete in itself and already there waiting to receive existence. It would in that way be represented as existing and not existing at the same time. Rather, the reason why nature cannot be regarded as complete in itself and lying there in expectation of further orientation comes from the order of factual finality. There is not and there never was any other final goal for nature than the supernatural. But in the approach from a physical standpoint, no reason appears why nature could not have been created just in itself. The matter and the form and the existence would be the same, from this viewpoint.[25] Nature could have been left to waste its sweetness on a desert air, or to lie in wait for a future elevation somewhat as the world waited for centuries for its redemption. Its purpose, as far as philosophy is concerned, would have been to provide a setting in which spiritual creatures could lead an intellectual life. Whether God in his infinite goodness would create such a universe as an external manifestation of his glory is hardly within philosophical competence to decide. It might seem to us to be without sufficient purpose, but a Leibnitzian sufficient reason is hardly admissible here—God is not obliged to create the best possible universe. Often in the events under present providence there is the temptation to remark how odd God's choices are. In any case, the incompleteness of nature as nature lies in its inability just by itself to indicate or to work towards the goal to which it is in fact oriented. No matter what explanation one gives of man's natural desire to see God, one cannot know philosophically that nature is able to receive the supernatural orientation. Divine intellection sees the possibility, but unaided human thinking does not.

V

Since nature is the source of action, incompleteness in nature may be expected to make itself somehow felt in operations to which it factually gives rise. There should be some kind of factual awareness of deficiency, even though the incompleteness of nature escapes philosophic scrutiny. The awareness would be based on affectivity, and be

25. Philosophically, there does not seem to be any insuperable difficulty on this issue. A review in *Theological Studies* 27 (1966), p. 278, suggested that de Lubac's unhesitating acceptance here (cf. supra, n. 20) showed "a sincerely meant bow to the magisterium, but no success at incorporating its positive meaning into his own point of view." The difficulties in regard to lack of "positive content," however, seem to be theological. Earlier another reviewer in the same journal, 11 (1950), p. 392, had noted: "Curiously enough, Catholic philosophers have shown much more readiness to accept de Lubac's major conclusions than have Catholic theologians."

able to find expression in art and poetry and literature.[26] It would bear on human activity, through which all lower types have their orientation to the ultimate factual goal. What eludes philosophy can nevertheless remain open to poetic vision.

In point of fact, people in ordinary life do not as a rule think their lives are all they would like them to be. The sentiment of reaching out continually for something that natural life does not provide may be found well expressed in Browning's *Andrea del Sarto*: "Ah, but a man's reach should exceed his grasp, or what's a heaven for?" Intellectually, man stretches his regard to the perfect and the eternal. Man has difficulty in being content with the imperfect and the fleeting, even though from the viewpoint solely of material nature he may tell himself grimly with Heraclitus (*Diels-Kranz, Fr.* 20) that in accepting life in birth one thereby accepts the fate of death. Lack of harmony between spiritual aspiration and material fact seems keenly felt. Death may cut life short before the fulfillment of one's deepest desires. In a now hardly remembered poem (*Charles Sumner*), the American poet Longfellow voiced trenchantly this ever-present yearning for completeness:

> Death takes us by surprise,
> And stays our hurrying feet;
> The great design unfinished lies,
> Our lives incomplete.

> But in the dark unknown
> Perfect their circles seem,
> Even as a bridge's arch of stone
> Is rounded by the stream.

As in religious intimation, heaven rounds to completion the circle of human life, so from the theologian's viewpoint supernatural grace fills out human activity to completion in the life of the wayfarer in the beatific vision. It elevates man's action to the plane on which the ultimate goal of creation may be attained. It makes fully operational all the dynamic orientation by which nature is completed as nature, that is, by which nature is rounded out in its capacity of providing direction towards its definite factual goal.

Though the completion remains a "dark unknown" to the poet, it is made sufficiently manifest to the wayfarer through revelation accepted on faith. Conclusions about it may then be drawn with the certainty that goes with theological reasoning. A place for sacred the-

---

26. Pegis, "Nature and Spirit," p. 62, very aptly applied Péguy's "O coeur inachevé" to the incompleteness in this human situation.

ology among the sciences is thereby safeguarded, in the sense in which the Latin term *scientia* was traditionally understood. Formal divine revelation, as handed down in the Judeo-Christian tradition, provides the stable basis for this theological science. Precise dogma, not vague affectivity, becomes its firm foundation. In Longfellow's simile the part of the circle located in the arch of stone was the solid and enduring structure. The shadow on the water was unsubstantial and passing. But in the theological perspective, the supernatural side of human life through grace is the facet that presents solidity and permanence. It is formulated with sufficient clarity, is eternal in its outlook, and is the deepest and most meaningful factor in human activity.

Hence, efforts to gauge human living solely from the viewpoint of nature are bound sooner or later to become frustrating. In point of fact, there is no condition of mere nature. In their actual state, spiritual beings are either endowed with grace or are in the contrary disposition, sin. There is in fact no neutral condition. Everyone who has the use of moral reason experiences the promptings of grace.[27] There is affective awareness of something more than nature. This may be found expressed in pagan literature. Man's deep longing for a homeland beyond and above the present world was voiced vividly in the Platonic myths. People were to be judged by Radamanthys and others for entrance into a new and wonderful life (Plato, *Apol.* 41AC). In Aristotle's *Eudemus* death meant return to one's real home.[28] The apostle Paul (Acts 17.28) reminded the Athenians that among their own bards there had been glimpses of divine parentage for the human race: "[A]s some of your own poets have said, 'We also are his offspring.'"

These were pagan traditions expressed in poetry and myth. After the advent of Christianity this affective awareness could continue to find voice, as in Wordsworth's lines: "Not in entire forgetfulness . . . but trailing clouds of glory do we come / From God, who is our home" (*Intimations of Immortality*). In the disappointments of life, Browning could see "On earth the broken arcs; in heaven a perfect round" (*Abt Vogler*), and express in the same poem the trust that through God's

27. "postquam uero usam rationis habent, tenentur salutis sue curam agere. Quodsi fecerint, iam absque peccato originali erunt, gratia superueniente; si vero non facerint, talis omissio est eis peccatum mortale." Aquinas, *De malo* 5.2.ad 8m; ed. Leonine, 23, 135a. For a discussion of the topic, see Salmanticenses, *Cursus theologicus* (Paris: Palmé, 1878), 9, 749–87.

28. "[I]n the fifth year thereafter, Eudemus himself would return home. . . . And so the dream had been interpreted as meaning that when Eudemus' soul had left his body, it had returned to its home." Aristotle, *Eudemus,* in *Select Fragments,* trans. Ross, *The Works of Aristotle* (Oxford: Clarendon Press, 1952), 12, 16.

power accomplishment will match inspiration, for who could "Doubt that thy power can fill the heart that thy power expands?"

Pagan myth and Christian poetry can accordingly perceive through affectivity the incompleteness that escapes the eye of the philosopher. Plato repeatedly burst into myth when philosophical reasoning fell short of his objective. Aristotle (*Metaph.* 1.2.982b18–19); cf. 12.8. 1074b1), too, noted that the lover of myth is in a way a lover of wisdom, a philosopher, as though the mythmaker had his own way of dealing with things that cause wonder. But in the context in the *Metaphysics* Aristotle was showing that wisdom means knowledge through causes. Precisely from this angle does the incompleteness of nature evade the philosopher's search, for he has no means of knowing about the elevation of nature through grace. In consequence, he measures nature by the goals with which he is acquainted through philosophical reasoning, and he finds nature adequate for them. But the great gap, between human life as actually lived and the perfection for which it longs so poignantly in poetry and myth, remains a problem for him.

He can face the problem in pessimistic or Sartrian fashion and maintain that nature is meant for the destructive or for the absurd. Nature would appear adequate in itself for this death-wish type of orientation. Or, human destiny could be located in an earthly paradise that man has been working towards through the past centuries of gradual progress in culture and civilization and that will gradually be attained through continued evolution, or, where necessary at any particular stage, through revolution. Again, nature is regarded as commensurate in itself for reaching this ultimate goal, provided the necessary time and human effort be at hand. In any case, the philosopher is measuring nature by philosophically known goals. He finds it adequate for them and, in consequence, regards nature as something complete in itself.

The affective awareness of the supernatural expressed in poetry and myth, then, does not radically alter the situation faced by Duns Scotus. It does not provide philosophy with access to the incomplete state in which nature is actually found, any more than did Avicenna's theological knowledge that being, in its full perfection, is the object of the human intellect. In spite of the difficulties that arise from actual human living, philosophers unaided by divine revelation will, by virtue of their method, continue to bypass the supernatural. In nature as nature, that is, in nature considered from the viewpoint of orientation towards an end, they will persist in seeing a finished whole.

This argument explains why so many people can say that, for them, philosophy does not come to grips with reality, while art and poetry and literature do; such people expect a rounded-out picture of the real not attainable in philosophy. It emphasizes Gilson's irritating claim that medieval philosophy, although genuinely philosophical in its procedure, has to be understood against a theological background. It shows how certain critics of medieval philosophy can allege that there was no philosophy at all in the middle ages but only an extended theology; for on each side the conception of nature is different. It helps to account for the need and place today of a thoroughgoing Christian philosophy, a philosophy specifically different from other philosophies and able to function in its own right as a genuine philosophy that reasons entirely from naturally knowable principles yet under the aegis of revealed truth. In these and other ways the observation of Duns Scotus (that the philosophers hold nature to be something complete) still has its relevance. Philosophy maintains its irreplaceable role as knowledge in terms of highest causes, but Horatio concedes to Hamlet that there are things in heaven and earth about which philosophy does not even dream.

3

THE NOTION OF CATHOLIC PHILOSOPHY

I

In the aftermath of the "secularistic sixties," and before predictions about the "superstitious seventies" are proven true or false, some serious reflections on the notion of Catholic philosophy may be in order. Notoriously, the *aggiornamento* of the sixties did not make any very observable use of Catholic philosophy.[1] The theologians of the decade showed comparatively little interest and still less enthusiasm for its role as a required training, preliminary to a theological or sacerdotal career. No distinctive place seemed assigned to it in the projected renewal of Catholic life. Unfortunately, this attitude continues. So, while there is no danger whatever that Catholic philosophy will succumb to superstition or be dominated by astrology in the years immediately ahead, there is a definite threat that its specific character may be misunderstood and its important functions neglected in the ongoing surge of Catholic intellectual life.

In this setting, both the elements of the expression, "Catholic" and "philosophy," are open to attack. On the one hand, the very notion of a specific Catholic philosophy may, in the wake of the secularizing mentality of the sixties, encounter bitter opposition from Catholic intellectuals. With some, the present ecumenical atmosphere tends to discourage the emphasis given by the designation "Catholic." On the

---

1. "The really deep 'sleeper" of the current *aggiornamento* is the issue of philosophy, that is, whether there is to be an updating of traditional philosophical concepts and methodology in Catholic circles, and how this is to be achieved." T. N. Davis, "Of Many Things," *America*, June 12, 1965, p. 841. During that period, however, there was no lack of concern among Catholic philosophers in regard to the live philosophical issues relevant to the renewal. This is amply testified to by the *Proceedings of the American Catholic Philosophical Association* throughout those years, and by the collection of papers edited by George F. McLean in *Christian Philosophy and Religious Renewal* (Washington, DC: Catholic University of America Press, 1966), and in *Christian Philosophy in the College and Seminary* (Washington, DC: Catholic University of America Press, 1966) and *Philosophy and Contemporary Man* (Washington, DC: Catholic University of America Press, 1968).

other hand, the current occupation with "relevance" may come to regard all independently based philosophy as something cut off from and meaningless for religion. The result, naturally, would be attempts to absorb the necessary functions of philosophy into theology. But philosophizing for theology will never build a genuine philosophy. Quite patently, then, there is need at the present moment for a careful reconsideration and assessment of the notion of Catholic philosophy, the "C" capitalized, not lower case.

During the nineteenth-century revival of philosophy in ecclesiastical circles, there was hardly any question that Catholic thought required a special type of philosophy, different from the Kantian and Hegelian and positivistic types that then dominated western thought, as well as from the traditionalism of the earlier part of the century. This special type was the officially promoted Scholasticism. Scarcely noticed was the now-apparent fact that Scholasticism is radically pluralistic in character, even though at the time sharp disagreements surfaced in controversies between thinkers with respectively Thomist or Scotistic or Suarezian backgrounds. The disputes were regarded as endemic to Scholastic tradition, and opponents were treated as though making mistakes in their reasoning from basic principles accepted as common. But that all the participants formed a group, cut off from and radically opposed to non-Catholic thought, did not even give rise to a doubt. The camps were different and opposed. They kept going their separate ways.

During the first quarter of the present century the division and opposition continued. The notion of a distinct philosophy for Catholic thinking kept on with its process of consolidation. On this continent it resulted in the organization of the American Catholic Philosophical Association in 1926. Again, the officially recognized Scholastic philosophy was being promoted.[2] It was quite optimistically offered to the world as the true basis for philosophic, scientific, educational, and cultural progress.[3] With the ensuing years the need and the difficulties of establishing communication with the outside philosophy became increasingly apparent. An attempt at direct encounter and collaboration, however, proved abortive and was never repeated.[4] Yet admonitions and encouragement to break outside the ghetto and achieve communication continued.[5]

2. See *Proceedings of the American Catholic Philosophical Association* 1 (1926), 15–17.
3. *Proceedings, ACPA* 1 (1926), 19–72.
4. The papers read at the joint session in New York may be found in the *Proceedings, ACPA* 13 (1937), 132–70.
5. The objective had been stated, in the course of a look at the first ten years of the

In the meantime, efforts were made in the other camp to bring Catholic philosophers into the main stream of American philosophy, notably through the Metaphysical Society of America, organized in 1950.[6] In the course of the last two decades these efforts have been supersuccessful. The great majority of the topics dealt with at the annual meetings of the American Catholic Philosophical Association are now no longer Scholastic but rather those of the non-Catholic philosophies. The articles appearing in the current issues of *The New Scholasticism* and *The Modern Schoolman* deal in large part with the same subjects and use the same vocabulary as the secular journals. A number of their articles are written by thinkers who have no Scholastic background at all. While the scholastic tradition has not been entirely absorbed into the modern, the predominance of the modern can on occasion reduce the scholastic content to a condition of near invisibility. The head of a philosophy department in a secular university, attending for the first time the annual convention of the American Catholic Philosophical Association in 1969, expressed openly his disappointment: "I made a special point this year to come to the ACPA meeting to hear some traditional philosophy, and all I have been getting is the same routine of 'conceptual frameworks' that I wanted to avoid."

Throughout this give-and-take, however, the label of a distinctive "Catholic philosophy" rarely became explicit.[7] In the nineteenth and

---

American Catholic Philosophical Association, as: "The day American philosophers begin to take us seriously as philosophers, that day the New Scholasticism has come of age in the United States"—James H. Ryan, "A Decade of Association," *Proceedings, ACPA* 11 (1935), 17.

6. Paul Weiss noted that through this society Catholic thinkers "who until then had held themselves apart from the main stream, talking only to one another and publishing mainly in highly specialized scholastically oriented periodicals, felt free to join in a continued discussion with fellow philosophers of the most diverse persuasions"—"Announcements," *The Review of Metaphysics* 22 (1968), 425.

7. It is used by Maurice Blondel, *Le problème de la philosophie catholique* (Paris: Bloud & Gay, 1932). On his reasons for preferring "Catholic philosophy" to "Christian philosophy," see ibid., p. 172, n. 1. In this preferential sense only should be applied the remark, "There was even a philosopher advocating a philosophy that could rightly call itself Catholic, such as was his own philosophy, but not Christian." Étienne Gilson, *The Philosopher and Theology* (New York: Random House, 1962), p. 179. "Catholic philosophy" occurs without much ado in *Christian Philosophy and Religious Renewal,* ed. George F. McLean (Washington, DC: Catholic University of America Press, 1966), pp. 30; 159–62. It is used by Avery Dulles in explicit confrontation with "Christian philosophy," as the seemingly more generic notion: "Just as there is a Christian philosophy, there is certainly such a thing as a Catholic philosophy"—ibid., pp. 158–59. The founding members of the American Catholic Philosophical Association were regarded as "students and teachers of Catholic philosophy" in the inaugural address by Edward A. Pace, *Proceedings, ACPA* 1 (1926), 14, and the part of laymen in "Catholic philosophy" was stressed, ibid., p. 17.

early twentieth centuries, Catholics may have admittedly and even belligerently prided themselves on possessing a philosophical tradition that was different. But they universally regarded this tradition as something that should be shared by all men, regardless of religious or cultural background. It was looked upon as, in principle, independent of religious belief. It was the "perennial philosophy"[8] that was the common heritage of mankind. The only problem was to get all men to see it and adopt it. The implications of this attitude, namely, that other views were philosophically invalid and that all philosophies could be definitively judged and excluded by the principles of one particular philosophy, did not come to light. If these implications had been brought to the fore, the difficulties involved in the attitude would have become patent and embarrassing.

With the first quarter of the present century, the acceptance of a religiously neutral mentality throughout philosophical reasoning had

8. The designation *philosophia perennis* was taken from the title of a book by Augustinus Steuchus (Eugubinus), *De perenni philosophia* (Basel: per Nicolaum Bryling et Sebastianum Francken, 1542). With him it meant a wisdom that was unitary (p. 6) and always possessed by the human race: "perennis haec fuit usque ab exordio generis humanae Philosophia"—ibid., p. 650. Its purpose was Christian piety (p. 649). The expression, clearly non-philosophic in its original meaning with Steuco, was brought into the stream of European philosophy by Leibniz (*Lettre III à Rémond: Opera philosophica*, ed. J. E. Erdmann [Berlin: G. Eichleri, 1839–40] 1, 704a), in the sense of a residue remaining from all the great traditional philosophies once their surface differences and worthless additions have been removed. A discussion of this topic may be found in Charles B. Schmitt, "Perennial Philosophy: From Agostino Steuco to Leibniz," *Journal of the History of Ideas* 27 (1966), 505–32. On the origin of the notion, see also Hermann Ebert, "Augustinus Steuchus und seine Philosophia perennis," *Philosophisches Jahrbuch* 42 (1929), 342–56; 510–26; 43 (1930), 92–100. For discusson and references in the modern situation, see Schmitt, pp. 505–506, nn. 1–10; James Collins, "The Problem of a Philosophia Perennis," *Thought* 28 (1953), 571–97. Though the designation "perennial philosophy" has been used by some non-Catholic philosophers, e.g., Wilbur Marshall Urban, *The Intelligible World* (London: G. Allen & Unwin, 1929), pp. 171–207, it attained its greatest popularity in Neoscholastic circles, where it continued the claims to a unitary character: "There is, we hold, only one *philosophia perennis*: and that means that if there is anything that deserves the name of philosophy outside our school, it also belongs to the *philosophia perennis*"—James A. McWilliams, "Presidential Address," *Proceedings, ACPA* 8 (1932), 7; cf. p. 13. The immediate objective was to "rediscover the perennial philosophy, the wisdom of European culture"—Mortimer J. Adler, "The New Scholastic Philosophy and the Secular University," *Proceedings, ACPA* 10 (1934), 164. The image from the use of "perennial" in gardening was not absent: "A perennial philosophy, like a perennial flower, must wake each year to new life and draw new resources from the fresh soil about it and the newly made garden in which it is destined to bloom"—James H. Ryan, "Presidential Address," *Proceedings, ACPA* 6 (1930), 23. "Perennial philosophy" is not listed as a topic in Paul Edwards's *Encyclopedia of Philosophy*, nor in the *New Catholic Encyclopedia*, nor in the *Enciclopedia filosofica*. It can hardly be regarded as an active notion at present. The orientation of "philosophy" as well as of "Christian philosophy" towards piety may be seen specified in the use of each of those two terms to designate the monastic life—see J. Leclercq, "Pour l'histoire de l'expression 'philosophie chrétienne,'" *Mélanges de science religieuse* 9 (1952), 221–26.

become ingrained in Neoscholastic thought, at least in principle. This front received an unwelcome jolt through the sudden prominence given by Bréhier and Gilson early in the third decade of the century to the term "Christian philosophy."[9] It was a term that had been in use here and there for centuries. Whatever it may have meant in the past, it now became exploited for a number of different senses all geared to contrast it with secular philosophy and bring it into some significant relation with the Christian faith. The notion, however, brought sharp reaction from some non-Catholic philosophers,[10] as well as from Catholic philosophers who were intent upon showing their

9. See discussion, "La notion de philosophie chrétienne," *Bulletin de la Société française de Philosophie* 31 (1931), 37–93; Émile Bréhier, "Y a-t-il une philosophie chrétienne?" *Revue de métaphysique et de morale* 38 (1931), 133–62; Étienne Gilson, *The Philosopher and Theology* (New York: Random House, 1962), pp. 175–99. For other references, see A.-R. Motte, "Le problème de la 'philosophie chrétienne,'" *Bulletin thomiste* 14 (1937), 230–55; É. Gilson, *The Christian Philosophy of St. Thomas Aquinas,* tr. L. K. Shook (New York: Random House, 1956), p. 441, nn. 19–20; Maurice Nédoncelle, *Is There a Christian Philosophy?* tr. Illtyd Trethowan (New York: Hawthorn Books, 1960), pp. 153–54; L.-B. Geiger, s.v. "Christian Philosophy," *New Catholic Encyclopedia*; L. Morati, s.v. "Filosofia cristiana," *Enciclopedia filosofica*. The religious differentiation may even be compounded: "Just as Europe has a Christian philosophy, it is necessary to have the humility to work towards Hindu-Christian philosophy, a Mohammedan-Christian philosophy, and a Buddhist-Christian philosophy"—S. Tissa Balasuriya, in *Christian Philosophy in the College and Seminary,* ed. George F. McLean, p. 34. On the differing attitudes of Christians towards philosophy, see Lawrence E. Lynch, *A Christian Philosophy* (New York: Charles Scribner's Sons, 1968), pp. 25–36.

The expression "Christian philosophy" is found, though rarely, in the middle ages and in the Renaissance. It occurs also in the seventeenth century. In these instances it has varied meanings. It did not acquire vogue until the nineteenth. For some nineteenth-century instances, see Nédoncelle, p. 85. The *Annales de philosophie chrétienne* continued publication from 1830 well into the twentieth century, with "philosophy" covering an exceptionally wide variety of subjects. "Christian philosophy" occurs in the accepted title of the encyclical of Pope Leo XIII, *Aeterni Patris,* 1879, in the philosophic context in which it was to become a controverted notion in the third decade of the twentieth century. A sketch of the controversy may be found in Nédoncelle, pp. 85–99. On Blondel's earlier denial that a "Christian philosophy" exists, see his own comments in his "Y a-t-il une philosophie chrétienne?" *Revue de métaphysique et de morale* 38 (1931), 605.

The term "Christian metaphysics" is used by Battista Spagnoli, *Opus aureum in Thomistas,* ed. Paul Oskar Kristeller in *Le thomisme et la pensée italienne de la Renaissance* (Paris: Vrin, 1967), p. 156.28. It may be found occasionally in modern writing, e.g. Bertrand Russell, *Why I am not a Christian,* ed. Paul Edwards (New York: Simon & Schuster, 1957), p. 26. It provides the title for Claude Tresmontant's *Christian Metaphysics,* tr. Gerard Slevin (New York: Sheed and Ward, 1965). "Christian metaphysic" is used by Nédoncelle, pp. 10; 151.

10. See infra, n. 24. Cf.: "Albertus Magnus and Saint Thomas had no choice. Even at the cost of crushing a possible Christian philosophy, they had to impose on Gothic evangelical inspiration the deforming tyranny of Aristotelianism. This deformation is what Mr. Gilson in another very recent book, *L'esprit de la philosophie médiévale,* called Christian philosophy"—José Ortega y Gasset, *Man and Crisis,* tr. Mildred Adams (New York: Norton, 1958), p. 118.

secular counterparts that Scholastic philosophy was autonomous in the sense of being in no way dependent upon religion or theology. The unfavorable reaction of the Louvain tradition, which had done so much for the progress of Neoscholasticism and prided itself on its ability to meet secular philosophy on its own ground, was particularly noticeable.[11] Today the opposition to the name and the conception is still strong.

Against this complicated background the notion of Catholic philosophy may be approached. What can it mean? At the 1970 business meeting of the American Catholic Philosophical Association, a proposal was made to change the name to the American Christian Philosophical Association. Without exception every speaker to the motion from the floor questioned the change. But the attitudes taken in opposition and the reasons given ranged widely over the spectrum's colors. The one extreme was that religious commitment radically affected one's philosophizing, the other that it made no difference to it at all. In the latter view, a Catholic philosopher was merely a philosopher who happened to be a Catholic, without undergoing any influence from religion upon his philosophical thinking. The adjective "Catholic" would have no more pertinent bearing in the phrase than it has in the notion of a Catholic goatbreeder. Scarcely different in essence was the stand that Catholic philosophy preserved a realistic tradition, even though the realism had nothing characteristically Catholic about it.

There is an acute problem, then, concerning the relations of "Catholic" and "philosophy" in the notion of Catholic philosophy. Does "Catholic" modify the philosophy in a way that gives rise to an enterprise specifically different from other kinds of philosophy? Or does it affect the philosophy so adversely that it destroys the philosophical character and absorbs the thought and reasoning into the wine of theology? Or does the notion "Catholic" remain entirely external to the philosophical undertaking and leave the union basically accidental and without distinctive effects on the genuinely philosophical level? Further, in the case that a specific difference is effected, what will be the relation of Catholic philosophy to Christian philosophy, to Jewish philosophy, to Islamic philosophy?[12]

---

11. Thomists in opposition to the notion of Christian philosophy may be found listed in *Bulletin thomiste* 14 (1937), 231–35. On the Louvain stand, see Nédoncelle, p. 94.

12. The difficulty, if not impossibility, of isolating at present a distinctively Protestant philosophy permits it to be passed over for the time being. Cf.: "[A]ny attempt to settle a philosophy on Protestantism is doomed to failure"—Nels F. S. Ferré, in "Philosophical Issues in Ecumenism," *Christian Philosophy and Religious Renewal,* ed. George F. McLean

These questions are raised by the very notion of Catholic philosophy. The considerations that follow will try to deal with them in the present-day context.

II

First, there should be a clear realization that what philosophizes is not a detached intellect but a whole human being, a person. The influences that from earliest years have given emotional and cultural formation mold the one who philosophizes. The object of philosophy, extending as it does over the totality of naturally knowable things, is correspondingly unrestricted in itself and lends itself readily to adaptation in the treatment given it according to each individual temperament. So much is this the case that, in the last analysis, philosophies turn out to be highly individual. In the whole history of philosophy it is difficult if not impossible to find two genuine philosophers who thought in exactly the same way. Rather, the differences among them are notorious. It is proverbial that philosophers never agree. To some observers philosophy has appeared for this reason to be more akin to poetry than to science. In point of fact, the contrast with the type of discipline that the mathematical and experimental sciences have developed with such astounding success is quite startling. Success of telephonic communication, of computer tabulation, of space travel, of gigantic engineering projects, all depend upon teams of workers understanding the same symbols in exactly the same way. Even a slight difference in the reading of the symbols by those engaged could cause disaster. All have to be trained to follow exactly the common grooves, without any individual variation.

In philosophy, on the contrary, each thinker uses terms in his own way and shades concepts in individualistic colorings that effectively prevent them from being merely transported out of one philosophy into another. Even among the commentators or exponents of a single thinker these individualist differences appear. Do any two exponents of Aquinas, for instance, present his thought in the same philosophical way? Rather, do not the leading commentators differ quite radically in what they find in the pages of their master? At least, the present writer, after more than four decades of acquaintance with Thomistic writers, has yet to meet two who understood Aquinas philosophically in exactly the same way.

(Washington, DC: Catholic University of America Press, 1966), p. 154. See also Avery Dulles, ibid., pp. 159–60, who nevertheless speaks of "Protestant philosophies," ibid., p. 161.

However, family resemblances do group philosophers in ever-widening or narrowing circles.[13] Western philosophy, no matter how variegated within itself, is markedly distinct from oriental philosophies. Greek philosophy as a whole differs sharply from medieval philosophy as a whole, even though there are all-pervasive intramural variations in each. Modern philosophy as a whole stands in clear enough contrast to either of them. Within the broader historical divisions, the doctrinal currents of Platonism, Aristotelianism, Scotism, Ockhamism, Kantianism, Hegelianism, pragmatism, positivism, existentialism, phenomenology, and linguistic analysis (and numerous other trends) bring thinkers together in groups in spite of their deeper individual differences.

Can the notion "Catholic" form one such bond in the context of the strictly philosophic community? Where profound differences in philosophies are found associated with various cultural backgrounds, such as oriental or occidental, Greek or medieval or modern, why should not the religious dimension be operative in describing similar divisions? If in the ultimate analysis each man's philosophy bears the stamp of his own personality and individuality, why should not the religious element in his formation play its part in making his philosophy other than that of anyone else, and at the same time be a bond that groups thinkers into a unity corresponding to the religious interest? If the religious element does so, will not the notions of Catholic philosophy, of Christian philosophy, of Jewish philosophy, of Islamic philosophy, make perfect and distinctive sense?

But how? In the field of practical philosophy, the influence of the religious bent is comparatively easy to see. In ethics, the starting points or first principles of the discipline are acquired on the basis of the habituation given through correct education.[14] The child is trained to be honest, self-restrained, courageous, kind, respectful and considerate of others. But the dynamics of ethical as well as of cultural thinking lead quickly to the notion of a dominating principle for the science in the strongest sense. In ethics, this first principle will be the ultimate end in virtue of which all other purposes or goals exercise their finality. It may be located variously in pleasure, in riches, in public standing, in a scientific or philosophic or contemplative life.

13. The term "family resemblances," used so frequently after Wittgenstein, had already appeared in English in 1910, for grouping scholastic thinkers, in Maurice De Wulf, *Scholasticism Old and New*, tr. Peter Coffey (Dublin: N. H. Gill & Son, 1910), p. 46. Cf. supra, "Introduction," n. 38.

14. See Aristotle, *Nicomachean Ethics*, 1.3.1095a2–11; 1.4.1095a2–8; 2.1.1103b23–25; 6.8.1142a11–20.

But once chosen, it dominates or, with consistency, should dominate the whole of one's conduct.[15]

With a Catholic, who accepts the beatific vision of God as the sole ultimate destiny of human life, the overall dynamics of ethical thinking will be understandably different from that of a morality in which the final end of man is philosophical contemplation or pleasure or temporal well-being. The differences will come out for instance in the sacrifices of time and money for building and maintaining churches and for religious educational institutions, in the refusal to be dominated by sociological and other this-worldly interest, in the resistance to secularistic thinking. Further, the inborn respect for human life will develop along different lines. The hierarchical subordination of all lower life to man, with man's proprietary dominion over these realms, may be accepted on Aristotelian grounds.[16] But the estimate of human beings as intellectual creatures will be significantly different. The destiny of the intellect to know God face to face, and of the will to love and enjoy God immediately, will mean that man is meant immediately for God. This will place the respect for human life and its procreation in a new light. Proprietary dominion over land and plant and animal will be accorded to human beings, but dominion over human life, in a proprietary sense, will remain with God alone. The whole situation now takes on a considerably different practical bearing for one who recognizes a church as the infallible voice of God to human beings. Where the divine will and plan become manifest through ecclesiastical tradition or pronouncement, the ultimate factor in questions such as duelling, suicide, capital punishment, mercy killing, hunger strikes, execution of hostages, contraception, divorce, celibacy, and the like, will not be sociological or naturally humanistic considerations. Rather, it will be the living voice of the church.

It is not at all the role of philosophy to determine what the teaching of the church or of tradition is on any of these questions. That is the task of the ecclesiastical magisterium to decide definitively and of theology to probe tentatively. But is it not easy to see how this situation will affect the purely ethical dynamics? Living a practical life that is ultimately directed towards the beatific vision, the Catholic philosopher is led to scrutinize carefully, in the light of his own reason, the nature of his intellect and will. On grounds naturally accessible to him he is brought to see that these faculties bear upon an infinite object, but that just in themselves they do not have the ability to attain it. In

15. Ibid., 1.12.1102a2–4.
16. See Aristotle, *Politics* 1.8.1256b15–20. Cf. *Nicomachean Ethics* 10.2.1173a4–5.

this light he sees that his nature lacks an ultimate end on its own level. He can understand how some other philosophers find that human nature is absurd or meaningless or nauseating. He sees that it is something radically incomplete, and that in the event of a divine revelation questions concerning the way his destiny is to be worked out and the extent to which he is to exercise dominion over human life have to take account of the revelation. This is philosophy, frank and straightforward. It makes no attempt to give the decisive answer in these questions, but it does show why they cannot ultimately be solved by philosophy alone in the concrete situation in which a human person recognizes himself as living. Even should naturally knowable reasons tip the balance in favor of duelling or of divorce or of abortion, the Catholic philosopher is able to recognize that these need not be the ultimately decisive reasons in the deliberation. On the purely ethical level he will be thinking in a manner different from his non-Catholic counterpart. This will hold even though the two may arrive at the same practical conclusions in particular cases. Is it not quite easy to see, accordingly, that the element "Catholic" will deeply influence ethical thinking on the purely philosophical level?

But also in the speculative realm differences become apparent. A person brought up a Catholic will naturally be inclined to think about the *Weltanschauung* given him by his faith. If he is a philosopher, he will make it an object of philosophical study. He will want to know how well this world outlook, accepted on faith, stands up against the questionings of reason. Many of his cherished beliefs in other spheres become shattered with experience. What about belief in God and in the immortality of the human soul? The importance of these two tenets prompts him to investigate them with a care and a penetration and a love not to be expected of nonbelievers, even when these react with corresponding or greater force against religious belief. The motive nevertheless is philosophic understanding, not apologetics.

Catholic philosophy will also serve for far more than a rational buttress of the faith. It will provide an intellectual deepening of spiritual life, a rational dimension in which a lived faith is able to work out its implications for the integral human being on the natural level. Philosophically, the Catholic may find that the existence of the things experienced around him and in himself comes always from something other than these things themselves and ultimately from subsistent existence, that it is being imparted continually by subsistent existence, that every action he originates comes into being through the concurrence of subsistent existence. The Catholic philosopher is accordingly engaged in seeing that this subsistent existence is the God in whom—

in words that, for all their possible background in Greek poetry, express thought according to the Scriptures—one lives and moves and has one's being. This genuinely philosophic understanding of God, rising as it does from deeply religious motivation, is patently different from the analyst's interest in "God-talk" or from any merely philosophical requirement of God as a necessary completion or explanation of the universe. It is part of the integral life of a Catholic philosopher. It proceeds from a concern that gives rise to a distinctive type of philosophizing.

Similarly, the interest in the nature and permanent existence of the human soul is understandably different in one who already believes on religious grounds that the most important objective in human destiny is the soul's eternal life. The intellectual urge to know what one can about it by reason prompts close study of the problem. It may turn out, as in Aquinas, that reason can show that the spiritual soul is subsistent and consequently imperishable, and yet that reason cannot demonstrate anything metaphysically about life for the soul apart from matter. To have any life apart, the human soul naturally has to have sensible images. These require bodily activity. New means of acquiring or making use of intellectual objects remain inaccessible to reason and have to be catalogued as belonging to the realm of faith and theology. But the philosophical knowledge that the human soul is imperishable follows from principles naturally accessible to human reason, once the religious interest leads to concentration of attention upon them.

The focus upon a special set of problems is in these ways apparent in ethics and in metaphysics. But it is also present in natural philosophy, as the long-disputed questions about material substance in the context of transubstantiation and the problems about extension in a glorified body show. Even logic is prompted by special interests regarding predication in the Trinity and Incarnation to delve into questions that emerge from the consideration of these mysteries. Minimal perhaps is the impact on the philosophy of science, yet even here questions arising from the creation of the material universe and the real presence of Christ in the Eucharist can spur the philosopher to closer scrutiny of the principles of experimental science.

This special focus, clearly, has to be ascribed to something outside the characteristic realm of philosophy. No matter what the philosophical principles of the admittedly Catholic philosopher are, the focus will be on these problems. The particular Catholic philosopher may be in the tradition of Plato or of Aristotle, or of Aquinas or Scotus or Suarez, or of Descartes, Kant, Hegel, Husserl, Heidegger, Whitehead,

Dewey, Marcel. Yet his philosophic interest in these special themes will characterize him as a Catholic philosopher. In point of fact, the membership of the American Catholic Philosophical Association is at present widely and radically pluralistic on the philosophic level. Yet, under the above criterion, all its members can be recognized as Catholic philosophers and as engaged in Catholic philosophy, even though they may not be professedly Catholic in religion.[17] From the focus on the themes of initial interest, the philosophic inquiry of course will branch out and extend over the whole range of recognized philosophical pursuits.

III

However, the thrust of the notion "Catholic philosophy" is not limited merely to the choice of the introductory themes. The religious element also involves constructive help. Religious problems, for instance, led Boethius to develop the notion of person as a distinct philosophical concept.[18] Creation, accepted on grounds of religious belief, inspired the Christian Neoplatonists to give being the primary role in the constitution of creatures.[19] The patristic interpretation of the *I am who am* of Exodus, in the sense that the proper name of God is being, appears to have led Aquinas to see that existence is the nature of God and is consequently distinct from the nature of any creature.[20] This

17. From the beginning the American Catholic Philosophical Association was firm in its stand that constituent membership is not restricted to Catholics—see *Proceedings, ACPA* 1 (1926), 5. If it understood "Catholic philosopher" merely as a Catholic who happened to be a philosopher, it could hardly bring its non-Catholic members under the notion. One might urge that the adjective "Catholic," just as the adjective "American" in its title, modifies the noun "Association." Surely by "American Philosophical Association" is meant not merely a society for the study of American Philosophy, but rather an association for the study of philosophy in general. Yet that need not imply that "Catholic" likewise bears merely on "Association" in the title. A Catholic association for philosophy seems fully open to the objection raised by Dupré's comparison with a Catholic association for goatbreeding. The import of the title is rather in the direction of an American association for Catholic philosophy. From the start the purpose of the association was to promote "Catholic philosophy" (see supra, n. 7). With this understanding of the title there is no incongruity in having a non-Catholic do Catholic philosophy. One speaks of a Greek paleographer or a Latin paleographer, even though the man be a fullblooded American. In the same vein one speaks of "our French professor" or "our German professor," even though neither is a Frenchman or a German. For discussion of "Christian philosophy" in the sense of "philosophy done among Christians," see Germain G. Grisez, "The Four Meanings of 'Christian Philosophy,'" *The Journal of Religion* 42 (1962), 106b–110a, and "The Christian Philosopher," in *Christian Philosophy and Religious Renewal*, ed. George F. McLean, pp. 28–30.

18. Boethius, *Liber de persona et de duabus naturis*, 2–3; PL, 64, 1342C–1345B.

19. E.g., Dionysius, *De divinis nominibus* 5.6; PG, 3, 819.

20. On the patristic tradition for the interpretation of Exodus 3.14, see Cornelia De

last tenet alone was enough to engender a radically new metaphysics. It is in principle a tenet able to be grasped by unaided human reason. Yet no one had seen it before Aquinas. In its light Aquinas was able to see that the existence of things is originally attained by a mental activity different from the activity by which natures are known. Existence in sensible things was seen to be a synthesizing actuality different from any finite nature, an actuality grasped originally not through conceptualization but through the synthesizing apprehension of judgment. In principle this philosophical understanding of existence is philosophically accessible. Yet even today it can easily be missed if approached by any other route than the one taken by Aquinas.

Similarly the scriptural revelation that man was created in God's image and likeness led Aquinas to find in the human soul a status different from that of an ordinary Aristotelian form, and to see in the spiritual soul a subsistent entity and a source of activities independent of matter.[21] Again, there is no question of using religious or theological principles to demonstrate conclusions. Rather, the religious or theological interest prompts closer scrutiny of the naturally knowable objects, and centers intellectual attention upon naturally knowable principles that stand in their own right without any religious or theological support. From these principles the strictly philosophical conclusions can then be drawn. In the present instance the religiously prompted inquiry can bring one to look for mental activities that function in a manner superior to the merely material, such as universality in knowledge and desire, complete reflexion upon one's own self, and freedom in choice. This leads to a substantial principle that maintains its existence independently of matter and is accordingly the principle that subsists. The immediate bearing upon existence, instead of relation to it merely as a co-principle in a subsistent composite, shows that the soul is naturally inseparable from its own existence and will in the course of nature retain existence forever. All this, again, is purely philosophical reasoning. Yet would it ever have been seen except for the religious context? In consequence, the religious interest,

---

Vogel, "'Ego sum qui sum' et sa signification pour une philosophie chrétienne," *Revue des sciences religieuses* 35 (1961), 346–54. For Aquinas, see *Sent.* 1.8.1.1; ed. Mandonnet, 1, 194–97.

21. "[Q]uia anima est forma absoluta, non dependens a materia, quod convenit sibi propter assimilationem et propinquitatem ad Deum, ipsa habet esse per se, quod non habent aliae formae corporales"—Aquinas, *Sent.* 8.5.2.ad 1m; ed. Mandonnet, 1, 230. "Dico igitur, quod animae non convenit movere, vel habere esse absolutum, inquantum est forma sed inquantum est similitudo Dei"—ibid., ad 5m; p. 231. The scriptural passage is Genesis 1.26–27.

though non-philosophical in character, can and does occasion significant philosophical penetration and progress.

The situation may be paralleled with philosophical interest that arises from considerations in experimental science. Modern scientific theories about the constitution of matter spark philosophical conceptions that go under the names of the various present-day cosmologies. Interest in organic evolution prompts the development on the philosophical level of evolutionary systems of the universe, in which even the terminology may indicate the scientific motivation, as in the notion of noosphere corresponding to the biosphere. Experimental science provides the inspiration and suggests general guiding lines. But the explanations are developed from wider philosophical principles. Similarly, in linguistic analysis, the motivation and general guidance may have come originally from philology. But what the analyst is doing is emphatically not philology but philosophy.

The fact that in experimental science and philology the knowledge is naturally accessible while in religion or theology it is of supernatural origin need not affect the parallel. In both cases the inspiration is from outside philosophy, while the philosophical development occasioned by it takes place from naturally knowable principles to genuinely philosophical conclusions. The frequently urged objection that the Catholic philosopher is not free to draw conclusions that contradict the tenets of his faith cannot have any more or any less validity than would the corresponding objection in the other two cases. The cosmologist, as an integrated scholar, is not free to disregard the facts established by experimental science, nor the analyst the findings of philology. The only conceivable reason for denying the parallelism seems to be the refusal to acknowledge divine revelation as an independent font of truth.

IV

From these considerations the distinctive notion of Catholic philosophy may be seen readily enough in relation to secular, Jewish, Islamic, and Christian philosophy. The Catholic philosopher is such because he is drawn to philosophy through a definite set of problems in regard to which his religious life inspires interest and concern. The religious motivation invites him to pursue them in definite ways that result in positive and distinctive help on the purely philosophical level. From these problems the philosopher branches out in the philosophical work into all the other intricacies of philosophical life. Accordingly, the dominant interest—in problems such as God, the immortality of the soul, the supernatural destiny of man, the life of grace, the sacraments, the magisterium, and other concerns of his religious life—prompts initial occupation with relevant philosophical problems. To the extent that this is his attitude, a person is a Catholic philosopher. As may easily be seen, this leaves room for degrees. But to the degree in which he genuinely has this attitude, the person is a Catholic philosopher and is doing Catholic philosophy. To that degree he is distinct from the secular philosopher, even though the secular philosopher may be dealing with the same problems from motives other than positive and personal religious concern. Quite frequently, on the other hand, the notions of a transcendent yet rationally demonstrable God, an immaterial soul, the need of a supernatural destiny for man, and the like, are regarded by secularistic philosophy as beyond the pale of rational consideration. In either case, however, Catholic philosophy is obviously distinct from its secular counterpart.

In common with Jewish philosophy, Catholic philosophy shares the interest in the philosophic inquiry into God's existence and nature and attributes, and his creation of the universe and his providence over human beings. Similarly, it has in common with Islamic philosophy an interest in God and the future status of the human soul. With Christian philosophy it has likewise these common interests, together with the philosophic issues that arise from considerations about the Trinity, Incarnation, and Eucharist. But it has also further and distinctively characteristic interests in regard to the philosophically scrutinizable aspects of the supernatural life of grace in the soul, about the beatific vision and the natural endlessness of man, about the eviternity of the separated soul in Purgatory and its relation to time, about the nature of belief in the context of ecclesiastical infallibility, and about numerous moral problems.

In a word, Catholic philosophy is not just religiously motivated philosophizing in general. It is not the only kind of philosophy that can be characterized by a religious designation. It sets itself off against other religiously motivated philosophies by its specifically Catholic interests. These, and not any differentia of purely philosophical origin, provide its specification. Yet all the principles from which it reasons are apprehended by natural intelligence alone. No principles from faith or theology are ever to be used in its reasoning process. It is a kind of philosophy that is set up by the factual union of faith and intelligence in the same person.[22] Accordingly, it is related to other religiously inspired philosophies in a way proportional to the specific or generic correspondence of the one religion to the other.

22. See Gilson, "La notion de philosophie chrétienne," p. 39. The role played by

V

The foregoing reflections should be enough to show quite definitely that there is a distinct type of thinking recognizable as Catholic philosophy. It is genuinely philosophy, in contrast to theology, for it bases its inferences solely on principles naturally accessible to human reason. It draws its conclusions exclusively from these principles. It does not ground any of its reasoning on divinely revealed principles or on theological conclusions. It is in no way a kind of theology or a dependency of theology. It stands in its own philosophic right. It remains water. It is to no degree changed into wine. It is philosophy through and through.

Yet its differentia as Catholic philosophy is not philosophical in origin. Rather, it seems to allow within its range an extremely wide variety of philosophical differentiations. In fact, one would be hard put to find any recognized type of philosophy that could not conceivably be found within its limits. The conclusions on religious topics may be different from what the originators of the respective philosophical trends reached in their own thinking, but the general tendencies and procedures of Epicureanism, Stoicism, Kantianism, Hegelianism, nominalism, realism, phenomenology, existentialism, analysis, structuralism, and many other types have been used with advantage in recognizably Catholic philosophy. One is loath to think there could be any limit. Any authentic philosophical procedure can hardly help having facets that can be exploited with success by an enterprising Catholic philosopher.

In each case, however, the philosophy will be characterized by distinctively Catholic interests. It arises from the natural wonder occasioned by intelligibly accessible aspects of Catholic beliefs and theological conclusions. This wonder is enough to spark the development of a fully rounded philosophy. The wonder centers upon topics that turn out to be introductory, but that keep leading further and further. Interest that reaches to being and form and nature, no matter what its origin, excludes nothing of philosophic range. Hence, a Catholic philosophy, even though it originates in topics of definitely Catholic concern, by its very nature extends to all themes of philosophic scrutiny. Just as with the medieval thinkers, the original Catholic interest leads to coverage of the whole philosophic field.

---

the religious belief is designated by Gilson as "morally necessary": "Ce seront des philosophies qui considèrent la révélation judéo-chrétienne comme un auxiliaire moralement nécessaire pour la raison. Elles pourront, grâce à ce guide, éliminer les erreurs, ajouter des vérités nouvelles aux anciennes, compléter des vérités anciennes, ou simplement les conserver"—ibid., p. 48.

This conception of Catholic philosophy amply justifies the philosophical pluralism among admittedly Catholic thinkers. Catholic philosophy can be Platonic or Aristotelian in cast, or with Maréchal can follow Kantian norms, or, with others, those of Hegel or of process philosophy or of phenomenology or of existentialism, and so on. As long as its basic motive is deeply religious interest in philosophical issues that arise in the ambit of Catholic intellectual life, it can be called Catholic philosophy.

The distinctive character of Catholic philosophy, then, does not arise from any particular philosophical bent or tradition, but from the religious interest that sets apart its problems and leads it to philosophically knowable aspects that otherwise might well have escaped philosophical notice. This interest can be had also by persons who are not professed members of the Catholic church, as experience shows clearly enough. These philosophers were welcomed into the American Catholic Philosophical Association from the start.[23] They have been concerned with the identical problems upon which the philosophic interests of their professed Catholic colleagues focused, and have been at home in the discussion of these topics. It is hard to see how they cannot be considered as doing genuinely Catholic philosophy in their part in the association's enterprise. The common interest undoubtedly arises from Catholic inspiration, and even in regard to the individual thinker no one can set limits to the working of grace. One may or may not hesitate in calling them Catholic philosophers, but about their genuine participation in Catholic philosophy there should be no doubt.

A more acute problem emerges in regard to those who say they are Catholic and are philosophers, but acknowledge no intimate connection between the two terms. They claim they are philosophers who just happen to be Catholics, or Catholics who just happen to be philosophers. It is not easy to discover why a Catholic with this mentality would want to be significantly known as a Catholic philosopher, or why he would bother taking out membership in a Catholic philosophical society. His interests could be served just as well, in fact a good deal better, by joining the American Philosophical Association, or one of its satellite organizations with which he has special doctrinal affiliations. It is difficult to see how he can fail to regard himself as supporting a splinter group through belonging to the American Catholic Philosophical Association. How, then, can he be at all looked upon as a Catholic philosopher? In point of fact, that is what he is called as a

23. See supra, n. 17.

member of the association. The accepted pluralism in the notion does extend that far. But will not the designation "Catholic philosopher," when applied to a non-Catholic in this setting, seem more equivocal than univocal?

Yet to what extent, if any, can this double personality be said at all in truth to be engaged in Catholic philosophy? If his philosophy is not at all affected by his Catholicism, it can hardly be characterized by it. The situation seems to leave no room for the notion of distinctly Catholic philosophy as a definite type of thinking. Or is this professed Catholic philosopher caught up in spite of himself in the ongoing current of genuinely Catholic philosophical thought? Is he making his contribution to it even though he maintains that he is doing nothing more than a secular philosopher would do? The latter involvement would seem in fact to be implicitly the attitude of Catholics who habitually associate themselves with Catholic philosophy while claiming that as philosophy it is not different from secular thinking. They would seem to have distinctly Catholic interests to justify their remaining part of an admittedly Catholic movement, and these interests can hardly help affecting their philosophical engagement. It is always the person, never a detached intellect, that is at work in philosophy. They would seem, in spite of themselves, to come univocally under the basic notion of people engaged in the distinctive type of thinking called Catholic philosophy.[24]

24. Often brought forward in the discussions on Christian philosophy is the stand expressed in the concluding words of Bréhier's article "Y a-t-il une philosophie chrétienne?" *Revue de métaphysique et de morale* 38 (1931), 162: "[O]n ne peut pas plus parler d'une philosophie chrétienne que d'une mathématique ou d'une physique chrétienne." On this objection in Feuerbach, nearly a century earlier, see Gilson, "La notion de philosophie chrétienne," 42–43. The reason back of it, namely, that philosophy is exclusively the work of reason and accordingly is incompatible with any theological influence, has been accepted, as Gilson (ibid.) notes, by some Neoscholastics. It would render the notion of Christian philosophy a contradiction in terms. Heidegger's comparison with wood and iron, expressed in English as a round square, brings out the point clearly. See Heidegger, *An Introduction to Metaphysics*, tr. Ralph Manheim (New Haven: Yale University Press, 1959), p. 7. In this regard, Duhem's vigorous defense against the charge that his Catholic faith affected his physics was directed against influence by metaphysics as well as religious belief: "But it might just as well be called the physics of a non-believer, for it does not render better or stricter justice to the arguments in favor of metaphysics or dogma that some have tried to deduce from physical theory"— Pierre Duhem, *The Aim and Structure of Physical Theory*, tr. Philip P. Wierner (Princeton: Princeton University Press, 1954), p. 287. The fact that physics or mathematics offers nothing of specifically Catholic interest does not imply the same for philosophy. Rather, Catholic interest in themes like morality, substance, and subsistent existence should be obvious, and also operative in a strictly philosophic inquiry.

The four options offered by Nédoncelle, pp. 100–113, for the notion of Christian philosophy may be more or less vulnerable to the foregoing objection. In Nédoncelle's

In the light of these considerations, the conception of Catholic philosophy as essentially a conserving and developing of some tradition of realistic or Aristotelian or Augustinian or Scholastic philosophy fades away. None of these currents, even Scholasticism, is necessarily Catholic.[25] The claim has been made that the American Catholic Philosophical Association was fully justified at the time of its organization, since it provided scope for traditional western philosophy in the face of positivistic onslaughts. From this the conclusion is drawn that the reason justifying its existence is no longer present. Particularly in regard to metaphysics the appropriate forum has since been provided by the Metaphysical Society of America and *The Review of Metaphysics*. Even apart from the Catholic enterprise—one is tempted to say without too much recent help from it—metaphysics now enjoys a respectable contemporary status.[26] Accordingly, interest in continuing traditional western philosophy does not in itself provide the expla-

---

words "the adjective and the noun do not make an altogether peaceful pair; they clash in spite of their attraction for one another, and they involve a paradox" (p. 114). The first option, namely, that Christian philosophy is a preparation for Christianity, would leave this kind of philosophy pre-Christian and accordingly pagan. It was pagan philosophy that *Aeterni Patris* regarded as the preparation for the Gospel. The second option is the notion of a philosophy that undergoes Christian influence, in this sense: "Reason would receive the aid of grace from within; philosophical reflection would be conducted with the categories of revelation themselves" (pp. 102–103). This is understood by Nédoncelle in its obvious meaning of a confusion with theology. It does not set up a philosophy as the term is understood today. The third option for the concept is a philosophy that inherits from Christianity. Clearly, Christian doctrine does not purport to offer philosophy, in its current understanding. The notion may explain a religious gnosis, but not a philosophy. The final option is that of a philosophy that relates itself to Christianity. But how can a philosophy just as a philosophy know anything about Christianity, especially in the intimate way required for specification by it?

The notion of Catholic philosophy as philosophical thinking prompted by genuine philosophical interest in themes of crucial concern to Catholic intellectual life is immune to the above objection. The procedure is from principles wholly accessible to human intellection, and the reasoning is entirely on the philosophical plane. This seems to correspond closely enough to "the outcome of the process of Christian wonder in a knowledge properly human"—Grisez, "Four Meanings," 117a. Grisez considers that type of knowledge to be basic in regard to the different notions of Christian philosophy.

25. On the different acknowledged kinds of Scholasticism, see *New Catholic Encyclopedia*, s.v. "Scholasticism." See also L. Gauthier, "Scolastique musulmane et scolastique chrétienne," *Revue d'histoire de la philosophie* 2 (1928), 230–32; 333–55. In regard to confusion with a perennial philosophy, cf.: "Only by refusing the idea of a *philosophia perennis*, and a philosophical tradition in which to simply integrate himself . . . will the Christian show how seriously he takes the renewing of the mind. . . . All Christian philosophy seems to us to reside in the Christian's decision to bear witness, in the philosophical field, to the reality of the renewing of the mind"—Roger Mehl, *The Condition of the Christian Philosopher*, tr. Eva Kushner (London: J. Clarke, 1963), p. 209.

26. "It is a pleasure to have lived long enough to see the desert becoming verdant, and to perceive the shrieks turning into faint echoes, hardly heard"—Paul Weiss, in *Philosophical Interrogations,* ed. Sydney and Beatrice Rome (New York: Holt, Rinehart and Winston, 1964), p. 313.

nation for any distinctive Catholic philosophy nor the justification for separate Catholic philosophical societies.

No, the reason for a distinctive type of philosophy called Catholic, and for the organization of Catholic philosophical associations, has to be frankly and admittedly religious, as the name itself should indicate. No probative force, it is true, comes to it from religious or theological sources. It needs no crutch to lean on from non-philosophical craftsmanship. It has its own authentic life, and that life is thoroughly philosophical. It is ready to offer what help it can to theology or politics or any other discipline when asked for it. But that is not its essential function. An ancillary function presupposes the personal life of the handmaid. This truth should not be difficult to grasp today when domestic help is so hard to come by and personal rights and dignity have to be respected before all else. A philosophy produced essentially as a handmaid for theology would be a robot, not a living thing. Rather, Catholic philosophy develops and leads its own autonomous life. It is not kerygmatic. It does not preach the Gospel. It is not apologetic. It makes no effort to reconcile faith with reason.[27] It ac-

---

27. Cf.: "We must renounce considering the Christian philosopher as man who seeks to establish harmony between his faith and the demands of his reason"—Mehl, *The Condition of the Christian Philosopher,* p. 208. That task is clearly apologetic and belongs wholly to theology. It raises, however, a question that at first might seem delicate but which is open to a straightforward answer on the basis of the conclusions just reached. A philosophy is a Catholic philosophy if it is motivated by genuinely religious interest in specifically Catholic themes. No requirement is made that its author profess religious adhesion to the Catholic church, or to its dogmatic or moral teachings. This raises the problem of how Catholic his philosophy can be if it reaches philosophical conclusions contradictory to the pronouncements of the magisterium, say, on the use of contraceptives or on the practice of abortion. Instances in the theoretical order of men whom one would like to call Catholic philosophers come readily enough to mind—Malebranche, Rosmini, Gioberti, Ubaghs. In this situation it becomes a *philosophical* problem for such a Catholic philosopher to explain why his conclusions differ from the teachings of the Catholic faith. In a context like that in which Duns Scotus (*Quodl.* 7.26; ed. Vivès, 25, 304b) granted that Aristotelian principles lead to a denial of Christian doctrine on divine omnipotence, a Catholic philosopher can show that the human intellect, while finite, is meant for infinite truth and that aspects beyond its unaided grasp might, if known, call for a revision of one's philosophical conclusions. There is no skepticism or double truth notion in this, but only an acknowledged restriction in the starting points used for drawing the conclusions. Today a Catholic philosopher may be found maintaining that the existence of God is not rationally demonstrable, in quite apparent conflict with the magisterium. This should hardly be a reason for denying his endeavors the status of Catholic philosophy. The faith can serve as the guiding star that prompts reexamination of the starting points and reasoning processes. Unlike Catholic theology, Catholic philosophy is not in any way grounded upon revealed tenets. Faulty conclusions made by it do not entail the rejection of any revealed dogmatic or moral teaching, as a faulty theological conclusion would. They point out rather the necessity for careful reassessment of the philosophical foundations and development. In this way, as *Aeterni Patris* pointed out, the faith is a positive help to Catholic philosophy precisely on the

knowledges both as independent sources of truth, quite as it acknowledges mathematics and experimental science as independent fonts. Only by leading authentically this life of its own is it in a position to render ancillary service to theology when theologians ask for it. But the ancillary function is not essential to it. It can easily lead its full personal life without ever being asked to provide assistance for theology. The history of the last decade should be enough to make this clear.

The notion of Catholic philosophy is accordingly a valid one. It deserves careful examination and evaluation at the present moment, when the justification for explicitly Catholic philosophical organizations is at stake. The notion is not an easy one to grasp against the Neoscholastic background of the past one hundred years, in which Catholics endeavored to show that they could be philosophers and scientists in exactly the same way as their non-Catholic colleagues, or against the secularistic background of the sixties, in which religion was oriented in toto towards this-worldly ends. The problem belongs to a type that, as Bréhier remarked,[28] is easier to solve than to draw

---

level of philosophical thinking. Conclusions of any philosophy are conditioned by the limitations of its own starting points, and the unacceptable conclusions render a closer scrutiny of them imperative.

Fidelity to the concrete situation in which the human intellect actually finds itself has even prompted the stand that, in the circumstances made known by divine revelation, philosophy becomes authentically itself: "En effet, bien que l'expression de *philosophie chrétienne* semble impliquer, dès l'abord, une contradiction, on verra qu'il n'en est rien et qu'au contraire, la philosophie n'est bien elle-même, c'est-à-dire ne respecte vraiment ses frontières et ne se situe parfaitement à sa place, que par l'aveu de la primauté de la foi"—Régis Jolivet, *La philosophie chrétienne et la pensée contemporaine* (Paris: Téqui, 1932), pp. 20–21. "Understood as Leo intended it, the adjective in 'Christian philosophy,' far from destroying the noun, would appear to strengthen and improve it"— Anton Pegis, *Christian Philosophy and Intellectual Freedom* (Milwaukee: Bruce, 1955), p. 42.

The concrete situation likewise permits the wide pluralism in Catholic philosophies. It shows how the limited scope of human intellection cannot be expected to grasp the whole of philosophic truth with any one set of principles, and that different principles allow this truth to be expressed in different and often verbally opposed ways. It similarly makes clear that Catholic philosophy is not merely trying to reach, on philosophical grounds, certain conclusions already accepted on faith. Through faith, for instance, one may believe that God exists, and yet not know that he is subsistent existence. Philosophical conclusions are not theological conclusions, and are not predetermined by one's faith. Hence arises the radical differentiation in the many philosophies that one would like to call Catholic. The pluralism is rejected, at least verbally, by some writers, e.g. Tresmontant, *Christian Metaphysics*, p. 19. On his stand, see infra, "Epilogue," n. 15. Apart from a pluralistic interpretation, deep philosophic disagreement is hard to understand. The radical difference in metaphysics between Aquinas and Scotus should be enough to cast doubt on Tresmontant's thesis. All Catholic philosophies, like philosophy in general, should aim at the truth. But they do not always succeed in attaining it in its fullness.

28. "En matière d'histoire des idées, les questions sont, en effet, souvent plus diffi-

up. Its solution may be expected to follow in one way or another in accord with the manner in which it has been set out. To draw it up correctly is not at all easy against the recent backgrounds. But the effort deserves to be made, in the interests of the philosophical thinking of Catholics who live in an integrated world, a single world whose different phases are accessible respectively by faith and by reason.

ciles à poser qu'à resoudre, une fois posées"—É Bréhier, "Y a-t-il une philosophie chrétienne?" p. 133.

4

THE DISTINGUISHING FEATURE IN CATHOLIC PHILOSOPHY

I

The notion "Catholic philosophy" is even more controversial than "Christian philosophy." With one notable exception it has not been stressed in book titles.[1] Seldom does it occur in the titles of articles. On occasion it has been brought to the fore in the discussions at meetings of the American Catholic Philosophical Association. There it has generally been given a quite cool reception. In spite of the fact that the association was founded with the express purpose of studying and teaching "Catholic philosophy" (*Proceedings, ACPA*, 1 [1926], 14; 17), many of its members down through the years have been repelled by the notion. Most have no serious objection to the designation "Catholic philosopher," in the sense of a philosopher who happens to be a Catholic. Even here, however, there have been attempts to have the word "Catholic" removed from the title of the association. The reason alleged is that the adjective has no more bearing on philosophers than it would have on goatbreeders in a Catholic goatbreeders' society. The label may be kept, it is allowed, because the great majority of the members are Catholic, or because they have special interest in Catholic themes, whether or not they happen to be Catholic in religion.

The deeply felt opposition to the title "Catholic" in connection with philosophy seems to be "the omnipresent fear that Catholics will introduce their religious beliefs at the expense of rigorous philosophical

---

1. It is found in Maurice Blondel, *Le problème de la philosophie catholique* (Paris: Bloud & Gay, 1932). Yet in Blondel "Catholic philosophy" is not contrasted with "Christian philosophy" by way of species with genus. Rather, the sole contrast is with secularistic philosophy. Blondel argues against giving "l'expression 'philosophie catholique' un sens qui la séculariserait en quelque sort." Ibid., p. 168. Only in Catholic philosophy does he find the "supernaturally Christian" character necessary for specification of the philosophy as "Christian." See infra, n. 7.

method."[2] Opponents like to envisage a situation in which Catholic and non-Catholic philosophers accept the same basic philosophical principles and discuss together the conclusions that may be drawn from them. The qualification "Catholic" would then mean no more to philosophy than it would to mathematics or biology.

Nevertheless, the title "Catholic philosophy" continues to be used, despite the opposition.[3] There seems to be an instinctive recognition that it can carry a meaning of its own. But it brings its inherent difficulties. A recent history of Canadian philosophy could remark that "writing about Catholic philosophy presents special problems."[4] The problems signalized arose from the two different backgrounds that shaped Canadian Catholic philosophy. One was the French tradition of the Lyons philosophy that in earlier times had formed the basis for the teaching of Catholic philosophy in both francophone and anglophone Canada. The other was the impulse given to Thomism by Leo XIII's encyclical *Aeterni Patris*. The problems were accordingly located in historical antecedents, prompting the unanswered question whether "with the new stance of the church . . . will there be no reason for there to be specifically Catholic philosophy?"[5]

That, however, is precisely the question at issue. Does "Catholic philosophy" denote a specifically distinct type of philosophizing, apart from any of the accidental influences that may have played their part in bringing it into existence? The designation "officially Catholic philosophy"[6] has been used to characterize the Thomism promoted by *Aeterni Patris*. But this characterization "official" lies outside the strictly philosophical order. It expresses nothing intrinsic to the nature

2. Louis Dupré, "Philosophy and the Religious Perspective of Life," *Proceedings of the American Catholic Philosophical Association* 45 (1971), 3.

3. E.g., Sr. M. Christine Morkovsky, "Catholic Philosophy in Latin America Today," *Proceedings, ACPA* 53 (1979), 36–44. Cf. infra, n. 23.

4. Leslie Armour and Elizabeth Trott, *The Faces of Reason* (Waterloo, Ont.: Wilfrid Laurier University Press, 1981), p. 479.

5. Armour and Trott, p. 506. As noted by Leonard Boyle, "A Remembrance of Pope Leo XIII: The Encyclical *Aeterni Patris*," in *One Hundred Years of Thomism*, ed. Victor B. Brezik (Houston: Center for Thomistic Studies, University of St. Thomas, 1981), pp. 21–22, n. 1, Pope Leo himself referred to its subject matter a year later as "Christian philosophy." However, the movement it promoted could readily be called "the return of Catholic Philosophy"—Hilaire Belloc, *Survivals and New Arrivals* (London: Sheed and Ward, 1929), p. 95.

6. Cf.: "able defenders both within and without officially Catholic philosophy." Alvin Plantinga, "The Reformed Objection to Natural Theology," *Proceedings, ACPA* 54 (1980), 49. "And let it be clearly understood above all things that the scholastic philosophy We prescribe is that which the Angelic Doctor has bequeathed to us, and We, therefore, declare that all the ordinances of Our Predecessors on this subject continue fully in force." Pius X, *Pascendi Dominici Gregis*, in *The Papal Encyclicals 1903–1939*, ed. Mary Claudia Carlen (Wilmington, NC: McGrath Publishing Company, 1981), pp. 92–93.

of Catholic philosophy, and obviously does not cover the entire range of the notion. Much thinking to which the epithet "Catholic philosophy" can equally well apply, on purely philosophical grounds, lies well outside the orbit of Thomism. Even within the thought inspired by the reading of Aquinas, the differences are often radical. From a philosophical viewpoint the "official" designation is not of any help towards finding an intrinsic specific distinction for the notion of Catholic philosophy.

The instances already cited, though, are sufficient to allow the expression "Catholic philosophy" to be used without apology in current discussions. The persistent recurrence of the phrase indicates a problem that has not been dying, and that still calls for close attention. To say that the title is not being evoked with enthusiasm today would of course be somewhat of an understatement. Catholic writers seem to shy away from it. It does not carry the élan that is observable in the promoters of Christian philosophy, of Islamic philosophy, of Jewish philosophy. These notions are now proudly put forward by their devotees. Apart from Maurice Blondel, the device "Catholic philosophy" does not seem to have been waved with any verve. Blondel preferred the phrasing "Catholic philosophy" to "Christian philosophy," on the ground that it specified more exactly what is meant. Only the notion of Catholicism, he claimed, could specify what is *supernaturally* Christian. In this setting he asked if there were in philosophy itself an aptness for being Catholic. Despite all the difficulties that had to be faced, he suggested that Catholic philosophy was still an important topic for discussion. It exhibited a rational worth and a unifying principle of organization that seemed to make it more comprehensive and coherent than any other doctrine.[7]

At that time the notion of "Christian philosophy" was fighting for recognition. It had to face the accusation of being a concept that is self-contradictory, like a square circle. Compounding the troubles by framing the question in a supernaturality beyond what the term

7. "Il ressort de tout ceci que l'alliance de mots '*philosophie chrétienne*' est moins précise et moins justifiable que l'expression 'philosophie catholique'; . . . le catholicisme, ainsi que nous le montrions en discutant les critiques de M. Bréhier, réussit seul à spécifier ce qui est surnaturellement chrétien." Maurice Blondel, *Le problème de la philosophie catholique* (Paris: Bloud & Gay, 1932), p. 172, n.1. Cf. "elle se présent à la discussion avec une valeur rationnelle, avec un principe d'unité organisatrice qui paraissent la rendre plus compréhensive et plus cohérente que toute autre doctrine." Ibid., p. 177. One might note that the expression "supernaturally Christian" bears upon the role of the supernatural clearly emphasized in the Catholic doctrines of the Mass, the sacraments, prayer, and papal primacy and infallibility, and so on. In this perspective Blondel was asking if there is an *attitude* (p. 159) belonging to philosophy itself that may or should be Catholic.

"Christian" itself expressed was too much for the epoch. But the problem has remained, with the result that the use of the expression "Catholic philosophy" does not cause too much surprise today. A reconsideration of the theme seems, accordingly, to be in order, and it could begin with a quick glance at the older theme that philosophy and religion should be sedulously kept apart.

II

The generic objection that philosophy and religion do not mix, however, is not felt so strongly at the present day. In recent decades religion has been the object of a flourishing branch of philosophy expressly called philosophy of religion. Religious experiences and beliefs are frankly recognized as important phenomena in human life. Philosophy has come to see that there is no reason why it should not deal with them thematically. Papal visits, World Council of Churches meetings, lively dialogue of Christians with Moslems, Jews, Buddhists, and others, as well as with Marxists, keep the topic of religion before the public eye. It is an intellectual interest that cannot be ignored. No longer may it be said that religion and philosophy are not on speaking terms. There is at first sight at least one very obvious way in which they do mix. The wonder that prompts all philosophical thinking has been playing a notable role in the religious area. Phenomenological and existentialist approaches especially have contributed to this interest. Religion is once more regarded as a respectable subject for intellectual consideration. It is no longer something just one's own business.

But much more than the role of a thematic object is required for the functioning of a Christian philosophy or a Catholic philosophy. What is meant by the terms is not precisely a type of philosophy that has religion as the object of its treatment. Rather, what is meant is philosophy that treats of any philosophical topic whatever, but in a Christian or a Catholic way. It is here that the difficulty arises. What is accepted on Christian or Catholic belief is taken on faith, without intrinsic evidence. What is known through philosophy is based on the intrinsic evidence of the object, immediate or mediate. The alleged contradiction seems at once to emerge. The object cannot be intrinsically evident and not intrinsically evident at the same time. The specter of the square circle or the wooden iron arises. The adjective and the noun clash. Either the one must absorb or eliminate the other, or the two must go their separate ways.

This was the objection that the proponents of Christian philosophy had to face earlier in the present century. It was discussed at considerable length. The specifying character, namely, the feature that makes Christian philosophy specifically different from any other kind of philosophy, was sought. The results of the discussion are applicable, proportionately, to the problem of Catholic philosophy. It will suffice to review them briefly, as far as the charge of self-contradiction in the phrase "Catholic philosophy" is concerned. Greater detail may be found in Nédoncelle's coverage.[8]

Nédoncelle, allowing for the moment "that the idea of Christian philosophy has a meaning," i.e., that it is not self-contradictory, finds that "the metamorphoses which it has undergone and the controversies which it has aroused are enough to show plainly that the meaning is far from clear" (p. 100). He sees four principal meanings, factual or possible, for it, with numerous degrees or variations within each. The first (pp. 100–102) is that of a philosophy preparing the way for Christianity. Against this one may well object that it is a difficult if not impossible notion to establish. Philosophy just by itself does not seem to prepare the way for Christianity any more than for Buddhism or for Jewish or Islamic belief. In any case, it would be something that precedes religious profession, while the present problem is concerned for the most part with someone who is already a Christian or a Catholic, and who undertakes to philosophize in a distinctive way that somehow corresponds to his religious belief. In a word, the religion is regarded as exercising its role before the philosophy starts.

The second type of explanation listed by Nédoncelle (pp. 102–104) for Christian philosophy makes it a kind of knowledge that owes its formation to Christianity. Under this caption he places Gilson's understanding of it as a philosophy "engendered" (p. 104) by Christianity. More recently this hostile critique leveled against Gilson has been interpreted to mean that "Christian philosophy was reduced to the philosophical moment of a Catholic theology."[9] Taken in the way

8. The best general survey of the modern problems on the topic is that of Maurice Nédoncelle, *Is There a Christian Philosophy?* trans. Illtyd Trethowan (New York: Hawthorn Books, 1960). On the various tendencies and positions regarding Christian philosophy, see A.-R. Motte, "Le problème de la 'philosophie chrétienne,'" *Bulletin thomiste* 5 (1937), 230–55. On the attitudes towards it, see Étienne Gilson, "La notion de philosophie chrétienne," *Bulletin de la Société française de Philosophie* 31 (1931), 37–39.

9. Gerald A. McCool, "How Can There Be Such a Thing as a Christian Philosophy?" *Proceedings, ACPA* 54 (1980), 132. "Philosophizing within theology" hardly makes the philosophy a "moment" of the theology, at least if the Hegelian signification of a phase in dialectical development is retained. Even while being used by theology, philosophy retains its own intrinsic nature, just as water does in the liquid mixture of wine. On that metaphor, see A. C. Pegis, "*Sub Ratione Dei,*" *The New Scholasticism* 39 (1965), 151–53. For a coverage of Gilson's engagement in the controversies on Christian philosophy,

meant by its critics, this manner of explaining Christian philosophy is obviously unacceptable. It would make the conclusions proceed from revealed premises and, in consequence, would absorb Christian philosophy into theology. The nature of the discipline as philosophy would be destroyed. Where Gilson uses the terms *engendre* or *génératrice* in this regard, he is careful to emphasize that the principles and methods of Christian philosophy are purely rational. There is no thought of drawing conclusions in it from revealed truths. In designating revelation as a source of light for Christian philosophy, he explains that the revealed truths are functioning only thematically, as an object of consideration.[10] This attitude occurs regularly in the philosophy of religion, where revealed truths are objects of study without being demonstrative principles. But where they are taken as principles for reasoning one no longer has philosophy: one has theology. Nédoncelle's understanding of this second attempt to explain Christian philosophy accordingly makes it a failure. While the first explanation in his list made Christian philosophy antecede religion, this second one destroys its nature by making its intrinsic procedure theological.

The third of Nédoncelle's listings (pp. 104–106) would explain the notion of Christian philosophy by the use of Christian tenets in the construction of a philosophy, after the manner of a gnosis. The mysteries revealed through faith cease to be supernatural. In this way they are absorbed into philosophy. In a manner opposite to the second explanation, this third attempt would make the Christian aspect entirely a function of philosophical speculation.

The fourth and last way listed by Nédoncelle (pp. 106–114) for explaining Christian philosophy is through relation to Christianity as to an order different from and superior to philosophy. Despite Né-

---

see Laurence K. Shook, *Etienne Gilson* (Toronto: Pontifical Institute of Mediaeval Studies, 1984), pp. 198–205. For Gilson's own presentation of the way Christian philosophy is so "engendered," cf.: "systèmes philosophiques, purement rationnels dans leurs principes et dans leurs méthodes, dont l'existence ne s'expliquerait pas sans l'existence de la religion chrétienne . . . une réalité historique complexe: celle d'une révélation génératrice de raison. Les deux ordres restent distincts, bien que la relation qui les unit soit intrinsèque. . . . la critique rationnelle pure, la seule dont la philosophie chrétienne soit justiciable, mais dont elle est entièrement justiciable, puisqu'elle se donne pour une philosophie." É. Gilson, "La notion de philosophie chrétienne," *Bulletin de la Société française de Philosophie* 31 (1931), 39. "que l'exercice d'une raison naturelle secourue par la révélation en soit encore un exercice rationnel, et si la philosophie qu'elle engendre mérite encore le nom de philosophie?" *Christianisme et philosophie* (Paris: Vrin, 1936, p. 128. Cf. supra, "Introduction," n. 17.

10. "[R]evelation simply proposes an object. . . . While allowing each knowledge its proper order, *the Christian philosopher considers revelation a source of light for his reason.*" Gilson, *The Christian Philosophy of Saint Augustine*, trans. L. E. M. Lynch (London: Victor Gollancz, 1961), p. 242.

doncelle's criticism of some of its versions, it is able in at least one of its forms to offer a satisfactory account of the notion of Christian philosophy. Though Nédoncelle does not discuss Gilson's explanation under this fourth caption, the proper place for it is here rather than under Nédoncelle's second listing. Gilson is adamant on the purely rational character of the procedure in Christian philosophy, which makes use of Christian beliefs as objects of consideration, not as principles for demonstration.[11] In that way it relates its philosophical discussion to Christian tenets. The result is a different type of philosophy in which concepts like person, nature, existence, and numerous others are given philosophical development they receive nowhere else. Gilson's explanation is accordingly historical. Philosophy remains essentially rational, revelation remains essentially above reason. The one requires intrinsic evidence, the other excludes intrinsic evidence. Yet, history shows they can combine in the one concrete human thinker in the way just noted, to produce a specifically distinct philosophical discipline in which both exercise *intrinsic* influence.[12] It is hard to see how this conception does not fit neatly under the caption of relating philosophical thinking to Christian belief already known as a superior object, even though it makes no claim to demonstrate the existence of the supernatural.

Aside from Gilson's own way of explaining this relation between Christian philosophy and Christian belief, the historical fact to which he points can scarcely be challenged. People philosophizing with Christian beliefs held steadily before their mind's eye have in fact produced philosophy different in type from what has emerged independently of the telling influence of those religious themes. Yet, in its formation, the religious beliefs have played the role only of objects of cognition. Thematically they are able to come under the object of philosophy of religion. They are an object of philosophical study, though their truth and certainty depend on sources above the penetration of philosophy. Known as objects, they inspire and guide philosophical penetration into topics upon which they draw attention. In that way only do they give illumination. Though their source originally was supernatural, they are now functioning in an entirely natural manner in their specifying role. They are naturally observable as religious phenomena, and as such can perform their task of specifying a type of philosophy. They may entail something more from the viewpoint of motivation as regards promoting and sustaining the efforts

11. See texts cited supra, nn. 9–10.
12. See texts supra, n. 9, and infra, n. 15.

necessary to bring about a full-fledged philosophy. But in respect of the present issue, namely, to show satisfactorily that Christian philosophy is not a self-destructive notion like a square circle or wooden iron, the manner in which the philosophical procedure is related to the Christian beliefs keeps it entirely on the philosophical level. Despite the faulty attempts at explanation listed by Nédoncelle, Christian philosophy has still kept on branching out, with a society formed under its name and a journal *Faith and Philosophy* promoting its interests. The historical fact invoked by Gilson has continued to pursue its course.

Nédoncelle's own conclusion was that "the adjective *Christian* could not be applied by the philosopher himself to the philosophy as such. In this respect the epithet would be extrinsic, like light falling upon an object" (pp. 111–12). The one exception he made was for Blondel's explanation, brought under the fourth of the above listings. Blondel had proceeded, from the insufficiency of nature, to infer the possibility of the supernatural, though not its fact. But this was claimed to be sufficient for the purpose, and accordingly kept the discussion intrinsic to philosophy. Nédoncelle (p. 112) found Blondel's attempt very attractive, but—quite rightly—difficult to accept in the way it brought the supernatural into the ken of natural reason.[13] But he concluded that apart from it, "it would be a vain hope to look for any watertight meaning of the expression 'Christian philosophy'" (p. 111).

This rapid glance at a controversy now over fifty years in the past has been necessary for acquaintance with the background of the pre-

---

13. The "avowal of insufficiency" is hardly what Nédoncelle excoriates as "the attitude of all pious agnosticisms" (p. 106). In its own order, nature is sufficient. But in itself it does not require that it be raised to the supernatural. See Henri de Lubac, *The Mystery of the Supernatural*, trans. Rosemary Sheed (London: Geoffrey Chapman, 1967), p. 65. Starting from the natural, one cannot reason to the supernatural. Showing that nature is finite while God is infinite provides a niche into which grace may fit when its existence is known from a supernatural source. But that nature has a potentiality to be elevated by the supernatural is not naturally knowable. The "obediential" potency can be established only through sacred theology. A Catholic philosophy, therefore, cannot be conceived as finding some sort of ground in nature for reasoning to the supernatural. The two sources of knowledge have to be kept carefully distinct. Any "philosophical necessity of the supernatural" (Nédoncelle, p. 112) is more than just a "weak point" in the explanation of the nature of a Catholic philosophy. If that philosophy is to be described as one "which tends of itself to indicate its relationship to a supernature and to utter an appeal to this supernature" (Nédoncelle, p. 150), the description has to be understood of the factual complex in which both phases are already united and contained, and not of the philosophical side just in itself. For Blondel's own explanation, see *Le problème de la philosophie catholique*, pp. 158–77. He regards the natural desire to see God as "une disposition congénitale, essentielle, la marque ineffaçable de toute intelligence finie" (p. 160), calling for explication by a doctrine that only Catholicism can furnish.

sent problem regarding the caption "Catholic philosophy." The difficulties of reconciling noun and adjective are the same, and are to be met in the same manner. The Catholic beliefs brought into play in the notion are seen to function here as objects of cognition, quite as they appear in their role of thematic objects for the philosophy of religion. But now these beliefs spur and guide the mind to deeper philosophic consideration of the topics they involve; the procedure then goes on to the study of any topic that comes under the range of general philosophy. In this way Catholic philosophy is not specifically a philosophy of religion, though it can have religion as one of its objects. It has a thematic range as wide as that of any other philosophy.

This point may be illustrated by a glance at any of the philosophies that may be readily recognized as Catholic. The instance that first comes to mind is the one that has been referred to (see supra, n. 6) as "officially Catholic." The Thomistic textbooks prompted by *Aeterni Patris* were motivated by deeply Catholic interest in philosophical themes. They gave ardent and distinctive attention to the rational demonstration of the existence of God and to the spirituality of the human soul. In regard to substance they were vitally concerned with the philosophical aspects of transubstantiation. On nature and person they were keenly sensitive to rational aspects involved by the religious doctrines of the Trinity and the Incarnation, together with the supernatural order of grace. In the ethical field their special interest was to find a rational account for Catholic morality, and even in logic there was added emphasis on predication of the divine names and on the avoidance of contradictions in speaking about mysteries above reason, as well as on the role of extrinsic evidence for acceptance of propositions through faith. Adequate philosophical treatment of these problems entailed the general coverage of philosophical themes. Starting from these special interests, the philosophy had as its object nature, being, thought, conduct, and the whole panorama of the philosophical order. It was philosophy that extended to everything that could come under philosophical inquiry. This was obvious enough in Neo-Thomism, and also in philosophies of Scotistic and Suarezian provenance. There is no apparent reason why any other of the philosophies that one would care to label "Catholic" could not go on to equally wide extension.

From these considerations the meaning of a specifically Catholic philosophy should emerge with sufficient clarity. The wonder that Aristotle (*Metaph.* 1.2.982b12–19) signaled as the beginning of all philosophy is in this case aroused by matters of Catholic belief, as faith spontaneously seeks understanding. The choice of topics on which interest is concentrated is in that way marked off. But in order to deal with these problems satisfactorily, the investigation of the whole philosophical area becomes necessary. What in this way is general philosophy can be Catholic specifically, on account of the specific choice of themes that prompt its basic interest. In its procedure it does not look to the authority of faith to support its conclusions. It reasons solely from what it sees as naturally evident in the objects facing it. Its principles are naturally known, and its conclusions follow according to the norms of logic. There are no intuitive jumps required, even though in an existentialist or phenomenological Catholic philosophy these may be included in the philosophy's normal procedure, in the manner of a philosophy of the heart. That type of procedure need not be excluded from a Catholic philosophy, yet the philosophy that uses it will have the task of justifying it and explaining its limits. But the reasoning always has to be from principles that are naturally evident or known through affectivity that is naturally observable, without any appeal to revealed authority for demonstrative support. The procedure remains entirely on the philosophical level. This conception of Catholic philosophy remains within the limits of Nédoncelle's conclusion that "in the face of Christianity" the duty of reason is "to enter into this new order by its own free choice: and on this showing an intrinsically Christian metaphysic is possible."[14]

III

But the question at once arises how the notion "Catholic" can be intrinsic to a philosophy, in a way that makes it a specifying characteristic. If choice of themes is what distinguishes Catholic philosophy from all others, why is there not question merely of an application of philosophy in general to Catholic themes, without affecting the intrinsic character of the philosophy? Kantian philosophy or Hegelian philosophy, for instance, can be applied to religious themes without thereby engendering a new and different type of philosophy. The same philosophy would merely be applied to different groups of objects already under its range. The philosophy itself would not be intrinsically affected in the way a genus is specified by an added differentia.

The question is important. What is involved is a new world outlook. Gilson commented, in a remark that has drawn considerable attention:

14. Nédoncelle, p. 151. The "free" connection with faith allows the "Catholic" element to enter the factual complex without any necessary sequence from the natural phase; cf. supra, n. 13.

"Once you are in possession of that revelation how can you possibly philosophize as though you had never heard of it?"[15] The world that faces you is in fact different. The whole observable universe, in the realms both of speculation and of action, takes on another aspect. Instead of nature itself being able to make manifest its own purpose, its full purpose and meaning have to be sought outside and above nature. As Aquinas (*CG*, 1.1,Finis) noted in this regard, the supreme purpose of anything is what its primary maker intends. A Catholic knows through his faith that the whole universe has been created by an infinitely powerful and provident God for a very definite purpose. Non-spiritual creatures are meant for the needs of spiritual creatures. Spiritual creatures are meant for the beatific vision of the divine substance and are raised by the habituation of grace to a level proportionate to this destiny. Grace makes them children of God and members of the one supernatural family of spiritual agents, with deep interpersonal relationship involved. This means facing a radically new world, in which man walks close to God in interpersonal communion and in spiritual association with realms beyond the terrestrial. The outlook can easily be caricatured as "the over-world of heaven and hell, angels and demons, transcendental cures and ecclesiastically induced changes in the weather."[16] But to one who is living a solidly Catholic life, this extension of the world beyond the immediately observable is as real and as unshakable as the sense of solidarity in Wordsworth's *We Are Seven,* in which the deceased brother and sister were as vividly present as the other family members to the cottage girl at the grave:

> My stockings there I often knit,
> My kerchief there I hem;
> And there upon the ground I sit,
> And sing a song to them.

> And often after sun-set, Sir,
> When it is light and fair,
> I take my little porringer,
> And eat my supper there.

No amount of dissuasion could veer her towards the attitude that only five were left in the family. The real situation was just as she saw it:

> The little Maid would have her will,
> And said, "Nay, we are seven."

15. É. Gilson, *The Spirit of Mediaeval Philosophy,* trans. A. H. C. Downes (New York: Charles Scribner's Sons, 1940), p. 5. Cf. supra, "Introduction," n. 17.
16. Brand Blanshard, *Reason and Belief* (New Haven: Yale University Press, 1975), p. 117.

In that way what is believed in can be as intrinsic to one's thinking and acting as are the cogently reasoned conclusions from evident principles. The intrinsic role played by appetitive habituation in ethical thinking is emphasized by Aristotle (*EN* 1.3.1095a2–4). But even in theoretical sciences, he notes (*Metaph.* 2.3.994b32–995a16), habituation plays its role. The reasoning may be from naturally evident premises to cogently drawn conclusions, but the attitude towards interests and objectives intrinsically affects the discipline. Greek philosophy means more than just a temporal and geographical designation. It contains intrinsically the notion of an attitude specifically Greek. Similarly, medieval philosophy involves intrinsically an attitude towards the world as known and life as lived in the middle ages. The notion of German philosophy expresses a propensity towards Idealism, that of Oxford philosophy an interest in the behavior of words. These characteristics are surely *intrinsic* to the notions. A man or woman need not be a German to be an Idealist, nor an Oxford graduate to be an analyst. Likewise, not every German is an Idealist, nor is every Oxford professor an analyst. It is something intrinsic to the philosophy itself that is specifically meant by these designations, rather than the accidental circumstances of time and place that give rise to them. The intrinsic feature keeps carrying the notion, even though the extrinsic origins of the designation cease to be present. So the designation "Catholic," when qualifying a philosophy, arises from a world view furnished by the Catholic religion. Once that world view is known as an object of cognition, it can continue to specify the philosophy even in somebody who is not a Catholic in religion. In a word, the reality from which the designation is taken may be extrinsic to philosophy, as is Greece or the Catholic Church. But the characterization thereby designated is something intrinsic to the philosophy, and marks it off as a specifically distinct type.

Catholic philosophy is in this manner intrinsically characterized by a propensity towards specifically Catholic themes, branching out from them to the consideration of all other philosophical topics. What renders all of them specifically Catholic is their integration into a real world known partly through natural cognition and partly through supernatural revelation. The reasoning in Catholic philosophy will start from the naturally known principles, and on them alone will the probative force of the reasoning rest. But the guiding and sustaining influence of the revealed knowledge will be continually present in and distinctive of its procedure. The prospect of heaven, believed in through faith, will not be a shadowy "over-world" notion of small relevance, but rather the supreme fact towards which all else in the real world is directed. This supreme fact, with its supernatural and interpersonal aspects, does not enter as a premise into the philosophical reasoning. But it keeps the Catholic philosopher alert to the consideration that nature itself is not a finished whole, and that purely natural reasoning cannot be expected to give the entire truth about it. Nature is not able of itself to show what it itself is meant for. Philosophers left to themselves may consider nature as something complete, as Duns Scotus observed,[17] but Catholic faith proclaims that its perfection lies in the order of grace. A Catholic philosopher, though not at all skeptical about the truth that follows from naturally known principles, will not expect unaided reason to tell the whole story. Rather, a strangely garbled version may well be the result. G. K. Chesterton, at a time when he was not yet a Catholic in religion, could remark: "The man who sees the inconsistency of things is a humorist—and a Catholic."[18] Existentialist or pessimistic philosophers have in fact come to the conclusion that the naturally knowable world is absurd or nauseating.

In matters of conduct, the difference in the world that faces the Catholic philosopher becomes even more accentuated. Because the supernatural destiny of man is the destiny of the whole observable universe, and because the relations between God and man are interpersonal rather than necessitarian, a distinctive outlook arises, for which there is not the least scandal in the prospect of miraculous intervention or in the ordinary influence of prayer on future events. A kindly agnostic farmer once said that he did not have the heart to tell his believing neighbors how he had seen the grasshoppers starting to leave the fields *before* the intercessory prayer had begun in the church. He benignly allowed them to go on thinking that the deliverance from the pests was something that followed upon the religious intercession. But the philosophical study of what divine providence and divine omnipotence mean, when approached from the habituation given by Catholic belief and Catholic life, leaves the regular influence of prayer quite what one should expect of interpersonal relations with God. Events should run their course in the way that had been planned from the beginning in response to the divinely foreseen prayers of individuals. In prayer life and sacramental life a very distinctive universe confronts Catholic philosophy. Neither magic nor serendipity nor fatalism reigns, but a profound belief in the reality

17. *Ordinatio*, Prol., 1.1.5; ed. Vaticana, 1, 4.14–16.
18. G. K. Chesterton, *George Bernard Shaw* (New York: John Lane Company, 1909), p. 46.

of the supernatural aspect of the universe as revealed through faith for both the theoretical and practical orders.

The entire panorama of the world so experienced and lived in becomes the distinct object that integrates Catholic philosophy. Yet no scriptural or traditional authority is invoked to ground or support its demonstrations. These sources remain extrinsic to its inferences. The probative force of the reasoning is based entirely upon naturally evident tenets. But the drive towards selection of topics and specified interest in them comes from within the philosophic wonder. It originates in the habituation of the Catholic philosopher, and in that way is intrinsic to the undertaking. It is much more than an external relation of the philosophical thought to a select set of objects. It contains within itself the principle of the selection. Just as Marxism proceeds from a distinct mentality towards social and economic conditions, or as Aristotelian practical philosophy proceeds from the virtuous habituation in the moralist, so Catholic philosophical thinking engenders intrinsically the features that gives it its specification. Philosophy is not an abstraction. It is the enterprise of a person, and the intrinsic habituation of the person is what brings it to bear upon its specific object. Intrinsic orientation towards themes of distinctly Catholic interest is the specifying feature in Catholic philosophy. The specification is thereby definitely intrinsic, while the divinely revealed doctrine, which is the "friendly star" that points for it towards those themes, remains entirely extrinsic to its reasoning processes.

IV

Two difficulties may arise quite spontaneously in regard to this conception of the distinguishing feature in Catholic philosophy. The first is that a mythology could exercise an equally specifying role, given that the truth or falsity of its contents does not enter into the probative force of the discipline's procedure. Mythological notions might function in the same purely guiding fashion as do supernaturally revealed notions in regard to constituting a distinctive type of philosophy. They seem on a par.

Yet there is a difference. True, there can be a philosophy of mythology, just as there can be a philosophy of religion or of art or of sport or of any other such human activity. Its thematic contents could be used to suggest points of philosophical inquiry, quite as myths were invoked by both Plato and Aristotle. But no matter how much a lover of wisdom may be a lover of myth, the two notions would obviously clash in the combination "mythical philosophy" or "mythological philosophy." Could mere myth engender a distinctive outlook on the real world, in the way a Marxist philosophy or a Catholic philosophy bears upon things other than myths? Myths open on reality only indirectly, through their symbolism. They do not literally present reality in itself. If possible remnants of a genuine religious tradition are left aside, the myths are but a poetically symbolic account of the naturally knowable world. Just in themselves they do not bring the mind to know any higher reality in things. Divine revelation, however, bears in literal fashion upon the real world as elevated supernaturally. Its literal discourse applies in one way or another to all the topics that come under the range of philosophy. Habituation to a universe really existing in the way taught by faith is in the Catholic philosopher as literal and at least as firm and unshakable as the cottage girl's belief in her seven-member family in Wordsworth. So viewed, the universe towards which Catholic philosophy is immediately oriented in distinctive fashion is the real universe as it actually is, described literally. The universe upon which a mythological philosophy immediately bore would be that of myth, even though the myths symbolize reality in their own characteristic way.[19]

The other difficulty is that, if the distinguishing feature in Catholic philosophy is the intrinsic habituation that prompts and guides it, philosophies that are not in accord with Catholic doctrine would not come under this designation. So, in the nineteenth century, philosophies like fideism, traditionalism, or ontologism could not be called Catholic philosophies. Yet they sprang from the Catholic habituation and Catholic interest, and can hardly be omitted from a history of Catholic philosophy. Intrinsically, according to the conception just outlined, they have the distinguishing characteristic that makes a philosophy Catholic, even though some of their conclusions may at least verbally clash with magisterial pronouncements.

This assessment seems fair from both angles. If Catholic philosophy is genuinely philosophy, its criteria as philosophy should be on the philosophical level. If its conclusions are opposed, even just verbally, to faith, they are certainly liable to religious censure, as in the nineteenth-century instances just noted. But it pertains to philosophers to probe how those philosophies went the way they did on the philo-

---

19. Cf.: "We should next distinguish what is said and what is expressed in a mythology from what is believed in the mythology by those who believe it. As symbolic, a mythology is open to constant reinterpretation." Richard T. De George, "Myth and Reason," *Proceedings, ACPA* 54 (1971), 34. "[T]he paradox of Christianity; that we can only really understand all myths when we know that one of them is true." G. K. Chesterton, *George Bernard Shaw*, p. 176.

sophical plane. Wrong Catholic philosophies they well may be. Yet, on the grounds of the criterion developed above, they still come under the notion of Catholic philosophy. Complete doctrinal orthodoxy, then, is not the decisive criterion for judging whether or not they are to be considered Catholic philosophies. If they are sincerely inspired by Catholic interests and bear upon Catholic themes, their mistakes do not deprive them of that title. It may well be that nobody who calls himself a Catholic philosopher will persist in maintaining conclusions that had been declared by the church to run counter to her beliefs. Yet theoretically the case is not impossible, as in the parallel instances of a theologian continuing to call himself a Catholic theologian in the face of ecclesiastical condemnation. The theologian has his own personal notion of ecclesiology to fall back upon. So, conceivably, an errant Catholic philosopher might invoke the tenet of the double truth. But where truth is regarded as one, the errors in the reasoning or in the understanding of the first principles, or in the interpretation of the philosopher's concepts, can be pointed out by strictly philosophical investigation. The matter is left to philosophical judgment. It conforms to the standard pattern of one philosophy criticizing another, even though in this case both philosophies are Catholic. As Gilson (text supra, n. 9) had emphasized in regard to Christian philosophy, the philosophy, because it is philosophy, is amenable *only* to purely rational critique. But it has to justify itself *fully* on that level.

V

The foregoing investigation has endeavored to isolate the specifying feature in Catholic philosophy. It has located the differentia in an intrinsic orientation towards philosophical themes that are of special interest to Catholic life and Catholic thought. From preceding inquiry it found that a philosophy is recognizable as Catholic by the selection of its topics, namely those of Catholic interest, and by its motivation towards increased philosophical understanding of them. It likewise concluded from a long drawn out debate that "Christian philosophy" is a viable notion, with the concomitant inference that "Catholic philosophy" is one of its species. Against that background it undertook the task of showing that habituation towards philosophical topics of Catholic interest is intrinsic to the enterprise of Catholic philosophy and functions as its distinguishing trait.

In this enterprise the revealed truths function only thematically as guides that point out items of further philosophical interest in objects already naturally known. Faith serves only as a "friendly star" leading the way to problems that are philosophical in nature. The revealed truths do not in any way serve as principles or starting points of demonstration. None of the reasoning processes in Catholic philosophy are based upon them. The reasoning runs its whole course on the level of natural intellection. But thematic acquaintance with the revealed truths as objects of belief makes a Catholic philosopher aware that he is facing a single real world that has both natural and supernatural facets. The result is a specifying object in which nature is regarded as incomplete in respect of its own factual purpose and meaning, and yet as possessing its own truth and manifesting its own certainty.[20]

The philosophy that emerges from this approach is in consequence a specifically distinct type. Its interests and motivation are distinctly Catholic. Yet its mode of procedure is thoroughly philosophical. Though guided to its characteristic problems by the friendly star of faith, it finds its philosophical starting points in naturally known reality. It reasons in strictly logical sequence from those naturally known principles to its conclusions. Its reasoning, though bearing upon points of special interest to Catholic belief, remains philosophical and in this way opens upon all topics of philosophical concern. Its range, therefore, is that of a general philosophy.

This assessment may readily be verified by a glance at the numerous monographs and manuals that were used in Catholic colleges and seminaries in the nineteenth and first half of the twentieth centuries. As developed for a general philosophic public, the meaning of Catholic philosophy may be observed in the vivid work of Jacques Maritain and Étienne Gilson and other such writers who directed their books and articles to the mentality of their contemporary cultured world. In a non-professional way it may be seen permeating the literary output of authors who were not professionally philosophers, such as G. K. Chesterton, Hilaire Belloc, Arnold Lunn, and E. I. Watkin. Its distinguishing characteristic becomes evident enough when writings such as these are set off against other philosophical literature and tendencies, even those in the more general area of Christian philosophy.

Catholic philosophy, then, is not entirely the same as Christian philosophy, though a focal reference interpretation can easily range them under the one notion. The supernatural in Christian revelation is the guiding star, and is most highly articulated in the Catholic dogmas of grace, sacraments, and ecclesiastical infallibility and jurisdiction.[21]

20. Cf. supra, nn. 13 and 17.
21. Cf. supra, n. 7.

From its own naturally knowable, though specially selected, starting points Catholic philosophy is able to range over the entire philosophical territory. It is thereby able to dialogue on equal footing with all other philosophies, for all the concepts it uses in its demonstrative procedures are accessible to unaided human reason. The naturally knowable content of its concepts is common, and in consequence permits profitable interchange of ideas. There is no fear, if the philosophizing is done properly, that revealed truths may surreptitiously replace rigorous observation and rational deduction.[22] Even though Catholic philosophy is trying to understand as far as philosophically possible a world that has been elevated to the supernatural, it keeps fully aware that nature, though elevated, has not been destroyed. It is a world in which weather forecasts have to be taken into account, the powder kept dry, and the most modern medical techniques utilized, while divine help is prayerfully invoked. Likewise, in regard to the supernatural aspects of that elevated world, the procedure of Catholic philosophy has to be genuinely rational in character, despite the fact that a person living a Catholic life cannot be expected to philosophize as though he or she had never heard of divine revelation.[23]

22. Cf. supra, n. 2.

23. Cf. supra, n. 15. A panel under the caption "What is 'Catholic Philosophy'? Reflections on 'The American Catholic Philosophical Association'" was held on the evening of the first day of the ACPA convention at Philadelphia, Friday, April 11, 1980. The panel was announced in detail on the program of the convention, but was given only a brief mention in the *Proceedings, ACPA* 54 (1980), 216, without any record of its discussions. Of the nine participants, only one, Andrew Woznicki, argued in favor of the notion. Woznicki's view, as published later, was: "Catholic philosophy, therefore, aims at an integration of truth in its totality. . . . In short, Catholic philosophy respects the autonomy of particular disciplines, but expects mutual interdependency among various ways of searching for truth." *Migrant Echo* 10 (1981), 184.

5

THE OBJECTIVES OF THE AMERICAN CATHOLIC PHILOSOPHICAL ASSOCIATION

I

The following address was given at Washington, D.C., in 1966, on the occasion of the fortieth anniversary of the founding of the American Catholic Philosophical Association. The address is cast in the mentality of the time. It reflects a deep sense of groping towards the meaning of the philosophy the association was intended to promote, accompanied nevertheless by full instinctive confidence in the worth of the project that had been undertaken. Notable difference in attitude had developed during the first four decades of the association's existence. In the years that have intervened since then the mood has continued to change, and the exact objectives of the association have kept coming under debate. One stand, for instance, has been that the association was necessary in the past to preserve traditional western philosophy by counteracting the monolithic tendencies of logical positivism or linguistic analysis, but that on account of today's ready acceptance of pluralism the association is no longer required. Some attention to the association's originally envisaged objectives would in consequence seem to have a place in the present collection of papers bearing on Christian philosophy.

The issue is whether in actual practice the philosophy pursued under the name "Catholic" was being sought for its own intrinsic and permanent worth, or was merely undertaken to satisfy the passing needs of a particular epoch. The American Catholic Philosophical Association saw itself at its founding as engaged in "Catholic philosophy."[1] The work of the association has been the most extensive cor-

---

1. Edward A. Pace, "Inaugural Address," *Proceedings of the American Catholic Philosophical Association* 1 (1926), 14; 17. For the original "Constitution" of the association, see *Proceedings* 1, pp. 9–11.

porate enterprise in America devoted explicitly to that purpose. What it has actually been pursuing in practice should therefore be most enlightening for the grasp of what Catholic philosophy means. An investigation into what it was intending at its foundation, and how it followed out that purpose during its early decades, seems, accordingly, to be of prime importance for understanding the nature of the philosophy in question. To bring out how the association kept feeling its way towards the meaning of the philosophy to which it was dedicated, the presidential address on that fortieth anniversary in Washington is here reprinted just as it was then given.

II

Forty years ago, in this historic and world-important capital, the founders of the American Catholic Philosophical Association launched with enthusiasm what seemed to them a thoroughly straightforward project. As appears clearly enough from their recorded proceedings, they were men of action, men of direct approach, of quick intuition. They were the breed that got things done. We, their cautious successors, have the advantage of standing on their shoulders to survey the philosophic panorama. Yet, if they could speak up, would they not find in many of us attitudes difficult for them to understand? Would they not be deeply puzzled by our more circumspect and pluralistic mentality? But by the same token, is it any easier for us today to achieve clear focus upon the object of their direct and unsophisticated intuition as they set afoot their enduring work? Is it even possible now to be in sufficient sympathy with their objective to know really what it meant? On this fortieth anniversary may we not well ask to what degree we continue to be in solidarity with their objective, or even if today we are at all still growing from our original roots? The answers of our members to these questions, it may be expected, will cover a broad spectrum, most likely extending to both extremes. But whatever the answers are, or how widely they diverge, the occasion seems appropriate for another look at the objective that motivated our founders, and at our present understanding of it.

The objective of our founders was stated plainly in the inaugural address of the first president, Msgr. Pace: "We approach our task with the conviction that the basic ideas of Scholasticism are living truths—firm enough to support the whole fabric of knowledge yet flexible enough to allow for every addition of ascertained fact."[2] That was

2. *Proceedings* 1 (1926), 16. The problem of justifying the separation of Catholic

their intuition. It was the magnificent vision of a thriving Scholastic philosophy that in the twentieth century would vivify the whole structure of human knowledge and ingest every new discovery or future creation of mankind into its vigorously pulsating life stream. That was the salvation the new association was to offer a baffled world. That was its objective. Its inaugural theme was "What the New Scholasticism Has to Offer Modern Thought."[3] The seven papers read on the topic showed how, from past wisdom,[4] through organized effort, the new

---

philosophers into a special organization was realized and faced. The answer was seen in the service rendered to philosophy by a distinctive association that would concentrate on Scholasticism: "Are we as students and teachers of Catholic philosophy . . . justified in forming a philosophical association apart from our fellow workers in this field? . . . Personally, I should hope to see our members take an active part in the discussion of other philosophical associations . . . At the same time, it seems to me that we can render important service to the cause of philosophy as a whole by a more specialized study and development of those principles and doctrines which we have inherited from our Scholastic predecessors." Pace, pp. 14–15. Scholastic philosophy, and not just Catholic philosophy in general, was accordingly regarded as the raison d'être of the new association. Moreover, although the above passage was addressed to "students and teachers of Catholic philosophy," any limitation of membership to Catholics alone was voted down from the very beginning; see "Organization Meeting," *Proceedings* 1, p. 5. Its general membership extended to "all who are interested in the teaching and spread of philosophical doctrines." Ibid., p. 9.

3. *Proceedings* 1 (1926), 7. Cf.: "Since every system of education is simply a philosophy in action . . . our hope of remedy for present evils and of a wholesome national life for the future depends largely, if not chiefly, upon education" and its failure or success rests on "the philosophical principles which underlie all education." Pace, p. 14. Accordingly: "The work to which we are now setting our hands marks an epoch. It opens a new era in the Catholic life of our country." Pace, p. 18. "[M]en will harken to religious teaching only when they are convinced of their own God-given origin and immortal destiny. This, I believe, is the great mission of Neo-Scholasticism in America. . . . in it we find too the master key to all the problems of contemporary concern. May this new American Catholic Philosophical Association under whose auspices we meet today be the agency here in America to turn that key and 'opening the doors let the light of day into the dark chambers of our modern thought.'" Patrick J. Waters, *Proceedings* 1, p. 42. For the titles of these crusading papers, see infra, nn. 5–11.

4. "We must, in the light of what I have tried to explain, reiterate our allegiance to this traditional philosophy." A. M. Schwitalla, *Proceedings* 1 (1926), 56. Charges of being "simply archaeologists" (*Proceedings* 1, p. 15) or purveyors of "antiquated" (p. 20) ideas, were vigorously repelled: "The greatest difficulty has been in finding ways of convincing modern thinkers that our offering is of genuine worth, is, in other words, something more than a relic of the days that have passed and are no more." C. C. Miltner, *Proceedings* 1, p. 62. Yet the notion of clinging to a traditional, common sense way of thinking was undoubtedly present: "[T]he spirit of common-sense philosophy, the only 'philosophia perennis' . . . It is the boast of its adherents that Scholasticism comes nearer to being the philosophy of common-sense than does any other." F. V. Corcoran, *Proceedings* 1, pp. 33–34. There was present something of the nostalgic air in Tennyson's verse, "Knowledge comes but wisdom lingers, and I linger on the shore" (*Locksley Hall*, 141). It was felt to be the age-old wisdom, in fact, adapting itself to the new knowledge: "It is precisely in its capacity for focusing newly discovered facts—a capacity which, under another figure of speech, is more properly designated adaptability, that a philo-

Scholasticism was to deliver to contemporary man "the firm unshakable foundations of all philosophy, nay of all science,"[5] and in particular in the fields of religion,[6] psychology,[7] epistemology,[8] biology,[9]

---

sophical system vindicates its right to the title 'philosophia perennis.'" A. M. Schwitalla, *Proceedings* 1, pp. 50–51.

On the unphilosophical attitude and tradition involved in the Neoscholastic notion that common sense can function as a criterion of truth in theoretical philosophy, see É. Gilson, *Réalisme thomiste et critique de la connaissance* (Paris: J. Vrin, 1939), pp. 9–39. As for the term "philosophia perennis," it can be traced back only as far as the Renaissance bishop Augustinus Steuchus. With its originator it meant that all philosophies of mankind tended towards the goal of the Christian religion: "In religionem veram cunctos Philosophos consensisse: Pietatem, Philosophiamque Christianam . . . omnes tacite collaudasse: Rerum humanarum finem esse, Philosophorum consensu, pietatem: Hanc autem esse solam Christianam." Steuchus, *De perenni philosophia* 10.1 (Basel: per Nicolaum Bryling et Sebastianum Francken, 1542), p. 649. This is hardly a philosophic notion of philosophy. For references to literature on this topic, see supra, p. 100, n. 8. The notion was transmitted by Leibniz as the perennial philosophy that remains after the differences have been removed. But what remains after the real differences have been taken away can hardly have any philosophical consistence. Nevertheless, the notion reappeared in Neo-Thomism as "une philosophie dont la perennité est le caractère propre," J. Maritain, *Antimoderne* (Paris: Editions de la Revue des jeunes, 1922), p. 19. Cf. "*la philosophia perennis*," ibid., p. 104; "après que la *philosophia perennis* eut magnifiquement fructifié en la synthèse thomiste," p. 161. Similarly: "It is inappropriate to attach the name of any man, be he the greatest of thinkers, to a philosophy which, identifying itself with the *philosophia perennis*, must renew itself from generation to generation." Maritain, *Moral Philosophy* (New York: Scribner, 1964), p. x. The perennial philosophy was regarded by Maritain as both "antimoderne" and "ultramoderne," *Antimoderne*, pp. 15–16. For a short sketch of the notion *philosophia perennis* in Neoscholastic philosophy, see R. F. Harvanek, "The Church and Scholasticism," *Proceedings of the American Catholic Philosophical Association* 32 (1958), 223–25.

5. F. P. Siegfried, "Neo-Scholastic Ontology and Modern Thought," *Proceedings* 1, p. 19.

6. "Scholasticism . . . is still the best instrument devised by human reason for the fruitful study of religious problems." F. V. Corcoran, "What the New Scholasticism Has to Offer Modern Thought from the Field of Religion and Theology," *Proceedings* 1, p. 34. "Coming now to the more specific question of Christianity, we confidently affirm that no other system of philosophy is at all comparable to Scholasticism in the services it has rendered that cause." Ibid., p. 30.

7. "[T]he psychological doctrines of the School, so long the object of ridicule, are demanded as a corrective of the anarchy and confusion prevailing in the modern intellectual world, . . ." P. J. Waters, "Neo-Scholastic Psychology and Modern Thought," *Proceedings* 1, p. 30. "The methods of Scholastic Psychology are greatly needed at the present time. Its precious truths, so long ignored, must be heeded if the pernicious influences of a soulless psychology are to be checked." Ibid., pp. 38–39. "If the American people are to be brought back to the recognition of religious values and respect for religious ideals, it will be, under God, through the doctrines of Thomistic psychology." Ibid., p. 42.

8. "The New Scholasticism thus finds itself in the pleasing role of welcoming home the prodigal son who has been wandering in a far country." J. T. Barron, "Contributions of the New Scholasticism to Modern Philosophy in the Field of Epistemology," *Proceedings* 1, p. 47.

9. "Scholasticism is the only system of philosophy . . . that can adequately serve as a background for biological thought and investigation." A. M. Schwitalla, "The Relation of Biology to Neo-Scholasticism," *Proceedings* 1, p. 56.

ethics,[10] and in philosophy of nature and experimental science.[11] It was an inspiring vista. In its spirit the founders stated officially in the beginning of the constitution that the object of the new association was "to promote study and research in the field of philosophy, with special emphasis on Scholastic philosophy."[12]

At today's meeting, forty years after, we are taking another look at "Scholasticism in the Modern World." Can we still see in this object the original inspiration of our founders? Has their unsophisticated intuition remained steadfast under the titantic tests of the intervening decades? The word "Scholasticism" has in fact disappeared from the opening article of the constitution.[13] In the most obvious details, the intuition of our founders has not brought about any of the ardently projected results. The experimental and social sciences have continued to make giant strides without benefit of stilts supplied by Scholasticism. The newer trends in Catholic philosophy do not bear its stamp. In practical fields, the operative influences have not come from its thinking. The *aggiornamento* within the church, the ecumenical movement among world religions, the surge of national and civil rights, social reforms and the new order of political dialogue among nations, have been neither sparked nor guided by Scholastic philosophy. All this is incontrovertible historic fact.

But in concentrating on the details in which the intuition has proven defective, may we possibly be missing the wood for the trees? Are we at all grasping the import of the original intuition when we view its objectives in that way? Today the phrasing "the field of philosophy, with special emphasis on Scholastic philosophy" may seem to express an authentic ecumenical commitment to appreciative encounter with all philosophies, some extra attention—presumably canonical in motivation—being given to Scholasticism. Those of us who learned our

10. "Let the problem be one of international or civil, domestic or personal dimensions; . . . to all these problems the New Scholasticism finds itself able to offer a set of principles readily and logically applicable." C. C. Miltner, "Neo-Scholastic Ethics and Modern Thought," *Proceedings* 1, p. 60.

11. "Where can science find an analysis and verification of the principles upon which it is based? In Scholasticism." J. A. Baisnée, "What the New Scholasticism Has to Offer Modern Thought in the Field of the Philosophy of Nature." *Proceedings* 1, p. 66. Need one remark that none of the dazzling projects envisioned in above nn. 5 and 7–11 can be used as enticements to Scholastic philosophy today?

12. *Proceedings* 1, pp. 4; 9.

13. In the 1956 revised constitution the article reads: "The objectives of this organization shall be to promote philosophical scholarship, to improve the teaching of philosophy, and to communicate with other individuals and groups of like interests." *Proceedings* 30 (1956), 213. The official journal of the association is still called "The New Scholasticism," though a strong movement has been afoot for some time to get rid of the word "Scholasticism" in its title.

Scholastic philosophy in the nineteen-twenties, however, will remember that what this wording meant against the then-prevailing background was thoroughly different. There was only one real philosophy, and that was Scholasticism;[14] and there was only one real Scholasticism, and that was the systematized Thomism of the commentators and of the theologically managed[15] textbook tradition in the nineteenth and early twentieth centuries. "Philosophy" meant that one system. All the rest came under "history of philosophy."[16] The field of philosophy was essentially covered by the systematized Thomism. Elsewhere and widely scattered were detached bits of truth, of which the owners might be legitimately despoiled[17] in the interests of a more

14. "Scholasticism, which we hold to be the true philosophy . . ." J. A. Baisnée, art. cit., *Proceedings* 1, p. 64. Cf. "La scolastique, précisément parce qu'elle est la vraie philosophie . . ." J. Maritain, *Antimoderne*, p. 111; see also ibid., p. 102.

15. See G. Smith, "Note sur l'avenir de la philosophie catholique," in *L'homme devant Dieu*, Mélanges H. de Lubac (Paris: Aubier, 1964), p. 284, n. 9. So, in retrospect: "I believe that the Church's mind in this matter can be stated in four propositions: 1) The first is the affirmation of a specifically Catholic Philosophy, which is the only true philosophy; . . . 4) The fourth is that the principal representative and the greatest teacher of this Catholic Philosophia Perennis is St. Thomas Aquinas . . .," R. F. Harvanek, "The Church and Scholasticism," *Proceedings* 32 (1958), 221. At the time of the organizational meeting, it was phrased, "There can be no question that, in the intellect of St. Thomas Aquinas, the Scholastic synthesis attained its highest and most complete realization." F. P. Siegfried, art. cit. *Proceedings* 1, p. 22.

16. A recollection of the manuals used in seminaries at the time is enough to make this clear. One manual, e.g., Lortie, was used for "Philosophy." Another, e.g., Turner, was used for "History of Philosophy." The notion back of this division was clearly expressed by Maritain: "Le caractère humain et collectif de la philosophie, . . . c'est dans la doctrine thomiste qu'il est réalisé. Par son universalité même . . . elle ne s'oppose pas aux systèmes modernes comme le passé à l'actuellement donné, mais comme l'éviternel au momentané." *Antimoderne*, p. 16. ". . . fragments détachés et périssables, ou brille un instant quelque parcelle de vrai . . . C'est pourquoi l'Eglise, connaissant la nature humaine, a toujours pris soin de protéger, selon la mesure de la prudence, et quelque prédilection qu'elle ait manifestée pour la doctrine de saint Thomas, qui est *sa doctrine propre*, la diversité des écoles philosophiques et théologiques." Ibid., pp. 18–19. Cf.: "systems which have their brief vogue, and are then committed to a merciful oblivion." F. V. Corcoran, art. cit., *Proceedings* 1, p. 34. In practice: "Mos est in Universitate Gregoriana, ut ultimo triennii philosophici anno Historia Philosophiae integra alumnis exponatur. . . . Quem agendi modum ipse scopus praescribit; hic est tum errores, qui in diversis partibus Cursus philosophici accuratam crisim obtinuerunt, tum veritates, quae ibidem ordine methodico propositae fuerunt atque probatae, iam in sua historica evolutione exhibere . . ." P. Geny, *Brevis conspectus historiae philosophiae* (Rome: Univ. Gregoriana, 1921), p. iii. Similarly, the study of the vicissitudes of Scholastic philosophy "maiorem persuasionem in mentibus discipulorum generabit, quanti momenti sit Philosophiae perenni firmiter adhaerere . . ." Ibid., p. iv.

17. Metaphor from Exod. 3.22; 12.36. See Maritain, *Antimoderne*, p. 113, for an instance of its use against the background of St. Justin Martyr and St. Augustine. Cf.: "Au contraire, toutes ces parcelles de vérité, disséminées dans l'innombrable quantité des systèmes philosophiques, et grâce auxquelles ces doctrines peuvent réussir pour un temps et gagner des adhérents, le Thomisme les absorbe et les assimile, les purifiant et en faisant ressortir la réelle valeur." P. Woroniecki, "Catholicité du Thomisme," *Revue thomiste* 26 (1921), 322.

appropriate place in the Thomistic synthesis. That was the import of the "special emphasis on Scholastic philosophy" in the original phrasing. The whole formula meant that the one system was mighty enough to absorb the incomparably lesser truths of all other systems, and that this process allowed what was worthwhile in the whole "field of philosophy" to lie waiting for absorption under the "special emphasis." That was what was understood by "the field of philosophy, with special emphasis on Scholastic philosophy." To the formula "One lord, one faith,"[18] the addition of "one philosophy" seemed to have been implicitly made.

This can be minutely documented.[19] Such was in fact the monochromatic lens through which the project of Scholasticism in the modern world was viewed at the inaugural meeting of the association. Today is there not keen sensitivity to the danger in a situation where one good custom would soon corrupt the world? Is there not militant awareness of the myriad approaches for profound and fruitful philosophic thought that are offered by the multivalent objects of human cognition? Can any sense be made today of the notion that all genuine philosophy is to be concentrated in a single system? Yet is this reflection, alone, enough to dismiss without further consideration the vision of our founders? Or is there still a possibility that a more circumspect approach may dissipate the monochrome and allow the object of their

18. Eph. 4.5. Cf. supra, n. 15.
19. "L'immense valeur du Thomisme aux yeux de l'Eglise, consiste précisement en ce qu'il n'est pas la doctrine d'un homme, mais la synthèse de la pensée humaine . . . Car dire Thomisme, ne veut pas dire la doctrine de tel homme qui s'appelait Thomas d'Aquin; mais la doctrine du genre humain élaborée pendant des siècles de réflexion" Woroniecki, art. cit., pp. 353–54. This was accordingly identified with Christian philosophy: "la philosophie thomiste ou la philosophie chrétienne" Maritain, *Antimoderne*, p. 98; "Saint Thomas seul apparaît aujourd'hui comme le représentant par excellence de la philosophie chrétienne," ibid., p. 110; "la *philosophia perennis* qui est la philosophie de l'Eglise," p. 126. Thomism, consequently, was Scholasticism in its purest form: "[E]n disant philosophie scolastique nous pensons à l'expression la plus pure et la plus universelle, la seule indéficiente, de la scolastique—à la philosophie thomiste," Maritain, ibid., p. 23; "la philosopie thomiste, c'est-à-dire la philosophie scolastique dans toute sa pureté formelle," p. 127. The notion of Scholastic philosophy as a single system culminating in Thomism had been spread by M. de Wulf, *Histoire de la philosophie médiévale* (Louvain: Institut Supérieur de Philosophie, 1900), pp. 288–90. De Wulf, in "Qu'est-ce que la philosophie scolastique?" *Revue néo-scolastique* 5 (1898), 293, stressed the "unité du système scolastique." For him, "Scholasticism is the *philosophia perennis* of the Western World," in the sense that it "is not a work that is ever finished,"—"Cardinal Mercier: Philosopher," *The New Scholasticism* 1 (1927), 14. Carried down to the level of seminary teaching, however, this unfinished aspect could easily be forgotten; e.g. "As a body of principles, Scholasticism was completed once for all by Thomas Aquinas in the 13 century; it is for modern Scholastics, or Neo-Scholastics, to apply these principles in the interpretation of the data of physical science." P. J. Glenn, *The History of Philosophy* (St. Louis: B. Herder, 1941), p. 359.

intuition, Scholasticism, to be seen in a yet fuller splendor of multi-colored and variegated meaning? In a word, did the object that really inspired our founders depend upon the systematized Thomism in which they expressed it? And is there not still among us a tendency, unconscious yet much more unpardonable after all these years, to identify the one with the other?

Our founders, in their pioneer efforts, had no independent background of their own to rely upon. They had no choice but to accept the then-current European interpretation of Scholasticism. In spite of their attachment to this systematized product of later centuries, however, they envisaged their work as based upon the spirit and texts of the great medieval Scholastics.[20] Their ultra-direct intuition penetrated that far, obscured though the vision was by the ephemeral monochromatic medium. The publication of those original texts was already under way.[21] The progress was slow, and has continued to be slow. But what happened when people followed the advice and delved critically into the medieval texts as they were made available? Was the advocated system found more deeply developed within them? Far from it. In the texts, rather, there is no *system* of philosophy at all.[22] They are texts of theologians, containing profound philosophical discussions of themes integral to theological teaching, or else commentaries on ancient philosophical treatises, and monographs on special philosophical subjects, but all geared to theological interests.[23] Of a

20. "Our first task, therefore, is to provide for ourselves and offer to others an accurate statement of what the Schoolmen taught. . . . It is only by going to sources that we can get the genuine spirit and letter of Scholasticism." E. A. Pace, "Inaugural Address," *Proceedings* 1, p. 15.

21. E.g., in critical editions like that of Quaracchi (1882–1902) for St. Bonaventure, and the Leonine (1882-) for St. Thomas Aquinas, and in series like the *Beiträge zur Geschichte der Philosophie des Mittelalters* (Münster, 1891-) and *Archives d'histoire doctrinale et littéraire du moyen âge* (Paris, 1926-).

22. On philosophical "system," see G. B. Phelan, "The Existentialism of St. Thomas," *Proceedings* 21 (1946), 25–26, n. 1. Cf.: "It was necessary to wait for Francis Suarez to "pull out" from the composite work a distinct system of philosophy." R. F. Harvanek, art. cit., *Proceedings* 32 (1958), pp. 222–23. So P. Duhem, *Le système du monde* (Paris: Hermann, 1913–59), 5, 569, could see no philosophical doctrine or synthesis in the writings of St. Thomas Aquinas. Yet the notion of a scholastic system or synthesis pervaded the mentality of the ACPA organization meeting: e.g. "First, then, we might survey metaphysics, that is, Ontology as a whole: as a relatively completed structure in the form it possesses in the Neo-Scholastic synthesis. From the system thus viewed . . ." P. Siegfried, art. cit., *Proceedings* 1, p. 19; cf. pp. 19–20. "A well-formed system of philosophy, such as Scholasticism" A. M. Schwitalla, art. cit., *Proceedings* 1, p. 50; cf. pp. 54 and 56.

23. For an explanation of this subordination in terms of intellectual habits, see A. C. Pegis, "Sub Ratione Dei: A Reply to Professor Anderson," *The New Scholasticism* 39 (1965), 141–57. As understood by Victor Cousin, *Histoire générale de la philosophie*, 9th ed. (Paris: Didier, 1872) pp. 218–25, the subordination rendered genuine philosophy impossible. For Cousin, accordingly, there were only two epochs of philosophy, ancient

comprehensive philosophy organized in its own right there is not a trace. The notion of a system of philosophy, so familiar since the time of Descartes,[24] just does not emerge from the original Scholastic texts. Philosophical discussion there is in abundance, but no system.

Nor is there any monolithic character to the philosophical thinking in the texts. The thought is radically pluralistic, and widely so. You are in different philosophical worlds as you read Anselm, Abelard, Bonaventure, Aquinas, Henry of Ghent, Duns Scotus, Ockham, to mention only a few. Agreement in vocabulary, even when present, does not affect the profound philosophic pluralism. The distinction between being and essence has a different meaning and is a different problem in Aquinas, for instance, on the one hand, and on the other in Giles of Rome.[25] The same holds for individuality and common nature in Aquinas and Duns Scotus.[26] The notion of a monolithic Scholastic philosophy—rising through the middle ages, reaching its perfection in Thomas Aquinas, and present in varying degrees of proximity in the others—is but a Neoscholastic myth.

Notwithstanding its radical and wide-ranged pluralism, however, there is a distinctive mentality that pervades the medieval scholastic thinking and gives it a clearly recognizable character, making it consistently differ from ancient thought as well as from the philosophies that have arisen in the wake of René Descartes. It does not offer itself as a salvation,[27] or as a closed and fully satisfying explanation of reality. This negative aspect is of course in solidarity with the theological setting in which medieval thought was cast. But the aspect has an important philosophical role. Realistically it permits philosophy, regardless of sapiential cast and universal embrace, to view itself modestly as one discipline or group of disciplines among a number of others,[28] and as one occupation and one intellectual preference among

---

and modern; see *Cours de philosophie* (Paris: L. Hachette, 1836), p. 1. Aside from these interpretations, however, the presumption is that the medieval writers meant what they said when they distinguished themselves from the "philosophers." Many of their treatises, such as the *De ente et essentia* of St. Thomas, may be read today as philosophy; and their writings on logic were meant to be instrumental to scientific knowledge in general. Nevertheless, it is not hard to show that their overall and dominating view was that of the theologian.

24. See É. Gilson, *The Unity of Philosophical Experience* (New York, 1937), pp. 179; 317.

25. See J. Owens, "The Number of Terms in the Suarezian Discussion of Essence and Being," *The Modern Schoolman* 34 (1957), 161–91.

26. See J. Owens, "Common Nature: A Point of Comparison between Thomistic and Scotistic Metaphysics," *Mediaeval Studies* 19 (1957), 1–4.

27. Cf. supra, n. 3.

28. Even the most all-embracing of scientific subjects, being, does not make the subject of any other science a part of the subject of metaphysics: "Unde proprie lo-

many. It allows no room for a philosopher-king, who would function above all tradition and all sentiment and all law, and would use philosophy alone to obliterate the evils of mankind. Further, philosophizing is seen to consist in "the plain hard work of demonstration,"[29] guided more or less obtrusively by the logic of the trivium. Finally, Scholastic philosophizing is characterized by the methodic subordination of speech to thought and of thought to sensible things.[30] It keeps *things* basic, sees them expressed in thought, and sees the thought about them expressed in speech. It involves no philosophic knowledge of spirit that is freed from the matrix of sensible experience, no plaguing subjectivity that escapes the controls of sensible reality and common traditional culture, no essential submission of philosophic thought to the laws of vocabulary.[31] This combination of characteristics gives a distinctive mold to Scholastic philosophical thinking, and suffices to set it apart from all other kinds of philosophy.

Was that distinctive concept of Scholasticism the real object of our founders' intuition? And is it a way of thinking that can serve as basic philosophy for our own age? Can we gaze upon it today with the enthusiasm of forty years ago? Or may not our vision of the same object, because more comprehensive, be even deeper and therefore much more modest, yet just as challenging and just as inspiring? These questions come under the general topic of our present meeting. For example, may not an epistemology based on the Scholastic texts explain the place and role and order of the marvelously developed modern sciences without attempting to be part of their work? Is not the logic in the medieval texts capable of using to the full the multiple and highly precisioned tools of the modern logics? Is not the natural philosophy of those texts able to be at home in an evolving universe? Can their metaphysics not underwrite the dynamic and currently stressed historicity of real existence? Are not their ethical principles equal to the task of functioning satisfactorily in complex modern cultures?

Negative answers to these questions have in no way become imper-

---

quendo subiectum illius non est pars subiecti metaphysicae; non enim est pars entis secundum illam rationem, qua ens est subiectum metaphysicae, . . ." Aquinas, *In Boeth. de Trin.* 5.1.ad 6m; ed. B. Decker, p. 171.20–24. Philosophy is not a master key to other doors.

29. Mortimer J. Adler, "The Demonstration of God's Existence," *The Thomist* 5 (1943), 189.

30. This order of things, thought, and speech is fundamental to Aristotelian method in philosophy; see Aristotle, *De interpretatione* 1.16a39.

31. Because things are so basic throughout the range of Scholastic thinking, it is hard to see how any of the numerous attempts to approach the Scholastics from viewpoints of phenomenology or linguistic analysis can hope to be successful.

ative. Positive answers we have not as yet established. But we do know enough not to look for any ready-made answers in the Scholastic texts themselves. We have to read the texts carefully, consider things under their guidance and inspiration, let them grow into a living matrix for our thinking, and with their aid give birth to our own philosophy. Here the anger becomes acute. Progress and development require cross-fertilization, the enlivening of old stock through the infusion of newer blood, the careful avoidance of inbreeding. This demands all the skill and professional knowledge of the expert. If added blood types are incompatible they will clash hopelessly, enervate the vital processes, and bring speedy dissolution. Wrongly placed injection of nucleic fluids will give rise to cancerous strains of cell-growth that will run wild and destroy the philosophical organism. Indiscriminate mixing of Husserl or Heidegger or Whitehead or Russell or Wittgenstein with the Scholastic notions will have the same disastrous effects as the earlier Neoscholastic attempts to incorporate Descartes or Wolff or Kant.[32] Yet the thinking inspired by the Scholastic texts today has to be done in a world colored by all those philosophers. The blazing splendor of reality has to be faced and probed as it is radiated through the fullness of preceding as well as contemporary thought, regardless of provenance.

This is hard work, and dangerous work. In Joyce Kilmer's lines:

It is stern work, it is perilous work, to thrust your hand in the sun,
And pull out a spark of immortal flame to warm the hearts of men.[33]

Yet that work is ours. To get into orbit in philosophy, we need the booster and control rockets of centuries-long thought. A human life span is just not geared to philosophic needs. It is long enough for growth to physical maturity, for bringing up children in one's own ethos, and for the final attempts at spoiling the grandchildren. But for a philosophic life, a span of seventy, eighty, or ninety odd years is ridiculously short. The work of the past becomes indispensable.[34] Even Descartes, who claimed to be starting anew and making philosophy the work of one mind,[35] is far from an illustration of his own claim.[36]

32. On some of these attempts, see É. Gilson, *Réalisme thomiste et critique de la connaissance*, pp. 50–212.

33. "The Proud Poet," in *Joyce Kilmer*, ed. R. C. Holliday (New York: George H. Doran, 1918), 1, 135–36.

34. See Aristotle's reflections, *Metaph.* 2.1.993b11–19.

35. *Discours de la méthode*, 6e partie; A–T, 6, 72.16–19. Cf. 2e partie; pp. 12.25–13.1.

36. On the Scholastic roots, see É. Gilson, *Etudes sur le rôle de la pensée médiévale dans la formation du système cartésien* (Paris: J. Vrin, 1930).

Like it or not, the natural shortness of human life makes us dependent on preceding thinkers. The only choice is which of them to make basic for our own development.[37]

There are many of us in the association today who are just as ardently convinced as its founders, perhaps more so, that the texts of the medieval Scholastics are eminently suitable for this need. There is now no question of going back to Scholasticism to find an organized philosophy. In that sense there never has been a genuine Scholastic philosophy and there is nothing to go back to. It is a question of going forward to Scholasticism, forward to philosophy that has not yet seen the light of day.[38] It is a question of taking the texts, living their spirit, using their riches, and under their guidance, their inspiration, working out philosophies that will be both full-blown and modern. For those of us who think this way, the admirable intuition of our founders remains intact in its splendor. It is even more brilliant when viewed in our multicolored pluralistic approach than in the seemingly straightforward and unsophisticated vision of forty years ago. Rid of the enervating monochrome, our members who think this way wish to continue working out the original intuition of our founders into the important influences that philosophy exercises in present-day thought and life. It is hard work, it is perilous work. But it is a challenge, and a challenge to be creative. It is work that will continue to give distinctive character to our association and accredit the association with a worthwhile function among the various philosophical societies of our land. This special characterization, moreover, has not, in the experience of these members, proven any impediment to dialogue. Rather, it has more frequently been an entrance card.

There are numbers of us, however, who think differently, whether from cherished interests of contemporary dialogue or from divergent philosophical bents. Even from the viewpoint of our founders' intuition, dissident views are always necessary for the health and survival of the association's project. More quickly even than the world, would an association such as ours be corrupted by the tyranny of one good custom. Within the ambit of the association's original intuition, a thriving Scholasticism needs continuous cross-fertilization from other philosophical tenets professed with conviction by thinkers within the

37. See É. Gilson, *History of Philosophy and Philosophical Education* (Milwaukee: Marquette University Press, 1948), pp. 21–28.
38. Cf.: "I hope indeed that the fragmentation of St. Thomas has come to an end. I hope that we shall undertake to build our own Christian philosophy, not by detaching fragments from his theology, but by risking our own intellectual lives in the world of today." A. C. Pegis, *St. Thomas and Philosophy* (Milwaukee: Marquette University Press, 1964), p. 88.

association itself. Present discontent with the external program of our founders is the result of progress. With only the then-extant European literature to guide them, our founders identified Scholasticism with the systematized Thomism of their day. Thanks in large part to their pioneer efforts, we have forty years of our own work now to show us differently. As interested and dedicated members, we all wish to take the course that will give maximum service to the association. That course will continue to be decided in true democratic fashion, according to the association's well-established tradition. The successful outcome of democratic procedure, however, rests on the clear thinking done by each of the individuals, coupled with the initiative and energy to have this thinking represented in the common decisions. The intuition of our founders was deep, deeper than they themselves were able to express. It deserves careful consideration before it is changed or abandoned. It should not be missed through concentration on individual trees that have long since lost all life. We should try to understand it in depth. In Msgr. Pace's words, it means that "the basic ideas of Scholasticism are living truths—firm . . . yet flexible."[39] It means that they are a comprehensive, penetrating, and inspiring school for sound, well-balanced philosophy. Whether or not we are now in agreement with that intuition, whether or not we wish to continue in its wake, the most philosophically appropriate tribute we can pay the revered founders of our association, on this fortieth anniversary of their pioneer achievement, is to *understand* what they were doing.

39. Supra, n. 2. Cf.: "the precious heritage of the great Christian thinkers of east and west, among whom the name of St. Augustine shines with a special lustre. The natural study of being and truth, as the faithful service of the word of God, is certainly not the exclusive prerogative of the Angelic Doctor." Pope Paul VI, "Address to the Thomistic Congress," trans. St. Thomas Aquinas Foundation, New York, in *The New Scholasticism* 40 (1966), 82–83. On the method for this "study of being and truth" in our own day, the reflections of A. C. Pegis, art. cit. (supra, n. 23), p. 145, deserve note: "I thought that the undertaking was possible if, in reading St. Thomas, we read as theology what he wrote as theology and *then* undertook on our own responsibility and in our own name, to develop a philosophy using his principles." Cf.: "Being guided into philosophy and theology by St. Thomas as the teacher, we could in turn become teachers and teach others, and perhaps become competent philosophers and theologians." John A. Oesterle, "St. Thomas as Teacher: A Reply to Professor Pegis," *The New Scholasticism* 39 (1965), 466. The need of competent present-day Scholastic literature becomes painfully apparent when one is asked to match in a college reading list the imposing array of the classics of analytical philosophy that are so readily available.

6

CHRISTIAN CONSCIENCE VS. ARISTOTELIAN RIGHT REASON

I

The phrase "right reason," in the sense of the basic general norm for morality, makes its earliest documented appearance in the treatises of Aristotle. In them it is presented without qualm as the commonly accepted designation for the standard or measure of goodness in human conduct.[1] Whether by this common acceptance Aristotle meant agreement within his own circle of hearers, or whether he was indicating a general prevalence that has left no other written record, is today difficult if not impossible to determine. In any case, the copious Platonic discussions on moral topics do not attest any notable adherence to the expression "right reason" for the function attributed to it by the Stagirite.[2] Instances of its use in this sense in other contemporary documents are lacking. The result is that its definitely known history begins only in the Aristotelian corpus. From that time on, however, it had a continuous and fruitful career down to the eighteenth century.[3] In that century the adjective "right" was dropped,

---

1. Aristotle, *Nicomachean Ethics*, 2.2.1103b31–32. The Apostle translation seems quite interpretation-free: "Now to *act* according to right reason is commonly accepted, and let it be assumed here." Irwin translates: "First, then, actions should express correct reason. That is a common [belief], and let us assume it." But the meaning in the Greek is not just that actions should *express* correct reason. It is their *performance* according to right reason that is at issue. Instead of right "reason," others have "rule" (Ross) or "principle" (Rackham). On this see infra, n. 15.

2. On this topic, see Karl Bärthlein, "Der ὀρθὸς λόγος und das ethische Grundprinzip in den platonischen Schriften," *Archiv für Geschichte der Philosophie* 46 (1964), 129–73. The Platonic instances are collected and analyzed on pp. 130–36. For the opposite view, see Ingemar Düring, "Aristotle on Ultimate Principles from 'Nature and Reality'; *Protrepticus Fr. 13*," in *Aristotle and Plato in the Mid-Fourth Century*, ed. Ingemar Düring and G. E. L. Owen (Göteborg: Studia graeca et latina Gothoburgensia, 11, 1960), pp. 36–37.

3. See Bärthlein, "Der 'ΟΡΘΟΣ ΛΟΓΟΣ' der *Grossen Ethik* des *Corpus Aristotelicum*," *AGP* 45 (1963), 213–58. I have not seen the typescript of J. Roeben, "De recta ratio in

quite in conformity with the Enlightenment, the Age of Reason. Reason, by the very fact that it was reason, had to be right.[4] The adjective was thereby rendered superfluous. In the Scholastic tradition, nevertheless, the phrase *recta ratio* continued to be used on into the twentieth century as the translation of the Aristotelian *ho orthos logos*, though without any very special emphasis on or concern for its original Greek background.

Yet the meaning of "right reason" as the norm of moral goodness had been made very clear in Aristotle. For him, choice is the origin of moral conduct.[5] In contrast to an object of theoretical study, which is determined by a stable essence in the order of being, an object of practical knowledge has nothing morally specified or definite prior to human choice.[6] Its basic characterization as good or evil is set up by its relation to a thoroughly flexible norm that is appropriate to free conduct. This norm is right reason. If what is chosen is in accord with right reason, the action is morally good. If chosen in opposition to right reason, the action is morally evil. Right reason becomes in that way the basic general norm by which the correct is distinguished from the erroneous in the moral order.

The formula "right reason" was carefully chosen. Reason directs characteristically human activity, parallel to the way sense and instinct guide performance on the animal level. On both levels the appetitive follows upon the cognitive, in proportional fashion. Accordingly, the appetite based upon reason is of its nature rational, and calls for guidance by reason. But with reason, as even a slight amount of experience testifies, error is not only possible but is also frequent in both the speculative and the practical orders. The mention of reason alone,

---

de *Ethica Nicomachea* en de *Magna Moralia*," Louvain diss. (1949). On the subsequent history of *recta ratio*, see Bärthlein, "Zur Lehre von der 'recta ratio' in der Geschichte der Ethik von der Stoa bis Christian Wolff," *Kant-Studien* 56 (1965), 125–55. For its more modern versions, see William K. Frankena, "The Ethics of Right Reason," *The Monist* 66 (1983), 22–23.

4. "Additur quidem vulgo, quod sit dictamen rectae rationis; sed per modum pleonismi: ratio enim non est, quae recta non est." Christian Wolff, *Philosophia practica universalis* 1.5.456; (Frankfurt: Off. Lib. Rengeriana, 1738), p. 351.

5. "The origin of action—its efficient, not its final cause—is choice, and that of choice is desire and reasoning with a view to an end." *EN* 6.2.1139a31–33; Ross trans. Cf. 3.5.1113b17–19. "Action" (*praxis*) in this context means human conduct, something that the lower animals do not share (1139a19–20). On the substantial level the man (*anthrōpos—De an.* 1.4.408b14–15) is the cause. On the level of faculties, choice is the efficient cause, with formal causality through reason and final causality through desire.

6. "The general account being of this nature, the account of particular cases is yet more lacking in exactness; for they do not fall under any art or precept but the agents themselves must in each case consider what is appropriate to the occasion, as happens also in the art of medicine or of navigation." *EN* 2.2.1104a5–10; Ross trans. Cf. 1.3.1094b12–16.

regardless of Wolff (supra, n. 4), is not enough to ensure the correctness of a judgment.

To be right in the speculative order, a judgment has to accord with existing reality. The judgment that Socrates is pale is correct if Socrates has that color in actual fact. The determination of the color is found first in the person or thing.[7] On the other hand, to be correct in the productive arts or crafts the agent's activity and its product must conform to a design or plan already existent in the mind of the producer.[8] To be rightly constructed, a house will have to be built in accord with the architect's blueprints. The determination is present first in a human mind. But it is a definite determination, based upon the nature of the thing to be produced. If the product is to be a house, the designing proceeds in conformity with the requirements of a dwelling place. An already fixed essence is there to determine the planning.

But for Aristotle there is in practical matters no essential determination prior to an agent's choice. There is nothing fixed in the nature of physical things that would specify the action as right or wrong. The physical act of taking human life, for instance, can be either morally good or morally evil. When necessary in defense of country, or for maintaining public order in the face of crime, it may be regarded as morally good. What, then, determines whether a particular act is right or wrong? For the Stagirite there was no Stoic law of nature or Christian divine law already established and able to serve as guide or pattern to which human conduct is obliged to conform. Neither in the real world nor in any intellect is the pattern already set. The moral mean that makes an action right has to be determined in each case according to the circumstances of the moment by the practically wise agent, the *phronimos*.[9] The *phronimos*, the individual man trained in the virtues, determines it on the basis of conformity to his own freely acquired habituation. Only then is there, with Aristotle, a norm for judging whether an action is morally good or morally evil.

The meaning of the term "moral" comes to the fore in this conception. In it the habituation or *mores* of the agent will ground the standard by which the quality of the characteristically human action is determined. Hence Aristotle insists strongly and repeatedly on the necessity of correct moral training or upbringing from earliest years.[10]

7. See *Metaph.* 9.10.1051a34–b9. Cf. *Int.* 9.18a33–b2.

8. See *Metaph.* 6.1.1025b22–23; 11.7.1064a11–13. Cf. 12.3.1070a13–15.

9. "[Ethical] virtue, then, is a habit, disposed towards *action* by deliberate choice, being at the mean relative to us, and defined by reason and as a prudent man would define it." *EN* 2.6.1106b36–1107a2; Apostle trans.

10. *EN* 2.1.1103b21–25. Cf. 10.1.1172a19–25; 9.1179b29–35.

The virtues are habits that essentially involve choice (supra, n. 9). They are brought about through the repeated performance of free acts. When the habituation is properly developed the agent is in a position to judge with truth and certainty whether or not an action conforms to it. Action in accord with it is seen to be morally right. Action opposed to it is seen to be morally wrong.[11] But this aspect of right or wrong comes into being only on the basis of relation to correct moral habituation, an habituation formed through freely chosen acts. Human choice, in consequence, is for Aristotle the origin of the whole moral order. The choice is not determined by anything that has gone before it, no matter how persuasive or influential the preceding factors may have been. If those antecedent causes had *determined* it, it could no longer be regarded as free.

In deciding what is in accord with his or her correct habituation, the practically wise person takes into consideration not only the nature of the act in question, but also all the accidents and circumstances of the situation, down to the last relevant detail. He or she weighs them all in the relations they bear to one another, and to the agent as a free cause. If the action conforms to correct habituation it has a profound intrinsic appeal that is expressed by the Greek term *kalon,* the word for "beautiful." The morally good act exercises proportionally the appeal that the beautiful engenders. But, over and above, it carries with the appeal the obligation to act in accord with it. In this way the *kalon* provides not only the motivation for morally good conduct, but also its obligatory character.[12]

Further, since the moral agent is aware that on account of his choice he himself is the origin of his free acts, fully as a parent is the origin of children, he sees thereby that he is responsible for what he has begotten.[13] But there is no hint of responsibility to any outside tribunal

11. "[S]ince moral virtue is a state of character concerned with choice, and choice is deliberate desire, therefore both the reasoning must be true and the desire right, if the choice is to be good, and the latter must pursue just what the former asserts. Now this kind of intellect and truth is practical; . . . of the part which is practical and intellectual the good state is truth in agreement with right desire." *EN* 6.2.1139a22–31; Ross trans. "State of character" translates the Greek *hexis* (a22), in the sense of moral habituation, and correct habituation is what makes the desire "right." The comparison between the two kinds of truth is meant to show that while speculative truth means conformity of one's judgment with reality, practical truth means conformity of the judgment with correct habituation.

12. The role of the *kalon* as the motive and the source of obligation for morally good conduct in Aristotle is discussed in my article "The ΚΑΛΟΝ in the Aristotelian *Ethics,*" in *Studies in Aristotle,* ed. Dominic J. O'Meara (Washington, D.C.: Catholic University of America Press, 1981), pp. 261–77.

13. *EN* 3.5.1113b7–21. At b25 *aitioi* has clearly enough the meaning of "responsible," and is so translated by Ross, Rackham, Irwin, and at b30 by Apostle. It is what the context, with its emphasis on the fact that the action is within one's power, requires.

or judge. Along with the motivation and the obligatory character of the act, the responsibility is grounded solely on the aspect of the *kalon*. It remains within the *kalon*. The *kalon* in its highest instance, the *kalliston*, constitutes the supreme happiness or *eudaimonia* of mankind.[14] But as first known to human cognition, the *kalon* is seen in individual actions that conform to correct moral habituation, with "right reason" as name for the form or design or constitutive character (Latin *ratio*, Greek *logos*) of an action so chosen. A morally good action in the Aristotelian setting is an action constituted by right reason understood in this sense. Its moral goodness requires no other explanation. Right reason, finally, turns out to be identical with human prudence or practical wisdom. It is the Greek *phronesis*, the Latin *prudentia*.[15]

However, even though the individual human agent makes the decisive moral judgment on the basis of his own particular habituation, the Aristotelian conception of morality envisages genuine universality for the *kalon*. The Stagirite's ethical doctrine is not a relativism. It (*EN* 2.6.1107a9–25) upholds, for instance, that stealing and adultery and murder are always wrong. Anyone correctly brought up, it implies, makes the same moral judgment in regard to these acts, no matter how much his or her individual propensities may vary. Every practically wise person, whether vigorous or feeble, will judge that a large amount of food is temperate for an athlete, but a much smaller

---

14. *EN* 1.8.1099a24–27; cf. 9,1099b22–24; 1101a2–5; *EE* 1.1.1214a5–8.

15. "But we must go a little further, for virtue is a habit not only according to right reason, but also with right reason; and right reason about such things is prudence." *EN* 6.13.1144b25–28; Apostle trans. The explicit identification of right reason with prudence or practical wisdom does away with the question whether Aristotle meant a faculty or a standard by the phrase "right reason." The faculty in its correct act *is* the standard. In the basic English commentary, John Alexander Stewart, *Notes on the* Nicomachean Ethics *of Aristotle* (Oxford: Clarendon Press, 1892), 1, 173, advised against the translation "right reason," on the ground that in the phrase the term "reason" has a wider sense than that of a faculty. Yet (p. 174) he acknowledges that there is here only a logical, and not a real, distinction between the two notions in Aristotle. Continental scholars have noted the subsequent tendency in anglophones to translate the phrase in the sense of standard or principle. In the *Eudemian Ethics* (1222a9; b7; 1227b17; 1231b33) J. Solomon's translation "right reason" is however allowed to stand in Jonathan Barnes's revision, though Michael Woods uses "right principle" for the first two passages, with "renders reason correct" for the third. The important point here is that the translation be free from any insinuation of an operative distinction between right reason and practical wisdom in Aristotle. His way of identifying the two has not, in fact, been entirely forgotten in modern writing, e.g.: "However, 'right reason' itself in the active sphere of moral life is prudence" –Kevin T. Kelly, *Conscience: Dictator or Guide?* (London: Geoffrey Chapman, 1967), p. 180. The identity of the two in Aristotle is recognized by Aquinas: "Et ideo *prudentia* quae in eis dirigit, dicitur in VI *Eth.* . . . *recta ratio agibilium*"—*Sent.* 3.23.1.4.qa 1, ad 4m; ed. Mandonnet-Moos, 3, 713 (no. 85). "*prudentia* . . . est directiva moralium virtutum, cum sit '*recta ratio agibilium*,' sicut dictum est." Ibid., qa.2, ad 3m; 3, 714 (no. 93).

amount for a weakling (*EN* 2.6.1107b1–8). Often this conformity with right reason is intuitively grasped. At other times it requires long and painstaking deliberation. It has to give consideration to the natures involved in the persons, things, relations, and circumstances that enter into the issues. But the end result is the determination that anyone with the proper habituation would make in regard to the same agent in the same particular situation. In this way genuine universality is guaranteed. The agent thereby learns to recognize moral goodness first in individual acts, and from them to see the *kalon* extended universally to all morally good actions.[16] But in no case could it be extended to something contrary to right reason.

The universality, however, is not cold or merely speculative in its application. Rather, it is something deeply felt, penetrating thoroughly the sensitive and rational appetites of the individual, and emitting everywhere an appealing warmth and glow. Right reason accordingly extends the aspect of the *kalon* through the whole of the individual's morally correct activity, and with empathy throughout the globally extensive range of human conduct.[17] It is profoundly universal, even though it does not base itself on anything beyond the natural reach of the human mind. Aristotle's moral optimism did not question in principle the power of human reason to bring to perfection the moral order it itself had generated.[18] In fact, a point to be stressed in the present issue is that the mutual involvement of the virtues (*EN* 6.13.1144b30–1145a5) requires Aristotelian right reason to mean conformity with perfect habituation by them all.

II

Obviously this is a very different explanation of morality from that of Christian tradition. The prospect of a life after bodily death, with accountability to a supreme and personal judge, does not enter into its consideration. Nor is there in it any notion of a natural or divine law anteceding human choice, or of a bond of filial love for a heavenly father. Esteem and respect for the *kalon* regulate everything in the Aristotelian moral order.

16. See *EN* 1.4.1095a32b13. The fact is first known (b6), the "reason why" comes later. The same procedure holds for Aristotle in speculative matters, *Apo.* 2.19. 100a1–b5.

17. Accordingly, John Herman Randall, Jr., *Aristotle* (New York: Columbia University Press, 1960), p. 248, can note that the Aristotelian ethical method can be applied to any culture, "to Soviet Russia, to medieval Christendom, to India, to New York City."

18. Aquinas, in his commentary on the *Nicomachean Ethics,* introduces the moral order as "ordo quem ratio considerando facit in operationibus voluntatis"—*Sent. Eth.* 1.1.21–22; Leonine ed., 47, 4. It is an order that reason *produces.*

For Christian belief, moreover, the Aristotelian ethics cannot help but remain circular. Its "right reason" depends upon correct upbringing. But correct upbringing depends in turn upon correct moral norms already possessed for its regulation. For Aristotle this could hardly pose even a theoretical problem. Just as the eternal successions of generation and perishing had no beginning, so in the rise and fall of civilizations there was always a preceding culture that had left its remnants.[19] The question of an absolutely primitive temporal "before and after" played no role in this philosophizing. The moral principles were in fact already present in the life of the Greek *polis*. For the procedure of Aristotelian practical science, this was all that counted. But in Christian belief the world had a beginning in time. There were indeed *first* human beings, who had no previously existing human culture to fall back upon for their moral principles.

Further, even within the presently given situation, serious objection to the Aristotelian universalizing of the *kalon* will necessarily arise. The Christian belief in original sin poses great difficulty for the prospect of building a universally acceptable moral order upon the presently factual habituation of each individual.[20] Passions are too difficult to control, and reasoning in the moral order is too obscure. The supreme purpose of human life on earth, namely, the meriting of the eternal happiness in the beatific vision of God through grace, is not known on the strength of unaided human reason. Ideologies vary widely and deeply, each convinced that it itself is the right one. Practically there is in the state of fallen nature no possibility for every individual to make what appears right to him the course that is right for all, as Aristotle (*Metaph.* 7.3.1029b5–7) had projected in his own outlook.

The Stagirite, however, without knowing the cause, was well aware of the difficulties in this regard. For him the *phronimos* had to possess

19. *Metaph.* 12.8.1074b10–14; *Pol.* 7.10.1329b25–31. Cf. *Cael.* 1.3.270b19–20; *Mete.* 1.3.339b27–30.

20. Though the doctrine of original sin may appear to a psychiatrist as "low self-esteem," it actually means that human beings function on a level far above what is knowable to unaided reason. On this orientation see Henri de Lubac, *The Mystery of the Supernatural*, trans. Rosemary Sheed (London: Geoffrey Chapman, 1967). It has not gone unnoticed that de Lubac's explanation has proved more interesting for Catholic philosophers than for theologians. The doctrine of original sin shows why unaided human reason fails to provide adequate moral guidance, and how there can be invincible ignorance without personal fault. But for this an explanation on the supernatural level is required. Insufficient is a natural habituation, such as the one seemingly implied in: "The 'inheritance' of Adam's sin means rather that sin, after its entrance into the world, so spread that consequently all men are born into a sinful world and in this sinful world become themselves sinners." Herbert Haag, *Is Original Sin in Scripture?* trans. Dorothy Thompson (New York: Sheed and Ward, 1969), p. 106. Cf. pp. 73; 93; 97.

all the virtues in a perfect degree, each virtue reciprocally involving all the others, as noted above at the end of the preceding section. That was the condition for making the truly universal judgment of right reason. Yet Aristotle does not refer to any such perfect individual by name. Moreover, for him the general run of human beings do not come under the class of the virtuous, or even under the class of the self-controlled. They are located in between the self-controlled and the uncontrolled, tending more towards the latter.[21] The perfect moral habituation required for judgments of right reason is in point of fact nowhere to be found among men in their present state. Aristotle (*EN* 10.9.1180a15 ff.) urged good laws to educate a better generation. But from the Christian viewpoint much more is required. Nothing less than divine revelation can make manifest the truth of the human condition, and without the continued help of divine grace a virtuous life is not possible.

On these counts, then, Aristotelian right reason just in itself does not satisfy the requirements for moral life in the world as known through Christian faith. Something more is needed for the correct guidance of human conduct.

III

The notion "conscience" (*syneidesis*) had already played a role in post-Aristotelian philosophy.[22] Instead of centering on whether an action is in conformity with the course of nature or with the dignity of a human being, the question in the Christian context bore upon re-

21. *EN* 7.7.1150a15–16; 7.10.1152a25–27.

22. On the Greek background in the Epicureans, Cynics, and Stoics, see J. Dupont, "Syneidesis: Aux origines de la notion chrétienne de conscience morale," in *Studia hellenistica,* ed. L. Cerfaux et W. Peremans (Paris: G. P. Maisonneuve, 1948), pp. 126–46, and on the Christian notion of conscience as "un retournement complet," p. 153. Literature on the question whether the New Testament use of the term *syneidesis* stems from Stoic vocabulary or popular parlance is given in note on pp. 123–24. The understanding of conscience as involving immediate relation of a person to God is stressed by Vatican II: "Our conscience is our most secret core, and our sanctuary. There we are alone with God whose voice echoes in our depths." *Pastoral Constitution on the Church in the Modern World (Gaudium et Spes,* no. 16). On this concept of conscience "come sacrario dell'incontro dell' uomo con Dio da solo a solo" (p. 113), see Domenico Capone, "Antropologia, coscienza e pesonalità," *Studia Moralia* 4 (1966), 93–113, and Thomas Srampickal, *The Concept of Conscience in Today's Empirical Psychology and in the Documents of the Second Vatican Council* (Innsbruck: Resch, 1976), pp. 360–75. A general coverage of the notion and history of the topic may be found in Philippe Delahaye, *The Christian Conscience,* trans. Charles Underhill Quinn (New York: Desclée, 1968), with bibliography of studies directly concerned with conscience, pp. 13–18. A list of medieval texts on conscience is given in Timothy C. Potts, *Conscience in Medieval Philosophy* (Cambridge: University Press, 1980), pp. 137–39.

lation to a personal God, in fact to a God who is in the literal sense a loving father. To God human beings owe everything they are and have. Much more than that, through sanctifying grace they are re-born in baptism into God's own nature. In this way they are in full truth his tenderly loved offspring.[23] As the best of fathers, God takes the deepest interest in the lives and well-being of each human agent. With believers, reciprocally, sensitivity through grace will be high in regard to whatever may please or whatever may offend God. Acquaintance with his wisdom as made known by religious instruction and belief will inspire appropriate insights for conduct in accord with this filial love.

Further, from Christian belief there springs awareness that an account has to be given to God as supreme judge for everything thought, said, or done during life on earth, with sanctions of eternal reward or eternal punishment. So strong and compelling is this awareness that it has been able even to serve as the starting point of a moral proof for the existence of God. Cardinal Newman expressed the situation eloquently: "If, as is the case, we feel responsibility, are ashamed, are frightened, at transgressing the voice of conscience, this implies that there is One to whom we are responsible, before whom we are ashamed, whose claims upon us we fear."[24]

23. The fatherhood of God through grace is real. This is definitely not a metaphorical use of the term "father." Rather, from the viewpoint of the actual order of things it is the primary instance of fatherhood, from which all other instances take the name (Eph. 3.15, with *patria* in the Greek).

24. John Henry Newman, *A Grammar of Assent* (London: Longmans, Green, and Co., 1913), 1.5.1; p. 109. Newman aimed to "show how we apprehend him, not merely as a notion, but as a reality" (Ibid., p. 104). In a recent phenomenological approach this has been expressed as the question, "Can moral obligation shake us like this to the roots of our being, if in being obliged we are only dealing with some finite good?" by John F. Crosby, "The Encounter of God and Man in Moral Obligation," *The New Scholasticism* 60 (1986), 334. For the contrast of conscience with right reason the consideration of infinity is paramount, for Christian conscience introduces a factor that is beyond the capacity of human reason to fathom. On the way Newman faces the problem of "false consciences" and "wide variety" in consciences, see Jay Newman, *The Mental Philosophy of John Henry Newman* (Waterloo, Ont.: Wilfred Laurier University Press, 1986), pp. 79–85. This book maintains that in constituting love the ultimate safeguard, "Newman has gone above and beyond the call of duty by assigning to it the highest place in his epistemology: he has argued that love is the safeguard of faith and reason" (p. 83). The immediate and vivid presence of God in conscience for Newman has been described as "God is obeyed because his presence is actually felt in the conscience binding one to obey him"—F. James Kaiser, *The Concept of Conscience According to John Henry Newman* (Washington: Catholic University of America Press, 1958), p. 99. On the authority of revelation for conscience with Newman, see Joseph Crehan, "The Theology of Conscience," in *Newman and Gladstone Centennial Essays*, ed. James D. Bastable (Dublin: Veritas Publications, 1978), pp. 214–19. Cf.: "Conscience gradually becomes that which it must be according to its nature—the living voice of God within us." Romano Guardini, *Conscience* (London: Sheed & Ward, 1932), p. 103.

Against the above background of faith, the touchstone for the morality of a particular human act is whether it pleases or whether it offends God. The deliberation about the act and the final decision in its regard become thereby the work of conscience. Conscience takes into consideration the relevant theoretical knowledge and the precepts of eternal and positive laws, and also attends to what prudence (Aristotelian right reason—supra, n. 15) has to say about their application in the particular circumstances. But conscience itself, not prudence, is what finally determines whether the action should be performed or avoided. It allows prudence the role of functioning as an intellectual virtue in seeking out correct means to the proposed end, but not the task of finally determining whether or not the action is right for the person who performs it.[25] The final decision is made on the basis of relation to the divine will, namely, on whether the action pleases or offends God.

This motive of conscience can be much stronger and psychologically much more compelling than right reason ordinarily is. In fact, a strong argument against the Aristotelian conception of morality is that it lacks teeth to enforce its conclusions.[26] Fear of eternal punishment

25. "Conscientia definitur sic. *Est judicium seu dictamen practicum rationis, quo judicamus quid hic et nunc agendum ut bonum, aut vitandum ut malum.*" Liguori, *Theologia moralis*, ed. Léonard Gaudé (Rome: ex typographia Vaticana, 1905), 1.1.1.2; 1, 3. Cf. I. Aertnys-C. Damen, *Theologia moralis*, ed. 17a (J. Visser), 1.3.1.64; 1, 75. Prudence, which for Aristotle (see supra, n. 15) was in this context identical with right reason, is defined in quite Aristotelian terms, but restricted to the application of principles to particular actions: "*Prudentia* est habitus sive acquisitus sive infusus perficiens intellectum practicum ad recte, idest convenienter virtuti, dirigendum appetitum in iis quae sunt ad finem, applicando principia ad operationes particulares;" Aertnys-Damen, 1.3.64 bis; 1, 76. So worded, this description seems to imply some kind of difference between prudence and conscience, over and above the extension of prudence to the supernatural order as an infused virtue. Yet the distinction remains vague, and is blurred still more by the acknowledgment that the act of prudence appears to be *the* act of conscience or at least *an* act of conscience: "Imo, ipse actus iudicii prudentiae videtur esse actus conscientiae," ibid., n. 3; 1, 76. With Aristotle (*De an.* 2.4.415a16–20), faculties are specified by their activities, and where there is the same activity there is the same faculty. The reference here seems rather to the often-noted decline in emphasis on prudence or right reason proportionately to the increased interest in conscience in Christian thought, described as "l'effacement progressif de la notion de la prudence devant celle de conscience"—M. Michel Labourdette, "Theologia morale," *Revue thomiste* 58 (1950), 210. Against the identification of right reason with conscience in Aquinas, see Léonard Lehu, "Si la 'recta ratio' de S. Thomas signifie la conscience." *Revue thomiste* 30 (1925), 159–69. Cf. infra, n. 40.

26. That inability was expressed forcefully by an Anglican bishop: "I cannot understand that any man's bare perception of the natural seemliness of one action and unseemliness of another should bring him under an obligation upon all occasions to do the one and avoid the other, at the hazard of his life, to the detriment of his fortune." Samuel Horsely, *Sermons*, 3rd ed. (Dundee: James Chalmers, 1812), 183. The reference was explicitly to Aristotle's doctrine "of the *seemly* and the *fair*" (p. 181) as the basis of morality, so described at *EN* 1.3.1094b14.

after death is a notably greater deterrent from evil than is the intrinsic attraction of the Aristotelian *kalon*. "Thus conscience does make cowards of us all" was Hamlet's (3.1.83; cf. *Richard III* 5.3.179 and 309) reflection on facing the prospect of escape through suicide. Aristotelian right reason, on the other hand, remains within the bounds of the human mind for its development and ultimate formation. It does not invoke the eschatological sanctions, or look to religious inspiration and teaching outside the sphere it itself controls.

One rather startling result of this raising of the moral norm above the level of the Aristotelian doctrine is the impossibility in principle of reasoning from one person's conscience to that of someone else. While from the Aristotelian right reason in one person you should in principle be able to see what is right for everybody in the same circumstances, you cannot do so from what an individual conscience dictates. From this viewpoint each conscience is independent of the consciences of others. According to the theological doctrine, each person has to abide by his own conscience in direct relation to God. St. Thomas More, facing death, could write: "I was very sure that mine own conscience so informed as it is by such diligence as I have long taken therein may stand with mine own salvation. I meddle not with the conscience of them that think otherwise, every man *suo domino stat et cadit*."[27]

This attitude could hardly be tolerated in the Aristotelian setting. The one decision of the Aristotelian *phronimos* was meant to hold universally when all the relevant circumstances were the same, no matter which particular individual was making the judgment. Yet consciences can give different decisions for different persons, as with Luther and Cajetan at Augsburg.[28] In stark contrast, there cannot be two opposed conclusions of right reason in regard to the same situation. For right reason the oath of adherence to the Act of Supremacy would have been either right or wrong for all the king's subjects, without exception. It could hardly, on the basis of right reason, have been right for some and wrong for others. Yet a deeply sincere Christian could allow place for divergent consciences about it. A person's conscience will be

---

27. Letter 64, in *St. Thomas More: Selected Letters*, ed. Elizabeth Frances Rogers (New Haven: Yale University Press, 1961), p. 253.

28. Significant in this regard is the remark, "Cajetan's meeting with Luther presents a prophetic microcosm of the whole Catholic-Protestant controversy." John M. Todd, *Martin Luther* (Westminster, MD: Newman Press, 1965), p. 151. But cf. qualifying observations in Hans Schär, "Protestant Problems with Conscience," in *Conscience: Theological and Psychological Perspectives*, ed. C. Ellis Nelson (New York: Newman Press, 1973), pp. 80–81.

right for himself, even though the act it prescribes is wrong according to the consciences of many others.

In the theology of conscience this gives rise to the distinction between what is objectively right, and what is subjectively right for a particular individual.[29] What is objectively right is that which is prescribed by moral law for all. But through invincible ignorance an individual person may think that the opposite is right. The latter course then becomes subjectively right for him or her. Common theological opinion, for instance, may consider death through hunger strike to be morally wrong. Yet it can respect the conscience of Terence MacSwiney, who regarded his hunger strike as the morally right thing for him under the circumstances of the moment. Though objectively wrong in the view of most theologians at the time, MacSwiney's course of action was not made an obstacle to his reception of the sacraments. Less sympathetic consideration today would be given to the killing of D'Esterre by Daniel O'Connell in a formal duel, although the acceptance of the challenge had its defenders in the last century. In a wider ambit, the execution of innocent hostages may be regarded as objectively wrong. Yet the officer in command or the soldier assigned to the firing squad may think that for himself the right course is to follow army orders. Genocide may be objectively wrong, yet a dictator may believe that he has a divinely given mission to exterminate a race. People may look upon the taking of human life in these cases as drastically wrong, and still allow that an individual conscience other than one's own could regard the action as right.

This situation turns out to be impossible for Aristotelian right reason, which is based on perfect habituation in all the virtues. Right reason gives the ultimate determination to the human act. It is in principle able to deal adequately with all the circumstances that enter into consideration for the act's morality. What it determines first and foremost as morally good is the individual act. It sees the moral goodness basically in the individual instance. That moral aspect is then universalized (see supra, n. 16). There is no Platonic Idea of the good or of virtue that would determine the morality antecedently to and independently of the individual act. If the individual act is right in the particular case, it is right without qualification, for every relevant circumstance is taken into consideration by right reason in deciding that it conforms to correct habituation. If that individual act is wrong,

---

29. For a comprehensive survey, see Karl Golser, *Gewissen und objektive Sittenordnung* (Vienna: Wiener Dom-Verlag, 1975). Lehu identifies the objective norm with the Thomistic right reason: "[I]l faut donc une règle objective qui n'est pas la conscience. C'est la *recta ratio* de S. Thomas." Art. cit., supra, n. 25.

it is wrong without qualification. There is in the Aristotelian context no fixed antecedent or "objective" pattern of morality from which an exception would have to be made for "subjective" considerations.

Aristotle, of course, allows for wrong habituation. But conformity to it makes the individual act an act that is wrong. Unacquainted with the inheritance of defective habituation through original sin, the Stagirite held the agent responsible for the resulting wrong act by having allowed the faulty habits to form. Against that background, habituation to exaggerated nationalism or false ideologies or too rigid a military discipline and the like would leave the act simply wrong, without qualification. It could not be subjectively right for any person, no matter how much an individual conscience might adhere to it.

Aristotle (*EN* 3.1.1110b31–1111a2) does allow for invincible ignorance. For him it merits pardon of the act. But in no way does ignorance make the action right for that particular moral agent. The action is wrong, without qualification. As wrong, it can be pardoned on account of the ignorance, but not regarded in any perspective as right. In that setting one could not say that genocide is right for those who engage in it with a good conscience, or that the starvation of millions was morally right for leaders blinded by an ideology, or that mistaken notions of racial inequality in the Scriptures make apartheid morally right for those who enforce it, or that abortion is right for those who in good conscience consider it a morally appropriate means of limiting population.

Right reason, then, because it takes all the relevant circumstances into consideration in determining what is right, provides the same standard for all. If it shows that an action in itself is wrong, it means that it is wrong for all, even though invincible ignorance calls for pardon. Defective or erroneous habituation, by the very fact that it is defective or erroneous, marks as morally wrong the action performed in accord with it. The possibility of a number of different and opposed conclusions by right reason in regard to the same individual action, in the way there can be different and opposed consciences about it, is in consequence excluded. The one "right reason" holds for all. It is highly flexible in deliberation, but once the determination is made it holds universally.

Christian conscience, on the other hand, functions in a personal way. It bases itself on the relations of a human person to a supernatural father and judge. At times it will center on the personal dispositions of goodwill in abstraction from facets that make right reason characterize the whole action as wrong. Crimes have been committed in the name of religion or of patriotism. According to the theology of conscience, the person who honestly thinks he is thereby pleasing God is, in that precision and for that reason, acting rightly and meritoriously.[30] What he does is regarded as subjectively right even though it is objectively wrong. But that is a far cry from Aristotle. Right reason does not allow the motive to be prescinded from the nature and relevant circumstances in determining the morality of the act. It requires that the act down to the last relevant circumstance be in accord with right reason, if it is to be morally good. What is utterly wrong in itself could not come under right reason for any particular person, no matter how much his or her conscience would allow it. In a word, conscience can be correct or erroneous, but by definition *right* reason can never be *wrong*. The conscience that allows something wrong in itself to be right for a particular person is in consequence aptly termed erroneous by the standards both of right reason and of natural or divine law.

All this may seem like a trivial matter of perspective. "Subjectively right," from the standpoint of conscience, suggests clearly enough that the action in itself is wrong. In that way it would seem to imply basic agreement with right reason. But the difference is that conscience may require the individual to perform the act, while right reason would forbid him to do so.[31] The framework of right reason avoids the anomalous and embarrassing situation in which one would have to acknowledge that extermination of millions in gas chambers, or burnings at the stake for religious dissent, could be the right thing for authorities convinced that their ideological or religious policy was correct. The Gospel statement (John 16.2) that the time would come when every

---

30. "Non solum autem qui operatur cum conscientia invincibiliter erronea non peccat, sed etiam *probabilius acquirit meritum*. . . . Cum vero operans prudenter agit, procul dubio mereri debet propter bonum finem quo operatur, nempe gloriae Dei aut caritatis erga proximum, etc." Liguori, 1.1.1.6; 1, 4. Cf. "[D]ictamen illud sequendo dum permittit, homo non peccet; immo opus formaliter bonum est et, si est in statu gratiae, meritorium peragit." Aertnys-Damen, 1.3.2.2.67; 1, 80. Restriction of "formal" to the act alone, as distinguished from the object, could give rise to the following critique: "Ergo, secundum *P. Cathrein,* homicidium, adulterium, furtum non habent malitiam formalem. Hic plane non intelligo"—Lehu, *Philosophia moralis et socialis* (Paris: Lecoffre, 1914), 1, 127 (no. 161). On the other hand, exclusion of "proprie dicta moralitas" from the purpose given the act by the agent's will could occasion the remark, "Certe non eamdem linguam loquimur" (p. 137, no. 170). In this context the way is left open for saying that the act of erroneous conscience is formally good on account of the intention (e.g., of pleasing God) even though it is formally wrong (e.g., as murder or dishonesty) in itself. From the viewpoint of Aristotelian right reason, however, it is difficult to see how an invincibly erroneous conscience can be called practically true (*practice* veram; Aertnys-Damen, 1.3.1.65, n. 5; 1, 77). For Aristotle it would *not* be in agreement with correct habituation.

31. See *EN* 7.3.1147a31–b3. With the acratic, right reason maintains up to the last that the wrong action should not be performed, and continues to do so during the act.

one who killed the apostles would think that he was rendering a religious service to God need not be taken to mean that persecuting the apostles was morally right for their adversaries just because those persecutors happened to consider it pleasing to God.

These observations stand out even more strongly when the question of the moral obligation to act in accord with an invincibly erroneous conscience comes to the fore. Persons responsible for law enforcement have at times seen as a duty the use of extremely cruel torture to ferret out information. Further, wholehearted zeal for religious belief or for an ideology have led authorities to persecute and even exterminate those who would not embrace the officially prescribed tenets. In accord with the doctrine of erroneous conscience, such persons, if following their own formed consciences, are not only subjectively right but also have the moral obligation to act in accord with the erroneous dictates.[32] The reason is apparent. They hold that the erroneously dictated action is required by God, or is what they are bound to by their ideology. To do something in itself morally wrong then becomes obligatory.

The inference turns out to be very incongruous if it is viewed in the setting of Aristotelian right reason. For Aristotle the moral obligation arises from the aspect of the *kalon*. But to a correctly habituated person, the deliberate infliction of torture upon innocent persons to obtain information they know they should not give does not radiate the *kalon*. The Aristotelian ground for moral obligation is lacking. For Aristotelian right reason there can be no moral obligation to perform what is in itself a morally evil act.

The obligation to follow an erroneous conscience arises only when the motive of pleasing God or of promoting an ideology is taken in precision from the nature or circumstances of the act. Right reason demands that all the relevant circumstances be brought into consideration, including the rights of individual persons and of particular groups. Only when the act takes account of all these factors does it glow with the obligatory attraction of the *kalon*. Right reason cannot disregard these other relevant factors if it is to remain *right*. True, this perfection of human reason by itself was not attained fully even in Aristotle's own view.[33] Yet wherever reason is right it cannot see that

32. "Qui conscientiam *invincibiliter* erroneam habet, non solum non peccat juxta eam operando, sed etiam aliquando tenetur illam sequi." Liguori, 1.1.1.5; 1, 4. *"Conscientia invincibiliter errans, si praecipiat aut prohibeat, obstringit ut sibi obediatur,"* Aertnys-Damen, 1.3.2.2.67; 1, 79.
33. Even Aristotle, in accord with his pagan outlook, approved legislation for infanticide: "As for exposure and rearing of children, let there be a law which forbids

an action is pleasing to God if the other relevant factors make it wrong. The erroneous conscience, however, does prescind from those factors, and can allow oppressors to think that they have a God-given obligation to do things that are abhorrent to a correctly habituated person. The motive of pleasing God or furthering an ideology grounds the "subjective" obligation, but only because this motive is taken in precision from the act's nature or relevant circumstances.

IV

Another situation that gives rise to contrast with right reason is a perplexed conscience. In the event of the perplexity the only two alternatives available appear wrong, yet one of them has to be chosen. If degrees are evident, the course with the lesser evil becomes the one for the person to follow. But if both appear equally wrong, either course may be taken with a clear conscience.[34] In the present context the relevant consideration for both the above contingencies is that something regarded as morally wrong is chosen and deliberately done. In the one case, the deciding consideration is the avoidance of a greater evil. In the other case it is the necessity of acting, even though both the available alternatives appear equally wrong. But in either case, something judged by the moral agent to be wrong is permissible for him under the circumstances.

The standard example given is a conflict of conscience between the neglect on the one hand of a religious obligation, say attendance at Sunday Mass, and on the other hand the remaining at home to fulfill the charitable obligations of looking after a sick person. The approach is obviously from the standpoint of law and its obligation. There is a law commanding each of the alternatives. There is a positive law of religious observance, and there is the natural law of necessary fraternal assistance. No matter which course the person chooses, a law appears to be broken and accordingly a wrong act performed. The moral agent in question lacks the philosophical sophistication or the instinctive judgment that would tell him how the obligation of the natural supersedes that of the positive law. Nor is he trained to weigh the

---

maimed babies to be reared. But whenever the established custom of the state is such as to forbid exposure of children, then, to avoid overpopulation in states which limit the number of births, let it instead be required to have abortion before sensation and life begin in the fetus . . ." *Pol.* 7.16.1335b19–259; Apostle-Gerson trans. "Sensation and life" will here be the criterion from Aristotle's viewpoint.

34. "Conscientia *perplexa* est ea, qua quis in medio duorum praeceptorum constitutis peccare credit, quamcumque partem eligat." Liguori, 1.1.1.10; 1, 6. Cf. Aertnys-Damen, 1.3.2.3.70; 1, 81.

intention of the legislator. His conscience may accordingly be mistaken in regard to one of the horns of the dilemma, in considering it to be wrong. But to him the other alternative appears equally wrong. In either case he has to do something he considers morally evil. Where in the case of erroneous conscience the wrong alternative appeared to be the only right course and thereby became obligatory, here neither course appears right. In consequence neither takes precedence vis-à-vis the other in imposing the obligation to follow it. The person is left free in conscience to follow either course.

The approach seems in principle to be the same in cases that today are much more under discussion—questions, for instance, of divorce, contraception, abortion, or euthanasia. There can be agonizing problems regarding the use of artificial contraceptives in face of the prospect of serious trouble in married or family life. The teaching of the Church, till recently unquestioned,[35] and still affirmed authoritatively and unambiguously for today's circumstances, is that the use of the contraceptives is immoral. To many, this would appear as a law or command of the Church, rather than as the expression of an already existent obligation to respect the integrity of the procreative act. If indications given by statistics can be trusted, the majority of European and American consciences would seem to be quite in line with dissentient theologians on the topic, and accordingly would be classed as erroneous rather than perplexed.[36] Nevertheless, consciences do seem troubled, as the strenuous efforts to defend the dissentient view would indicate. Often the question still seems faced in terms of whether or not a definite law or command of the Church should be observed in this matter, or whether the question comes at all within the Church's competence. This tends in practice to promote the attitude of leaving the decision to the individual conscience. Somewhat similarly, the Church's teaching in regard to the unborn child's right to life is definite. But in the case of a pregnancy that threatens great psychic harm

35. See John T. Noonan, Jr., *Contraception* (Cambridge, MA: Harvard University Press, 1967), p. xix.

36. In assessing this situation, strong and definite expressions of contemporary Catholic experience in favor of *Humanae Vitae* should not be ignored, e.g., Joyce Markes Russell, "Contraception in a New Context," *America* 145, no. 9 (Oct. 3, 1981), 182–83, and Juli Loesch, "From the Council to the Synod," *Commonweal* 112, no. 18 (Oct. 18, 1985), 572–74. But as the practical judgment is made in accord with the person's habituation, the ignorance can be invincible as long as the wrong habituation lasts, and, as with Aristotle's (*EN* 7.3.1147b6–9) acratic, may require physiological or psychological intervention for its cure. Similarly, the ignorance can be invincible in a person who sincerely takes pride in homosexual orientation, during the time the wrong habituation dominates.

to the mother, the possibility of a perplexed as well as of an erroneous conscience may be present.

The situation of perplexity should not have any place in the context of the Aristotelian right reason, which in principle is meant to function smoothly and definitively in the moral order it itself evolves and dominates. But where with revelation a higher authority comes into play, with its laws and commands, perplexity does in fact make its appearance. Instinctive respect for human life is seen, in the context of faith, to be grounded on the divine dominion over it. In some cases, such as necessary defense in war or as punishment for crime, the right to take it may be looked upon as divinely allowed to public authority. But can that permission be seen extended to suicide, duelling, hunger strike, euthanasia, medical experimentation, or termination of life support? Does the divine dominion hold also in regard to the procreation of human life in questions of marriage, polygamy, divorce, contraception, and genetic engineering? In all these areas perplexity does in fact arise. Here divine guidance and authoritative interpretation should be welcome, if an effective moral order in the incessantly changing maelstrom of divergent human views is at all to be maintained. For a believer, this magisterial mission has been confided to the Church.

Yet even so, perplexity can be alleged. Academic freedom and enterprise can be poised against authoritative decision, and abuse of authority can be feared. Occasion for perplexity can in fact continue to be frequent. In the face of the objections, the believer has to stay aware that the human intellect unaided by faith is not capable of knowing the particular goal for which man has been created, or the sacramental road by which the goal is to be reached.[37] He will realize that in these respects his intellectual vision is darkened, and his moral habituation is left weak. He will not be surprised when he finds that God's ways are different from human ways. He will see that his own personal habituation just in itself is not sufficient in the actual human condition to ground the sweep of universality required for Aristotelian right reason. He will acknowledge that in moral outlook men differ from one another sincerely, giving rise to the adage "quot homines tot sententiae" (Terence, *Phormio* 2.4.454). He will in consequence appreciate divinely given guidance by revealed doctrine and its interpretation through the Church. Against the volatile background of human thought he will not be too disturbed at claims of "loyal opposition" on

37. Cf. supra, n. 20. In this respect, the way of the *viator* is "covenantal" rather than jejunely rational.

the part of heresy, schism or dissent, for he knows that one's own individual judgment, often proved fallible, can go off on many tangents. He will realize that some theologians allege a duty to oppose the decisions of the magisterium, and will recognize in saints like Joan of Arc and Catherine of Sienna a divinely inspired mission. Yet, with all this in mind, he will be strongly oriented to preference for the authoritative teaching of the Church wherever it is available, when cases of perplexity arise.

Given the immaturity of the *viator* in regard to the divine destiny towards which earthly life is directed, perplexities may be expected to continue making themselves felt. They have to be acknowledged in the Christian context, with the choice left to conscience in each individual. Aristotelian right reason, on the other hand, taking every relevant circumstance into consideration, would claim to show that at least one of the two alternatives comes under the *kalon*. The Aristotelian procedure is based on the constitution of the human act in accord with correct moral habituation, and not on the aspect of law or command. Consequently, in the Aristotelian setting, rational activity is able to specify what it itself brings into being. The result may be the same as with conscience in allowing either alternative to be chosen. Yet right reason would do this by showing that the alternative chosen is morally good in itself. It would not accede to the acceptance of something that is believed to be in itself morally wrong. Rather, it would be showing that the alternative is morally right.

Again, this may seem a trivial question of viewpoint just as in the case of erroneous conscience. But it frees one from having to hold that a morally wrong act can sometimes be right for a particular individual. Where faulty habituation or invincible ignorance is at the source of the trouble, the general considerations of blame through having allowed wrong habits to form, or of pardon on account of ignorance, would come into play in the case of perplexity quite as in the case of error. But in no case could Aristotelian right reason say that what is wrong in itself can be right for a particular person.[38]

---

38. "Conscientia potest esse erronea, recta ratio non potest." Lehu, *Philosophia moralis,* p. 106 (no. 151). This consideration can evoke different reactions, e.g.: "[I]l faut donc une règle *objective* qui n'est pas la conscience. C'est la *recta ratio* de S. Thomas," Lehu, *Rev. thomiste* 30 (1925), 161. "And conscience is always stunted unless it transcends itself. Civilization, consequently, lies somewhere beyond conscience," Thomas Vernor Smith, *Beyond Conscience* (New York: McGraw-Hill, 1934), p. vii. What needs to be kept in mind in this regard is that from the theological viewpoint, the viewpoint of Christian conscience, right reason is concerned with the malice or evil of the act. This, as a privation of human goodness, is something *finite* (see Aquinas, *ST* 1–2.87.4c). But conscience is concerned with sin—"a theologis consideratur peccatum praecipue secundum

V

In the light of these considerations the contrast between Aristotelian right reason and Christian conscience is based obviously enough on the difference between the natural and the supernatural orders. It is to be explained in accord with that difference. Though the truths of revelation are above human reason they are not contrary to it. Rather, they supplement it. The mist of prima facie opposition between conscience and right reason should be dissipated once the full light of Christian truth is allowed to focus upon a given situation. The revealed doctrines accepted on supernatural faith, and the promptings of grace sensitively responded to, may be expected to fill the deficiencies of unaided human reason and round out the awkward contours of the problems involved. But another measure has come into play, and right reason will thereby cease to be the sole or independent standard for human conduct.

In treating of the theological virtues of faith, hope, and love, St. Thomas Aquinas (*ST* 1–2.64.4c) called attention to the two different measures by which their acts are regulated:

The first is taken from the very nature of its virtue. And thus the measure and rule for theological virtue is God himself; . . . This measure surpasses all human power, so that we can never love God as much as he ought to be loved. . . .

Another rule or measure for theological virtue is relative to us: for although we cannot be borne towards God as much as we ought, yet we should come to him by believing, hoping and loving according to the measure of our condition. And so in theological virtue it is possible to find a mean and extremes incidentally and in reference to us (Blackfriars trans.).

---

quod est offensa contra Deum" (*ST* 1–2.71.6.ad 5). Here the offense is *infinite*—"erit peccantis mortaliter contra Deum infinita offensa ex parte dignitatis eius cui per peccatum quodam modo inuria fit" (*De ver.* 28.2.168–71). Seen merely as "the enticement of the will by a good which is not in accordance with right reason . . . sin is not some contortion of the will whereby it somehow rebels against God (as the idea of formal disobedience to conscience would suggest) but it is rather an objective lack of order in the human act due to the object adhered to." Kevin T. Kelly, *Conscience*, pp. 187–88; cf. pp. 181–85. Such a "right reason" context for the explanation of sin is hardly sufficient for Christian conscience. Yet conscience requires both divine revelation and right reason for its guidance. Of itself, and not just in its act, it *can* be erroneous, quite as reason, just in itself as a faculty, can err. It seems going too far to say, "Conscience itself as faculty or power cannot be erroneous, but its decisions may be in error. Conscience as vital power can be dulled, but it cannot err"—Bernard Häring, *The Law of Christ*, trans. Edwin G. Kaiser (Westminster, MD: Newman Press, 1963), 1, 154. The traditional way of referring to "erroneous conscience" instead of just "erroneous decision" seems correct enough, for if conscience is *able* to make an erroneous decision, it itself is able to err. On the failure of an invincibly erroneous conscience to attain practical truth, see supra, n. 30.

This implies that the standard based on human habituation is applicable to distinctively Christian conduct, and has to be followed in the way a Christian practices love of God. But Aristotelian right reason is not sufficient, in itself and just alone, for giving the ultimate balanced judgment. A "double standard" (*mensura . . . duplex*) is indeed at work, though without injustice to any party concerned.

Instead of having his or her ultimate orientation to a *eudaimonia* that consists in the highest exercise of the intellect during a full lifetime on earth, with the Christian conscience each human being is meant directly for God through supernatural elevation. A man or woman is thereby related to God as to a father, instead of just as a citizen to public justice. The simultaneous application of the two standards may often turn out to be surprising. To the laborers who had for one hour of comparatively easy work received the same recompense as those who had toiled through the long hours of blazing sun, the master of the vineyard could say: "My friend, I am not being unjust to you; did we not agree on one denarius? . . . I choose to pay the last-comer as much as I pay you. Have I no right to do what I like with my own? Why be envious because I am generous?" (Matthew 20.13–15). From the Christian viewpoint, God may dispense his goods and share his dominion in a spirit of family love, with himself as the measure or standard. This dispensation of his love is not arbitrary or despotic, for God himself, the highest instance of goodness and of the *kalon,* is the standard by which his own actions run their course. The prodigal son (Luke 15.12–34) may be showered with much more elaborate attention and beneficence than his steadily faithful brother. Aristotelian right reason, based only on human standards, might require the opposite. The role of Mary (Luke 10.38–42) is given approval over that of Martha. Aristotelian right reason might dictate that, for the moment, both women should share the family labors. Quite similarly, even if not always correctly, Christian conscience functions in a spirit of family relationship in which the wishes of the father are not only respected but are loved precisely because they are his.

In this perspective the desire to please God predominates. With ardor it emphasizes love of God as the first and greatest (Matthew 22.38) norm of Christian conduct. True, love of God in practice requires the other virtues. But the habituation in those virtues, including that of prudence or right reason, may remain very weak even after sacramental regeneration or reconciliation. Experience makes this only too evident. In the state of fallen nature the virtues do not work together with the harmony that would be attributed to them in the states of integral or sanctified nature. The result is that the unbounded desire to please God can be carried into strange vagaries, trampling roughshod over the most basic human rights of persons held up as enemies of God or as standing in the way of what is considered a God-given destiny. The impulse that originates in dedication to the divine will can in fact be pursued inordinately "with more zeal than discretion," as illustrated in More's newly converted Utopian.[39] Conscience erroneously allows the rational standard to fade out of vision and dictates as obligatory what right reason will condemn as wrong. In the present state of human nature the ignorance may be invincible, or the virtuous habituation too weak to stand strain. The invincible ignorance may often be grounded on the deficient habituation. Nevertheless, in such cases the conduct will be condemned unequivocally as wrong by the tribunal of Aristotelian right reason, quite as it was by the Nuremberg court in the case of war crimes. Pardon for invincibly erroneous conduct may be accorded, but that does not make the conduct right.

At times, then, in the family atmosphere of Christian conscience, the gaze is in point of fact kept fixed solely on the motive of pleasing God. A wrong course of conduct comes thereby to appear right to the person involved. Refusal to pursue it would mean for him that he was deliberately flying in the face of a heavenly father by failing to do what was regarded, though wrongly, as something required by the divine will.

This is hard for reason to grasp apart from faith. Instinctively, though, one comes to feel that something more deeply rooted than reason is at work. A mother may find herself threatened with violence and even death by a wayward son forcing money from her to sustain his drug habit. Yet she will insist fervently, "I love him," and close her eyes to all else. Aristotle himself (*EN* 3.6.1115a24–35) could uphold the virtue of bravery in facing death on the battlefield even though it cut off the full lifetime required for a man's *eudaimonia* or ultimate goal. Pascal could write: "The heart has its own reasons which Reason does not know; a thousand things declare it. . . . You have cast away the one and kept the other; Do you love by reason?[40] Francis William Bourdillon could express the contrast as

39. "[H]e spoke publicly of Christ's religion with more zeal than discretion . . . he condemned all the rest outright." More, *Utopia* 2, ed. Edward Surtz (New Haven: Yale University Press, 1964, reprint 1978), p. 132.

40. *Pensées* 277; trans. H. F. Stewart. Accordingly, right reason takes into consideration many aspects and circumstances that the individual conscience may miss. So "it is possible at least in some instances for the judgment of right conscience to exist apart from the judgment of prudence in a given act. This is possible because the judgment

> The mind has a thousand eyes,
> And the heart but one,
> Yet the light of the whole world dies
> When love is done.[41]

Ever alert activity by the thousand eyes would be required to keep human conduct in continuous accord with right reason. But such multifaceted and exact performance is not found in the present human milieu. Reason does not function perfectly. The ultimate decisions, accordingly, have to be left to conscience. Conscience of its own nature is obliged to make all the use it can of right reason or prudence. But it can be erroneous or remain perplexed, and through error or perplexity it may bring into human life much drama and agony, even though this is sublimated by Divine love, mercy, and redemption.

The spirit of family compassion engendered by grace has therefore to be kept in mind when one is assessing an individual act performed in the state of fallen nature. In the theological perspective the "subjectively good" intention in the case of invincible ignorance may be accepted for the individual act's moral specification, even though the act in itself is condemned by right reason and is merely tolerated in fact by the divine will as a regrettable lapse in the exercise of human intelligence and freedom. This attitude may not seem coldly reasonable. But it fits in with the ardor of love. One need only compare the way a child's unhelpful, and in fact hindering, aid is fondly relished by an otherwise rationally minded parent. While right reason cannot see the *kalon* in any act opposed to itself, Christian theology can regard as subjectively good something that in itself is contrary to the divine goodness. It is able to disregard the agent's blindness to the evil character of the act, and class as "subjectively good" an act that is contrary to right reason yet meant without personal fault to please a loving God.[42]

---

of conscience does not express the entire reality present in the judgment of prudence." Reginald Doherty, *The Judgments of Conscience and Prudence* (River Forest, IL: Aquinas Library, 1961), p. 112.

41. See John Bartlett, *Familiar Quotations*, 15th ed. (Boston: Little, Brown and Company, 1980), p. 670, no. 8. In regard to this epistemological functioning of love, cf. Jay Newman's remark cited above in n. 24.

42. Here the vocabulary becomes difficult, as in the question "Utrum bonitas concordans rationi erranti sit bona?"—Salmanticenses, *Cursus theologicus* 11.19.6; 6, 186. According to the theological doctrine, an evil deed done through invincible ignorance may be supernaturally meritorious on account of the motive of pleasing God or helping one's neighbor. In consequence, the oppression of others or the destruction of their property, if done in *good* conscience, should be morally *good*. The reservation may be added "actum bonum, saltem inadaequatum"—Liguori, 1.1.1.6; 1, 4. But in any case, the aspect of evil is allowed to drop out of the act's specification, on the ground that

Aristotelian ethics (*EN* 1.2.1094b10–11) is a political science. It treats individuals as members of a civic community rather than as family. Christian theology, on the other hand, takes into consideration the weakened state of human intellect and will. It knows that the roots of ignorance and of deficient habituation can lie beyond the personal responsibility of the individual. In some situations the good intention may be accepted for the act's specification, even though just in itself the act is condemned as wrong. The motivation of love for God is allowed to predominate in the specification of the individual's act, and the objectively wrong action becomes meritorious and even obligatory for a particular person in a particular case. But in so regarding the act, theology poses a philosophical problem. Hence, while not attempting to add anything to the theology of conscience, philosophy of religion has within its purview the task of studying erroneous and perplexed consciences as religious phenomena, in an endeavor to understand their contrast with Aristotelian right reason.

---

the evil is involuntary. Nevertheless, the two aspects clash in a way hard to express correctly in language. The identical act assessed as good by the measure of conscience is not good as measured by Aristotelian right reason. The same situation holds in regard to the designation "right": "licet in se actio recta non sit, recta tamen est juxta conscientiam operantis"—Liguori, 1.1.1.5; 1, 4. In the event of invincibly erroneous conscience the two measures cannot be made to coincide. They give rise to the difficulties in language noted supra, n. 30. The same linguistic problem occurs in referring to God as the highest instance of moral goodness. The true ultimate end is the highest instance of the Aristotelian *kalon* (supra, n. 14). But when *kalon* is rendered "morally good," there is difficulty in applying the designation to God. Cf.: "Does this make the ultimate end a *moral* good?"—Robert W. Schmidt, "Moral Good and Ontological Good," *The New Scholasticism* 52 (1978), 425.

PART TWO

SOME THEMES IN
CHRISTIAN PHILOSOPHY

7

GOD IN PHILOSOPHY TODAY

I

The term "God" occurs in bona fide philosophical language. It is used without hesitation by Plato, Aristotle, and other pagan writers. Accordingly, by being mentioned it need not in a Christian milieu elevate the discussion to the plane of sacred theology.

Even among pagan philosophers, however, the term "God" was introduced from manifestly religious traditions. It did not express a notion formed from basically philosophical concepts, as did "separate substance" or "primary movement." In fact, though God in the religious context may turn out to be identical in reality with what the philosophical concepts signify, this identity is not immediately evident. The identity of the two was expressly rejected by Pascal, and has to be established by a reasoning process.[1]

Today the interest in God arises obviously enough from religious and theological sources. The current discussions in philosophy are not sparked by purely philosophic interest in the notions of subsistent being or primary efficient cause, but by issues developing from "the death of God" or other theological and religious concerns. Nevertheless, these issues can be discussed on a genuinely philosophical level, just as topics originating in experimental research can be dealt with in contemporary philosophy of science. The relevant point is that for anyone brought up in Jewish or Christian or Moslem culture, interest in God antedates interest in philosophy and is carried over from religious and cultural spheres into the range of philosophic scrutiny.

---

1. E.g.: "Our forefathers in the most remote ages have handed down to their posterity a tradition, in the form of a myth, that these bodies are gods and that the divine encloses the whole of nature. The rest of the tradition has been added later in mythical form. . . . But if one were to separate the first point from these additions and take it alone—that they thought the first substances to be gods, one must regard this as an inspired utterance." Aristotle, *Metaph.* 12.8.1074a38–b10; Ross trans. For Pascal's attitude, see his *Le Mémorial.*

There need be little surprise, then, that on the threshold of modern philosophy the notion of God occurs as something already familiar through religious belief—"We have heard that there exists a God, who can do all things, and by whom we have been created."[2] On the strictly philosophical plane Descartes required God as a guarantee for naturally known truths,[3] and proceeded at once to establish the existence and attributes of God according to the new methodical sequence.[4] What previously had been done by sensible existents in serving as the ground of truth now required philosophically the divine guarantee.[5]

This prima facie infringement on today's principle of subsidiarity was followed by more drastic violations in subsequent thinkers. In Malebranche, God became the universal reason in which the human mind sees all things.[6] God was philosophically required in order to house the objects of human intellection. Moreover, since for Malebranche creatures both corporeal and spiritual entirely lack efficacy, God was also required philosophically in order to perform the activities of which creatures can be only occasions.[7] In Berkeley, God was required philosophically in order to provide a mind in which the external world would continue to exist when other minds were not perceiving it.[8] With Kant, God was required by practical reason in order to safeguard the moral world.[9]

2. René Descartes, *Principia Philosophiae* 1.5; A–T, 8, 6.14–15 (IX², 27).

3. On the divine guarantee as a necessary supplement to intuition for Descartes, see Henry G. Wolz, "The Double Guarantee of Descartes' Ideas," *The Review of Metaphysics* 3 (1950), 471–89. The solidarity of this doctrine with Cartesian thought in general is emphasized by Wolz: "[N]or is the divine guarantee an artificial device introduced by force from without in order to relieve a philosophic difficulty. As the entire body of Descartes' philosophy, it rests on the conception of the divine will as the source and foundation of all truth and all reality." Wolz, pp. 488–89. On the compatibility in Descartes of "full practical commitment" in faith with "theoretical open-mindedness" on the philosophical level, see John Baillie, *Our Knowledge of God* (Oxford: University Press, 1939), pp. 136–37. Yet the separation from theology tends to widen. In the "Preface to the Eighth Impression (1959)" of the work, Baillie (p. vii) notes "that there is at present much less mutual understanding between the philosophers and the theologians of the English-speaking world than at any previous period. . . . They no longer talk the same language."

4. *Principia* 1.14–41.

5. E.g., for Aquinas truth consists "in the being of the thing, and in the apprehension of the cognitive power proportioned to the being of the thing." *Sent.* 1.19.5.2.Solut.; ed. Mandonnet, 1, 491. Cf. *De ver.* 1.4. In these articles the Augustinian requirement of divine illumination for truth is faced, and the notion of God as the truth by which all things are true is explained in terms of efficient and exemplar causality.

6. *Entretiens sur la métaphysique et sur la religion*, 1.9–10. See also the "Préface."

7. *De la recherche de la vérité* 6 (2e partie).2. Cf. "[T]here is also a contradiction in your being able to move your footstool. That is not enough, there is a contradiction in all the angels and demons joined together being able to rustle a straw." *Entretiens* 7.10.

8. *Three Dialogues between Hylas and Philonous* 3; in *Works*, ed. Luce-Jessop, 2, 230–31.

9. *Critique of Practical Reason* 2.2.5.

In all these thinkers, however, the God envisaged was the traditional God of revelation. He was the God who in the beginning had created heaven and earth,[10] who was proclaimed each Sunday in the Christian *Credo* as the maker of all things visible and invisible. He was the supreme and intelligent being whom men everywhere in the west continued to call their maker, and to whom people considered themselves responsible for all their words and deeds. Under the catalysis of Hegelian idealism this background rapidly changed. Instead of being created in the image and likeness of God, man now becomes the one who creates God after man's own image and likeness.[11] God becomes a product of human thought, for some unnecessary, for others something that man for various reasons just has to invent. Such a God, the invention and product of human ingenuity, could scarcely be expected to take on the serious duties that had traditionally been required of him in the religious, moral, and social orders. Before the end of the nineteenth century the proclamation that God is dead had been put into the mouth of Zarathustra by Nietzsche.[12] A similar failure to satisfy these needs could be expected in the later process philosophies, in which God, though not a creation of the human mind, turned out to be a creation of nature.[13]

In this complex setting, against an immediate background of logical positivism, linguistic philosophy was able to focus its attention on "God-talk" sentences and analyze them as especially delectable bits of odd use of language.[14] Existentialism, in the wake of Kierkegaard,

10. Gen. 1.1. Even though this verse may not be chronologically the earliest, it is the way God is introduced in the order that became traditional in the Scriptures. Similarly, as creator and as able to do all things, he is brought into philosophical consideration by Descartes—see supra, n. 2. "Ground of being" seems inadequate to express this notion fully, just as one does not say that the carpenter is the ground of the house. "Cause of being," on the other hand, is satisfactory. On "Provident Creator of the universe" as a nominal definition of God, see Fernand Van Steenberghen, *Hidden God*, trans. Theodore Crowley (Louvain & St. Louis: B. Herder, 1966), pp. 36–38.

11. See Ludwig Feuerbach, *The Essence of Christianity*, trans. George Eliot, reprint (New York: Harper, 1957), pp. 12–32.

12. *Thus Spake Zarathustra* Prologue, 2. On the origin of the phrase in Johann Rist's chorale, see Martin E. Marty, "Whenever God Dies: Protestant Roots of the Problem of God," in *Speaking of God*, ed. Denis Dirscherl (Milwaukee: Bruce, 1967), p. 76. The line in German with Rist is "Gott selbst ist tot," Marty (p. 76, n. 1) recalls.

13. This wording is of course an over-simplification of the process philosophies in their bearing on God. The essential point is that for them God keeps developing in one way or another with the universe. For a discussion see the chapter on "God Finite and in Process" in James Collins, *God in Modern Philosophy* (Chicago: H. Regnery, 1959), pp. 285–324. The best known process philosophy, that of Whitehead, expresses the main tendency as follows: "Neither God, nor the World, reaches static completion. Both are in the grip of the ultimate metaphysical ground, the creative advance into novelty." *Process and Reality* (New York: Macmillan, 1929), p. 529.

14. On this situation, see W. Norris Clarke, "Linguistic Analysis and Natural Theology," *Proceedings of the American Catholic Philosophical Association* 34 (1960), 110–26.

sought on the other hand a personalistic approach that could dispense with the difficult and apparently inadequate way of trying to reach God through concepts.[15] At the present moment, strictly philosophic interest in the topic among English-speaking thinkers is predominantly logical. The ontological and cosmological arguments for the existence of God are receiving extensive discussion. Interest centers either on establishing their validity in old or new ways, or in trying to show the flaws that lie in them, or in pointing out the flaws that lie in the attacks upon them, but without any commitment to accepting the arguments themselves.[16] Occasionally, new proofs, allegedly different from the traditionally recognized arguments, have been brought forward. But these do not seem to have had success in making themselves the focal points of general discussion.[17]

II

Against this extensive and sharply articulated background, what can be the role of philosophy today in regard to the problem of God?

To answer the question, the first step has to be clear agreement on

15. For short surveys of these existentialist trends, see Collins, pp. 340–76; Cornelio Fabro, *God in Exile*, trans. Arthur Gibson (Westminster, MD: Newman Press, 1968), pp. 865–957; 1039–1042. On the context in which the proofs "merely develop the content of a conception," see Kierkegaard, *Philosophical Fragments*, trans. David F. Swenson (Princeton: Princeton University Press, 1962), pp. 49–55.

16. See the two issues of *The Monist* 54 (1970), 159–459, on the topic "The Philosophic Proofs for God's Existence." A collection of outstanding discussions on the arguments may be found in *The Existence of God*, ed. John Hick (New York: Macmillan, 1964).

17. Instances of professedly new proofs may be seen in Josef Gredt, *Elementa philosophiae aristotelico-thomisticae*, ed. 7a (Freiburg i. Briesgau: Herder, 1937), 2, 199–200 (no. 790); Jacques Maritain, *Approaches to God*, trans. Peter O'Reilly (New York: Harper, 1954), pp. 72–83; John E. Smith, *Experience and God* (London: Oxford University Press, 1968), pp. 149–57. The "anthropological approach" in this last proof aims "to return to the way of Augustine and the Platonic tradition; the self must retire into itself, for the conception of God is first realized in this self-reflective encounter"—Smith, p. 150. It starts "with an experience which contains in itself the presence of a reality not immediately known as such"—ibid., p. 151. The problem "is generated by man's encounter with the world and himself . . . we should begin with the origin of the question of God in experience which all men share"—Smith, *Religion and Empiricism* (Milwaukee: Marquette University Press, 1967), p. 62. Doubts, however, may be raised whether such an "encounter" with the transcendent is an experience that all men actually share, and about its philosophic relevance to theism: "Thus a theism grounded in experience is both realistic and metaphysical rather than subjectivistic and nominalistic. . . . It does not demand a personal experience of God himself, an "encounter" with the transcendent that leaves behind all argument"—Harry R. Klocker, *God and the Empiricists* (Milwaukee: Bruce, 1968), p. 159. In any case, the "encounter" would seem to be above the level dealt with by philosophy. It is rather "an objective, grace-given experience of God"—Karl Rahner, *Do You Believe in God?* trans. Richard Strachen (New York: Newman Press, 1969), p. 111.

the meaning assigned to the term "God" in the context. In general philosophic discussions at the present time, one does not have to probe very deeply to find that under variations in terminology and twisting in conceptual frameworks, the basic topic at issue is still the God of Jewish, Christian, and Moslem revelation, the God of kerygmatic tradition. The focus is not upon Persian or Hindu or far eastern conceptions, nor upon Greek or Roman or Celtic or Nordic divinities, nor upon Aristotelian unmoved movents or the Plotinian One or the Spinozan substance. The interest bears definitely enough upon the God traditionally believed in by Jews, Christians, and Moslems, a God who made the world and who exercises providence over it and to whom men are responsible. This conception of God may be attacked or defended in the discussions. The effort may be to change it even in its most essential features. But the basic subject that attracts the philosophical interest remains sufficiently recognizable. In fact, if the notion at issue were anything else, it would not be approached today in philosophy under the caption of "God."

In explicitly Christian philosophy, of course, there is no doubt even prima facie about the notion involved by the term. While not apologetics or any other type of sacred theology, Christian philosophy approaches the topic with a definite notion of God in mind. Before entering philosophy, anyone brought up in a Christian setting has learned to believe in the God of revelation. On taking up philosophy, he naturally wishes to understand the notion to the extent available to philosophic reasoning.[18] The same, I presume, holds equally for the professedly Jewish or Islamic philosopher.

If the subject at issue, then, is clearly the creator of heaven and earth, the maker of all things visible and invisible, does it not itself determine the immediate philosophic parameter under which it may be approached? What other way is suggested than that of the making of things? In philosophical terminology, this means the way of efficient causality.[19] The fact that efficient causality as a genuine philosophic category has been neglected for the past few centuries need not act as a deterrent, if it is now obviously indicated as the path on which the present subject is to be approached. Nor does the limiting and restricting character of efficient causality as immediately known to men require that it be viewed as anthropomorphic and imperfect

18. Cf. Anselm's "fides quaerens intellectum" *Proslogium,* Proem.

19. Cf.: "[W]hile this older metaphysical idea of an efficient cause is not an easy one to grasp, it is nonetheless superior and far closer to the truth of things than the conceptions of causation that are now usually taken for granted." Richard Taylor, "Causation," *The Monist* 47 (1963), 291.

wherever it is found outside this context. Rather, efficient causality as traditionally understood instantiates itself in differing ways. It can mean the painting of a fence, the running of a race, the hearing of a sound, the imagining in a daydream, the writing of theology, the procreating of offspring, the creation of the whole universe. The notion is open to functioning as a parameter that can take on in turn the definite meanings required in the various subjects in which it is found.

To follow this indicated way of efficient causality, the philosophic approach has, of course, to be from the side of things. The sensible things of the external world, and the internal workings of one's own cognitional and appetitive processes, are the objects immediately known. They present themselves, accordingly, in a twofold existence. They exist in themselves. They exist also in one's thought as one is thinking of them. Since they remain the same things under both ways of existing, they do not involve either way of existing in their own natures. Nor could they involve the existence as something consequent upon their natures. Without existence the natures would be actually nothing. Nothing would be there upon which anything could follow. Existence, though not part of these natures, is accordingly accidental to them in a way that is prior, not subsequent. This means that its dependence as an accidental characteristic is upon something other than the nature it is actuating. It means that the existence is from something else, and ultimately from something in which existence is in no way accidental but entirely subsistent.[20] Through this procedure in the line of efficient causality the primary efficient cause is cogently established in the conclusion of a long demonstration. It is a demonstration whose starting point, the existence of observable things, is originally grasped, not through any kind of conceptualization, but through a radically different intellectual activity known technically as judgment.[21]

The philosophic understanding of God emerges almost immediately from this conclusion reached in the line of efficient causality. As the subsistent existence that efficiently causes all accidentally shared existence, the being that is reached in the conclusion is clearly the creator of heaven and earth, the maker of all things visible and invisible. He is in the full sense the creator, because as the primary efficient cause he cannot presuppose materials to which he himself has not given

---

20. For this reasoning, see St. Thomas Aquinas, *De ente et essentia* 4; ed. Roland-Gosselin, pp. 34.7–35.19.

21. See Aquinas, *Sent.* 1.19.5.1.ad 7m; ed. Mandonnet, 1, 489. Also 1.38.1.3.Solut.; 1, 903. *In Boeth. de Trin.* 5.3c; ed. Decker, p. 182. Existence and thing have to be grasped together. Accordingly, each can be represented separately only as an existent (*ens*).

existence. He is the maker of all things other than himself, for subsistent existence is necessarily unique. Anything else, on the contrary, is not its own existence but receives its existence from something other than itself and ultimately from subsistent being.

The philosophical understanding also shows that the efficient causality, namely the giving of existence, is not something done and finished once for all, like the building of a house or the casting of a bronze statue. The carpenter or the artisan ends his work, yet the product continues years after in existence. The dependence upon subsistent existence, on the other hand, never ceases as the caused thing remains in being. Any received existence, because it is always prior to the finite thing's essence, has to be coming throughout all its duration from subsistent existence. This explains on the philosophical level the revealed notion of the God who sustains all things by the word of his power.[22] Likewise, the occurrence of each new action, the drawing of each breath, the raising of a finger, the thinking of a thought, all mean new existence brought into the universe. They take place therefore under the ever-present efficient causality of subsistent being. Again one is enabled to understand philosophically the meaning of the scriptural notion that in God we live and move as well as have our being.[23]

The subsistent being reached by way of efficient causality further presents the divine nature itself as essentially existence, in accord with the patristic understanding of the Exodus verse "I am who am" as the proper name of God.[24] Everything of which existence can be the actuality (and, accordingly, all perfections, including intelligence, will, freedom, and power) will be found in unlimited degree where existence subsists in itself, unlimited by any finite nature.[25] The revealed notion of God as perfect is in this way borne out by the philosophical procedure. But in subsistent being, all these different perfections are existence itself. There they are, in consequence, on a level beyond the grasp of conceptualization, in keeping with the inaccessible light in

22. Hebrews 1.3. As noted at the beginning of this section, the current discussions about God in philosophy are concerned with the God of scriptural revelation, e.g. "the belief in the existence of God as He is conceived in the Judeo-Christian tradition"— Alvin Plantinga, *God and Other Minds* (Ithaca, N.Y.: Cornell University Press, 1967), p. vii.

23. Acts 17.28.

24. Exod. 3.14. In the Platonic tradition, see Cornelia De Vogel, "'Ego sum qui sum' et sa signification pour une philosophie chrétienne," *Revue des sciences religieuses* 35 (1961), 346–54. This "first name" by no means excludes other names. Rather it is a ground for them, somewhat as "maker of heaven and earth" is a ground for the currently used introduction of God as "supreme object of worship."

25. See Aquinas, *ST* 1.4.1–2, where the reasoning is meant to explain the scriptural assertion (Matt. 5.48) that the heavenly Father is perfect.

which God is revealed as dwelling.[26] The infinite intelligence and providence, in accord with which existence is bestowed in the course of
events, are in this way understood to extend far beyond human scrutiny, quite as the Scriptures portray.[27] Further, the possibility of genuinely free action, which the scriptural doctrines of merit and sin and
reward and retribution presuppose, is given its required source in the
unlimited efficient causality of God, and in a way that safeguards the
scriptural notion of divine providence even in respect of human conduct.[28]

III

The attention given to existence over the last twenty-five years accordingly provides philosophy today with extremely helpful insights
for explaining on its own level the problems set before it by the scriptural notion of God. It also helps to face the problems that arise from
modern philosophy itself and from contemporary culture in general
in regard to God's life and "death." The widespread problem of the
agnostic type of atheism, for instance, takes on very definite lines in
its sharply etched grooves.[29] Since the philosophical way to God is
through existence grasped in judgment, the notions originally obtained through conceptualization are of their nature insufficient to
form a basis for cogent reasoning to his nature or being or attributes.
Consequently, the most complete development of the mathematical
and experimental sciences may take place without at all leading the

26. I Tim. 6.16. On God as "utterly unknown" and "entirely unknown" see Anton
Pegis, "Penitus manet ignotum," *Mediaeval Studies* 27 (1965), 212–26.
27. Cf.: "'For my thoughts are not your thoughts, nor are your ways my ways,' is
the oracle of the Lord. 'But as the heavens are higher than the earth, so are my ways
higher than your ways, and my thoughts than your thoughts.'" Isa. 55.8–9.
28. Prov. 21.1.
29. See Étienne Gilson, "La possibilité de l'athéisme," *Atti del XVI convegno del centro
di studi filosofici tra professori universitari* (Brescia: Morcelliana, 1962), pp. 41–42. On
"Natural Atheology" see Plantinga, pp. 113–83, and on the current understanding of
"atheism," Jean Lacroix, *The Meaning of Modern Atheism*, trans. Garret Barden (New
York: Macmillan, 1965), pp. 13–63. Cf.: "l'ateismo avrà sempre i suoi seguaci, potrà
anche essere imposto et accettato per un certo tempo da interi gruppi, ma non pre-
varrà"—Gennaro di Grazia, *Ateismo e esistenza di Dio* (Naples: Fausto Fiorentino, 1964),
p. 263. In this whole context the exact meaning of God as that handed down in scriptural tradition has to be kept in mind, since "everyone is, in some accepted senses of
God, an atheist"—Antony Flew, *God and Philosophy* (London: Hutchinson, 1966), p. 15.
On the term "Stratonician atheism" (from Strato of Lampsacus, 3rd century, B.C.) for
the sufficiency of nature without a transcendent God, see Flew, p. 69. On the other
hand, cf.: "Mais il n'existe pas encore, à notre connaissance, de philosophie cohérente
qui ait pensé le monde dans une perspective athée"—Claude Tresmontant, *Comment se
pose aujourd'hui le problème de l'existence de Dieu* (Paris: Editions du Seuil, 1966), p. 386.

mind to God. Likewise, philosophies that do not proceed from an existential basis may round themselves out to completion without entailing anything divine. The agnostic type of atheism, rather, is indicated for merely human reasoning when its basis is exclusively conceptual. Similarly, the mystic tendencies in Christian thought that proclaim God to be utterly unknown and entirely incomprehensible, yet produce extensive treatises describing his nature and his dealings with men, find their philosophical explanation in rich existential knowledge of God. But they totally lack express conceptual development of that knowledge, at least according to what they themselves claim.[30]

Further, since existence as the basic actuality is most intimate in regard to the whole thing, the continued bestowal of existence makes the divine presence and activity the most intimate of all influences for creatures. The much-satirized idea of a God "out there" appears as an incredibly ridiculous fantasy. But even the notion, sometimes found in scientific and philosophic circles, that the individual creation of each human soul and the performance of miracles would be unwarranted interference from outside, vanishes as unfounded. The divine activity in these cases is seen as from within, and far from interference in the case of direct creation for the human soul it is rather what the course of nature itself demands as the stage for rationality is reached in the development of animal life. In the line of final causality, on the other hand, the existential understanding of the divine nature shows how this infinitely subsistent object is beyond the unaided natural grasp of human intellect and will, even though these two faculties can be satisfied by nothing less than it. Hence it is quite possible for human nature and human life, when considered solely on the philosophical level, to appear as intrinsically purposeless, absurd, and nauseating.[31]

There are other types that in comparison with the agnostic may be called positive atheism, if the designation can be allowed any sense. These types deny the existence of God on the grounds of the evil in the universe or of the nonsensical character of propositions that lack

---

30. I.e., the *via negativa* has to be balanced by a positive way in which the divine nature and attributes are asserted and described. So Aquinas, after stating that one cannot know what God is but what he is not (*CG* 1.14), proceeds to explain the divine attributes at great length. In this context the "reality" of God is only a secondary consideration in respect of his existence. Metaphysically, one reaches the existence first, and afterwards shows that it is subsistent and accordingly is a thing. The tendency of preferring the phraseology "the reality of God" to "the existence of God," made current by Peirce, is therefore misleading if the etymological signification of "reality" (*res*, 'thing') is respected.

31. On the nature of man as "naturally endless" see Anton Pegis, "Nature and Spirit: Some Reflections on the Problem of the End of Man," *Proceedings of the American Catholic Philosophical Association* 23 (1949), 73.

sensible referents. With regard to the first ground, the relevant consideration is that through the existential understanding of God one knows that the intelligence and power in subsistent being are infinite. One knows that this intelligence and this power are impenetrable to conceptual knowledge. One thereby becomes hesitant in pronouncing the final verdict about the way the universe runs its course. With regard to the second ground, the alleged nonsensical character of propositions about God, the answer is clear. From the standpoint of human cognition the referent for subsistent being is the existence of sensible things that is immediately grasped in the act of judgment. Far from allowing any positive assertion of the non-existence of God, this sensibly attained existence leads rather to the startling conclusion that God is the existence of all things,[32] or that the only way to avoid dispensing with existence is to declare that it is God.[33]

Likewise the radically distinct basis required for existential conclusions enables one to assess the ontological arguments. It means that conceptually apprehended natures, even when these are expanded to the infinite, can never justify inference to the existential order. Similarly, the reason emerges why cosmological arguments will have to envisage an efficient cause of things, and not just a "ground of being" that would follow from some necessity found in concepts and would with Kant reduce these arguments to the ontological type. Also, the teleological argument will have as its operative feature the actual directing and guiding of things in the universe by divine providence, rather than the static analogy of house with blueprint in the notorious argument from design.

Finally, the Cartesian requirement of God to guarantee truth may be assessed in this existential framework. Every existential actuality in the universe sufficiently grounds the truth corresponding to it. It itself can completely fulfill this subsidiary role, even though, as a nature upon which all essences depend, existence is located in God alone.[34] In regard to Malebranche, the efficient causality of creatures is safeguarded in all aspects corresponding to their natures, while the coming to be of new existence, which corresponds to the nature of God, is accounted for by the divine causality under which creatures act. Against the claims of Malebranche and Berkeley, the immediate ob-

---

32. "Esse est ergo omnium quae facta sunt ipse factor eorum, sed causale, non materiale." St. Bernard, In Cant. 4; PL 183, 798B.

33. See Donald C. Williams, "Dispensing with Existence," The Journal of Philosophy 59 (1962), 754.

34. The first consideration of a nature is from the viewpoint of its existence in the divine intellect, an existence presupposed by the absolute consideration of the nature just in itself. On this point, see Aquinas, Quodl. 8.1.

jects of human intellection are sufficiently presented in sensible things themselves, in full subsidiarity to the way their natures are shown to be identified with subsistent existence in a basic exemplar role. Correspondingly, the intimate activity of God within all human consciousness lays the ground for philosophical appreciation of the moral argument or the argument from conscience, even though the argument offers no strictly rational proof of God's existence. Further, the infinite perfection of subsistent existence renders impossible any real identification of God with the results of natural process, results that admittedly will continue to be finite. The philosophic way to God through efficient causality, moreover, proves just as clearly as did Aristotle that supreme perfection comes first, not last, in the universe.[35]

Philosophy, all these considerations show, has an exceptionally important role to play in regard to God in contemporary thought. But the role must be accurately gauged. It is not to preach, not to persuade, not to pressurize, but quietly and genuinely and sincerely to *understand.* The role of philosophy today in respect of God calls more than ever for literal application of Aquinas's reflection: "doctrina debet esse in tranquillitate."[36] The role of philosophy is modest. It is frankly restricted. But is it not obviously vital for the contemporary *fides quaerens intellectum?*[37]

35. "Those who suppose, as the Pythagoreans and Speusippus do, that supreme beauty and goodness are not present in the beginning . . . are wrong in their opinion. For the seed comes from other individuals which are prior and complete, and the first thing is not seed but complete being"—Aristotle, *Metaph.* 12.7.1072b30–1073a1; Oxford trans.

36. *In ev. Joannis,* 13.3.1; ed. Vivès, 20, 209a. The text continues: "Sedendo enim et quiescendo anima fit sapiens et prudens." Cf. infra, "Epilogue," n. 18.

37. Anselm, *Proslogium,* Proem. For Anselm, the "understanding" meant sacred theology—see Jean Daniélou, *God and the Ways of Knowing,* trans. Walter Roberts (Cleveland & New York: Meridian Books, 1957), pp. 191–94. Nevertheless, the "understanding" in regard to the existence of God can also be had on the level of Christian philosophy— on the notion of Christian philosophy in this context, see Michele Federico Sciacca, *Il problema di Dio e della religione nella filosofia attuale,* 4th ed. (Milan: Marzorati, 1964), pp. 153–85. Studies of this general way of understanding the existence of God in medieval settings may be found in Anton C. Pegis, "St. Anselm and the Argument of the 'Proslogium,'" *Mediaeval Studies* 28 (1966), 228–67; "The Bonaventurian Way to God," ibid., 29 (1967), 206–42; "Towards a New Way to God: Henry of Ghent," ibid., 30 (1968), 226–47; 31 (1969), 93–116. For readings on the ontological argument from the viewpoint of modern interests, see *The Ontological Argument,* ed. Alvin Plantinga (Garden City, N.Y.: Anchor Books, 1965); and *The Many-Faced Argument,* ed. John H. Hick and Arthur C. McGill (New York: Macmillan, 1967). The ontological argument may be found developed from starting points in moral experience, e.g.: "[L]'existence de Dieu est affirmée ontologiquement. Non par déduction de l'existence à partir de l'essence conçue, mais par saisie terminale de la liberté absolut impliquée dans la relation originaire—originaire en nous—du désir et du langage"—Claude Bruaire, *L'af-*

firmation de Dieu, Essai sur la logique de l'existence (Paris: Editions du Seuil, 1964), p. 168; "The ontological approach must be taken in conjunction with the anthropological approach, . . . each individual must attempt to recover in *his own* experience the *presence* of the divine in the crucial experiences"—John E. Smith, *Experience and God,* p. 156. So, after a survey of the various forms of the moral argument, the question has been asked: "La personne, l'être au sens fort, que nous connaissons, ne devrait-elle pas nous offrir le point de départ parfait pour nous élever à la connaissance de l'être parfait?"— John Henry Walgrave, "La preuve de l'existence de Dieu par la conscience morale et l'expérience des valeurs," in *L'existence de Dieu,* ed. Collège Dominicain à La Sarte-Huy (Tournai: n.p., 1961), p. 130. But this bolstering of the ontological argument can hardly extend to the existential starting point emphasized in the present paper. Though in cognition a nature is always grasped with its existence, the nature and the existence are two radically different starting points for reasoning processes. From existence the way is by efficient causality only, until the nature of existence, namely God, is reached. There is no question here of starting from the nature of existence, which is infinite. The starting point is in finite things, where existence is not found as a nature or as "something," but only as actuating something finite. There is, accordingly, no "leap" from something finite to something infinite when the apprehended existence allows one to reason along the route of efficient causality to existence as a nature.

8

THIS TRUTH SUBLIME

I

As Christian faith gradually sharpened its confrontation with western metaphysics, the tendency to present God in terms of being took progressively deeper roots. Whatever may have been the original meaning of Exodus 3.14, a current of patristic and Scholastic thinking was stimulated by the scriptural verse to identify the nature of God with being.[1] Very strangely—from the viewpoint of the history of philosophy—this tendency developed in contrary direction to the elsewhere prevalent Neoplatonic background of Christian philosophical thought, a background that in Plotinus had expressly denied the character of being to the first principle of all things. Still more strangely—from the same viewpoint of the history of philosophy—the tendency reached a high point with St. Thomas Aquinas in the identification of the divine nature with existence. True, as far as words are concerned, St. Thomas still speaks as a rule in the vocabulary of being, not of existence. But for him, being is an actuality experienced by men as contingent and incessantly changing from moment to moment, fading out into the past as it stretches on into the future.[2] St. Thomas clearly meant what in present-day vocabulary is called existence.

There was no precedent in earlier western thought for this reasoning in terms of existence. Furthermore, it ran counter to the traditional Greek understanding of being as permanence, fully as much as the identification of the omnipotent God with being had run counter to the spirit of Plotinus. Nor, as one reads St. Thomas, does one encounter attempts to tincture the "existential hyaline"[3] with anything

---

1. See Cornelia J. De Vogel, "'Ego sum qui sum' et sa signification pour une philosophie chrétienne," *Revue des sciences religieuses* 25 (1961), 346–54.

2. See especially *Sent.* 1.8.1.1.Solut.; ed. Mandonnet, 1, 195. Also 1.19.2.2.Solut.; 1, 470–471.

3. "the direct interest in fattening Existence at the expense of essence. Some such

else in order to endow it with an intelligibility not its own. Rather, existence is taken just as grasped in sensible things. It is known in judging[4] that a man or a stick or a stone exists, while in contrast a phoenix does not exist in the real world. A man has no other original knowledge of existence. No mixture of the knowledge by which he apprehends the natures of things enters into his grasp of their existence. Nothing is added to existence in its role of starting point for a long and intricate demonstration that finally reaches existence in its own nature, a nature in which the dynamic progress from past to future has vanished in the still more dynamic actuality of eternal self-possession. St. Thomas rises to lyric tones, scarcely audible through the English translation, in contemplating the God of Christian worship now brought before his intellect in terms solely of existence: "This sublime truth Moses was taught by our Lord. . . . The Lord replied 'I am who am. . . . Thou shalt say to the children of Israel: He who is hath sent me to you'" (Contra gentiles 1.22.10; trans. Pegis). Found scattered through the theological texts of St. Thomas, this penetrating metaphysical doctrine has in our own day seen its philosophical primacy stressed by thinkers like Fabro and Gilson. It has been given, in an initial way at least, genuine philosophical presentation. It still awaits much painstaking metaphysical development.

II

Against so profound and inspiring a background of traditional Christian thought, what is to be made of current assertions that the existence of God is unimportant, that it can be neither proven nor disproven, that to assert the existence of God is just as atheistic as to deny it,[5] that to attribute existence to God is absurd or possibly ungrammatical,[6] or that the Christian today should not seek the certain

---

loading is perhaps necessary for contemplating the existential hyaline at all, somewhat as a microscopist must stain the transparent tissues to make them visible, . . ." Donald C. Williams, "Dispensing with Existence," *The Journal of Philosophy* 59 (1962), 754.

4. There seems to be no satisfactory word to express this immediate grasp of existence. "Perception of existence," "intuition of existence," "apprehension of existence," "knowledge of existence," and the like, may be used. "The second operation of the intellect" and "judgment" are standard Thomistic designations for it.

5. "Thus the question of the existence of God can be neither asked nor answered. If asked, it is a question about that which by its very nature is above existence, and therefore the answer— whether negative or affirmative—implicitly denies the nature of God. It is as atheistic to affirm the existence of God as it is to deny it." Paul Tillich, *Systematic Theology* (Chicago: Chicago University Press, 1951), 1, 237.

6. "And modern views make it self-evidently absurd (if they don't make it ungrammatical) to speak of such a Being and attribute existence to Him." J. N. Findlay, "Can God's Existence Be Disproved?" *Mind* 57 (1948), 182.

assurance of God's existence?[7] Surely, if the nature of God is existence, to deny existence to him is to deny any nature to him. It is not only the "death of God," but the stultification of the very notion. It is the reduction of the name "God" to the category of contradictions like a square circle.

To ask whether God exists, on the other hand, is undoubtedly a correctly framed question in the tradition of Christian theology. As a question, it is attested by innumerable theological treatises down through the centuries. But can it also be a proper question for a metaphysician to ask? For some thinkers today, to identify God with what is concluded by a metaphysical demonstration seems little short of blasphemous. Certainly, that distrust of human reason for proving God's existence clashes sharply with the attitude found in Augustine, Anselm, Bonaventure, and Aquinas. It is quite true that the great majority of present-day writers seem to accept without much question Kant's disposal of the traditional arguments for God's existence. Yet one has but to compare the text of Kant with the text of St. Thomas to see that there is not even verbal resemblance between the latter and the arguments refuted by the German philosopher. In St. Thomas the demonstration starts with sensible things existent in a real external world, and finds that these things are caused efficiently, or, in plainer language, made to exist by a cause that is existence itself. The demonstration reaches subsistent existence first, and then finds this existence identified with the God of Christian belief.[8]

In this metaphysical procedure, consequently, the question becomes worded in reverse order, when compared with the theological context. Having reached existence that is itself a thing and not the existence of something else, the metaphysician has still to ask, "Is this subsistent existence God?" And yet, need that prevent a Christian metaphysician from legitimately posing for himself the question with the wording, "Does God exist?" As a believer, he has already accepted on religious faith, with his earliest instruction, the truth that God exists. But as his intellectual scrutiny expands, is he not prompted by the desire to live this truth intellectually to the full extent of his science? If, with

7. Eugene Fontinell, "Reflections on Faith and Metaphysics," *Cross Currents* 16 (1966), 39.

8. See *De ente et essentia* chap. 4, and the frequent occurrences of the argument in *Sent.* 1. The identity of this proof with the "five ways" of the *Summa theologiae* 1.2.3c, has been a subject of sharp and varied controversy. For a discussion, see Michel Guérard des Lauriers, *La preuve de Dieu et les cinq voies* (Rome: Università Lateranense, 1966), with the stages of the proof itself outlined on p. 37. Cf.: "Le rapport entre la preuve et les cinq voies est donc, simultanément, oeuvre de Dieu créant la nature raison, et oeuvre de l'homme exerçant sa propre raison." Ibid., p. 6.

St. Thomas, he takes the path of existence in developing the science, he is led to see that the nature of being is found in subsistent existence. He does not have to be a theologian to conclude that the perfections of subsistent existence identify it beyond doubt with the God he has accepted as a believer. Has he not thereby answered his question, "Can I demonstrate by reason that the God in whom I believe exists?"

The opening words of the sacred Scriptures read: "In the beginning God created the heavens and the earth" (Genesis 1.1; Conf. ed.). Likewise, the first statement of the Nicene Creed is: "I believe in one God, the Father almighty, maker of heaven and earth." Similarly in the traditional catechisms the first introduction to formal Christian doctrine comes in the words "Who made the world?" or "Who made us?" with the answer "God made us," and with God presented as "the Supreme Being, infinitely perfect, who made all things and keeps them in existence" (New Baltimore Catechism). Aside from all theology, in point of fact the initiation into Christian faith through the Bible, through the creed, through traditional instruction, has been in terms of the maker of the world. The procedure takes for granted that the world in front of people is evident and admitted. The world had to be made, the reasoning then follows, and its maker is called God. In this way God has been for centuries presented initially to the Christian mind. In the creed the notion of omnipotence is stressed by the insertion of the word "almighty."

Is not this a process easy enough for the as-yet-undeveloped mind to follow? The child knows that his building-block castles have himself as their builder. He sees oatmeal being made in the morning, dinners being cooked, houses being constructed, machines being assembled. Without his own activity his castles would not have come about, without the activity of others the things around the world would not have been made. The notion that everything in front of him requires a maker, a maker who can do everything or is almighty, is not difficult for him to grasp. The whole visible world in all its broad expanse does not appear as an exception to his notion that a visible thing requires a maker. On the authority of parents and instructors he has no hesitation in accepting the identity of its maker under the name of God.

Nothing more is required for awakening the virtue of Christian faith. Reasonably, the child believes those who teach him. A sufficient and satisfactory condition is present for allowing the grace of faith to become operative and to give its firm certitude to the child's belief. As mind develops and scrutinizing questions arise, however, further intellectual equipment becomes imperative. Without regret the child drops his belief in a white-bearded Santa that puts the presents under

the tree, his belief in the fairies that leave a quarter under his pillow
after a tooth has been extracted, his belief in the omniscience of parents and teachers, and even, after having grown up and become sufficiently mature, his belief in the essential superiority of his own race.
He is faced with the question, "Is my belief in the existence of God
to follow the same pattern?" This turns out to be of much tougher
fiber, and it faces tremendously complicated issues. As he reads Hume,
the status of the causal proposition, upon which his understanding
of God's existence rested, comes to require deeper scrutiny. He is
brought to see that he does not perceive any causing or being caused
in things external to himself. Nor is he in possession of any immediately known and universal principle that would establish the need of
a cause for every observed thing. As he reads Kant, the imposing of
forms of his own thought upon a sensible manifold, with all its consequences of paralogism, antinomy, and incapacity to apply principles
outside the world of sensible experience, offers a global challenge to
his acceptance of God as the maker of the world. The still later restrictions, by which logical empiricism confines human thought to the
sensible world, by which phenomenology remains within the eidetic
and finite, by which existentialism grounds philosophy on human in-
tentions, or by which linguistic analysis models human reasoning upon
the structure of verbal expression, all have to be faced and overcome.

Does not his faith now require an intellectual framework capable
of dealing with all these considerations? Is it not vitally in need of
understanding? Has not the *fides quaerens intellectum* become a real and
lived experience? Does not the initial formula "God made the world"
require penetration and clarification on a metaphysical level? Does it
not have to be understood now in a way that can move with ease in
the intellectual circles activated by Hume and Kant and Husserl and
Heidegger and Tillich and Kaufman? Does not the more profound
intellectual equipment become mandatory as an integral part of the
educated Christian's life? In this intensely modern and highly developed cultural milieu the problem posed by the opening words of Genesis, of the creed, and of the catechism has to be met today. Against
that background does the demonstration of God's existence have to
be worked out.

Where is the required mental formation and depth to be sought?
Where is the training and the ability to breathe easily on the high
level of contemporary thought to be obtained? Face to face with the
full impact of modern culture, Leo XIII and his successors have in-
culcated the necessity of mastering the thought of St. Thomas Aquinas. It is one thing, however, to divine the direction or to catch a faint

glimmer of "the light at the other end of the tunnel." It is quite another and much more difficult thing to follow the path step by step. Need one wonder at the impatience with the comparatively meager results of the efforts to reach St. Thomas's thought, at the end of nearly a century of intense work and devoted endeavor? Yet should one be surprised? Not only the gigantic work of establishing a critical text, as yet but half accomplished, and the editing of enough thirteenth-century writers to supply an adequate background for assessing its thought, but also the intricate and hazardous task of reading the Thomistic principles in their theological setting and then developing them on a strictly metaphysical plane in accord with contemporary exigencies, will require labor for many years to come. It is a long and difficult work, a work to be faced seriously and carried on perseveringly.[9]

III

But is the task really worth the effort? Does it actually offer sufficient promise for satisfying the *fides quaerens intellectum*? What advantages does it claim over other and less laborious possibilities? At least, it provides a starting point that does not automatically preclude its attaining the desired goal. It does not base itself upon any finite nature, a nature that would condemn it irrevocably to remain within the finite order. In accord with Aristotle, it acknowledges no other origin than sensation for the human knowledge that comes within the orbit of philosophy. In sense experience, moreover, it sees with Aristotle that what is directly known is an external sensible thing. The sensation itself, as all other cognitional activity, is known only concomitantly and reflexively. Epistemologically, there is no possibility of human thought becoming a starting point for reaching reality external to itself. It is already too late for that. Rather, external reality is the first object known. Known immediately and directly, it is basic for human reasoning.[10] Human cognition itself is grasped in terms of what exists

9. "In this way we declare the importance of your work whose purpose is to confront contemporary philosophy with the thinking of St. Thomas on the problem of God. . . . [T]he writings of St. Thomas have not ceased to excite the interest of great minds and to promote the formation of fruitful schools, and all the while the magisterium of the Church has been lavish in its approbation and support of the thought of St. Thomas." Pope Paul VI, "Address to the Thomistic Congress," Sept. 10, 1965, printed in *Osservatore Romano* (Sept. 13–14, 1965), trans. St. Thomas Aquinas Foundation, in *The New Scholasticism* 40 (1966), 81.

10. For reflexive consideration of perception, the end product of the stimulus and of the reaction of the sensory apparatus is seen to be immediately known. But in that

externally. Far from rendering unthinkable anything that really exists outside thought, thought itself becomes thinkable only in terms of sensible things that exist externally in themselves. The starting point is not at all restricted to human thought and its forms.

Yet are not the sensible things themselves all likewise finite in nature? How can they provide a starting point that does not, in advance, limit the results of the demonstration to the finite order? The sensible things are immediately known in a twofold way. Through conceptualization one grasps what they are; through judgment one knows that they exist. Neither of these two cognitive activities is reducible to the other, even though they always accompany each other. Through conceptualization one knows objects like man, animal, tree, color, distance. All these are finite natures. They offer no possibility of reaching out to the infinite God believed in by Christian faith, the omnipotent maker of the world. The *fides quaerens intellectum* need not waste time probing them for means of understanding what it believes about God's existence. By judgment, however, one grasps the existence of these things. The typewriter, the desk, the wall, the door in front of you exist. You have but to "look out and see" in order to know that they exist. The "look out and see" is what is meant here in the technical use of the word "judgment." It is an act of knowing, an act of apprehension. What it apprehends is not part of the nature of any finite thing.[11] Existence is nowhere grasped immediately as a nature, and accordingly is not a starting point that predetermines the conclusions to remain in the finite order.

The existence grasped by judgment, moreover, is intimately conditioned by time. A cloud formation that existed for a while is gone a few instants later. Its fleeting existence was known through judgment at the moment, but when the formation is reconstructed by the mind it is now judged nonexistent in reality. The existence of things in the sensible world is in continual change, incessant change, always going from the past through the present into the future. There is nothing static in it, not even for the smallest part of time. It is continually changing. It is radically incomplete, radically open to development. It requires the novelty of the future.

---

end product the external thing's form, the cause of its being, has already made the percipient be the thing itself cognitionally. In this way the external thing is directly and immediately perceived. Distance and plurality of objects are judged as a result of habituated interpretation. But those are problems for physics and experimental psychology. The object with which the metaphysician at this stage is concerned, namely, something external to human cognition and immediately known, is not affected by the further determinations and precisions. It remains basic.

11. See St. Thomas, *Sent.* 19.5.1.ad 7m; ed. Mandonnet, 1, 489. Also *Sent.* 1.38. 1.3.Solut.; 1, 903–904. Cf. *Sent.* 1.8.4.2.Solut.; 1, 222.

The existential actuality, moreover, is what is deepest and most intimate in anything.[12] None among the many specific or generic natures is indispensable for a being. The thing does not have to be a stone, or a stick, or a horse, or a man. It can be some other nature. You can do away with any particular nature in turn, and still have some other nature that is able to exist. But you cannot do away with existence and then have anything. You can abstract from all the other aspects in turn, and still be able to have a thing. No one of them is absolutely required. Accordingly, existence is the most basic of all. Yet this most intimate actuality, the actuality on which all the other aspects are based, is in continual change. In its innermost depths any sensible thing is radically and unavoidably mutable. Small wonder St. Augustine and the long tradition following him saw mutability as the fundamental characteristic of creatures, the characteristic that primarily distinguishes creatures from God. In the very foundation of its own self, a sensible thing is changeable. It is always tending towards something new in the future. Further, insofar as existence is not part of the sensible thing's nature, what is deepest and most intimate in the thing and most required by it is accidental to it.

The combined accidentality and priority of existence to nature show that sensible things are dependent upon something else for their existence. Because it is accidental, in the wide sense of not belonging to their nature, the existence has to be dependent. Otherwise, the existence would be grasped as something there in itself and not as the existence of the stone or other sensible thing. Because it is prior, it cannot be dependent on the thing it makes exist. It is, in consequence, dependent on some other thing. Something other, then, is making the thing exist, something that is existence itself and not the existence of something else. Even though one may conjure up a series of intermediate causes, even a series that is circular or infinite, all the existence concerned is coming from something whose existence is neither prior nor accidental to itself, something that is identical with its own existence, something that is existence itself.

This means that subsistent existence is causing, by its activity, the existence of all the things perceived in the external universe. Without it, they just would not be there, they would not be existing. The fact that a stone or a stick is present in the world, and is known by the

---

12. "During the whole period of a thing's existence, therefore, God must be present to it, and present in a way in keeping with the way in which the thing possesses its existence. Now existence is more intimately and profoundly interior to things than anything else. . . . So God must exist and exist intimately in everything." St. Thomas, *ST* 1.8.1c; Blackfriars trans.

human mind, grounds the cogent reasoning to the conclusion that existence subsists in their ultimate cause. The consequences are apparent. Only in subsistent existence is existence to be found as a nature. As long as other things are present in the world, they are being kept in existence by the action of subsistent being. All new existence, likewise, is caused by virtue of its action. No new being comes into the world, no event happens, except by means of the action of subsistent existence. Anything that exists in the external world, as well as anything that happens, attests the existence of subsistent being, at least to a mind that takes cognizance of the thing or event and reasons to the entailed metaphysical conclusions.

It is not too difficult to show that subsistent existence is identical with the God of Christian worship, the God introduced in the opening verse of Genesis, professed in the first words of the creed, and taught in the initial question of the catechism, the God in whom "we live and move and have our being."[13] As the ultimate source of existence for everything else, subsistent being is clearly identical with the God who made heaven and earth. As concurring in every action, from the standpoint of all new existence produced, subsistent being is unmistakably the God in whom we live and move. As the conserving cause of all existence outside itself, it is equally the God in whom we have our being. In giving being to all things and events, subsistence existence is likewise identical with the divine providence without which no sparrow falls to the ground. As most intimate to every thing and every action, subsistent being is obviously one with the searcher of hearts and with the Lord who inclines a human heart in whatever direction he pleases. It is the cause of every free action and decision. In all these aspects, subsistent being shows itself to be identical with the revealed God of Scripture.

Yet all this metaphysical knowledge of subsistent being is founded upon what is originally known through judgment. It is not founded on anything first known through conceptualization. In consequence, one has no authentic concept of existence. To be thought about and discussed, what is known through judgment has to be conceptualized under other notions, such as something, or actuality, or perfection. All the more, then, does one lack an authentic concept of subsistent being, or of anything one attributes to it on its own level. What subsistent being is, what goodness or truth or justice is when attributed to subsistent being and thereby identified with it, we just do not know.[14]

13. Acts 17.28. For St. Thomas's use of this scriptural text, see *Sent.* 1.36.1.3.ad 4m; ed. Mandonnet, 1, 837, *ST* 1.18.4.ad 1m.

14. See St. Thomas, *ST* 1.13.2.ad 2m. St. Thomas frequently (e.g., *De ver.* 2.11c; *De*

From the viewpoint of conceptual knowledge one's ignorance of subsistent being and everything in it is total. From this standpoint one
can apply to the full the negative theology of Christian tradition, that
God remains utterly unknown, entirely unknown, is as nothing, and
so on. In terms of conceptual knowledge, one's ignorance is complete.

In terms of what is originally known through judgment, however,
one's knowledge of God can become extremely rich. The whole positive theology, as found developed at such great length in St. Thomas,
follows from the demonstrated conclusion that existence subsists. Existence in its first and literal sense is thereby shown to be the nature
of God. There is no possibility here of symbol or metaphor. Existence,
as we know it in sensible things and in ourselves, has its nature only
in God. It has its nature solely in subsistent being. Literally, *what* existence is can be found nowhere except in is primary instance. The
existence found in creatures, while of course existence in a literal
sense, is only a secondary grade of existence. The primary, the first
literal sense of existence, is found solely in God.

This reflection holds likewise for all other perfections that are capable of actual identity with subsistent being. In their primary and
model sense they are literally present in it. So truth, in its literal sense,
is present in God—as are goodness, and justice, and wisdom. The
instances of these that we immediately experience in the world around
us are only secondary instances. Other attributes, attributes that involve imperfection in their very notion, are in God only causally or
metaphorically, as when God is called a tower of strength or a rock of
salvation. But existence, and perfections like intelligence, action, providence, and justice, are in God in their literal and primary meaning,
a literal meaning known to us through its secondary instances.

In all the really important things, therefore, the metaphysical principles of St. Thomas enable one to speak literally in applying perfections to God. Even though one does not know what these perfections
are when identified with subsistent being, one knows nevertheless that
they are present in God in their full and literal sense. The tendency
to lump together the two adjectives in the statement "anything said
about God is immeasurably inadequate and symbolic"[15] does not at all
follow when faith finds understanding in the light of St. Thomas's

---

pot. 7.5c; *CG* 4.7) stresses that everything in God is God's being or substance. On the
background for the Thomistic doctrine of the divine unknowability, see A. C. Pegis,
"Penitus Manet Ignotum," *Mediaeval Studies* 27 (1965), 212–26.

15. Eugene Fontinell, "Reflections on Faith and Metaphysics," p. 38. For a discussion
of the Thomistic way of predicating concepts of God, in contrast to the symbolic, see
Lewis S. Ford, "Tillich and Thomas: The Analogy of Being," *The Journal of Religion* 46
(1966), 229–45.

metaphysical principles. "Immeasurably inadequate" our knowledge of God certainly is. But in the really important metaphysical characteristics, it is not at all symbolic. It is literal, and indicates the primary literal sense of these characteristics.

In this way, then, the *fides quaerens intellectum* penetrates metaphysically into the content of the faith's most primitive teaching, the teaching that God made the world. The profound reasoning of St. Thomas is but an amplification on the philosophical level of the first truth learned in catechism. Mastering St. Thomas's principles is the intellectual process of growing up in the life that received its infant nourishment through authoritative instruction from parents and teachers. Developing them to their far-reaching conclusions is the work of intellectual maturity in the Christian seeking understanding of what he or she believes. The Thomistic metaphysical principles show upon scrutiny that they do not restrict conclusions to the sensible or even the finite world. They accordingly offer prospects of reaching metaphysical knowledge of God. Examination of their actual performance shows that they accomplish this objective, even though they still require long years of painstaking development. Found in St. Thomas in theological contexts, they await thoroughly metaphysical organization. But even in their original setting they are clear enough in their philosophical message, when they are patiently collected and compared and studied. From the existence known directly through judgment in sensible things, they proceed with sure step to the sublime truth that in God existence and nature are identical.

IV

Will not this truth sublime, with its manifold implications, have real bearing upon a Christian's spiritual life? The realization that existence is the nature of God both shocks routine complacency and stimulates appreciation of one's own shared existence. Explaining St. Bernard's dictum, "God is the being, not essential but causal, of all things," St. Thomas concludes: "[T]herefore divine being, from which all created being flows by way of efficiency and exemplification, is called the being of all things."[16] In saying that existence flows from God, one may have difficulty in avoiding the notion of formally determined sequence, as water flows from a spring, conclusions from premises, consequences from ground, or instantiation from a basic notion. In logic one be-

---

16. *Sent.* 1.8.1.2.Solut.; ed. Mandonnet, 1, 198. On the topic, see G. B. Phelan, "The Being of Creatures," *Proceedings of the American Catholic Philosophical Association* 31 (1957), 118–25.

comes accustomed to think in terms of formal sequence of one truth from another, and may tend unwittingly to reduce existential sequence to that type. Or in thinking of existence as participated, one may unconsciously represent it as form shared by all existents, quite as the color red is shared by all things red. A distinct effort is required to show oneself that one shares existence not by the addition of any new quality of form, but entirely by being made to be. When subsistent existence makes anything exist, it adds nothing by way of nature. It just makes the thing itself exist, by way of efficient causality. This is altogether different from the addition of a new form, as in the case of grace. Yet the existence that all creatures possess has its nature only in God. The very existence regularly taken for granted, squandered at times, often unappreciated, is the very being of God—not formally, but in the sequence of efficient causality. Existence, however, is what is most intimate to oneself. It is the very core of all else. As giving it continually, God is understood to be working most intimately within us, interiorly to all we are, at the very center around which all else in us evolves. Existence is most intimate in our make-up, and God is its interior cause. Can the notion of the presence of God be brought any closer or made any more manifest? Where existence is exercised, there is God.

Likewise, does not the realization that one's existence continually depends upon the exercise of God's conserving causality drive home the Christian notions of one's continued and total need for the divine power? Does it not strongly support and make intelligible the specifically Christian teachings about the virtue of humility? Since all new existence comes from God, and is imparted in virtue of the divine activity, one cannot raise a finger, draw a breath, speak a word, except in the causality of the God in whom one lives and moves and has one's being. The very fact that one raises an eyebrow means, under metaphysical scrutiny, that God is here and now exercising his activity as primary movement, and is doing so as the intimately present subsistent existence from which all new existence flows. How can the realization of all this help but make one walk more closely with God? Where new existence is being imparted, there is God working as its efficient cause, interiorly and intimately.

These considerations enter even more forcibly into the understanding of one's own free activity. A nature that is existence is not confined by any formally determining limits. Operating in an order superior to and transcending the alternatives of necessity and contingence,[17] it

17. See St. Thomas, *In Periherm.* 1.14.22 (Leonine). To say that existence as a nature

moves the free will of man infallibly to the smallest detail of every decision and action without in any way forcing or determining. Every finite cause, on the other hand, determines the caused activity's course, as it moves something else to action. But subsistent existence is not a finite nature. In causing the activity appropriate to a free agent, it does not determine the activity. Rather, it gives the exercise of the creature's freedom. A free action would be unintelligible if its actuality, as free, had its ultimate explanation in a finite nature like man or angel. It could be merely accepted as a psychological fact, and left without philosophical explanation. But as understood through primary origin in the motion by an infinite nature, subsistent being, its entire freedom is philosophically guaranteed. True, one cannot know *what* God's moving of the free will is, any more than one knows *what* anything else in God is. One cannot conceptualize it. But one knows that it is there, and that to act in this way pertains to the nature of subsistent being. The sublimity, the responsibility, of a free decision and free activity are thrust home with pertinent force under these considerations.

Illumined by this metaphysically known truth, how can the omnipotence of God fail to be of importance for one's daily life? The thought that every wave of a finger, every breath, is so intimately dependent on God's omnipotence, working interiorly at the core of one's self and one's activity, will sharpen one's appreciation of routine undertakings. The realization that every act of free choice is taking place only in virtue of the divine omnipotence, will make one sensitive to the presence of God and to his providence. Does not this enable one to understand the traditional Christian prayer of petition? Even the smallest thing, like a sparrow falling to the ground, comes under the all-embracing scope of divine providence and omnipotence. To pray for the quick finding of a misplaced note, for relief from an ailment, for courage to face a difficult situation, becomes readily intelligible. Nor is there anything odd, when one views things in the light of the divine omnipotence, in believing that the course of natural events has been from all eternity adapted to fit the object one prays for, and that the course of nature would have been different if one had not so prayed? To the divine omnipotence the task of arranging the sequence of events in accord with the objects prayed for is no more difficult than

---

operates or performs activities need not run counter to good grammar. An abstract form of a word stands without difficulty as the subject of a transitive verb, e.g. "Kindness wins friends." As existence in creatures is never a nature, it cannot in them be the subject of any operation or activity. But where it is subsistent as a nature, there is no reason why it should not be the subject of the sentence, even when the verb is transitive.

to arrange it in some other way. What is particularly surprising about that? The understanding of all other existence as caused by subsistent existence makes the Christian teachings on the necessity of abundant prayer of petition readily acceptable. The power of the Pantokrator,[18] as accepted in Christian tradition, is shown to be fully adequate to the task of answering the prayer of petition. Why should not that power be continually exercised even in the smallest details?

Similarly, the metaphysical grasp of existence, in accord with the principles of St. Thomas, safeguards intellectually the traditional Christian motivation of eternal reward and avoidance of eternal punishment. It provides the understanding of the Christian virtue of hope. Existence, grasped through judgment, is conceptualized as a perfection upon which transcendental properties follow. These are attributes like truth and goodness and beauty. To have any of them, you must first have a thing, a thing that exists. Upon the thing's existence the transcendental properties are based. In this way truth and beauty and goodness are understood not as detached "values," but as real properties of real things. To have them, one must first have the things. Without the things, the properties just cannot be possessed. The desire for the things, then, becomes the rational way of striving for the enjoyment of the properties. The possession of the things is the reward. Accordingly, the *fides quaerens intellectum* is able to understand and retain the traditionally instilled Christian motivation. One lives and works for the reward of heaven. One strives to avoid the eternal punishment and horror of hell. Such is the way God wishes to be served, according to the practice of Christian faith. He wishes man to be united with him in the beatific vision of heaven, and not separated from him in an abyss of everlasting frustration. Knowing through faith that God has so planned things, one is able to give full intellectual acceptance to the reward-punishment type of motivation, even when acting through the supernatural virtue of charity for the supreme overall purpose of pleasing God.

Nor is one's appreciation of human life in any way diminished by regarding people as objects that share existence through the causality of God. One reasons to the spiritual nature of man from his intellectual activities. Man thinks on the plane of the universal and with complete reflection. The grasp of the universal calls for scientific knowledge and for freedom of will and action. It signalizes man as a free and independent agent, whose every authentically human action is a fresh start, a novelty. Brought directly into actuality by the divine

18. On this notion of the Pantokrator as expressing the "common heritage," see John Courtney Murray, *The Problem of God* (New Haven: Yale University Press, 1964), pp. 34–35.

omnipotence, without possibility of intermediate cause, the new beginning in the order of events, as introduced by a human act, attests both the superiority of men over non-intellectual agents, and the essential immediacy of man's relation to God. Meant to know God through intellect and to serve him freely through will, every individual man is raised above the conditions that allow merely material things to be possessed as property. Over human life and its procreation man does not have proprietary dominion. In questions of homicide, including suicide, war, legal execution, mercy killing, duelling, abortion, and hunger strikes, in questions of mutilation and slavery, in questions of marriage and education, the divine will as known through the authority that speaks for it on earth calls for respect. The philosophical principles of St. Thomas are of crucial significance here for *understanding* the attitude of the Church in regard to all these questions, even when her stand runs counter to almost universally accepted social opinion, such as with duelling in the eighteenth century or with today's controversial issues on human life and its procreation.

The need for Thomistic metaphysical principles is just as urgent for bringing about a wholehearted acceptance, by the Christian faith, of today's scientifically established views on the nature of the sensible universe. In these Thomistic principles, does not the evolutionary concept of nature and of man find a most appropriate metaphysical setting? Existence, as grasped through judgment, is continually changing in man and in sensible things. It is always progressing. It does not stay still for a moment. The deepest core of visible things is consequently in unceasing flux, and it is being given continually from within. When scientists, in explaining on their own level the evolution of nature, say they brook no interference from without, one can fully agree. But the action of subsistent existence is emphatically from within. Far from interference, it is what is most essentially required by the natures of things. One may therefore expect God to give existence as the natures of things demand. If they require evolution, existence will be given them in exactly that way. When the proper moment comes for animation by a spiritual soul, the soul will be created without any interference from outside, without any discontinuity from the viewpoint of orderly progress. God continues to dispense existence as the natures of things require. For his omnipotence there is no more interference in creating a human soul at the moment the natural evolution of the body demands it than in imparting new existence in the rustling of a leaf brought about by atmospheric conditions. From the viewpoint of his omnipotence, there is nothing stranger in the one exercise of his activity than in the other.

The *fides quaerens intellectum*, then, urgently requires a deep appreciation and a correct understanding of the divine omnipotence, in the face of today's intellectual problems about both man and nature. It has in this regard a strong need that can be satisfied by the metaphysical explanation of omnipotence in terms of subsistent being, the existence that gives being to all else. In the principles of St. Thomas it finds this explanation. These reflections underscore the necessity of more widespread and deeper understanding of the Thomistic metaphysical principles for the practice of the faith, as lived in today's culture.

Nor does the adhesion to St. Thomas's principles with full accord exclude in the least the much-appreciated contributions of other philosophies. The intricate tools of modern logics, the phenomenological approaches that escape dichotomies such as subjective and objective, the studies of the various existentials like dread and ultimate concern, the close scrutinies of language, do not at all supplant or hinder the progress of Thomistic metaphysics. They are quite compatible with it. There is, of course, no question of absorption of any one of these philosophies into the others. Each stands on its own feet. Each can understand, appreciate, and learn from the others, without being overwhelmed or suffocated. Eidetic aspects can be abstracted and studied and used as starting points for profitable development of thought, with existence in the Thomistic sense disregarded. Existentials are there. They can be explored and used as a basis for thinking, with fascinating and helpful results. Language may be analyzed, and logic applied, with increased light on human thought processes.

Preference for Thomistic thinking, then, need not have the least fear that new philosophies or sciences will in the future undermine or alter its metaphysical principles. New discoveries will always be welcome and stimulating. Yet as long as there is a stick to move a stone, as long as a flame or an element warms a pot of water, as long as a leaf rustles in the wind, and a human intellect takes cognizance of any of this, the way remains paved for reaching subsistent existence in accord with the principles of St. Thomas. Even if the universe and man evolve to a point where everything as now known has changed beyond surface recognition, even if all material things be sublimated into the pure subjectivity of human thought, nevertheless, as long as the human intellect notes the consummation of the process and reflects upon its own cognition of it, it has still all the necessary equipment to reason demonstratively to the existence of God.

These views, one may object, judge all knowledge by the principles of St. Thomas. That is true. But nobody can philosophize in a vacuum. You have to take your start from some principles. But the principles should be broad enough and deep enough to allow recognition of the legitimacy of other principles as primary starting points, even though personally one cannot accept them in that role. One can nevertheless acknowledge them as positions with their own inherent intelligibility. In point of fact, things exist in reality, are conceived in thought, and are expressed in language. Principles found in things, principles found in thought, and principles found in language have accordingly been used by the many different philosophies as their respective starting points. In the way in which these different principles are given the basic position in the different philosophies, they will mark the subsequent course of the thought with a characteristic direction and spirit. They will give rise to radically different philosophies. But in each case the principles should be open enough to allow a clear-sighted vision of other starting points for other intellectual worlds. At the same time they should keep one keenly and uncompromisingly aware of the all-pervading differences between one's own philosophy and other philosophies. The hundred eyes of Argus are constantly required to enable a philosophy to see in all directions at once and to be alert in maintaining a balanced outlook in a pluralistic universe.

The metaphysical principles of St. Thomas eminently satisfy this last criterion. As the noosphere, to use Teilhard de Chardin's apt coinage, spreads with increased opportunities for education, the necessity of providing for the *fides quaerens intellectum* in cultured Christian circles becomes greater. Not the least is the requirement of knowledge about God. Particularly in this respect are the broad and ever-open principles of St. Thomas the answer to the challenge in the recent versions of the Zarathustrian tidings that God is dead.

V

What, then, is God, literally, in terms open to philosophical understanding? God is existence, and existence, where it subsists, is God. That is the *sublima veritas* reached in the conclusion of the Thomistic demonstration that God is his existence. The collocation of the words in the Latin gives "sublime" the emphatic place in the expression. This would be matched in English by correspondingly reversing the usual collocation and translating *haec sublimis veritas* by "this truth sublime." It is truth that brings intellectual maturity to the *fides quaerens intellectum*. Faith no more depends upon one's understanding in maturity than in childhood, but it does seek the understanding appropriate to each successive stage of life. The Catholic intellectual does wish to understand what he believes, as far as human reason can go. In tenets open to intellectual scrutiny he does wish to be intellectually secure. In St. Thomas are to be found the satisfactory principles for this task. Confronted with the broad and ever-developing expanse of modern thought, should the educated Catholic, seeking to understand his faith, be cut off from this invaluable assistance? Should the *fides quae-rens intellectum,* endeavoring to probe in the crucial contemporary circumstances the literal meaning of God as maker of the world, as presented in the opening words of Genesis and of the creed, be deprived of the intellectual penetration afforded by the truth sublime that *what* God is, is his existence?

9

"DARKNESS OF IGNORANCE" IN THE MOST REFINED NOTION OF GOD

I

Ever since the time of Parmenides, western philosophical thought has been conscious of difficulties in the notion of being. Parmenides began by showing that the stable way of being is required by thought itself. He emphasized that outside being there is only not-being, a way that can yield no knowledge at all. A mixture of the two ways was forbidden him, since this results in unstable and deceptive appearance, not truth. In following the sole way permissible for philosophic thinking, Parmenides claimed to be taking part in a journey directed towards light.[1] He could contemplate being as a luminous object. He could deduce conclusions from its nature just as from any object open to penetration by human thought. The conclusions, irrefutable in the Eleatic context, made impossible any genuine differentiation or plurality or change. There could exist only one being. It could not change or be differentiated in any way whatever.

In their extreme form, these conclusions were unacceptable to subsequent philosophers. By some, being was retained as indestructible, yet as differentiated in elements or atoms. By Plato, its true nature was placed in differentiated Ideas outside perceptible things. By Aristotle, being was regarded as multisignificant and consequently as a plurality. It was given secondary status after a primal One by Plotinus. It was denied by Gorgias, as non-existent and unknowable and inexpressible. In numerous currents of modern thought it has been set aside as an empty or meaningless concept, a surd or a blank. On the other hand, being in its own nature was identified with God in patristic and scholastic tradition. In fact, the formula "God is the being of all things" was, with appropriate qualifications, defended in medieval times.[2]

---

1. *Fr.* 1.9–10 (Diels-Kranz, 28 B). Cf. *Frs.* 6 and 9.
2. See Aquinas, *Sent.* 1.8.1.2; ed. Mandonnet, 1, 197–98. Cf. *Summa contra gentiles*

In the thirteenth century this problem of being was faced by Thomas Aquinas against a proximate background of patristic speculation and a remote background of Neoplatonic, Aristotelian, and Parmenidean thought. In solidarity with the patristic understanding of a verse in Exodus (3.14), the first and characteristic name of God was for Aquinas "he who is."[3] For him, in spite of a reservation drawn from a comment by John Damascene, "being" was regarded in the context as signifying what God is, namely God's quiddity or nature.[4] Yet for Aquinas, being did not confront the mind in Parmenidean fashion as a luminous object. Rather, in accord with the background in Exodus (19.9; 20.21), it was enshrined in dense darkness (*caligo*). The notion, in its application to God, could be best attained through the gradual removal of all ordinarily understood aspects, even of the "is":

The reply to the fourth is that all other names mean being under some other determinate aspect. For instance, "wise" means being something. But this name "he who is" means being that is absolute, i.e. not made determinate by anything added. Therefore Damascene says that it does not signify what God is—rather, it signifies an infinite (as though not determinate) ocean of substance. Hence when we proceed to God by "the way of removal," we first deny to him corporeal aspects; and secondly, also intellectual aspects such as goodness and wisdom, in the way they are found in creatures. Just "that (he) is" remains then in our understanding, and nothing more—hence it is, as it were, in a state of confusion. Lastly we remove from him even this very being itself, as present in creatures—and then it remains in a darkness of ignorance. In that ignorance, as far as the wayfaring state is concerned, we are best joined to God, as Dionysius says; and this is a dense darkness, in which God is said to dwell.[5]

1.26. Besides Dionysius and Bernard, as cited by Aquinas, the Boethian tradition likewise gave expression to this tenet; see: Gilbert of Poitiers, *In I de trin.* 52; ed. Nikolaus Häring (Toronto: Pontifical Institute of Mediaeval Studies, 1966), p. 89.5–6. Thierry of Chartres, *In Boeth. de trin.* 2.56; ed. Häring (Toronto: PIMS, 1971), p. 173.44; and *In de hebd.* 24; ed. Häring (Toronto: PIMS, 1971), p. 409.48–49.

A discussion of the metaphysical issues involved in the tenet may be found in Gerald B. Phelan, "The Being of Creatures," *Proceedings of the American Catholic Philosophical Association* 31 (1957), 118–25.

3. *Sent.* 1.8.1.1 and 3; 1, 194–95; 199–201.

4. "But in God his very being is his quiddity; and therefore the name that is taken from being properly denominates him, and is his proper name, just as the proper name of man is that which is taken from his quiddity." *Sent.* 1.8.1.1.Solut.; 1, 195. In Aquinas, no distinction is made between essential being and existential being. Accordingly, in a context like the present, *esse* and *est* may be translated in terms either of being or of existence, in the way English idiom requires. E.g., "Unde per suum esse absolutum non tantum est, sed aliquid est" (*Sent.* 1.8.4.1.ad 2m; 1, 220) may without hesitation be rendered in English: "Hence by his own absolute being he not only exists, but is something."

5. "Ad quartam dicendum, quod alia omnia nomina dicunt esse secundum aliam

In this passage two overall considerations stand out. The first is that on the metaphysical level God is reached in terms of being. The second is that here the notion of being is not luminous, but rather is in a kind of darkness, a darkness resulting from ignorance. The passage is found in the earliest major writing of Aquinas, the *Scriptum super Libros Sententiarum Magistri Petri Lombardi*. It is meant to answer an argument taken from John Damascene.[6] Damascene, in accord with patristic tradition,[7] listed the first name of God as "he who is," in the sense of "an infinite ocean of being." As what is infinite is incomprehensible and therefore unknowable—so the argument is made to run—"he who is" cannot stand as a name for God. In replying to this argument, Aquinas claims that for Damascene "he who is" did not express God's nature but only an indeterminate ocean of substance. Even though all determination by corporeal and intelligible aspects had been removed, the residue still is not immediately capable of

---

rationem determinatam; sicut sapiens dicit aliquid esse; sed hoc nomen 'qui est' dicit esse absolutum et non determinatum per aliquid additum; et ideo dicit Damascenus, quod non significat quid est Deus, sed significat quoddam pelagus substantiae infinitum, quasi non determinatum. Unde quando in Deum procedimus per viam remotionis, primo negamus ab eo corporalia; et secundo etiam intellectualia, secundum quod inveniuntur in creaturis, ut bonitas et sapientia; et tunc remanet tantum in intellectu nostro, quia est, et nihil amplius: unde est sicut in quadam confusione. Ad ultimum autem etiam hoc ipsum esse, secundum quod est in creaturis, ab ipso removemus; et tunc remanet in quadam tenebra ignorantiae, secundum quam ignorantiam, quantum ad statum viae pertinet, optime Deo conjungimur, ut dicit Dionysius, et haec est quaedam caligo, in qua Deus habitare dicitur." *Sent.* 1.8.1.1.ad 4m; 1, 196–97. Though "aliquam" might be expected for the "aliam" in the opening sentence, the "aliam" gives an acceptable sense, for being has a determination proper to itself, e.g.: "Ita etiam divinum esse est determinatum in se et ab omnibus aliis divisum"—*Sent.* 1.8.4.1.ad 1m 1, 219. "Intellectus" is used regularly in the objective sense of "notion"; see ibid., p. 219, and "non est de intellectu ipsius quidditatis," Exp. 1ae partis textus, p. 209. The "wayfaring state" was a customary theological designation for man's life on earth; cf. supra, chap. 2, n. 23.

   With the passage as a whole, one may compare Radhakrishnan's presentation of Buddha's teaching: "The primary reality is an unconditional existence beyond all potentiality of adequate expression by thought or description by symbol, in which the word 'existence' itself loses its meaning and the symbol of nirvāna alone seems to be justified." Sarvepalli Radhakrishnan, *An Idealist View of Life* (London: George Allen & Unwin Ltd., 1932), p. 100.

   6. *De fid. orth.* 1.9.1–2 (PG, 94, 836); Burgundio trans., ed. Eligius M. Buytaert (Louvain: E. Nauwelaerts, 1955), p. 48. On the medieval translations of Damascene, see Buytaert's Preface, p. v, and Introduction, pp. ix–xx.

   7. A survey of the patristic tradition may be found in C. J. De Vogel, "'Ego sum qui sum' et sa signification pour une philosophie chrétienne," *Revue des sciences religieuses* 35 (1961), 346–53. The description "an infinite and indeterminate ocean of being" has its source in Gregory Nazianzus, *Orat.* 38.7 and 45.3 (PG, 36, 317B and 625C). On the meanings of "infinite" and "indeterminate" in this phrase, see L. Sweeney, "John Damascene's 'Infinite Sea of Essence,'" *Studia patristica VI*, ed. F. L. Cross, in *Texte und Untersuchungen zur Geschichte der altchristlichen Literatur* 81 (1962), 248–63.

signifying the divine nature. The notion of being that remains in it, even though freed from quidditative limitations, manifests only the imperfect being that is known in creatures. Yet with the removal of this final restriction, the last glimmer of light seems to die. The first and most characteristic name of God has been attained, but what it signifies is englobed in darkness.

What is the situation here? Damascene had meant that the dominantly significant and first name of God is "he who is." In this context the name "God" holds only second place. Damascene does not say in so many words that "he who is" does not signify what God is, but rather "an ocean of substance." Yet Aquinas seems justified in interpreting the meaning of his statement just that way, since Damascene had made the general assertion that all designations of God fail to signify what God is in substance, and then had listed "he who is" as the first of these designations. But what background does Aquinas use for the inference? Damascene had commenced his discussion by emphasizing the simplicity of the divine nature and the lack of any composition in it, in contrast to whatever consists of multiple and differing components. No characterization of God, accordingly, implies substantial differences in him, and from that viewpoint does not express anything in the order of substance.[8] For Aquinas this was sufficient to allow the conclusion that anything implying composition could not signify what God is. The reason had just been given in the reply to the immediately preceding argument: "[S]ince the being of a creature imperfectly represents the divine being, also the name 'he who is' signifies it imperfectly, because it signifies in the manner of a concrete union and synthesis." Concrete being, in fact, in itself expresses imperfection, "as in this name 'he who is.'"[9] The being immediately known to the human mind is in that way regarded by Aquinas as involving composition and therefore imperfection. It is apparently considered by him as still luminous for the human intellect, since there is as yet no mention of darkness. But it is not sufficient to signify the divine nature.

Against that background the steps outlined for progress in knowledge of God may be examined, as they are sketched in the passage in question. The first step is to reject corporeal attributes from the notion

8. "Oportet igitur singulum eorum, quae in Deo dicuntur, non quid secundum substantiam est significare estimare." Damascene, *De fid. orth.* 1.9.1; Burgundio trans., p. 48.8–10. Cf.: "[N]on ipsam substantiam comprehendimus, sed ea quae circa substantiam." Ibid., 1.10.2; p. 51.10–11.

9. "[C]um esse creaturae imperfecte repraesentet divinum esse, et hoc nomen 'qui est' imperfecte significat ipsum, quia significat per modum cujusdam concretionis et compositionis; . . . sicut in hoc nomine 'qui est.'" *Sent.* 1.8.1.1.ad 3m; 1, 196.

"he who is." This is fully in accord with the basic Aristotelian tenet that only sensible things are immediately apparent to human cognition. They are the only starting point for philosophical procedure to God. From them the human mind has to reason to their primary cause and to show that the primary cause cannot be a body. The procedure required had already been sketched in an earlier article in the commentary on the *Sentences*: "But from the seeing of perceptible things, we reach God only through a reasoning process, insofar as those things are caused and everything caused is from an agent cause and the primary agent cannot be a body."[10]

What is the process by which corporeal attributes are removed from the original conception? The basic human conception of anything that is, is that of a perceptible existent. Such was the Presocratic notion of things,[11] and such is the notion of reality that is most readily acceptable in ordinary human discourse. In fact, to express anything other than the corporeal, one has to use negative notions. Incorporeal, immaterial, inextended, non-quantitative, are the notions employed. They presuppose what is corporeal and quantitative, and then negate the characteristically corporeal aspects. How is this possible? It cannot be achieved by a simple process of abstraction, in the way the notion "man" is abstracted from John and Dick and Harry and the other observable individuals. The abstraction merely leaves out of consideration the individual characteristics observed in each man and focuses upon what is common in them all, the notion "man." "Man" is an object already seen in each, and now focused on in isolation from the individual traits. The same holds as in ascending scale the generic natures of animal, living thing, and body are isolated. These specific and generic natures are objects that confront the intellect in the individuals observed.

But can one go further and see within the notion "body" a still wider notion that would have "corporeal" and "incorporeal" as its differentiae? The schematizing in the traditional Porphyrian tree would seem to give that impression. From individuals "man" is abstracted, from man and brute "animal," from animals and plants "living thing," from animate and inanimate "body," and allegedly from bodies and spirits "substance." But is that what has actually happened at the last step? In all the other steps the different instances were observable before one's intellectual gaze. But were the instances "bod-

10. "Sed visis sensibilibus,non devenimus in Deum nisi procedendo, secundum quod ista causata sunt et quod omne causatum est ab aliqua causa agente et quod primum agens non potest esse corpus." *Sent.* 1.3.1.2.Solut.; 1, 94.

11. See Zeno, *Fr.* 1 (Diels-Kranz, 29 B); Aristotle, *Metaph.* 4.5.1010a2–3.

ies and spirits" equally observable? No. There were no instances of spirits before one's direct gaze, from which one could abstract a notion common also to bodies, as "man" was seen in Dick and Harry, and "animal" in man and brute. Even the word "spirit" betrays its corporeal origin. Etymologically it means "breath," and as denoting something invisible it has lent itself to signifying an incorporeal substance. But it does not present any simple concept beyond the corporeal order, nor does it offer positively a new differentia comparable to life, sensation, or rationality.

Yet the human mind is able to distinguish between the corporeal and the substantial in the instances of body that it immediately encounters. Body is originally conceived as able to have the three dimensions of length, breadth, and thickness. But the same thing can also be conceived as capable of existing or ceasing to exist. A table is made and destroyed, a tree grows and decays, and an animal is born and dies. The two ways of conceiving the same thing can be distinguished. Conceived in relation to its being or its existence, a body is known as a substance. In fact, the original designation of the Aristotelian category was in terms of being. It was *ousia,* and meant a being in the primary sense of the notion. To say that a body is a substance was merely to say that it was a being in the basic sense of the term "being."

With Aquinas, already at the time of the first book of his commentary on the *Sentences,* the quiddity or nature of a thing and the being of the thing were regarded as known through two different though always concomitant activities of the intellect.[12] As regards its nature, the thing was known through simple conceptualization that could be expressed in language by a single word, such as gold, mountain, man, or phoenix. As regards its being, it was known through a synthesizing act of judgment that required a proposition and a sentence for its

12. "[S]ince there is a double operation of the intellect, of which one . . . consists in the apprehension of simple quiddity, . . . the other . . . in the composition or division of a proposition, the first operation regards the quiddity of the thing, the second regards its being." *Sent.* 1.19.5.1.ad 7m; 1, 489. Cf. 1.38.1.3.Solut.; 1, 903. The Latin infinitive *esse,* which signifies the actuality originally grasped in the second operation of the mind, may be translated in this context by either "being" or "existence," without any change in the meaning of the term (see supra, n. 4). Being as encountered in sensible things is known through a synthesizing type of cognition because this being *consists in* a synthesis of form with matter or of accident with subject: "consistit in quadam compositione formae ad materiam, vel accidentis ad subjectum." *Sent.* 1.38. 1.3.Solut.; 1, 903. This immediate knowledge of being is intuition, in contrast to inference and to conceptualization. It is in the form of a judgment, as in the ordinary intuition that something is so, or in the philosophic sense that something is true. The use of "intuition" to describe the grasp of being through judgment may be seen in Maritain's posthumous work *Approches sans entraves* (Paris: Fayard, 1973), pp. 264–68.

expression. In relation to what was known about it in the latter way the thing was regarded as a being. Accordingly, the ground for the distinction between body and substance in the same thing is clear-cut. As a result of the highest type of simple conceptualization and abstraction in the first traditional category, the object is known as a body. As a result of reference to the actuality grasped through judgment, it is known as a substance.

But this recognized distinction allows for the play of further judgments in regard to the notions involved. The notion of something able to exist or to be is open to separation from the notion that originally accompanied it, the notion of body. Through a judgment one can negate the notion of body and retain the notion of existent. There is no question of leaving out the corporeal aspect, as would be the case in simple abstraction. It is not left out by abstraction, but it is negated by judgment. The object still appears corporeal but is judged to be incorporeal. The judgment is one of separation.[13]

Two instances in which this judgment is made in the metaphysics of Aquinas are the subsistent existence that is reached as the primary efficient cause of all perceptible things and the human soul that functions as the substantial principle of intellectual activity.[14] These are shown to be existents through reasoning processes in which the conclusion is drawn that they transcend the corporeal order. They are accordingly judged to be spiritual substances. To the extent the corporeal has been negated in them by judgment, the formation of a composite concept "incorporeal existent" follows. There is no simple abstraction from the corporeal, but its deliberate negation by judgment and the formation of the subsequent negatively expressed composite concept. The basic notion of an existent is retained from perceptible objects, and the negation of corporeality is joined to it.

Is this what has been taking place in the passage under consideration? Its wording is: "Hence when we proceed to God by 'the way of removal,' we first deny to him corporeal aspects."[15] "He who is" had been proposed as the first name for God. The object brought before the mind by the expression "he who is," is prima facie a perceptible existent, a man. This object has to be purified if it is to stand for the

13. A discussion of this topic may be found in my article "Metaphysical Separation in Aquinas," *Mediaeval Studies* 34 (1972), 287–306.
14. "But the most perfect of forms, that is, the human soul, . . . has an operation entirely rising above matter. . . . Insofar therefore as it exceeds the being of corporeal matter, since it is able to subsist and operate by itself, the human soul is a spiritual substance." *De spiritualibus creaturis* 2c. Cf. *De pot.* 3.11c; *Summa theologiae* 1.75.2; *Q. de an.* 1 and 14.
15. See text supra, n. 5.

divine nature. The way designated is a way already dealt with in the commentary. It consists in taking something that is imperfect, and then removing the imperfections in order to reach something perfect.[16] In the present case the corporeal attributes are removed from the object "he who is," and the process is that of negation—"negamus ab eo corporalia." This is quite obviously the judgment of separation.

The first step in "the way of removal," accordingly, frees the notion "he who is" from the imperfections involved in corporeality. Basically, the object still appears as corporeal. But the corporeal characteristics in it have been explicitly negated by judgment, and in this way removed from the conception. In this whole process no mention is made of any darkness. What is retained in the object is still treated of as luminous. In it the notions of "substance" and "existence" keep their full meaning. Though all sensible characteristics are deliberately set aside, the specifically intelligible traits seem to preserve their luminosity in entirely undiminished fashion. The conception, by and large, is now that of ordinary instructed Christians, who believe that God has no body while still regarding him as good and wise in the manner familiar to them, though raised to an infinite degree.

II

The second step in the procedure to God rejects from the notion "he who is" even intellectual attributes as they are found in creatures. The designation "intellectual" means, obviously enough, the kind that cannot be distinguished by the senses but only by the intelligence. The examples given are goodness and wisdom. The two seem rather disparate, but together they may illustrate an important facet of the reasoning in this passage. For Aquinas, goodness is a transcendental property of being.[17] It follows upon being, and is present wherever being is found. Since no creature is identified with its being, still less can it be identified with its goodness. Accordingly, goodness as dif-

16. "Secunda ratio sumitur per viam remotionis, et est talis. Ultra omne imperfectum oportet esse aliquod perfectum, cui nulla imperfectio admisceatur." *Sent.* 1.3.div. 1ae partis textus; 1, 88.

17. On the transcendentals in this context, see *Sent.* 1.8.1.3.Solut.; 1, 199–200. On the medieval background, see H. Pouillon, "Le premier traité des propriétés transcendantales," *Revue néoscolastique de philosophie* 42 (1939), 40–77. A coverage of the transcendentals is given by Karl Bärthlein, *Die Transzendentalienlehre der alten Ontologie* 1 (Berlin: Walter de Gruyter, 1972). Unlike Aquinas, it does not accept goodness and truth as properties of being. Goodness and wisdom were used together by Peter Lombard as examples of the attributes of God in the text upon which Aquinas (*Sent.* 1.8; 1, 190) was commenting.

ferent from the thing's nature is removed from the notion "he who is."

Since goodness is meant to serve as an example, it would indicate that the other transcendental properties of being, such as truth and beauty, are being negated in the sense in which they are different from the subject that possesses them. But in the context the intelligible attributes negated have to be restricted to transcendentals that are properties. The basic notion from which they are being removed has to remain. It is that of something existent, "he who is." The transcendental subject of being, namely "thing," and its first actuation as "a being," are transcendentals that remain for the third step in the procedure. In a word, only the intelligible attributes that *follow* upon an existent nature are in question in the second step.

The other example given is wisdom. This is a different kind of attribute, not common to all creatures, and following upon a definite type of nature rather than upon existence. It had just been used to illustrate the way being can be determined under a definite aspect, for it "means to be something,"[18] namely, to be wise. It had also been given as an example of a divine name that in its meaning designated the source of God's activity in the created world, and as an instance of a notion that in creatures implied imperfection.[19] In creatures, of course, wisdom belongs to the category of quality and has the imperfection of an accident.[20] What it is meant to illustrate in the context is a determination or limitation of being. All natures other than being itself come under this designation—"all other names mean being under some other determinate aspect."[21] The attribute "male," implied by the Greek masculine article and participle, and by the masculine relative pronoun in Latin, is no exception.

The general situation, as it is at this stage, seems described clearly enough in the text. The notion from which the start had been made found expression in the words "he who is." To have this notion stand for the divine nature, bodily aspects are first negated in it. Secondly, transcendental properties and definite natures, as these are known in

18. "sicut sapiens dicit aliquid esse." *Sent.* 1.8.1.1.ad 4m; 1, 196.

19. *Sent.* 1.8.1.1.ad 2m; 1, 196. Cf. *Sent.* 1.2.1.2–3 (1, 61–72), where goodness and wisdom are likewise the examples used.

20. "[S]icut quod hoc nomen 'sapientia' imponitur cuidam qualitati, et hoc nomen 'essentia' cuidam rei quae non subsistit: et haec longe a Deo sunt." *Sent.* 1.2.1.3.Solut.; 1, 69.

21. "alia omnia nomina dicunt esse secundum aliam rationem determinatam." *Sent.* 8.1.1.ad 4m; 1, 196. Cf.: "Praeterea, quidquid est in genere, habet esse suum determinatum ad illud genus. Sed esse divinum nullo modo determinatum est ad aliquod genus; quinimo comprehendit in se nobilitates omnium generum" *Sent.* 1.8.4.2, contra; 1, 221.

creatures, are removed from it. What remains now in the original notion? Its content is described as only "that (he) is (*quia est*) . . . and nothing more."

How should the *quia est* be translated? It is reminiscent of the Parmenidean route of being, namely *hoti estin,* and presents the same barrier to exact translation. No subject is expressed, yet English requires the insertion of a subject term. The translation will read "that it is." In Parmenides this would imply a subject other than being, though there cannot be anything other than being for the Eleatic when traveling the way of truth. Further, in the thirteenth-century background, "that a thing is" was an expression that stood in contrast to "what a thing is." It designated the existence of the thing in contrast to the thing's nature, and was for Aquinas what the act of judgment attained.[22] Here it is meant to signify "being itself, as present in creatures"—"ipsum esse, secundum quod est in creaturis." It is the existential actuality that confronts the mind whenever something is known to exist.

But what is this "being itself, as present in creatures," when taken just alone? It is the synthesizing actuality known through judgment, and expressed in proposition and sentence. However, all quidditative determinations have been removed from it in this second stage. From that standpoint it is entirely indeterminate. "Existing" is all that can be left in the object. That is, of course, wide enough to extend to everything. Yet, as known to the human intellect, it remains an actuality making something else exist. It has to imply, besides itself, an indefinite "something" that does the existing. The notion accordingly is "that which is" in the all-embracing universality to which existing can extend. It means something that exists without limits—quite in accord with the simile of a boundless ocean.

There need be little wonder, then, that the description of this second stage concludes with the assertion, "Hence it is, as it were, in a state of confusion." There is no reference to a Greek source for that notion. Elsewhere the term *confusio* is found used by Aquinas in its various ordinary senses. It is directly opposed to *distinctio,* and in the concrete may signify a mingling in which each component keeps its own identity and yet is known in a way that does not distinguish it from the others.[23]

22. See supra, n. 12.
23. Cf.: "Distinctioni autem opponitur confusio." *ST* 1.66.1.contra 2. There, and in the reply to the argument, *confusio* was used for the *chaos* of the ancients; see also *Phys.* 4.1.Angeli-Pirotta no. 800. In the text from the *Summa*, "sub quadam confusione" describes the instances under the universal as well as the parts in an integral whole: "scientia imperfecta, per quam sciuntur res indistincte sub quadam confusione. . . .

In the present context it bears on the patristic description of God as "an infinite ocean of being." Aquinas is facing the interpretation that this does not signify what God is, in the sense that it does not express the divine nature. Yet it does name God in terms of being only, and being is the nature of God. Why, then, does not "he who is," in the meaning of an infinite ocean of being, signify the divine nature? What is meant by saying that the notion is in a state of confusion that does not as yet permit it to signify what it intends?

Since no Greek source is indicated, the answer has to be sought in Aquinas's understanding of being. For him, being is the primary actuality of anything whatsoever.[24] Its range is accordingly unlimited. Where it subsists, it will actualize every aspect of reality. In this way it may be regarded as an indeterminate ocean of being, containing the totality of being in a way that leaves each aspect indistinct from every other. But is the notion so formed as facile as it appears at immediate encounter? Why should any problem at all arise about distinction within it, if it satisfactorily subsumes everything under the one characteristic of being?

First, there is the question how being is originally grasped by the human intellect. For Aquinas, being is originally known through the synthesizing act of judgment. It is known as an actuality that itself consists in a synthesis, a synthesis that joins matter, form, and accidents into a single existent, and thereby determines and individuates. It should not allow indistinctness.[25] On the other hand, what is actuated

Manifestum est autem quod cognoscere aliquid in quo plura continentur, sine hoc quod habeatur propria notitia uniuscuiusque eorum quae continentur in illo, est cognoscere aliquid *sub confusione quadam.* Sic autem potest cognosci tam totum universale, in quod partes continentur in potentia, quam etiam totum integrale; utrumque enim totum potest cognosci *in quadam confusione,* sine hoc quod partes distincte cognoscantur." *ST* 1.85.3.c. Cf.: "in quadam communitate et confusione." Ibid., 1.89.1c. See also 1.117. 1.ad 4m. In the commentary on the *Sentences,* the opposition was described through contrast to arrangement of parts in place: "[C]onfusio opponitur ordini partium qui pertinet ad rationem situs." *Sent.* 4.10.3.3.ad 2m; ed. Moos, 4, 418 (no. 87). The overall meaning is that the components of something are not distinguished here from one another. The adjective "indeterminate" in the text of Damascene seems to have been what suggested Aquinas's use of the term "confusion" in his explanation of the passage. So the ocean metaphor is explained at *De pot.* 7.5c, as "significat esse indeterminate."

24. Being (*esse*) is presented in this sense as "the actuality of essence" (*actu essentiae*). *Sent.* 1.33.1.1.ad 1m; 1, 766. In later works the universal range is made explicit: "the actuality of all acts, and on this account it is the perfection of all perfections." *De pot.* 7.2.ad 9m; "[B]eing is the actuality of every form or nature." *ST* 1.3.4c. Cf. *Periherm.* 1.5.Leonine no. 22.

25. Where being is a nature, namely in God, it determines and distinguishes just by itself. Cf.: "Ita etiam divinum esse est determinatum in se et ab omnibus aliis divisum, per hoc quod sibi nulla additio fieri potest." *Sent.* 8.4.1.ad 1m; 1, 219. "Deus enim per essentiam suam est aliquid in se indivisum, et ab omnibus quae non sunt Deus, distinctum." *De pot.* 8.3c. On sensible being as a synthesis of matter, form, and accident, see text supra, n. 12.

by existence may be considered in indefinite fashion, extending to everything that may possibly exist. In this way every aspect of being may be included under the notion "he who is," when all quidditative determinations have been separated from it in "the way of removal." The content of the notion may be expressed metaphorically as an indeterminate ocean of being, including as it does drop after drop of water in indefinite sequence, each spatially apart from the others but without any definite limits appearing between them.

Why is this concept unable to signify the divine nature, the nature of being? Quidditative knowledge, in the noetic already at work in Aquinas at the time of writing the commentary on the *Sentences,* is knowledge through conceptualization, knowledge through the first operation of the intellect. Through this type of knowledge the being of the thing is not grasped. Yet, in the notion of "he who is" as an indeterminate ocean of being, the representation is that of something conceived as existing in indefinite fashion. It is basically the notion of an existent nature, even though all quidditative limitations have been separated from it by deliberative thought. In Heideggerian terminology it would still be regarded as an ontic conception. It is the notion of something that has being, a common notion that is now applied to a single subject by the removal of all quidditative limits. It does not represent properly the subsistent existence reached when the existence of perceptible things is traced to the primary efficient cause.

Why does this anomaly arise? Being, in the noetic of Aquinas, is nowhere immediately attained by the human intellect as a nature. It is a facet that remains outside the natures of things. It is not known as a quiddity or nature, but as another actuality that synthesizes all the components of a thing. In the designation "he who is," this actuality is still regarded as present in what is designated, but it is not the nature that is thereby represented. It has the status of an actuality outside the nature envisaged, on account of the way in which it was originally known by the intellect. The nature thereby designated is not the nature of being, but rather the common nature of anything that can be, taken now without limitation. It is a melding of all possible natures, that is, all natures other than the nature of being, into a something that is regarded as existing. The one nature that is not included is the nature of being. But that is the nature it would have to express if it were to designate the nature of God. There need be little wonder, then, that "he who is" may be characterized as signifying not what God is, but rather an indeterminate ocean of substance. The nature represented is still other than the nature of being, and does not include being in any quidditative way. It is the notion of an existent substance that has no quidditative limitations, containing in indistinctive fashion every possible quidditative perfection.

The situation is the same as in the case of the Anselmian argument, already discussed by Aquinas in a preceding article in the commentary on the *Sentences*.[26] The concept of a being greater than which nothing can be thought does not tell whether or not it exists. It can be thought not to exist. The meaning is that quidditative perfection, even though extended indefinitely, does not include existence. Existence has to be known through judgment. The sum total of all conceivable perfections does not result in the nature of existence, the nature of God. Just as there is no necessary sequence from the greatest conceivable perfection to the existence of God, so the indeterminate ocean of substance does not express what God is, or what the nature of being is.

Although the object "he who is" is now found to be in a confused state, it is not said to be in darkness. It is still luminous. All concepts of definite natures have been removed from it, but the concept of "nature" or "something" in general remains. It is luminous in the way of a universal notion. It is represented as actuated by being, the actuality known through judgment. "He who is" is conceived as something that exists. The notion of "something" is an ordinary notion accessible to conceptualization, and the notion "is" continues to be that of the actuality expressed ordinarily in the synthesis of a proposition. Both elements in the notion "he who is" are still accessible at this stage to ordinary human cognition, and in that way remain luminous even though, through metaphysical separation, the ordinary quidditative determinations have been removed from the notion. The notion contains the whole of being (*"Totum . . . esse"*—Burgundio trans., p. 49.2) in the confused way in which a universal contains all that comes under it. "Sicut in quadam confusione" describes well enough the knowledge thereby given.

The luminosity in the notion "he who is" does not, accordingly, yield knowledge about the nature of being. It makes manifest only the synthesizing being that is found in creatures, being that is not present as a nature. Aquinas has no hesitation in making the statement: "And similarly this name 'he who is' names God through the being found in creatures."[27] If the distinction between the two original ways of knowing (namely, conceptualization and judgment) is not kept in

---

26. "[P]otest cogitare nihil hujusmodi esse quo majus cognitari non possit; et ideo ratio sua procedit ex hac suppositione, quod supponatur aliquid esse quo majus cogitari non potest." *Sent.* 3.1.2.ad 4m; 1, 95.

27. "Et similiter hoc nomen 'qui est' nominat Deum per esse inventum in creaturis, quod exemplariter deductum est ab ipso." *Sent.* 8.1.1.ad 2m; 1, 196.

mind, the cognition of being may be looked upon as an intuition of its nature and accordingly the Parmenidean consequences may be drawn. Being is then regarded as entirely luminous, in the way it was viewed by the Eleatic. But in the noetic of Aquinas, the being that is known in the act of judgment does not manifest the nature of being. The being of creatures is of course derived from subsistent being not only by way of efficient causality but also by way of exemplar causality. Yet it reflects its exemplar too imperfectly to represent it in the way in which any nature is known. The light that "he who is" provides is that of a synthesis, not that of a nature.[28]

The knowledge reached at this stage is no longer that of the ordinary instructed Christian, but rather that of the metaphysician. The ordinary Christian does not remove from his notion of God the intelligible attributes as found in creatures, such as wisdom and goodness. He thinks of God as being good and wise quite as he sees these attributes in creatures, though on an infinite scale. He does not attempt to regard them as rendered indistinct in the one concept of being. He does not push his thought that far. This second stage is one for a metaphysician. There need be no surprise at finding it neglected by mystical writers. Unless he is a metaphysician the mystic does not subsume the other perfections under the one notion "being." He need not encounter the confused state on his way to the dark cloud.

III

In the third and final step, even the synthesizing type of being is removed from the notion "he who is." Immediately the object is in darkness. The light thrown by the being that is known through judgment, even though it is but a very imperfect reflection, was sufficient to represent the totality of being in indistinct fashion. But when it disappears in the process of removal, it takes with it all that it actuates. There is nothing luminous left in the object "he who is." Yet, according to the text, it is in this situation that cognitional union with God best takes place.

Dionysius, there seems no doubt, was referring to mystical union.[29]

---

28. Text supra, n. 9.
29. On this topic, see Charles Journet, *The Dark Knowledge of God*, trans. James F. Anderson (London: Sheed & Ward, 1948), pp. 70–81. Dionysius uses the description "the darkness of true mystical nescience." Dionysius, *Myst. theol.* 1.3.85; PG, 3, 1001A (Journet, p. 78). The union (*henōsis*) that takes place with God in this darkness is regarded by Dionysius (*De div. nom.* 7.3; PG, 3, 872) as a knowledge (*gnōsis*) that surpasses our understanding. For Aquinas, any knowledge is a union of knower and known. In

With the symbolism of perceptual cognition removed, and the limiting force of concepts out of the way, the obstacles to mystical knowledge would be set aside. There is nothing in the text to indicate that Aquinas was not understanding Dionysius in this way. Yet the text occurs in a theological school treatise, in which communicable knowledge is being passed from master to students. The immediately preceding stage was one of metaphysical reasoning. Does the present one remain open also to interpretation on the metaphysical level? Does it proceed in metaphysical sequence from what has already been established? No matter how well Aquinas appreciates the setting in which Dionysius speaks, is he here applying these considerations to a situation present also on the philosophical plane? Specifically, what will the "darkness of ignorance" mean, if it is interpreted in a metaphysical context?

First, it will inevitably mean lack of conceptual knowledge. The subsistent being that was reached by "the way of causality" is not known in quidditative fashion. It was attained by travel on the route of existence. The sensible thing's existence, grasped through judgment and not through conceptualization, was the basis for reasoning to its primary efficient cause, subsistent existence. No quidditative knowledge of the existence was present at any stage of the reasoning. Having demonstrated that existence subsists in this primary instance, one has thereby shown that it is in this instance a nature. It is *what* exists. But that nature has been reached in terms of existence, and not through any elaboration of quidditative concepts. The result is that one cannot *conceive* it as a nature, even though one knows that it is a nature. The lack of any conceptual content in the object now before one's mind can surely be termed a darkness. More specifically, it is a darkness resulting from ignorance, since in the notion all quidditative content remains a blank. The notion can be developed to an incomparably rich content, by showing that each of the transcendental and quidditative perfections known to the human mind is included in one way or another in subsistent existence. But there each of them is identified with subsistent existence. What they are at that level is existence itself.[30] What the existence is remains unknown. Accordingly

---

consequence, the metaphysical knowledge of God likewise achieves a union on its own level, in darkness but with richest philosophical content. On "homo conjungitur Deo" in this sense, see Aquinas, *ST* 1–2.3.2.ad 4m.

30. "quidquid est in simplici, est ipsum suum esse." *Sent.* 1.8.exp. 1ae partis textus; 1, 208. Cf.: "Quidquid autem est in Deo, hoc est suum proprium esse." *De ver.* 2.11c. Nevertheless, the formal meaning of the different attributes remains intact in this identity with subsistent existence, both because their meaning in creatures is derived from

one can demonstrate that each perfection is present in subsistent existence, yet not know *what* the perfection is when it is found identified with existence. The light of conceptual knowledge is utterly and completely lacking. The question is not the same as in the problem of uniting in one concept the corpuscular and the wave notions of elementary particles and light, when both aspects have been proven to be there. Rather, it is the impossibility of any concept at all in regard to the nature of being.

Consequently, the intuition of existence in sensible things, as experienced through the act of judgment, cannot focus upon subsistent existence. It cannot give knowledge of any quiddity. But here the object is a quiddity as well as existence. It therefore cannot come under the human intuition of existence, the intuition of a synthesizing actuality. True, one can show that what is uppermost in that sensible existence is actuality and not the synthesizing aspect that existence in created things involves.[31] That is enough to allow the existence of creatures to serve as the starting point for reasoning to subsistent existence. But it does not permit one to see what existential actuality is in the status of a nature instead of a non-quidditative synthesizing of something other than the existence itself.

A blind person guides himself by touch and hearing, a pilot makes an instrument landing just by panel readings. Neither can see the place to which he is going. But each has the respective kind of knowledge that suffices to get him where he wants to go. So a metaphysician demonstrates that the primary efficient cause is subsistent existence and that it contains all perfections in the highest degree. But he cannot conceive either its nature or any of its perfections as they are in themselves, and he cannot intuit its existence. The ordinary light in which nature and existence are apparent to him has disappeared. Surely this merits the appellation "a darkness of ignorance." Yet in this darkness the whole positive metaphysics about subsistent existence, in all its richness, attains its best development.

IV

The passage in Aquinas about the "darkness of ignorance," in which God is best known, is open accordingly to thoroughgoing metaphysical interpretation. It means that subsistent existence, though concluded

---

the divine model, and because that meaning would be there even though no creatures ever existed, as already explained at *Sent.* 1.2.1.2; 1, 63.

31. See *Periherm.* 1.5.Leonine no. 22.

to by demonstration from sensible things, cannot be conceptualized; and it cannot be represented through the model of the existence immediately known by the human mind. On both these counts the notion of subsistent existence remains dark. Yet, in the realization of this darkness, metaphysical knowledge reaches its highest point, for then the infinitely rich attributes it predicates of subsistent being are not tarnished or diminished by the built-in deficiencies of the human cognitive processes. The "darkness" provides the way of rising above these otherwise unavoidable limitations. It blots out what is imperfect and deceptive.

At the same time, the passage illustrates how genuine metaphysics is operative in the theological reasoning of Aquinas. The setting of the passage is theological, occurring as it does in the course of a commentary on a theological text. God's name has been revealed as being, yet according to the same revelation he is best known in a dense darkness. The theological introduction of the notion "being" prompts the metaphysical inquiry how God, elsewhere represented as light, has to be known in darkness. Does being furnish the answer? Somewhat as the calculations of Adams and Leverrier led to the turning of a telescope on Neptune, so these theological considerations focus attention on the anomaly in the object "being." The closer metaphysical scrutiny then reveals that being was attained as a synthesis in judgment, and not known originally by way of conceptualization. The result shows that what is intuited as "being" cannot be used in Parmenidean fashion as a nature from which the conclusions of unicity and unchangeableness may be deduced. The nature of being is in no way intuited. It is *concluded to,* and only in darkness. It is not immediately the being that is known in the light of intuition.

In this manner, being is located as a nature in a unique and unchangeable primary instance, while the being that is intuited by the human mind remains multiple and varying. Even with the consequent tenet that God or subsistent being is the being of all else,[32] the relation of subsistent being to all the other instances of being is that of exemplar and efficient, not formal, cause. The being that is luminous to human cognition remains accordingly multiple and variable, while the nature of being in its unicity and unchangeableness is eminently respected. But the condition is a "darkness of ignorance" in which the nature of being is attained only by way of a conclusion to something beyond the human intellect's power to intuit or conceive. The priva-

---

32. See supra, n. 2.

tion of both intuitional and conceptual light requires that the most refined notion of the primary efficient cause be enshrouded in this darkness in order to permit, on the metaphysical level, the successive predication of its infinite richness without the hindrance of finite restrictions.

10

"CAUSE OF NECESSITY" IN AQUINAS'S *TERTIA VIA*

I

The *tertia via* in Aquinas's *Summa theologiae* for proving the existence of God continues to be puzzling. Along with other difficult points in its procedure, the insertion of the notion "cause of necessity" for one class of necessary beings seems to complicate the argument and open diverse ways of interpretation. Yet this notion is an integral part of the background against which the final conclusion is drawn: "Therefore it is necessary to posit something that is necessary of itself, not having a cause of necessity from some other source, but which is the cause of necessity to the others; and this all call God."[1] The conclusion of the arguments is precisely the positing of a cause of necessity for whatever other necessary things there may be.

The importance and timeliness of a correct understanding of this argument from the *Summa theologiae* should be obvious enough today. After some three decades of sharp and searching controversy in the present century on the ontological argument for God's existence, interest turned towards what Kant had called the "cosmological argument."[2] By this designation was meant immediately the reasoning from the contingency of the world, in the sense of the basic outline of all the proofs in the traditional natural theology (Kant, *Critique of Pure Reason*, B 632–33). Since the *tertia via* of Aquinas argues from the contingency in the things of the visible world to a first necessary being, may it not be classed straightway under the cosmological argument and be brought into the current discussion about it?

---

1. "Ergo necesse est ponere aliquid quod sit per se necessarium, non habens causam necessitatis aliunde, sed quod est causa necessitatis aliis, quod omnes dicunt Deum." *ST* 1.2.3c.

2. For a short survey of its "importance in the history of ideas and its extraordinary resilience under criticism," see Ronald W. Hepburn, in Paul Edwards's *Encyclopedia of Philosophy,* s.v. "Cosmological Argument for the Existence of God."

Some hesitations arise, however, when the *tertia via* is placed in this setting. A cosmological argument should, from the general pattern, reason from a contingent being or contingent beings to a necessary being. Once the necessary being has been reached, its task should be completed. Such is not the case in the *tertia via*. It arrives at a necessary being or necessary beings, but still has to inquire about the cause of their necessity. Not precisely a necessary being, but the cause of necessity for all other necessary beings, is its terminus. This consideration seems enough to alert an historian of philosophy to a possible deepseated difference between the notion of the cosmological argument that is in vogue today and the spirit of the *tertia via*. The problem consequently deserves some careful investigation.

The investigation will have to take account of the different concepts of necessity and the way the necessity is caused. Category mistakes, in confusing the necessity of propositions with necessity in things, have to be avoided. What functions in the argument is a necessity found in things, regardless of what propositions people may make about them. Logical necessity, understood as necessary relations between propositions, is accordingly not at stake. Is the necessity meant here, then, to be found in the way a real essence necessarily contains its own notes and necessarily grounds the properties that follow upon it? In this way human nature is necessarily rational and sensitive, and grounds the abilities to reason and to decide. Insofar as the essence is their necessary source, it may readily be looked upon as the cause of necessity in their regard.

Or is the "cause of necessity" in this case something existential rather than a necessitating feature in the order of essence? The possibility of an existential or voluntaristic interpretation cannot be ruled out a priori when one considers the background against which Aquinas was writing. He was well aware of the passage in Plato's *Timaeus* (41AB) in which the demiurge proclaimed to the gods that, though generated, they were by his will indissoluble.[3] The bond in his so willing was greater and more dominant than the condition given them by their birth. The possibility, then, that a thing could be necessarily existent on account of the decision of its maker, even though it itself is perishable on the ground of its own essence, has to be taken into consideration. In this case the introduction of the notion "cause of necessity" will have an important bearing on the interpretation of the *tertia via* vis-à-vis the cosmological argument constructed and demol-

---

3. "Plato, qui de corporibus caelestibus Deum loquentem inducit in hunc modum: *Natura vestra estis dissolubilia, voluntate autem mea indissolubilia:*" Aquinas, *Summa contra gentiles* 1.20, Ad hoc.

ished by Kant. Under Kant's analysis the cosmological argument turned out to be but a version of the ontological. Though claiming to start in experience, it abandoned experience after the first step and argued from mere concepts (*Critique*, B 634–635). This or any other reduction of the cosmological to the ontological argument obviously will not hold in regard to the *tertia via*, if the necessity in question comes not from the exigencies of concepts or natures but from the will of an external efficient cause. On the other hand, the difficulties are just as obvious. What philosophical means are available for knowing the will of the maker? Further, if pushed to the extreme, will not this view exclude all serious functions of essences and even ultimately, with Descartes,[4] make all necessary truth depend on the will of God?

Further difficulties arise from the nature of Aquinas's own involvement in the *tertia via*. The argument occurs in a professedly theological work, the *Summa theologiae*. In the method of sacred theology, the existence of God is obviously presupposed from the start, since the basic principles of the science are accepted on his word. The ways for demonstrating his existence are brought under a consideration of the divine essence, as though the real question at issue were the relation of God's existence to his essence: "Primo considerabimus ea quae ad essentiam divinam pertinent. . . . Circa essentiam vero divinam, primo considerandum est an Deus sit" (*ST* 1.2.init.). In the *Summa contra gentiles*, the ways of demonstration are expressly introduced as arguments that have been drawn up by other thinkers: "procedamus ad ponendum rationes quibus tam philosophi quam doctores Catholici Deum esse probaverunt" (*CG* 1.13.Ostenso igitur). There is no reason to doubt that the same status is accorded them in the *Summa theologiae*, since its procedure at this stage parallels in general lines the treatment given in the *Contra gentiles*.

One point, however, might prima facie cause some hesitation in admitting the parallelism for the case of the *tertia via*. In the *Contra gentiles* this argument is not listed under the ways for demonstrating God's existence. Rather, it occurs two chapters later as a proof for the divine eternity. It exhibits the same general structure as the *tertia via* in the *Summa theologiae*, as far as the intermediate conclusion that a first necessary being has to be posited: "Ergo oportet ponere aliquod primum necessarium, quod est per seipsum necessarium. Et hoc Deus

---

4. "Do not be afraid, I ask you, to affirm as certain and publish everywhere that it is God who has established these laws in nature just as a king establishes laws in his kingdom." R. Descartes, *Correspondance à Mersenne*, 15 avril 1630; Adam & Tannery, 1.145.13–16. Cf. *à Mersenne*, 27 mai 1630 (pp. 151–52); *à l'Abbé Picot*, 2 mai 1644 (4, 118–19).

est" (*CG* 1.15.Amplius). It then proceeds to draw the further conclusion that the divine eternity follows from this necessity.

Just because the argument here goes on to an ulterior conclusion it need not be rejected as a proof for the existence of God. Rather, it requires for its validity the demonstration that it contains of the divine existence. Only by proving that God is necessarily existent, according to the method followed in the *tertia via*, does it demonstrate the divine eternity. Parallel cases are easy to find in Aquinas. For instance, in the commentary on the *Sentences* the argument from motion, listed in first place among the different ways in the *Summa theologiae* and the *Contra gentiles,* is not brought under any of Dionysius's three "ways of reaching God from creatures" (*Sent.* 1.3.div. 1ae partis; ed. Mandonnet, 1, 88–89), but is given as a preliminary argument for the divine immutability: "Ergo oportet devenire ad primum motorem, qui movet et nullo modo movetur; et hic est Deus. Ergo est omnino immutabilis" (8.3.1.contra; p. 211). The argument reaches the primary movent with all the cogency of the *prima via* of the *Summa theologiae* and the first two ways of the *Contra gentiles.* The fact that it goes on to draw a further conclusion does not at all keep it from being the same argument used in the two *summae* as a way of demonstrating God's existence. Likewise, the reasoning in the *De ente et essentia* to prove the entitative composition of creatures uses the argument from efficient causality to reach God: "Patet ergo quod intelligentia est forma et esse, et quod esse habet a primo ente quod est esse tantum, et hoc est causa prima que Deus est" (*De ente* 4; Leonine ed., *Op. Om.* 43, 377.143–46). The purpose of a further inference does not infringe upon its cogency as a proof of the divine existence. For its own purpose it has to arrive at the nature of existence. But to reach the nature of existence, in the metaphysical procedure of Aquinas, is to prove the existence of God.[5]

The way of arguing in the *tertia via,* then, is found in the *Contra gentiles* outside the list of arguments by which others, namely, both philosophers and Catholic teachers, have proven that God exists. It is no longer expressly placed in a list of the reasons used by others. It is rather offered as an argument by Aquinas in his own name, regardless of source.

---

5. Since existence is not grasped in the conceptualization of any nature, its own nature is not known till one has worked out the conclusion that in a single instance it subsists in itself as existence only. But that is to have proven the existence of God. According to Aristotle's (*Metaph.* 5.5.1015a34–36) basic sense of the necessary, namely, "what cannot be otherwise," God could be called a necessary being because he is his own existence. But this existential meaning is not included in Aristotle's list. For Aristotle, however, necessity and eternity were convertible (*De gen. et corr.* 2.11.337b35).

This twofold status indicated for the argument from contingency need not at all be disconcerting. Rather, the importance of the twofold relation (to himself and to the reasoning of others) is emphasized in regard to the interpretation and understanding of the argument as used by St. Thomas. The ways he lists for proving the existence of God, even though taken from other thinkers, he quite obviously accepts as valid. He may not understand them in exactly the same way as in their original context. The argument from motion, for instance, he elsewhere characterizes, speaking in his own name, as most efficacious for proving the existence of the first principle.[6] It is the argument used in his own procedure in the *Compendium theologiae* (c. 3). But he does not understand it in its Aristotelian sense, in which it involves the eternity of cosmic motion and the animate nature of the heavenly bodies.[7] Likewise, the way of efficient causality, though expressly attributed to Aristotle,[8] he understands in a way that finds efficient causality in separate substance. It is an argument used frequently by Aquinas in his own name in the commentary on the *Sentences*.[9] The same openness to new interpretation can be shown for the arguments from the grades of being and from the teleology of the cosmos.[10] It should accordingly be looked for in the argument from the contingency of observable things. The express rejection of the

6. *In Phys.* 8.1.Angeli-Pirotta no. 1991. A discussion of the way the skeletal argument is revivified by Aquinas may be found in my article, "The Starting Point of the *Prima Via*," *Franciscan Studies* 5 (1967), 249–84.

7. See *CG* 1.13.Praedictos; *In Phys.* 8.1.1991; *In Metaph.* 12.5.Cathala nos. 2496–99.

8. *CG* 1.13.Procedit. The Aristotelian separate substance is regarded by Aquinas as an agent cause: "[Q]uod non solum sit aliqua substantia sempiterna movens et agens, sed etiam *quod eius substantia sit actus." In Metaph.* 12.5.2494.

9. In his own way Aquinas explains the first reason given by Peter Lombard for knowledge of God: "Prima ergo ratio sumitur per via causalitatis, et formatur sic. Omne quod habet esse ex nihilo, oportet quod sit ab aliquo a quo esse suum fluxerit. . . . Ergo oportet quod sint ab aliquo uno primo, et hoc est Deus." *Sent.* 1.3.div.1ae partis textus; ed. Mandonnet, 1, 88. This consideration was regarded as basic for all three ways given in Dionysius: "Et ratio hujus est, quia esse creaturae est ab altero. Unde secundum hoc ducimur in causam a qua est" (ibid). The consideration likewise underlies the Thomistic doctrine of participation as sharing in existence rather than in form; e.g., "Reliquitur ergo quod omnia alia a Deo non sint suum esse, sed participant esse. Necesse est igitur quod omnia quae diversificantur secundum diversam participationem essendi, ut sint perfectius vel minus perfecte, causari ab uno primo ente, quod perfectissime est." *ST* 1.44.1c.

10. The *quarta via* cites Aristotle, but concludes to a cause of existence (*causa esse*). The argument from the directing of things to a purpose is taken (*CG* 1.13.Ad hoc) from John Damascene (*De fid. orth.* 1.3; PG 94, 795D) and Averroes, who explains its denial of efficient causality: "ex quo sequitur ipsum negare agens: generans enim non generat, nisi propter aliquid, et similiter movens movet propter aliquid" (*In II Phys.* text 75 [Venice, 1562], fol. 75v2, L). Aquinas (*ST* 1.2.3.ad 2m) understands the argument in the framework of the first and third *viae*.

Anselmian argument, and the omission of arguments from the consensus of peoples or instinctive human knowledge and moral tendencies, suffice to show that the arguments given by philosophers and Catholic teachers are not placed indiscriminately in the list.

This manner of dealing with arguments constructed by other thinkers suggests that the structure of the demonstration in each case has to be examined in the writer from which it was taken. The argument from motion, for instance, clearly has its structure in the Aristotelian treatises. The new meaning infused into the structure, however, will be from Aquinas's own thought. It is a new meaning that will conclude in the *prima via* to a unique immobile movement, instead of to a possible fifty-five. Correspondingly, in the *tertia via* the background from which the structure may have been taken will have to be probed in its alien sources. The meaning breathed into it, however, will need to be studied in the preceding works of Aquinas himself. From this double standpoint one will be able to gauge what the argument owes to its alien structure and what it owes to the original thinking of its new proponent.

In Aquinas himself the version of the argument in the *Summa contra gentiles* lies behind the *tertia via* of the *Summa theologiae*. Probably between them is a basic discussion of possibility and necessity in the *De potentia* (5.3.), in which Arabic sources are used as a framework. Still further back are enlightening reflections in the commentary on the *Sentences*. These will have to be investigated for Aquinas's own thought. The role played by the framework in which the Arabians had placed the discussion of contingency and necessity will require examination, with their Aristotelian background and the possibility of other influences. Only then will one be in a position to assess the structure of the demonstration and the meaning given to the argument in the writings of Aquinas.

II

The version of the argument in the *Contra gentiles* (1.15.Amplius) commences with the observation that some things in the world have the possibility to be or not to be. This openness to both being and not-being requires that if they have being, they have it from a cause. Of themselves, they could just as well not exist. Infinite regress in efficient causes had just been shown through Aristotelian reasoning to be inadmissible. Accordingly, something that is a necessary being has to be posited:

Omne autem quod est possibile esse, causam habet: quia, cum de se aequaliter se habeat ad duo, scilicet esse et non esse, oportet, si ei approprietur esse, quod hoc sit ex aliqua causa. Sed in causis non est procedendum in infinitum, ut supra probatum est per rationem Aristotelis. Ergo oportet ponere aliquid quod sit necesse esse (*CG* 1.15.Amplius).

The force of the argument is that the perishable things in the observable world are of themselves as equally open to existence as to non-existence. This determination has to come from a cause. What kind of a cause? The text does not specify. But there need not be the least doubt that here an efficient cause is meant. Everywhere for Aquinas, a cause that gives existence is an efficient cause, or at least requires efficient causality to achieve its effect.[11] Further, the backward reference to the impossibility of an infinite series is concerned expressly with efficient causes: "Procedit autem Philosophus alia via in *II Metaphys.*, ad ostendendum non posse procedi in infinitum in causis efficientibus" (*CG* 1.13.Procedit). Also, the use of the verb *approprietur* for the bestowal of existence indicates influence of the Latin Avicennian text in its notion of agent causality.

What the argument has proven, then, is that where there are contingent things there is some necessary being as their efficient cause. The argument goes on to show that ultimately there is a cause that does not have its necessity from anything else:

Omne autem necessarium vel habet causam suae necessitatis aliunde; vel non, sed est per seipsum necessarium. Non est autem procedere in infinitum in necessariis quae habent causam suae necessitatis aliunde. Ergo oportet ponere aliquod primum necessarium, quod est per seipsum necessarium. Et hoc Deus est: cum sit causa prima, ut ostensum est (*CG* 1.15.Amplius).

The caused necessary things, as is clear elsewhere in Aquinas and has been stressed in some modern articles, include angels, spiritual souls, and celestial bodies.[12] In virtue of the impossibility of infinite

11. Aquinas frequently uses the Aristotelian formula "forma dat esse," in the sense that the form specifies the existence and is accordingly its cause in the order of formal causality, orienting the thing to existence only and not to non-existence. But the exercise of this function presupposes efficient causality: ". . . esse per se consequitur formam creaturae, supposito tamen influxu Dei; . . . Unde potentia ad non esse in spiritualibus creaturis et corporibus celestibus, magis est in Deo, qui potest subtrahere suum influxum, quam in forma vel in materia talium creaturarum." *ST* 1.104.1.ad 1m.

12. On this topic, see C. Fabro, "Intorno all nozione 'Tomista' di Contingenza," *Rivista di filosofia neoscolastica* 30 (1938), 132–49; T. B. Wright, "Necessary and Contingent Being in St. Thomas," *The New Scholasticism* 25 (1951), 439–66; P. Brown, "St. Thomas' Doctrine of Necessary Being," *The Philosophical Review* 73 (1964), 76–90. The doctrine of St. Thomas on the question was sharply criticized in the middle ages—see A. Maurer, "Henry of Harclay's Questions on Immortality," *Mediaeval Studies* 19 (1957), 79–89, and "St. Thomas and Henry of Harclay on Created Nature," *Atti del III congresso*

regress, these caused things require a first cause, a cause that is in consequence necessary, not through any other cause, but by reason of itself. Again, the thinking of Aquinas is clearly enough in terms of efficient causality. The backward reference is to the same passage already cited, in which "a first efficient cause" was reached (*CG* 1.13.Procedit). The force of the reasoning lies in the bestowal of existence though efficient causality. If there are contingent things, there is a necessary efficient cause that is making them be; and if that cause is made to be necessary by something else, there is ultimately a first efficient cause that is thereby necessary without undergoing the influence of any efficient causality itself. The notion of necessity seems bound quite closely with efficient causality. As efficient causality is the bestowal of existence, the notion indicated for necessity in this context would seem to bear upon existence. The first efficient cause is existence, and is thereby necessary in virtue of itself. By it, existence is caused here in a way that cannot be otherwise. This would seem to be the meaning of the text if necessity retains its Aristotelian sense of what cannot be otherwise.

But is not something more than efficient causality involved in the argument? The bestowal of existence would seem to be the same, as far as the force of the reasoning is concerned, whether the caused beings are contingent or necessary. Accordingly, it would be superfluous to make the notions of contingency and necessity suggest a new way for proving God's existence. The *Contra gentiles,* aside from any reasons from its historical background, would be right in not listing this way among those by which philosophers and Christian teachers had proved it. But why, then, would the *tertia via* have been admitted into the *Summa theologiae?* Who would be the philosophers who had used it, and does it involve something more than the efficient causality of the *secunda via?* "Cause of necessity" seems a different notion from "cause of existence." Do the sources of the notion offer any explanation of the difference?

In both the *Summa theologiae* and the *Contra gentiles* the argument is presented in terms of possibility. The relevant meanings of possibility are outlined briefly in the *De potentia* 5.3c: "Dicendum quod in rebus a Deo factis dicitur aliquid esse possibile dupliciter. *Uno modo* per potentiam ágentis tantum. . . . Alio mode per potentiam quae est in rebus factis; sicut possibile est corpus compositum corrumpi." The instance given for the first type of possibility is the possibility of the

---

internazionale di filosofia medioevale (Milan: Vita e Pensiero 1964), 542–49. On the Neo-scholastic misunderstandings of the *tertia via* from this angle, see Wright, pp. 439–45; and in regard to misunderstandings in other modern writers, see Brown, pp. 76–78.

world before it was created. For it to be created was possible. But the possibility did not lie in any creature, since as yet no creature existed. The possibility lay solely in the power of God, who was able to bring the world into existence. From this reasoning, one may conclude that the distinction is between a type of possibility on the one hand that is located in an efficient cause different from the thing called possible, and on the other hand a type of possibility that is found within that thing itself.

The latter type of possibility is then discussed against a twofold Moslem background. The question centers on whether things already in existence have in themselves any possibility for non-existence. The first view given is that of Avicenna:

Avicenna namque posuit, quod quaelibet res praeter Deum habebat in se possibilitatem ad esse et non esse. Cum enim esse sit praeter essentiam cuius libet rei creatae, ipsa natura rei creatae per se considerata, possibilis est ad esse; necessitatem vero essendi non habet nisi ab alio, cuius natura est suum esse, et per consequens est per se necesse esse, et hoc Deus est.[13]

What is meant by possibility within the thing itself for existence, becomes clear enough from this description. The essence of a creature is its nature considered as a potentiality for being, while the being is over and above the essence.[14] Considered just in itself, then, the nature

13. *De pot.* 5.3c. The necessity of existing holds here for all created existents, though "a certain ambiguity in this regard" in both Alfarabi and Avicenna is noted by E. Fackenheim, "The Possibility of the Universe in Al-Farabi, Ibn Sina and Maimonides," *Proceedings of the American Academy for Jewish Research* 16 (1947), 40, n. 4. On the view that the two Arabian thinkers were attempting to harmonize the necessary emanation in Neoplatonism with the Moslem theology of creation, and on Averroes's charge that this actually happened with them, see Fackenheim, pp. 42–52. In their philosophical context, Fackenheim emphasizes, "the convertibility of the terms 'eternity' and 'necessity' appears to be beyond question," p. 47. A schematic presentation of the terms involved—*possibile, potentia, necesse-esse, necesse-esse per se, necesse-esse non per se*—may be found in Avicenna's *Metaphysices compendium* 1.2.1.1, trans. Nematallah Careme (Rome: Pont. Institutum Orientalium Studiorum, 1926), 66–68. See also *Algazel's Metaphysics,* ed. Joseph T. Muckle (Toronto: St. Michael's College, 1933), 1.1.8; pp. 46–47. Algazel regards the basic division as standard: "Iam autem convenerunt philosophi in hoc ut appellarent primum possibile, secundum vero debitum vel necesse esse" (ibid., p. 46.16–18). On its ground in the accidental character of existence in creatures, see ibid., 1.5; p. 120. On its relation to the equally basic theological distinction between God and creatures, see Fackenheim, pp. 39 and 52.

14. "Tamen nomen nature hoc modo sumpte uidetur significare essentiam rei . . . ; sed essentia dicitur secundum quod per eam et in ea ens habet esse." Aquinas, *De ente et essentia,* 1; Leonine ed., *Op. Om.* 43, 370.45–52. Cf. "esse preter formam"—ibid., 4; 377.124–25. For Aquinas there is likewise a sense in which contingent things have a purely existential necessity, in the way that it is necessary for Socrates to be seated while he is seated. See *De pot.* 5.4c. Aristotle, *Cael.* 1.12.281b9–12, stresses on the other hand the formal or essentialist aspect—to say that a man standing is not standing is false but not impossible. Alfarabi, *Philosophy of Plato and Aristotle,* trans. Muhsin Mahdi (New

of a created thing is something that is able to be, but of itself it does not have that being. Any necessity of being that may be found in it will, accordingly, have to come from something else whose nature is its own being. In consequence this latter is in virtue of its own self necessary being—*per se necesse esse*. It is identified with God.

This throws considerable light on the terminology of the argument drawn up in the *Contra gentiles* (1.15.Amplius). The possibility for existence and non-existence in perishable things is their natures or essences. The reason, namely, that existence is over and above their essences, holds for all created things. Where a created thing has necessary existence, it has this necessity of existence not from itself but from a being that is necessary in virtue of the identity of its existence with its essence. In this view, no ground for necessary being is located within the creature itself. At the same time, however, the Aristotelian eternity or necessity of the heavens and their immaterial movements is safeguarded within the framework of accepted theological doctrine.

Likewise, the meaning of "cause of necessity," as used in the *tertia via* and in the corresponding argument in the *Contra gentiles*, begins to emerge. The context is that of existence. The nature of any created thing, considered just in itself, does not involve existence. Of itself, in consequence, it is something possible. Whatever necessity of existing it may have, it will have from the being that is itself existence. To have necessity of existing from something else means that the necessity is caused by the other being.

In the Avicennian view, then, the causality is efficient. The being that is necessary in virtue of itself efficiently causes whatever necessity any other beings may have. In the framework of Avicenna's terminology the situation becomes clear enough. In the eighth treatise of his *Metaphysics* he was showing that in every series of causes there is a first principle that is one and separate from all, and that alone is necessary being (*necesse esse*) and is that from which every existent thing has the source of its existence.[15] After reaching the first efficient cause (the first cause absolutely), he proceeds without further ado to deal with the first cause under the designation of *necesse esse*.[16] The

York: Free Press of Glencoe, 1962), 83, could understand the Aristotelian division of propositions as into necessary, possible, and existential.

15. "Primum . . . ut ostendamus quod causae omnibus modis finitae sunt, et quod in unoquoque ordine earum est principium primum, et quod principium omnium illorum est unum, et quod est discretum ab omnibus quae sunt, ipsum solum ens necesse esse, et quod ab ipso est principium sui esse omnis quod est." *Metaph.* 8.1; ed. S. Van Riet, *Liber de philosophia prima sive scientia divina* (Leiden: Brill, 1980), p. 376.10–15.

16. *Metaph.* 8.3–4; ed. Van Riet, pp. 393–404. Étienne Gilson, *History of Christian Philosophy in the Middle Ages* (New York: Random House, 1955), p. 211, notes that the

divisions of things in general into the possible and the necessary, and the necessary in virtue of itself, and the necessary in virtue of something else, he accepted as basic.[17] The remote background may without too much hesitation be seen in book *lambda* of Aristotle's *Metaphysics,* in which the first principle is reached from the starting point of perishable substances and established as eternal and incapable of being otherwise than it is. It is accordingly declared to exist "of necessity," for one of the senses of necessity is that just mentioned, namely, where a thing is not capable of being otherwise but has to be in one way only. On such a first principle, for Aristotle, depend the heavens (imperishable) and the world of nature (perishable, composed of matter and form).[18] In this Aristotelian passage may be found the elements of Avicenna's general framework, though his special emphasis on the unicity of the first principle and the location of the necessity in the relation of existence to essence spring clearly enough from interest in the revealed doctrine of creation.

The Avicennian background for introducing the notion of a "cause of necessity" into the proof for God's existence is accordingly straightforward and verifiable in detail. It locates the cause of necessity outside creatures and solely in their first efficient cause.[19] On the other hand, a reason within creatures is found in the doctrine of Averroes:

Commentator vero contrarium ponit, scilicet quod quaedam res creatae sunt in quarum natura non est possibilitas ad non esse, quia quod in sua natura habet possibilitatem ad non esse, non potest ab extrinseco acquirere sempiternitatem, ut scilicet sit per naturam suam sempiternum. Et haec quidem positio videtur rationabilior. Potentia enim ad esse et non esse non convenit alicui nisi ratione materiae, quae est pura potentia.[20]

Latin translation of Avicenna spread the formula *causa agens* for the cause of existence, while the Latin translation of Algazel popularized the formula *causa efficiens.* Both formulas were used as equivalent by Christian writers in the thirteenth century.

17. See above, n. 13.

18. Aristotle, *Metaph.* 12.6–7.1071b3–1072b14. Comparison of the formulas used shows that the type of necessity listed at 1072b13 is the type attributed to separate substance at b8, "that which cannot be otherwise." This basic sense is not understood existentially by Aristotle—see supra, n. 5. The thrust is not on the existing but on the "one way only."

19. On the Koranic background in "Everything goes to destruction except His Face" (Sura, 28.88), see Fackenheim, art. cit., 51–52. Regarding existence, for Avicenna, as an accident in creatures, see F. Rahman, "Essence and Existence in Avicenna," *Mediaeval and Renaissance Studies* 4 (1958), 1–16. R. L. Franklin, "Necessary Being," *The Australasian Journal of Philosophy* 35 (1957), 99, notes that the theist's model for the dependence is "the way in which a man may influence matters by an act of will." But the model seems also to include intellection and other conscious acts that need not be free. It allows the efficient causality to be a necessary emanation as well as a free creation.

20. *De pot.* 5.3c. Accordingly in this context, as A. Forest, "Comptes-rendus," *Bulletin thomiste* 4 (1927), 147, notes, to say that spiritual substances have no potentiality for

In this continuation of the article in *De potentia,* Aquinas regards the view that locates within the creature the lack of possibility for non-existence as the "more reasonable" of the two. Lack of possibility for non-existence is dealt with in terms of eternal duration, sempiternity. But a thing cannot be naturally sempiternal if it has within itself the possibility of non-existence. This calls for an examination of the principle by which a thing has potentiality for existence or non-existence, namely, its matter.[21]

Strictly speaking, the potentiality of matter is in regard to form, and not at all directly to non-existence. Only through its potentiality to other forms is matter a tendency to non-existence under the form that presently actuates it:

Materia etiam, cum non possit esse sine forma, non potest esse in potentia ad non esse, nisi quatenus existens sub una forma, est in potentia ad aliam formam (*De pot.* 5.3c).

Consequently the role played by matter allows a twofold intrinsic lack of possibility in a creature for non-existence. Either there is no matter in its constitution, as in spiritual forms, or the possibility of the matter is exhausted by its present form, as in the heavenly bodies. In the first case the form subsists in its own being, and can no more be separated from its being than from itself.[22] In the second case there is no contrariety of forms to initiate any process of corruption or perishing.[23] The result is that only things with matter subject to contrariety have in their own nature possibility for non-existence. All

---

non-existence does not entail that it is impossible for them not to exist, where the latter clause is understood in the sense of logical impossibility.

21. For Aristotle, matter coincided with potentiality, as form did with actuality. Aquinas extends potentiality and actuality to spiritual substances but not as matter and form in any univocal sense: "[E]rgo oportet quod ipsa quidditas uel forma que est intelligentia sit in potentia respectu esse quod a Deo recipit, et illud esse receptum est per modum actus. Et ita inuenitur potentia et actus in intelligentiis, non tamen forma et materia nisi equiuoce." *De ente* 4; p. 377.149–54.

22. *De pot.* 5.3c; *ST* 1.75.6c.

23. Because the only motion observable to the ancients in the celestial bodies was the circular, which has no contraries, the traditional view expressed by Aristotle in *De caelo* 1.2–5.268al ff., left these bodies unalterable and accordingly imperishable. They were in consequence included among necessary beings. P. Brown (art. cit. supra, n. 12), pp. 80 and 88, adds primary matter on account of its imperishability. But for Aquinas, primary matter just in itself—the viewpoint from which it is imperishable—does not subsist and cannot have any kind of being: "Est etiam quaedam creatura quae non habet esse in se, sed tantum in alio, sicut materia prima, sicut forma quaelibet, sicut universale; non enim est esse alicujus, nisi particularis subsistentis in natura." *Sent.* 1.8.5.2.Solut.; 1, 227. Similarly, the species do not subsist as such. An attempt to bring them under necessary things that have a cause of their necessity may be seen in A. Dondeyne, "De tertia via S. Thomae," *Collationes Brugenses* 30 (1930), 196–97.

other things have *naturally* "necessitas essendi," with no possibility for non-existence in their nature (ibid.).

"Necessitas essendi," a term used regularly in the Latin Avicenna, is in this way regarded against the background of Averroes as the opposite of possibility for non-existence. If possibility for non-existence is taken away from a thing, the thing's existence has thereby the character of necessity. The thing can consequently be regarded as a necessary being,[24] and not a possible one. The reason for the necessity is located in the created thing's nature in these cases, and not just, as with Avicenna, in the divine causality.

This view, for which the background mentioned is the doctrine of Averroes, finds accordingly in the creature itself the cause of necessity for existence.[25] The cause is the creature's nature, when the nature is either form alone or form that exhausts the potentiality of the matter. But this does not mean that the necessity for existence escapes the divine causality, since the nature itself is caused by God:

Nec tamen per hoc removetur quin necessitas essendi sit eis a Deo, quia unum necessarium alterius causa esse potest, ut dicitur in V *Metaphysic*. Ipsius enim naturae creatae cui competit sempiternitas, causa est Deus (*De pot.* 5.3c).

Necessity of existing, understood in this passage as sempiternity, has to be caused by God in a way that is not merely the bestowal of being. It pertains to the created nature itself. The cause of the created nature is thereby the cause of the sempiternity, not only by giving it existence, but by fashioning it in such a way that it requires perpetual existence.

The theme of the part played by nature is rounded out in the article of the *De potentia* by the observation that, even in things that have the possibility of non-existence, the matter is permanent and in it the form of the thing that perishes is reduced to a potential state. In all nature, therefore, there is no potentiality by which anything could tend towards nothingness. This seems meant to emphasize the point that the natural tendency of all things is towards existence. So there should be no surprise in finding that, in natures where there is no tendency to

24. "Sunt enim quaedam in rebus creatis quae simpliciter et absolute necesse est esse." *CG* 2.30.Licet. Aquinas, however, seems to avoid express application of the term "ens necessarium" to creatures, even though he has no hesitation in using the adjective of the term *res*: "Nihil igitur prohibet res quasdam divina voluntate productas necessarias esse." Ibid., Item.

25. See Averroes, *In VIII Phys.*, comm. 83 (Venice: apud Junctas, 1652), fol. 432rCD. Cf. *De substantia orbis* 2; ed. Arthur Hyman (Cambridge: Mediaeval Academy of America Press, 1986), pp. 82–84. For the Aristotelian passage referred to by Aquinas, see infra, n. 31.

any other substantial existence, the existence should be naturally permanent, and in that sense necessary.

Having in this way established a cause of necessary existence in created natures, the article of the *De potentia* returns to the causality exercised by the power of God. Anything that in itself is impossible (for instance, something that involves a contradiction) may be called impossible for God. From this viewpoint non-existence is not impossible for creatures, since none have existed from all eternity. Because a creature is not its own existence, there is no logical contradiction in predicating non-existence of it. In that sense there is no creature whatever of which one may now say its non-existence is impossible. Likewise there is no intrinsic necessity compelling the divine power to keep anything in existence, nor are creatures necessary in order to ensure the divine goodness and happiness. Only on the supposition of his own plan to keep things perpetually in existence can their being be regarded as necessary:

Relinquitur ergo quod non est impossibile Deum res ad non esse reducere; cum non sit necessarium eum rebus esse praebere, nisi ex suppositione suae ordinationis et praescientiae, quia sic ordinavit et praescivit, ut res in perpetuum in esse teneret. (*De pot.* 5.3c)

Does not this throw the whole question back to the position just ascribed to Avicenna? In the last analysis, the sempiternity of any creature depends upon the divine causality that keeps it in existence. Even though its nature should call for perpetual existence, it could be reduced to nonexistence by the divine will. Does its sempiternity then depend just on the divine will, as Plato described the immortality of the gods in relation to the will of the demiurge, or does a further dependence upon an established order and foreknowledge allow also the creature's nature to play its role in causing the perpetuity of its existence?

The answer is not spelled out in this article of the *De potentia*. It seems left implied in the notion of divine foreknowledge and providence. It is apparently allowed to follow from the understanding that the divine plan respects the natures of things and requires that existence be imparted according to the exigencies of these natures. The reasoning proceeds as though the natures of the heavenly bodies and of spiritual subsistents can be the cause of perpetuity for the existence of these things, even though the natures themselves are caused by God and the bestowal of their existence depends upon his free will. In the reply to one of the arguments, the necessity caused in them by the divine will is in fact termed absolute:

licet creaturae incorruptibiles ex Dei voluntate dependeant, quae potest eis esse praebere et non praebere; consequuntur tamen ex divina voluntate absolutam necessitatem essendi, in quantum in tali natura causantur, in qua non sit possibilitas ad non esse; talie enim sunt cuncta creata, qualia Deus esse ea voluit, ut dicit Hilarius in libro *De synodis* (*De pot.* 5.3.ad 12m).

What Aquinas presupposes in this article, apparently, is a framework in which imperishable creatures have in themselves absolute necessity in regard to their existence, yet have that existence in dependence upon a will that is free to continue imparting it or to withdraw it. The absolute necessity is acquired from the divine will, yet is absolute because these creatures are caused by God in a nature that has no possibility for non-existence. But the reason they have that nature is that God willed it to be such. Is there circularity in this reasoning, or does the earlier thinking of Aquinas provide a framework in which it proves to be cogent?

III

In this, as in most of the important questions in Aquinas, the basis of his philosophical thought may be looked for in the commentary on the *Sentences*. There it is often worked out in vivid detail and with a welcome freshness that in the later works gradually gives way to more mature and settled terminology or established discussion. For instance, at the philosophical root of an issue that has been crucial in the topic just considered lies the radical distinction between simple apprehension and judgment. Through the first, conceptualization, things are known from the standpoint of their natures. Through the second, they are apprehended from the viewpoint of their existence. The Arabian background for the way these two different acts of intellection were related respectively to nature and to existence, and the character of judgment as an act of apprehension as well as of composition, emerge most clearly in the early terminology used in the commentary on the *Sentences*.[26] The vital bearing of these considerations on the tenet that existence is known as an actuality over and above the content of a thing's nature should be readily apparent. From that tenet the reasoning to subsistent existence and the real distinction between nature and existence in creatures took place, as well as to the

26. *Sent.* 1.8.1.3.Solut.; 1, 200, for *imaginatio intellectus* and *credulitas*. For *imaginatio intellectus, formatio, fides*, see 1.19.5.1.ad 7m; 1, 489. For *formatio, indivisibilum intelligentia*, see 1.38.1.3.Solut.; 1, 903. On the translation of the Arabic equivalents as "concept" and "judgment," see Rahman (art. cit. supra, n. 19), p. 4, n. 2. On a Stoic background, see M.-D. Chenu, "Un vestige du Stoicisme," *Revue des sciences philosophiques et théologiques* 27 (1938), 63–68.

total dependence of creatures on the first cause, and their consequent possibility in that respect.[27]

In regard to the way the nature and existence of creatures are respectively related to their first cause, the Prologue of the commentary on the *Sentences* outlines a special type of "analogy":

aut ex eo quod unum esse et rationem ab altero recipit; et talis est analogia creaturae ad Creatorem: creatura enim non habet esse nisi secundum quod a primo ente descendit, nec nominatur ens nisi inquantum ens primum imitatur; et similiter est de sapientia et de omnibus aliis quae de creatura dicuntur (*Sent.*, Prol., 1.2.ad 2m; ed. Mandonnet, 1, 10).

A creature, according to this text, receives both its existence and its aspect (*ratio*) as a being from the creator. Both are involved in the relation to its maker that goes under the designation "analogy" for Aquinas.[28] The creature has its existence from its creator, as is shown in the commentary by arguments among which that from Avicenna has the most prominent place.[29] But it also has from its creator the aspect that characterizes it as a being, just as it has the characteristic and existence of wisdom or any other quality from the creator as the ultimate source. Only insofar as it imitates the first being may a creature be called a being.

The language of imitation throws the problem into the framework of exemplar causality. The first efficient cause, according to this doctrine of analogy, makes creatures imitations of itself through imparting existence. Yet the imitation takes place according to different aspects, such as being or wisdom. The first cause functions as a form, after which the effects are fashioned. The exemplar causality is spelled out clearly:

Unde ipse est exemplaris forma rerum, non tantum quantum ad ea quae sunt in sapientia sua, scilicet secundum rationes ideales, sed etiam quantum ad ea quae sunt in natura sua, scilicet attributa. Quidam autem dicunt, quod ista attributa non differunt nisi penes connotata in creaturis: quod non potest esse: tum quia causa non habet aliquid ab effectu, sed e converso (*Sent.* 1.2.1.2.Solut.; 1, 63).

Here the first efficient cause is presented as a form according to which all other things are modeled. In this way it produces effects

27. *De ente* 4; pp. 376.90–377.152. *Sent.* 1.8.5.2.Solut.; 1, 229–30.

28. This two-term relation is not made clear by the present-day use of the English word "analogy." A medicine is not said to be "analogous" to health because it causes health, nor is a color described as "analogous" to health because it is a sign of health. But these were grounds for the use of *analogia* in medieval philosophical vocabulary.

29. See *Sent.* 1.3.1.2.Solut.; 1, 94. Ibid., 1.8.4.2.Solut.; 1, 222. Also *Sent.* 2.3.1.1. Solut.; 2, 87.

similar to itself, though in the fashion that Aquinas calls "analogous": "[C]um secundum formam suam producat effectus similes, non univoce, sed analogice; sicut a sua sapientia derivatur omnis sapientia" (ibid.). But this exemplar form is regarded as containing both aspects that are attributes and aspects that are ideas. These latter are the forms of created things:

ita etiam formae materiales habent duplex esse, ut dicit Commentator in XI *Metaph.*: unum in actu secundum quod in rebus sunt; et aliud in potentia activa secundum quod sunt in motoribus orbium, ut ipse ponit, et praecipue in primo motore, loco cujus nos in Deo dicimus. Unde apud omnes philosophos communiter dicitur quod omnia sunt in mente Dei, sicut artificiata in mente artificis; et ideo formas rerum in Deo existentes ideas dicimus, quae sunt sicut formae operativae (*Sent.* 1.36.2.1.Solut.; 1, 839).

The notion of divine ideas for all created things is accordingly accepted by Aquinas as a position common to all philosophers, and is interpreted by him as a doctrine of "operative forms." This means that the divine power, in imparting existence, is operating in accordance with these forms. The basic exemplar for the products, however, remains the divine essence: "[S]i essentia sua exemplar omnium rerum ponatur: quia, sic intuendo essentiam suam, omnia producit" (ibid., ad 2m; p. 840). This is carefully explained:

Unde cum hoc nomen "idea" nominet essentiam divinam secundum quod est imitatum a creatura, divina essentia erit propria idea istius rei secundum determinatum imitationis modum . . . et ex hoc sunt plures rationes ideales, secundum quod Deus intelligit essentiam suam ut imitabilem per hunc vel per illum modum" (*Sent.* 1.36.2.2.Solut.; 1, 842).

The divine activity is in this way understood as imparting existence in a manner that is fashioned or guided by exemplar causality. Here, as elsewhere in the commentary on the *Sentences,* the two phases are kept together,[30] and there is no thought of ever separating them. Existence is bestowed upon a creature in the way that the creature imitates the divine essence. This ability to imitate the divine essence comes however from the divine essence itself, because the divine essence can be imitated in the particular way. The cause does not depend upon

30. E.g.: "[C]um creatura exemplariter procedat ab ipso Deo sicut a causa quodammodo simili per analogiam ex creaturis potest in Deum deveniri tribus illis modis." *Sent.* 1.3.1.3.Solut.; 1, 196. The reason for all three ways is that a creature has existence from something else, p. 88. Cf.: "[N]ominat Deum per esse inventum in creaturis, quod exemplariter deductum est ab ipso." *Sent.* 1.8.1.1.ad 2m; 1, 196. "a quo omne esse creatum effective et exemplariter manat." Ibid., a.2; p. 198. "rationem causae exemplaris et effectivae tantum in Deo." Ibid., a.3.Solut.; p. 200. "per modum efficientis exemplaris." *Sent.* 1.38.1.1.Solut.; 1, 898. See also *Sent.* 1.19.5.2.Solut.; 1, 491–92; 1.22.1.2.Solut.; 1, 535.

the effect, but vice versa. In both orders, that of existence and that of essence, the divine causality will remain supreme.

What consequences will this view have for the problem of possibility and necessary existence? Its tenets would indicate that existence is bestowed in the way required by the essence of the created thing, even though that essence depends ultimately upon the exemplar causality of the divine essence for its exigencies. If an essence such as a spiritual form exhibits absolute necessity, it will have the cause of this necessity in God:

Necessarium autem absolute dicitur quod est necessarium per id quod in essentia sua est; sive illud sit ipsa essentia, sicut in simplicibus; sive, sicut in compositis, illud principium sit materia, sicut dicimus, hominem mori est necessarium; sive forma, sicut dicimus, hominem esse rationalem est necessarium. Hoc autem absolute necessarium est duplex. Quoddam enim est quod habet necessitatem et esse ab alio, sicut in omnibus quae causam habent: quoddam autem est cujus necessitas non dependet ab alio, sed ipsum est causa necessitatis in omnibus necessariis, sicut Deus (*Sent.* 1.6.1.1.Solut.; 1, 166).

Here the notion "cause of necessity" emerges from a discussion of the basic Aristotelian divisions of the necessary. The range given the concept of necessity is accordingly broad and is located firmly in the tradition that goes back to the Stagirite. But the influence of the Arabian developments is apparent in the coupling of existence and necessity in a context in which a cause of necessity is sought for some absolutely necessary thing. This is located in the necessity of the first cause: "necessitas primae causae quae non dependet ab alio, sed ipsa potius est causa necessitatis in omnibus aliis" (ibid., p. 167).

The framework, accordingly, of a "cause of necessity" is not regarded as an ad hoc device for the construction of an argument to prove God's existence. It is introduced in the discussion of a Trinitarian problem and is seen as extending to all types of necessity, including logical necessity that is based on form. It follows the Aristotelian text in distinguishing between things that are necessary in virtue of themselves and others that are necessary by reason of something else: "Now some things owe their necessity to something other than themselves; others do not, but themselves are the source of necessity in other things."[31] The preoccupation with existence in connection with necessity, and the funneling of the final division towards a single cause of the necessity in all other necessary things, indicate a metaphysical background that is no longer Greek. As with the Arabs,[32] the division of being into the necessary and the possible or contingent is accepted

31. Aristotle, *Metaph.* 12.5.1015b9–11; Oxford trans. The Greek text uses the word *aitia*, 'cause': "the cause of their being necessary."
32. See supra, n. 13.

as basic by Aquinas: "Necessarium enim et possibile divident ens. Si igitur Pater non genuit Filium necessitate, genuit ipsum contingenter vel possibiliter" (*Sent.* 1.6.1.1.arg.1; 1, 165). In the context of this discussion, then, contingence and possibility show no appreciable distinction from each other in their contrast to necessity. They are not taken as sub-contraries.

With the terminology and divisions and background of the topic determined in the early thinking of Aquinas, one may now proceed to the discussion of possibility and the opposed necessity in the commentary on the *Sentences*. The discussion takes place in regard to the mutability of creatures, an Augustinian theme with an Aristotelian parallel. The introduction to the reasoning comes from the Aristotelian connection of movement with potentiality:

motus, quodumque modo dicatur, sequitur potentiam. Cum igitur omnis creatura habeat aliquid de potentia, quia solus Deus est purus actus, oportet omnes creaturas mutabiles esse, et solum Deum immutabilem (*Sent.* 1.8.3.2.Solut.; 1, 213).

The notion of passive potency, which in Aristotle was synonymous and coextensive with that of matter, is in this way extended to all creatures including immaterial ones. With pure actuality limited to one instance only, God, the notion of passive potentiality now includes all possibility, and is immediately taken up under the latter designation. Every creature, because its existence is from another, according to Avicenna's reasoning "quantum est in se, est possibile, et ista possibilitas dicit dependentiam ad id a quo est" (ibid.). Upon this dependence or possibility there follows a mutability that consists in the allowing of annihilation (*vertibilitas in nihil*). But here there is no mutability in the strict sense of the notion, since there is no substrate that changes. Another reason may be added:

Alia ratio est, quia nihil dicitur possibile cujus contrarium est necessarium, vel quod non potest esse, nisi impossibili posito. Esse autem creaturae omnino deficere non potest, nisi retrahatur inde fluxus divinae bonitatis in creaturis et hoc est impossibile ex immutabilitate divinae voluntatis, et contrarium necessarium (*Sent.* 1.8.3.2.Solut.; 1, 214).

The wording is strong. Any withdrawal of God's goodness in regard to the bestowal of existence is impossible. The word "impossible" is used three times in these few lines to characterize the notion. Its contrary, the continued bestowal of existence to which the creature's essence is a potency, is in consequence necessary. Since its contrary is necessary, it cannot be described as "possible." The reason lies in the immutability of the divine will.

What does this mean? On the one hand, from a metaphysical viewpoint every creature in virtue of its own essence is a possible, because it is a potency in respect of the being it receives from something else. On the other hand, its annihilation is impossible, because the condition required for its annihilation is impossible. The condition would be a change in the divine will. But that change is precluded in the present perspective.

All this makes a consistent picture. The annihilation of a creature is logically possible, since its existence is from one relevant point accidental to its nature. The annihilation is impossible, however, from the viewpoint of the divine goodness and unchangeable will. As with Plato's demiurge, the will of the maker is dominant. As with Avicenna, all creatures have their being and necessity from their first cause. But the immutable will of the maker here enters the question. As with Averroes, the natures of things are respected. Essence is the potentiality for existence, and where it requires permanent existence, it is given existence in just that way. Where the essence has a principle that tends towards different existence, existence is bestowed accordingly. In all nature, consequently, there is no direct tendency to nonexistence. The divine goodness respects this condition, and annihilation becomes impossible. These views on annihilation explain clearly enough how Aquinas could say in the *De potentia* (5.3.ad 12m) that imperishable creatures acquire from the divine will an "absolute necessity of existing."

IV

Do these considerations from the earlier works of Aquinas clarify sufficiently the notion "cause of necessity" as used in the *tertia via* of the *Summa theologiae*? They certainly explain the historical genesis of the terminology and overall framework of the argument. Its starting point, the presence of generable and destructible things in the world, is Aristotelian in terminology but is at once thrown into the Arabian background of possibility for existence, instead of being left just in the context of potentiality for form: "Invenimus enim in rebus quaedam quae sunt possibilia esse et non esse, cum quaedam inveniantur generari et corrumpi, et per consequens possibilia esse et non esse" (*ST* 1.2.3c). The text then offers a difficulty. The Leonine edition gives the meaning, "It is impossible for all things that are of this nature to exist always." What seems to be the better reading, however, runs: "But it is impossible for all existent things to be of this kind"—"Impossibile est autem omnia quae sunt, talia esse."[33] With this reading,

33. On the readings here, see Thomas C. O'Brien, *Metaphysics and the Existence of*

the time factor does not take on any more significance than it has in the Aristotelian background, in which motion has always existed.[34] Aristotle could, in the context, speak of the supposition that potentiality existed before actuality: "But if this is so, nothing that is need be; for it is possible for all things to be capable of existing but not yet exist."[35] The time adverbs in the *tertia via* seem merely to take up the Aristotelian formulation:

quia quod possibile est non esse, quandoque non est. Si igitur omnia sunt possibilia non esse, aliquando nihil fuit in rebus. Sed si hoc est verum, etiam nunc nihil esset, quia quod non est, non incipit esse nisi per aliquid quod est; si igitur nihil fuit ens, impossibile fuit quod aliquid inciperet esse, et sic modo nihil esset, quod patet esse falsum (*ST* 1.2.3c).

This reasoning holds equally in the supposition of a beginning of these things in time as in that of their existence from eternity. If everything were perishable in nature, there would have been nothing that was determined to existence. In that case there would have been a time in which nothing existed. The "aliquando nihil fuit in rebus" cannot, with Aquinas (for whom time follows upon motion and existence), mean that there was an absolute time without any things. Rather, it parallels the way he can speak of the possibility of the world *before* it existed, even though time is dependent upon mobile being,[36]

God (Washington: Thomist Press, 1960), p. 82, n. 305; 226, n. 83. For Neoscholastic discussions of the *tertia via*, see list in Étienne Gilson, *Le thomisme*, 6e ed. (Paris: Vrin, 1965), pp. 79–80, nn. 40–44, and footnotes in John F. X. Knasas, "Making Sense of the *Tertia Via*," *The New Scholasticism* 54 (1980), 476–511.

34. *Metaph.* 12.6.1071b6–7. Cf. *Ph.* 8.1.250b11–252a5.

35. *Metaph.* 12.6.1071b25–26; Oxford trans. In Aristotle the verb *estai* is in the future to signify "need be." In Maimonides, with whom the argument is drawn up in the same general lines as in Aquinas, the verb (*remanebit*) in Latin translation is likewise in the future: "Quod si ita fuerit, nihil remanebit: ergo nec dator esse, et sequitur quod nihil esset omnino." See text in Réne Arnou, *De quinque viis sancti Thomae* (Rome: Università Gregoriana, 1932), p. 80. Aquinas, however, uses the past tense, *fuit.* This wording has lent itself to the interpretation of the argument as envisaging possible things first existing and then all finally perishing in the infinite course of past time. See P. Brown (supra, n. 12), pp. 86–87. This is open to mathematical objections. But with Aquinas, there does not seem to be any recourse to a calculus. The argument rather is open to the interpretation that there never would have been any existents to balance one against another in terms of their recurring possibility. Cf.: "Aussi bein, ne voyons-nous pas que S. Thomas ait pensé à la disparition des êtres en acte; il nous semble, au contraire, qu'il envisage plutôt leur non-apparition. Du moins nous croyons pouvoir interpréter sans peine dans ce sens le texte en litige." L. Chambat, "La 'tertia via' dans Saint Thomas et Aristote," *Revue thomiste* 32 (1927), 335.

36. "Dicendum quod antequam mundus esset, possibile fuit mundum esse." *ST* 1.46.1.ad 1m. Cf.: "Vel dicendum quod designat aeternitatem temporis imaginati, et non realiter existentis." Ibid. ad 8m. For the stand that the *quandoque* in the *tertia via* has "un sens purement métaphysique, nullement temporel," see H. Holstein, "L'origine aristotélicienne de la 'tertia via' de Saint Thomas," *Revue philosophique de Louvain* 48

or the way in which Aristotle (1071b24), after saying that without time there can be no before or after (b8–9), can speak counterfactually of potentiality existing before anything was actual.[37] Aristotle is concerned with motion, Aquinas with existence. Aristotle's objective is to show that the eternal motion in changeable things requires for its explanation other and eternally unchangeable beings. Without these entirely actual beings, the potentiality in changeable things would never have been actualized and there would not be anything at all. The objective of Aquinas is to show that, without necessary being, nothing would now exist. In corresponding fashion a case may be made that here he is in no way envisaging a situation in which contingent things had existed and then, for lack of continued support by necessary being, finally passed out of existence. Rather his meaning is that, without necessary being, the contingent things would never have come into existence at any time.[38] In this light the thrust of the reasoning is the same as that in the formulation of the *Contra gentiles* (1.15.Amplius): "Omne autem quod est possibile esse, causam habet: quia, cum de se aequaliter se habeat ad duo, scilicet esse et non esse, oportet, si ei approprietur esse, quod hoc sit ex aliqua causa."

The problem for Aquinas, consequently, is the bestowal of existence upon things that do not have existence in virtue of their own essence. The remote background is the Aristotelian requirement of eternally actual things to explain the successive actualizing of perishable things in the eternity of cosmic motion. Since for Aquinas the ultimate actuality of anything is existence rather than form, the change to the existential framework is understandable. The influence of the "third philosophical speculation" of Maimonides, with the tenet that if all the individuals of a species are perishable the species itself is likewise perishable, may have played its own role in having Aquinas include the argument in the *Summa theologiae* among the standard ways to

---

(1950), 367. On the controversy, see also P. Descoqs, "Métaphysique," *Archives de philosophie* 3.3. (1926), 98–103; A.-D. Sertillanges, "Le P. Descoqs et la 'tertia via,'" *Revue thomiste* 31 (1926), 490–502; "La troisième 'Voie' thomiste," *Revue de philosophie* 32 (1925), 24–37; Ch.-V. Héris, "Comptes-rendus," *Bulletin thomiste* 5 (1928), 317–20.

37. Hippocrates G. Apostle, *Aristotle's Metaphysics* (Bloomington: Indiana University Press, 1966), p. 399, n. 13, takes the "before" to mean priority "in existence (or in nature, or in *substance*)," as though priority in time were not included. Yet priority in time is included by Aristotle in his discussion of the impossibility in the counterfactual hypothesis, and he shows that though potentiality can be prior in an individual to actuality, in an overall sense actuality has to be prior in the order of time (*Metaph.* 9.8.1049b11–1050a3).

38. For this way of understanding the text, and for its verbal resemblances to the Aristotelian passage, see Chambat (art. cit. supra, n. 35), pp. 335–37. But Aristotle, *Cael.* 1.12.281a28–30, would support Maimonides.

prove that God exists.[39] However, no source is mentioned in the *tertia via*. Placed nowhere else among the formal lists of arguments directed to this purpose, it can hardly help but reflect some concern at the time of the *Summa theologiae* with the immediate creation and conservation of all finite things by a unique first cause. For Aristotle, a plurality of necessary beings could account for the actuality of perishable things; for an Arab, the necessary finite causes could bestow on them their existence.[40] The argument had to be structured to show that,

39. "Now it is indubitable, as you know, that what is possible with regard to a species must necessarily come about." Maimonides, *The Guide of the Perplexed* 2.1; trans. Shlomo Pines (Chicago: University of Chicago Press, 1963), 247. This obviously enough envisages a situation in which things already existent would have perished: "Now if all of them have undergone corruption, it would be impossible that anything exists, for there would remain no one who would bring anything into existence" (ibid.). Maimonides expressly takes over this "third philosophic speculation" from Aristotle, though realizing that its purpose is different with the Stagirite. However, as Arnou (op. cit. supra, n. 35), p. 79, n. 2, observes, Maimonides took the construction of the argument as a proof for the existence of God from Avicenna. Cf. Avicennian formulations in Arnou, pp. 59–71. The formulation of the *tertia via* of Aquinas follows closely enough that of Maimonides, even to the point of giving perhaps most readers the impression that he, like Maimonides, is envisaging a hypothetical situation in which things existed and then all perished. P. Gény remarks: "Celle de Maimonide présente de telles ressemblances avec le troisième voie de la *Somme*, que celle-ci paraît bien n'en être qu'un résumé." "A propos des preuves thomistes de l'existence de Dieu," *Revue de philosophie* 31 (1924), 587. On the other hand, Chambat, art. cit., pp. 334–335, rejects the influence of Maimonides because of the different viewpoint in the situations envisaged by the two thinkers as just noted, and observes that Aquinas makes no use of the principal part of Maimonides' reasoning in the passage, that what is possible for the species comes about necessarily. The latter notion, however, might be difficult to see in the Latin translation included by Arnou (p. 80) in the source material for Aquinas's five ways: "possibile autem in genere necessario est."

Chambat has no hesitation, though, in allowing (p. 337, n. 1) the Aristotelian background for Maimonides' phraseology in this matter. There is general agreement, then, that Aristotle's argument for the eternity of the world is the ultimate source of the reasoning. With Avicenna the argument was placed in the Arabian framework of the possible, the necessary through a cause, and the necessary in virtue of itself. In the *Metaphysices compendium*, 1.2.2.1 (trans. Carame, pp. 91–100), the argument is used to prove the existence of uncaused necessary being. In the Avicennian texts available to Aquinas this orientation was not so explicit. Accordingly the Avicennian structure, as found in the *Contra gentiles*—"Celle d'Avicenne, reprise par Dominique Gundissalvi, est acceptée et traduite presque littéralment par saint Thomas au *Contra gentiles*, I, 15," Gény, art. cit., 586–87—need not be included among the arguments by which philosophers had proven the existence of God. It could be used rather for demonstrating that God was eternal. Where Maimonides was the immediate source, as in the formulation in the *tertia via* of the *Summa theologiae*, the argument was ready to be included in the ways of proving that God exists, ways that had already been used by others.

40. Existence of the material forms in the active power of the movements for the celestial bodies is presented as the doctrine of Averroes by Aquinas, *Sent.* 1.36.2.1.Solut.; 1, 839. Sources for the doctrine of mediate creation are listed in the Ottawa edition of the *Summa theologiae* 1.45.5; 1, 288a36. For Aquinas the celestial bodies remained intermediate causes of generation: "sicut caelestia corpora sunt causa generationis inferiorum corporum dissimilium secundum speciem." *ST* 1.104.1c.

even when these eternal and necessary beings had been reached, it had still to proceed towards establishing why they themselves existed necessarily.[41] Since their essences are not existence, they also have to have their existence from something else. But since their essences contain no principle that would make them perishable, they can never, as far as their essences are concerned, lose their existence. The divine goodness requires that existence be imparted according to the way the creatures imitate the divine essence. All these components add up to the notion that the first efficient cause is the cause of necessity for all other necessary beings.

V

"Cause of necessity" in the *tertia via,* then, has facets in both the existential and essential orders. It includes both efficient and exemplar causality. Beyond doubt it is concerned with the imparting of existence. But it is also preoccupied with the bestowal of existence in the way the essences of the different types of creatures demand. For Aquinas there are finite essences that possess existence necessarily, once existence has been bestowed upon them. These are the angels, human souls, and, for the medievals, the celestial bodies. In the basic Aristotelian reasoning that arrived at separate substances, finite necessary beings would be sufficient to account for the eternity of cosmic motion. To the existence of finite necessary beings Aquinas could have no objection. If the Aristotelian framework was to be accepted for the demonstration of God's existence, it would in consequence have to be structured in a way that went beyond finite necessary beings to a unique first cause. This first cause had to be the cause not only of the existence of these creatures, as in the *secunda via,* but also the cause why their existence was necessary or sempiternal. The exemplar causality of the first cause met this further requirement. Not only the existence of the created world, but also the necessity found in it, can provide a way of demonstrating the existence of God.

One may readily admit, then, that against the Arabian background the basic Aristotelian argument for reaching separate substance required the presentation given in the *tertia via* of Aquinas. A quite

---

41. L. Charlier, "Les cinq voies de Saint Thomas," in *L'existence de Dieu,* ed. Collège Dominicain de Théologie à La Sarte-Huy (Tournai: n.p., 1961), 207: "Dire qu'ils ont une cause de leur necessité, c'est reconnaître qu'ils ne sont pas éternels au sens fort du mot." Aquinas, it is true, requires real identity of essence and existence for his own notion of eternity, of which eviternity is a participation, but he recognizes that the traditional teachers (*doctores*) hardly give notice to any distinction between the two types of duration. See *Sent.* 2.2.1.1.Solut.; 2, 64.

different question is whether the framework of the *tertia via* has any relevance in the modern setting. Surely no one today would, after establishing the contingence of the observable world, attempt to account for it by angels or imperishable heavens or spiritual souls. The direct character of the path from things that have existence contingently to a single necessary being seems accepted by both advocates and adversaries of the cosmological argument.[42]

From the viewpoint of demonstrating the existence of God, which is the one real concern of the argument, the foregoing objection is well taken. The probative force of the argument lies in the consideration that no nature except the unique subsistent existence contains being as one of its essential notes. Whether the existence of a creature is temporal or eternal, it requires subsistent being as its efficient cause. Necessary being is not a starting point for the demonstration, and is not required as an intermediate stage. Subsistent existence, reached without the intermediary of necessary beings, can at once be established as necessary and eternal because of the identity in it of essence with existence. But that is a consequence, not a stage of the argument. The force of the proof itself lies in the bestowal of existence upon contingent things, and is complete when the first cause of existence is reached. From the start it proceeds in the order of existence, and not in the order of merely logical necessity. It cannot be reduced to the ontological argument.

In another way, however, the *tertia via* does have relevance for modern thinking. The Platonic dominance of the mere will of the demiurge over the natures with which things are endowed, the Avicennian stand of allowing no necessity at all to spring from the natures of created things, the Cartesian dependence of even the eternal truths on the divine will—all exhibit a voluntarism that ill accords with any appeal of God to modern man. "The cause is in my will," alone and blunt, is no more conciliatory or attractive in real life than in Shakespeare's *Julius Caesar* (2.3.71). In its jejune outlines, as in the *secunda via,* the argument from the bestowal of existence brings to the fore only the power of the first cause. The *tertia via,* proceeding as it does through the different types of essences, shows in a fuller and more satisfactory way how the existence is imparted. It is imparted not arbitrarily or despotically, but as the natures of the various things require, and out of an infinite goodness that ensures the immutability of the divine will in this way of providing for creatures.

42. On modern encounters with the notion "necessary being" in this context, see for example J. Hick, "God as Necessary Being," *Journal of Philosophy* 57 (1960), 725–34; T. Penelhum, "Divine Necessity," *Mind* 69 (1960), 175–86.

11

THE SPECIAL CHARACTERISTIC OF THE SCOTISTIC PROOF THAT GOD EXISTS

I

The radically special characteristic of a proof that God exists may quite readily be expected to differ in accord with the different types of thought that undertake the demonstration. The proof may be physical, as in Averroes, or moral, as in Kant and Newman. Even the proofs that lay claim to a metaphysical character may be variously based on the stability and permanence of essences, or on the existence of sensible or spiritual being, or on the possibility or character or content of human intellection. In accord with radical difference in the respective basis, then, may not each proof of God's existence show a corresponding difference in the special characteristic that, even within the particular philosophy in question, distinguishes it sharply from all other proofs? A look at the well-known Scotistic demonstration may serve to illustrate quite strikingly this philosophically important issue.

II

In the preamble to the proof for God's existence, John Duns Scotus examines in his major commentary on the *Sentences* the Anselmian argument on the theme.[1] He refers it explicitly to its author, and treats it under the general heading, "Is it immediately evident that some-

---

1. *Joannis Duns Scoti Ordinatio,* in *Opera Omnia,* ed. Commissionis Scotisticae (Vatican City: Typis Polyglottis, 1950–   ), 1.2.1–2.11; 2, 129.4–10; and nos. 35–36, pp. 145.11–146.14. For Scotus, just as for Aquinas, there is no thought of interpreting the Anselmian argument as a passage from thought to reality. St. Anselm is mentioned as the author at 1.2.1–2.11; 2, 129.5; and at no. 35, p. 145.11; and similarly at *Reportata parisiensia,* in *Opera Omnia,* ed. L. Wadding (Paris: Vivès, 1891–95), 1.2.3.8; 22, 73b, and 1.3.2.1; 22, p. 97b.

thing infinite exists?"[2] The Franciscan theologian has no quarrel with the reasoning: "That than which nothing greater can be thought exists."[3] He maintains that this major premise of the Anselmian argument is *true*. He is concerned only with insisting that it is not *immediately* evident.[4] It has therefore to be proven. After the development of his own proof, he allows that Anselmian argument to be "colored" by the addition of "*sine contradictione*" twice in its formulation, and he proves the major premise by the reasoning contained in his own demonstration, namely, that absolutely perfect being is of its nature uncausable.[5]

This view of the Anselmian argument obviously sets aside any properly existential characteristic as a necessary consideration for the proof that God exists. It presupposes a metaphysics that permits reasoning to the order of existence from the nature of supremely perfect being as the object of human conceptualization. In the Scotistic context, the univocal concept of being, when taken with the intrinsic mode of infinity, involves real existence without *requiring* the intervention of any originally existential judgment. Against that background, the Anselmian argument can proceed quite smoothly.

In point of fact, Duns Scotus formulates the question of God's existence in terms of infinite being. He asks: "Is there among beings any actually infinite existent."[6] That type of formulation might be expected from the characteristic Scotist doctrine that "infinite being" is the most perfect concept of God naturally attainable by men in their present state.[7] But does it also point to infinity as the operative notion

2. "Utrum aliquod infinitum esse sit per se notum, ut Deum esse." *Ord.* 1.2.1–2.10; 2, 128.11.

3. "Praeterea, quo majus nihil cogitari potest, illud esse." *Ord.* 1.2.1–2.11; 2, 129.4.

4. "[D]ico quod major est falsa quando accipitur 'illud esse per se notum est,' tamen major vera, non tamen per se nota." *Ord.* 1.2.1–2.36; 2, 146.7–9.

5. *Ord.* 1.2.1–2.137–38; 2, 208.16–210.11. The reasoning is: "[S]umme cogitabile non est tantum in intellectu cogitante, quia tunc posset esse, quia cogitabile possibile, et non posset esse, quia repugnat rationi eius esse ab aliqua causa, sicut patet prius in secunda conclusione de via efficientiae." Ibid., no. 138; p. 210.3–7. E. Bettoni, *L'ascesa a Dio in Duns Scoto* (Milan: Vita e Pensiero, 1943), p. 25, remarks: "Quel doppio 'sine contradictione' è necessario, perché fonda e mette in evidenza, la prima volta, la possibilità de ciò che si pensa come Dio; la seconda, l'impossibilià de ciò che si vorrebbe pensare maggiore di Dio."

A second way (*Ord.* 1.2.1–2.139; 2, 210.12–211.1) of "coloring" the Anselmian argument is based on the Scotistic doctrine of cognition. What exists is a *maius cogitabile*; for it is a *perfectius cognoscibile*, because it is knowable by intuitive and not merely by abstract intellection. Therefore the most perfect knowable thing must be knowable by intuitive cognition—it is an existent, it exists.

In both "colorings," actual existence follows from the supreme perfection of the real object of thought.

6. "[Q]uaero . . . primo, utrum in entibus sit aliquid existens actu infinitum." *Ord.* 1.2.1–2.1; 2, 125.6–8.

7. "Et istud est perfectissimum conceptibile et conceptus perfectissimus, absolutus,

and special characteristic in Duns Scotus's proof for God's existence? The answer to this question is to be sought in an examination of the Scotistic proof, first as regards its external structure, and secondly as regards its probative content.

As regards external structure, Scotus proposes to show in the first stage of the demonstration a threefold primacy. Among beings there is an absolutely first efficient cause, an absolutely ultimate final cause, and an absolutely ultimate supreme nature.[8] In the infinite being, each of these stands as a "property" relative to creatures.[9] The second stage is to show that each of the three properties is uncausable. The third step is to demonstrate that each of the three *exists* in reality.[10] Apparently the process by which they are first established does not immediately show their real existence. This indicates that what is first attained is their nature, and that from their nature their existence is to be proven. It does not seem to allow existence any operative role in the first two stages of the demonstration. The fourth stage undertakes to show that these three relative properties coincide in one being. Even then the identity of this one existent being with God has still to be demonstrated by a fifth and final step. The being is shown to be infinite. Since that being exists, God, in the highest way conceivable by man, exists.[11]

Does this external structure indicate any special characteristic for the demonstration? The structure implies, evidently, that the first efficient cause, the ultimate final cause, and the supreme nature do not immediately reveal themselves as identical with the Christian God. If those three results had been reached on the basis of existential actuality, as in Aquinas, the identity would be immediately apparent. But with Scotus, the question still remains open. All three processes reach the instance that is most perfect respectively in each of the three orders. Aristotle had used similar processes. But in true Greek fashion he had equated the notion of perfection with finitude. He had located his first efficient cause, his final end, and his supreme being in finite form.[12] Duns Scotus, apparently, is reaching in this stage of his ar-

---

quem possumus habere de Deo naturaliter, quod sit infinitus." *Ord.* 1.2.1–2.147; 2, 215.1–3.

8. *Ord.* 1.2.1–2.41–42; 2, 149.13–151.3.

9. "[I]deo primo declarabo esse de proprietatibus relativis entis infiniti." *Ord.* 1.2.1–2.39; 2, 149.1–2.

10. "[P]rima est quod aliquid sit primum, secunda est quod illud est incausabile, tertia est quod illud actu existit in entibus." *Ord.* 1.2.1–2.42; 2, 151.1–2.

11. "Et sic probatum est Deum esse quantum ad conceptum vel esse eius, perfectissimum conceptibilem vel possibilem habere nobis de Deo." *Ord.* 1.2.1–2.147; 2, 215.4–6.

12. Hence Aristotle (*Metaph.* 12.8.1073a14–b17) can ask if separate substance is one

gument a result somewhat between Aristotle and Aquinas. The being that is so attained does not appear as finite form, nor is it yet seen as existent. It is rather a nature that appears for the moment as neither finite nor infinite nor existent, but which can be shown by further reasoning first to exist, and then to be infinite.

The structure of the demonstration, in consequence, indicates that Scotus is not at all proceeding from a properly existential starting point, but rather from a quidditative object that can be the basis for reasoning to actual existence. But even with this actual existence established, the structure of the argument indicates that the notion of infinity has to be applied to the existent reality in order to make the demonstration bear on the Christian God. This would suggest that infinity is at least the special characteristic that enables the Scotistic demonstration to prove that *God* exists.

But can infinity be the characteristic that proves the *existence* of the first efficient cause, ultimate end, and supreme being? In the Anselmian argument, as accepted by Scotus, infinity of perfection seemed required to prove actual existence. But here in Scotus's own demonstration the existence is proven in the third stage, and therefore before the infinity. The infinity is demonstrated only in the fifth stage. The actual existence, however, is regarded as proven from the nature of the first cause, ultimate end, and supreme essence. Is there some characteristic common to these three properties that proves existence just as does infinity, and if so, what is the relation of that common characteristic to infinitude?

The answer to these queries can emerge only from a careful and detailed examination of the Scotistic proof. This study should reveal to what extent the indications from the structure of the demonstration are borne out in the actual reasoning.

III

In accordance with the proposed structure, Duns Scotus commences by showing that there is an efficient cause holding absolutely first place.[13] As his starting point, he takes something that is manifestly evident even though it is contingent. It is something "causable" by way

---

or many, and reply that there are as many as are necessary to account for the original movements in the heavens. Scotus (*Rep. par.* 1.2.3.2; ed. Vivès, 22, 69b) regards the Aristotelian first being as actually infinite. See also *Ord.* 1.2.1–2.120; 2, 197.2–3.

13. "Prima autem conclusio . . . est ista, quod aliquod effectivum sit simpliciter primum." *Ord.* 1.2.1–2.43; 2, 151.4–5.

of efficient causality, that is, something *capable* of being caused.[14] In so designating his starting point, he is focusing not on the contingent *existence* of the thing, but on its causability, that is, on its *nature* as causable. Unlike Aquinas, he is starting in the quidditative or essential order, not in the existential. True, Scotus has in mind real being, and for the most part being existing in the actual world.[15] He is not commencing in thought. But he is giving the existential characteristic no genuinely operative role. He is basing his demonstration as a whole on the *nature* of contingent things, a nature which, even though really existing, is of itself common and therefore entirely indifferent to being, either in the intellect or in reality.

Upon that type of quidditative basis the argument is developed. The nature so understood is causable, and in consequence has to be caused by something else. But it cannot be the result of an infinite series of causes. The argument establishes in that way the nature of an absolutely first cause.[16]

There are only two points that Scotus feels called upon to defend in the reasoning given in this first stage of the demonstration. One concerns the starting point. The reasoning, it might be objected, is based upon contingent things and accordingly is not a demonstration.[17] Scotus answers that one *could* argue that a certain truly contingent nature is the *effect* of change and therefore by the *nature* of correlatives requires an *efficient* cause. This obviously means that the contingent existence accompanies the nature, but only as a fact. It does not enter the probative force of the argument. It can in consequence be disregarded. Nevertheless, Scotus continues, in using the contingent to establish by contrast the necessary, one can take the proof as dealing with quidditative being or possible being, and not with actual existence, even though later in the third stage of the demonstration actual existence is to be proven. In this way the argument

14. Ibid., p. 151.6–7. The specific term used by Scotus is "effectibile." "Causabile," however, is frequently substituted for it in the course of the argument. "Causabile" is the quasi-generic term, applicable to the results of formal, material, and final causality as well as efficient. Cf.: "Illud est ineffectibile, ergo incausabile, quia non est finibile, nec materiabile, nec formabile." *Ord.* 1.2.1–2.57; 2, 163.1–2. In English, "causable" and "causability" are recognized by the *O.E.D.*, s.v., though as rare.

15. Scotus (*Ord.* 1.2.1–2.58; 2, 164.12–14) notes that four of the five reasons used in the proof *can* involve existence. But as he is starting from the nature of causable things, which as a common nature is indifferent of itself to being either in the intellect or in reality, he would have no special point in either emphasizing or excluding its actual existence.

16. *Ord.* 1.2.1–2.43; 2, 151.7–152.9.

17. *Ord.* 1.2.1–2.45; 2, 153.3–5.

proceeds from necessary objects.[18] Contingent existence is eliminated from its starting point.

These two answers leave no doubt regarding the essentialist preoccupation to base the demonstration in the quidditative order. The first reply allows the contingent existence to be disregarded, the second eliminates its role. This is in sharp contrast to the procedure of St. Thomas, in which the contingent existence of sensible things is the starting point.

The other notion to be defended is the impossibility of an infinite series in efficient causality. An infinite series of essentially subordinated causes is impossible for five reasons: 1) The cause of the totality of essentially subordinated caused things must be outside that totality. 2) The number of essentially subordinated causes cannot be infinite. 3) Essential priority presupposes a principle that is first. 4) The increasing perfection of causes in a proposed infinite series would imply a cause of infinite causal perfection in a sense in which infinity excludes imperfection and therefore dependence of that cause on any other. Here the power of the first cause is established as infinite, infinity implying perfection without imperfection. 5) Causative power does not necessarily involve any imperfection, and therefore can be present in some nature without imperfection. For the moment, the existence in reality of this cause does not enter the argument, though later it will be shown that the possibility thus established is the basis for concluding to its existence.[19]

---

18. "[R]espondeo quod posset sic argui: aliqua natura est effecta quia aliquod subiectum mutatur, et ita terminus mutationis incipit esse in subiecto, et ita ille terminus vel compositum producitur sive efficitur; ergo est aliquod efficiens, per naturam correlativorum, et tunc potest esse secundum veritatem prima contingens, sed manifesta. —Potest tamen sic argui, probando primam conclusionem sic: Haec est vera 'aliqua natura est effectibilis, ergo aliqua est effectiva.' Antecedens probatur, quia aliquod subiectum est mutabile, quia aliquod entium est possibile distinguendo possibile contra necessarium, et sic procedendo ex necessariis. Et tunc probatio primae conclusionis est de esse quidditative sive de esse possibili, non autem de exsistentia actuali. Sed de quo nunc ostenditur possibilitas, ultra in conclusione tertia ostendetur actualis exsistentia." Ibid., no. 56; pp. 161.10–162.8. Regarding the argument in the first of the two alternatives, cf.: "Notandum vero, pro demonstratione demonstrante disjunctam de subjecto aliquo, quod si disjungantur correlativa aliqua, ut causa et causatum, prius et posterius, ex praemissa quae dicit unum illorum inesse alicui, sequitur alterum illorum inesse alii, non de existentia, sed de esse quiditativo." *Quaestiones subtilissimae super libros Metaphysicorum Aristotelis* 1.1.49; ed. Vivès, 7, 37a.

19. *Ord.* 1.2.1–2.53; 2, 157.6–159.6. The last two reasons are: "Tum quarto, quia superior causa est perfectior in causando, ex secunda differentia; ergo in infinitum superior est in infinitum perfectior, et ita infinitae perfectionis in causando, et per consequens non causans in virtute alterius, quia quaelibet talis est imperfecte causans, quia est dependens in causando ab alia. —Tum quinto, quia effectivum nullam imperfectionem ponit necessario: ergo potest esse in aliquo sine imperfectione. Sed si nulla

The first four of these arguments, Scotus himself points out, can bear on the existence of the first cause; in this case they are dealing with manifest contingent things. But they may also be taken as dealing with "nature and quiddity and possibility," and in that way as proceeding from necessary objects.[20] The fifth, of course, is not concerned with contingent things at all, but only with objects that are necessary. Scotus shows no interest whatever in the proof of existence upon the contingent basis. He merely mentions it, without letting it enter into the sequence of his demonstration as a whole.

The defense of the proposition is completed by showing that an infinite series of accidentally subordinated causes has to be dependent upon the first cause in an essentially subordinated series.[21] The reasoning is based entirely upon the *nature* of accidentally subordinated causes. It does not enter the existential order.

The demonstration then goes on to its second stage. It proves quite easily that the nature of the absolutely first efficient cause is uncausable, by reason of being *first*. Because it is absolutely first, this cause cannot have any prior efficient cause. Nor can it have a final cause, for a final cause exercises its causality only through an efficient cause. Having no extrinsic cause, it cannot have any intrinsic cause, for the nature (*ratio*) of extrinsic causality is prior to the nature (*ratio*) of intrinsic causality.[22] The point stressed in the reasoning is that extrinsic causality expresses perfection without imperfection.[23]

The third stage in the demonstration proves that such a first cause

causa est sine dependentia ad aliquid prius, in nullo est sine imperfectione. Sed si nulla causa est sine dependentia ad aliquid prius, in nullo est sine imperfectione. Ergo effectibilitas independens potest inesse alicui naturae, et illa simpliciter est prima; ergo effectibilitas simpliciter prima est possibilis. Hoc sufficit, quia inferius ex hoc concluditur quia tale efficiens primum, si est possibile, est in re." Ibid., pp. 158.3–159.6.

20. "Aliae autem probationes ipsus *a* possunt tractari de exsistentia quam proponit haec tertia conclusio, et sunt de contingentibus, tamen manifestis; vel accipiantur *a* de natura et quiditate et possibilitate, et sunt de necessariis." *Ord.* 1.2.1–2.58; 2, 164.12–15. On the first alternative, cf.: "Uno modo sumendo pro antecedente propositionem contingentem *de inesse*, quae nota est sensui, scilicet quod aliquid sit productum in actu, quod notum est sensui, quia aliquid est mutatum, quod nec negaret Heraclitus, et sic ex veris evidentibus, non tamen necessariis, sequitur conclusio." *Rep. par.* 1.2.2.7; 22, 65–66.

Whatever may be said about the proof when taken as proceeding from contingent existence, it is certainly not *the* characteristic proof of Duns Scotus, with which the present study is concerned. Cf. "[L]a *sua* dimostrazione di Dio è quella che parte dalla possibilità." E. Bettoni, *L'ascesa a Dio in Duns Scoto*, p. 59.

21. *Ord.* 1.2.1–2.54–55; 2, 159.7–161.8.

22. *Ord.* 1.2.1–2.57; 2, 162.9–164.4.

23. "[C]ausalitas causae extrinsecae dicit perfectionem sine imperfectione." *Ord.* 1.2.1–2.57; 2, 163.10–11.

is actually existing, that is, it is a nature truly existing in actuality.[24] The nature (*ratio*) of the absolutely first efficient cause has already been established as uncausable. It cannot exist through another. If it *can* exist, therefore, it can exist of itself; and it can exist, as the first stage in the demonstration has shown. But if it *can* exist of itself, it *does* exist of itself; otherwise non-being would be able to make something exist, and moreover the first cause would then be causing itself and so would no longer be uncausable.[25] "What does not exist of itself is not able to exist of itself, because in that case non-being would produce something in being, which is impossible, and besides, in that case it would cause itself and thus would not be entirely uncausable."[26]

The reasoning is as follows. The first cause *can* exist of itself. Suppose, then, that it does not exist. What could produce it? Certainly no other cause, for then it would exist by virtue of that cause and not of itself. So it would have to be produced by itself as non-existent. But what is non-existent cannot produce anything whatsoever. If it does not exist, the first cause *cannot* exist. Yet it *can* exist, as has already been established. Moreover, even if as non-existent it could produce itself, it would then be causing itself and therefore would no longer be absolutely uncausable. Accordingly, if the first cause is a nature that can exist of itself—and that has been proven on the basis of quiddity and possibility—it *does* exist in actual reality.

There is not the least doubt about this way of concluding to actual existence. The text is crystal clear. The nature and possibility of a first cause have been established on the basis of the nature and quiddity and possibility of manifest things; and this possibility of the first cause proves that its nature actually exists.[27]

Scotus continues to press home the same point in two other ways. The existence of the first cause is shown by the consideration that it would not be fitting for the universe to lack the supreme possible degree of being.[28] Moreover, the existence of the first efficient cause

24. "Tertia conclusio de primo effectivo est ista: primum effectivum est in actu exsistens et aliqua natura vere exsistens actualiter sicut est effectiva." *Ord.* 1.2.1–2.58; 2, 164.5–7.

25. *Ord.* 1.2.1–2.58; 2, 164.7–165.3.

26. "Quod non est a se non potest esse a se, quia tunc non-ens produceret aliquid ad esse, quod est impossibile, et adhuc, tunc illud causaret se et ita non esset incausabile omnino." *Ord.* 1.2.1–2.58; 2, 164.16–165.3.

27. É. Gilson, *Jean Duns Scot* (Paris: Vrin, 1952), pp. 142–43, notes that this reasoning makes the actual existence of God the source of his possibility. Nevertheless, as far as the demonstration is concerned, "Il est vrai que l'existence du Premier soit atteinte au moyen de l'essence" (ibid., p. 148).

28. "Illud ultimum, scilicet de exsistentia primi effectivi, aliter declaratur, quia inconveniens est universo deesse supremum gradum possibilem in essendo." *Ord.* 1.2.1–2.58; 2, 165.3–5.

follows from its character of "first"; this means that it is uncausable, and since it is not contradictory to entity (i.e., it is possible), as shown in the initial stage of the demonstration, it can exist of itself and therefore does exist of itself.[29] The common characteristic in these three ways of expressing the argument is that actual existence follows from possibility.

Scotus then proceeds to establish the existence of an absolutely final cause and an absolutely supreme nature, using, as he repeatedly insists, the same or similar arguments. He shows that the second stage in each case concludes that such a nature is uncausable efficiently, and so allows the third stage to conclude to actual existence in the manner just shown.[30]

Existence, therefore, follows from possibility. But what is the characteristic in possible being that allows this conclusion? That characteristic was designated, respectively, in the three ways of expressing the argument, as "uncausable," "supreme," and "first." Common to these three concepts is the notion of perfection. The three, in the sequence of the demonstration, manifest their content in the proof's second stage, where efficient causality was shown to express perfection without imperfection.[31] Because it was unrestricted by any imperfection, the first efficient cause is uncausable and supreme in perfection. The perfection without imperfection of this cause is the characteristic that permits and requires the reasoning to actual existence.

In Duns Scotus, therefore, when the univocal quidditative being seen in manifest things is extended to its supreme degree of perfection, it thereby involves actual existence. In St. Thomas, on the other hand, perfection established on a merely quidditative basis, no matter what degree it might reach, could never include the least existential actuality.

The fourth stage in the Scotistic demonstration is to establish the identity of the first efficient cause with the ultimate final cause and with the absolutely supreme nature. This is done briefly and without difficulty. The first efficient cause cannot act principally on account

29. "sic in quantum primum exsistit. Probatur ut praecedens; nam in ratione talis primi maxime includitur incausabile, probatur ex secunda; ergo si potest esse (quia non contradicit entitati, ut probatur ex prima), sequitur quod potest esse a se, et ita est a se." *Ord.* 1.2.1–2.59; 2, 165.9–13.

30. *Ord.* 1.2.1–2.60–67; 2, 165.14–168.11.

31. See supra, n. 30. Likewise, the fifth reason in the first stage of the demonstration was: "effectivum nullam imperfectionem ponit necessario." Text supra, n. 19. Cf.: "Sed sunt aliae primitates, quae non dicunt imperfectionem, ut primitas eminentiae et independentiae triplicis, puta duplicis causalitatis, effectivae et finalis." *Rep. par.* 1.2.2.3; 22, 64a.

of anything other than itself and, in consequence, is the ultimate final cause. Since its causality is equivocal in respect of the other causes, it must, being first cause, also be most eminent.[32]

Even with the threefold primacy located in one and the same being, however, the identity of this being with the Christian God is, in accordance with the Aristotelian background of the reasoning, not yet apparent. The fifth stage of the demonstration proves that such a being is infinite. This is done in four ways.

The first way is through the nature of its efficient causality. Although the infinite causal perfection of the first efficient cause had been established in the initial stage of the demonstration,[33] this infinite power is now shown by adapting an Aristotelian argument. The first efficient cause, as far as its power is concerned, can produce effects through infinite time. Therefore Aristotle's proof regarding infinite substance seems conclusive in showing that the first cause has total causative perfection.[34] This infinite power, which is naturally demonstrable, is not, however, omnipotence in the full theological sense; for that is an article of faith, and not provable by reason.[35] The notion of creation, namely, passage to being from non-being absolutely, so important in the demonstration of St. Thomas,[36] is not taken as a source of argument. The reasons are, first, because it is accepted only on faith, and second, because created being is not infinitely distant from absolute non-being, but only to the extent of the quidditative being of the creature, which is finite.[37]

The second way, also in the line of efficiency, is that the first efficient cause actually knows intelligibles in infinite number, numerical infinity in this case involving infinite perfection. Since it is infinite in cognoscibility, it is infinite in being; for the two correspond, according to Aristotelian doctrine.[38] The third way is that the human will desires an infinite good. Infinity, accordingly, is not contradictory to the nature of the good.[39] This means that the ultimately final good has to be infinite, for the greater the good, the greater the finality. The fourth way is that the supreme being must be infinite in perfection; for being does

---

32. *Ord.* 1.2.1.268–73; 2, 168.12–173.18.
33. "infinitae perfectionis in causando," *Ord.* 1.2.1–2.53; 2, 158.5–6. Text supra, n. 19.
34. *Ord.* 1.2.1–2.111–124; 2, 189.1–201.10.
35. *Ord.* 1.2.1–2.119; 2, 194.8–13.
36. See Aquinas, *Scriptum super Sententias*, 2.1.1.3; ed. Mandonnet, 2, 20–23. Also 4.5.1.3.56–70; ed. Moos, 4, 209–11.
37. Scotus, *Ord.* 1.2.1–2.121–124; 2, 198.1–201.10.
38. *Ord.* 1.2.1–2.125–129; 2, 201.11–205.7.
39. *Ord.* 1.2.1–2.130; 2, 205.8–206.4.

not exclude infinity, and, as every infinite is greater than the corresponding finite, infinite perfection is greater than finite perfection.[40]

Infinity, therefore, is proven from perfection. The most perfect nature, the greatest good, the most perfect efficient causality, imply for Scotus infinite being. In being, apparently, "most perfect" and "infinite" coincide, because the infinite is greater than any finite instance, in being, just as in quantity.[41] In this way Scotus presses home the consideration that actual existence can be proven from infinity in being. If such infinity is possible, it actually exists, according to the third stage of the demonstration. In this way also the Anselmian argument is to be explained.[42]

In the Scotistic reasoning, therefore, infinity does not follow logically from existence, but rather precedes it. The fifth stage of the demonstration could logically have preceded the fourth. In fact, the infinity is just an explicit realization of what the second stage of the demonstration proved, namely, perfection without imperfection.[43] It is an application of the norm that the infinite is greater than the finite. The causal perfection was understood as infinite, even in the second stage of the demonstration. But at that stage Scotus, true to the Aristotelian form of the arguments, did not call attention to the fact that this perfection implied infinity in being. He showed first that the perfection implied actual existence, and then without reference to that existence, that it implied infinity in being. Perfection, without imperfection, in consequence, is what established actual existence. But perfection in the Aristotelian sense would establish neither existence nor infinity. Perfection for Aristotle had meant finitude. Only when su-

---

40. *Ord.* 1.2.1–2.131–136; 2, 206.6–208.15.

41. "[F]inito autem non est incompossibile esse aliquid perfectius: . . . quia infinitum non repugnat enti; sed omni finito maius est infinitum." *Ord.* 1.2.1–2.131–132; 2, 206.8–11. "[E]rgo perfectissimum ens est infinitum." Ibid., no. 132; p. 207.1. Cf. text infra, n. 55.

42. "Item sic suadetur: infinitum suo modo non repugnat quantitati, id est in accipiendo partem post partem; ergo nec infinitum suo modo repugnat entitai, id est in perfectione simul essendo.

Item, si quantitas virtutis est simpliciter perfectior quam quantitas molis, quare erit infinitum possibile in mole et non in virtute? Quod si est possibile, est in actu, sicut ex tertia conclusione patet, supra, de primitate effectiva, et etiam inferius probabitur." *Ord.* 1.2.1–2.134–135; 2, 208.1–7.

43. Cf.: "Si autem intelligas absolute 'summum,' hoc est quod ex natura rei non posset excedi perfectio illa, expressius concipitur in ratione infiniti entis. Non enim 'summum bonum' indicat in se utrum sit infinitum vel finitum." *Ord.* 1.3.1.1–2.60; 3, 41.12–16. Against this background is to be understood the remark of E. Bettoni: "È chiaro però che già (i.e., in the third stage) a questo punto l'essere trascendente è raggiunto: il balso fondamentale dal finito all'infinito, dall'essere diveniente all'Essere indiveniente è già compiuto. E la vera prova dell'esistenza di Dio sta qui." *L'ascesa a Dio in Duns Scoto,* p. 56.

preme perfection is considered as infinite may it be offered as a reason for actual existence. Infinity, therefore, is the special characteristic which in the procedure of Duns Scotus proves both that God *exists* and that the existent is *God,* according to the highest concept of God that is naturally attainable.

IV

The content of the Scotistic demonstration, then, bears out what its introduction and its external structure indicated. The Franciscan thinker bases his reasoning entirely in the quidditative order, allows the contingent existence of the manifest things to be neglected or eliminated, and reaches a being whose nature is not immediately recognizable either as existent or as divine. The perfection of that nature then proves both that it is existent and that it is God. But to allow either of those conclusions, supreme perfection has to be understood as infinite. In infinity, therefore, lies the answer to the question of the special characteristic in the Scotistic demonstration of God's existence.

But "infinity" in regard to God has for Scotus a twofold sense. In one sense it is naturally knowable to man, but as the basis for the immediacy of the divine omnipotence, and for the Trinity, it is known only by revelation.

To what extent, then, does the application of the univocally common notion "infinity" identify with God the result of the Scotistic demonstration? Certainly it does not express the intrinsic constituent of the divine nature as treated in theology, namely that nature as *haec,* a nature that of itself is individual. The whole conceptual content of "infinite being," as conceived by the human mind in the present state, is universal in character and univocal to creatures. It is a combination of univocal and universal concepts that in extension is limited to God and is in this way proper to him. But it does not exhibit any simple nature that is proper to God. It is identified with God only incidentally (*per accidens*). Of itself it does not show that identity. Aristotle, in fact, would be led to deny in it the infinity even of power that is proper to the God of revelation. The Christian theologian, however, can see in it a notion to which all theological truths can be referred, even though it does not contain those truths within itself. The theologian can use it as a substitute for the primary notion in theology, and in this way see that it is identified with God in the sense that it can apply to no other being than God.[44] That is sufficient for the purpose of Duns Scotus in the commentary on the *Sentences.*

44. "Sic etiam de ente infinito, quamvis enim uterque conceptus simpliciter simplex

The Scotistic demonstration, therefore, from its basis in univocal quidditative natures, does not claim to express the intrinsic constituent of the divine nature, nature of itself individual. The Scotistic basis for such predication, namely real community, is in this case entirely lacking.[45] The proof of St. Thomas, on the other hand, from its basis in contingent existential actuality, does express the metaphysical constituent of God's nature as existence, for existence can be the nature of no creature whatever and is therefore univocal to no finite nature. The Scotistic proof, by applying the univocal notion of infinity to the univocal notion of being, does not rise to any content above created nature, but pinpoints its objective by allowing two univocal natures to cross. The Thomistic demonstration, on the other hand, does not start with any created nature, but with an actuality that is not grasped as

---

sit communior conceptu Dei, conveniens univoce deo et creaturis, tamen post determinationem uterque conceptus particularisatur, et fit conceptus proprius Deo, sic quod solum illi convenit." *Rep. par.* 1.3.2.10; 22, 97a. After giving the example that if one does not know what a triangle is one can abstract from other figures the notion of figure and from numbers the notion of primary, and thereby have a concept restricted to triangle without knowing the nature of a triangle, the text continues: "Sic in proposito, possum abstrahere conceptum a creatura, qui communis est Deo et creaturae, licet a conceptu proprio Dei illum conceptum communem abstraherem; et sic verum est quod in conjungendo illos simul, tantum convenit ille conceptus totalis Deo, quem possum cognoscere, licet non cognoscam hanc essentiam, ut haec est, cui convenit talis conceptus." Ibid., p. 97ab.

45. "'Deus et creatura non sunt primo diversa in conceptibus'; sunt tamen primo diversa in realitate, quia in nulla realitate conveniunt." *Ord.* 1.8.1.3.82; 4, 190.17–19. It is here that Scotistic concepts lose their seemingly immediate contact with reality. Their universal predicability is based upon the real and positive community of the common nature in sensible things. That nature is quidditatively being and is grasped by the metaphysician in its natural priority to all individual and existential differences. See *Ord.* 2.3.1.1.34; 7, 404.4–17. Unitive containment would make it contradictory for the nature to be found anywhere whatever without the pertinent differentia. Cf. *Quaest. metaph.* 7.13.20–21; 7, 420–21. The result is a metaphysical order that is utterly unknown to Thomistic thought, and that establishes a different basis of predication and gives an altogether special sense to the notions of "univocal" and "common." But the divine nature is of itself individual and in consequence is a nature that excludes any real community with other beings. Hence, in the present state, natural thinking alone cannot show that there is any per se basis for including the divine nature within the range of one's concept "being." According to merely natural knowledge in the present state, that concept is not seen to extend beyond sensible quiddity and its derivatives. But through revelation the theologian knows God and knows that the human intellect is of its nature meant to include God in its primary object. He knows that God is the first being, etc., and therefore he sees that his common and univocal concepts of "first being," and so on, apply only to God, even though they do not express the divine nature. In this way only is he able to know God through naturally formed concepts, and in this perspective he can apply those concepts to God in their full univocal nature. Hence in this case there can be community of concepts without a corresponding community of nature.

a nature, and that leads to a nature above the whole order of created natures. That nature, however, is not attained as it is in itself, but only insofar as it corresponds to the truth in human judgment.[46]

V

In the light of the foregoing considerations, one may well ask two questions regarding the starting point of Duns Scotus. First, how does his initial concept of being, unlike that of St. Thomas, allow a conclusion to the existential order? Secondly, how does it, so differently from that of Aristotle, allow its supreme perfection to consist in infinity and not in finitude?

As regards the first question, Duns Scotus as a matter of fact sees no altogether special type of being in existential actuality. He continues to interpret existence, as used by Thomistic reasoning, according to the alleged Avicennian conception of an accident naturally subsequent to essence.[47] Why? There may well be ample psychological and historical reasons. The natural propensity of the human intellect renders extremely difficult any thinking in terms above the essential order.[48] The doctrine that the proper actuality and source of being in sensible things escapes the act of conceptualization and is grasped originally only in judgment appears in St. Thomas without progenitors and has been seen by very few who have lived after him, even among those who have read his texts extensively. But even apart from all such reasons, would not Scotus's belief in the impaired capacity of the human intellect in its present state prevent him from admitting that any higher level of being was grasped in the act of judgment?

Duns Scotus maintains that the intellect in the present state of fallen nature does not know by natural means what its own first object is. That object is being as being, even though to Aristotle it appeared to be sensible being.[49] True, the intellect in its present state cannot under-

---

46. *Summa theologiae*, 1.3.4.ad 2m. The rest of the Thomistic procedure in treating the divine nature—*quid non sit* (1.3.preamble)—is by way of negation.

47. "Nec possunt dicere quod esse angeli finitet essentiam eius, quia secundum eos est accidens essentiae, et posterius naturaliter." *Ord.* 1.2.1–2.141; 2, 211.8–10. Similarly: "[E]sse est quid posterius essentiae." *Rep. par.* 1.2.3.3; 22, 70a.

48. On this point, see H. Bergson, "Introduction à la métaphysique," *Revue de métaphysique et de morale* 11 (1903), 27. É. Gilson, *Le thomisme* 5th ed. (Paris: Vrin, 1944), pp. 60–61.

49. "Ad aliud negandum est quod assumitur, quod scilicet naturaliter cognoscitur ens esse primum obiectum intellectus nostri, et hoc secundum totam indifferentiam entis ad sensibilia . . . Non sic Aristoteles; sed secundum ipsum, primum obiectum intellectus nostri est vel videtur esse quiditas sensibilis, et hoc vel in se sensibilis vel in suo inferiori; et haec est quiditas abstrahibilis a sensibilibus." *Ord.* Prol. 1.1.33; 1, 19.12–

stand anything that is not contained in the quiddity of sensible things.[50] But this consideration does not allow the *theologian* to hold that the first object of the human intellect is the quiddity of a material thing. According to faith, the same intellect in a beatified soul, unchanged in its nature by the *lumen gloriae,* can know immaterial substance.[51] Rather, this means that the nature (*ratio*) of being is common and univocal to all things.[52] If it were not thus univocal, there would be no way for the human intellect naturally to know God.[53] The concept of being, even as taken from sensible things, is of itself indifferent to the finite or the infinite.[54]

The human intellect, therefore, in its very first act grasps without naturally realizing it the nature of being as such. No matter what its state, it can know nothing whatever except in that first object, being as being. Knowing in its initial act the full univocal nature of being, it has nothing more in this regard to attain in any further act. To look for such special significance in the second act, that of judgment, would be nugatory. In such a doctrine the judgment may state a mode of being in the sense of actual presence. But it can add nothing whatever in the nature of being as such.

From this initial conception of being likewise emerges the answer to the second question. Aristotle, confined to sensible nature as the full extent of his starting point, could see the perfection of being only in limit. Scotus, believing that the first object of the intellect had a much wider scope, saw the nature of being, even when known in sensible things, as neutral to limit and to infinity. Such being, therefore, since it allowed the infinite, could find its supreme perfection in nothing less.[55]

20.8. Cf. "Sed primum obiectum intellectus nostri naturale est ens in quantum ens." Ibid., no. 1; p. 2.8. "si ideo non cognoscitur quid sit obiectum primum intellectus." Ibid., no. 36; p. 21.6–7. On this question see É. Gilson, *Jean Duns Scot,* pp. 12–35.

50. "Tamen ei pro statu isto adaequatur in ratione motivi quiditas rei sensibilis; et ideo pro statu isto non naturaliter intelliget alia quae non continentur sub illo primo motivo." *Ord.* 1.3.1.3.186; 3, 113.4–7.

51. *Ord.* 1.3.1.3.113; 3, 70.14–18.

52. "[O]mne per se intelligibile aut includit essentialiter rationem entis, vel continetur virtualiter vel essentialiter in includente essentialiter rationem entis." *Ord.* 1.3. 1.3.137; 3, 85.14–16.

53. "Deus non est cognoscibilis a nobis naturaliter nisi ens sit univocum cum creato et increato." *Ord.* 1.3.1.3.139; 3, 87.1–2.

54. "[S]ed intellectus viatoris potest esse certus de Deo, quod sit ens, dubitando de ente finito vel infinito, creato vel increato; ergo conceptus entis de Deo est alius a conceptu isto et illo, et ita neuter ex se et in utroque illorum includitur." *Ord.* 1.3.1.3.27; 3, 18.14–17.

55. See supra, nn. 41–42. Also: "[C]ognito ente non statim occurrit intellectui finitas." *Rep. par.* 1.2.3.8; 22, 73a. The transcendentals therefore need not be identified

The theology of Duns Scotus, in consequence, compels him as a Christian to see in the object grasped by the first act of conceptualization the full univocal nature of being. This nature extends to everything that has the aspect of being, existence not excluded. When so understood in the fullness of its perfection, that is, in its intrinsic mode of infinity, it necessarily, though without immediate evidence, includes existence. It can be the starting point for reasoning to the existence of infinite being. St. Thomas Aquinas, on the other hand, sees in the first act of abstract conceptualization only the nature of sensible things, which in no way includes the actuality of being. Unlike Aristotle, Aquinas looks to judgment for the original knowledge of existential actuality. Only by reasoning from that actuality as grasped by judgment can he reach the nature of being as such, which is the *I am who am* of Exodus.

---

with any specific nature: "[O]mnis pars essentialis in quocumque genere, et omnis species cuiuscumque generis, includit limitationem, et ita quodcumque transcendens esset de se finitum, et per consequens repugnaret enti infinito, nec posset dici de ipso formaliter, quod est falsum, quia omnia transcendentia dicuntur 'perfectiones simpliciter' et convenient Deo in summo." *Ord.* 1.3.1.3.135; 3, 84.9–14. The different cultural backgrounds of Aristotle and Duns Scotus require consideration here. The aim of Greek culture was to express form, and accordingly it tended to see perfection in the finite only. But with Scotus, in the wake of centuries of Christian and Neoplatonic tradition, the highest and the most perfect had come to be placed above the limited.

12

SOUL AS AGENT IN AQUINAS

I

In treating of the human soul, as is well enough known, St. Thomas Aquinas seems to want the best of both worlds. He is first and foremost a Christian thinker. Accordingly he requires a spiritual soul that continues in existence after separation from matter in death, and that at least in some way or other is able to exercise the vital functions of intellection and volition in its separated state. But he is also a metaphysician whose reasoning on the soul has been in large part inspired by Aristotle. From this standpoint he is led to think in terms of a soul that is essentially the form of a material substrate, and that in consequence should not be capable of any real existence apart from its body.

Aquinas is well aware of the emerging anomaly. He regards it in fact as the initial problem to be faced in his own *Questions on the Soul*. The first query is whether the human soul can be both a form and a singular thing. The answer, given after penetrating consideration of the history and the difficulties of the problem, is affirmative and unqualified. The human soul is a singular thing to the full extent of being able to subsist by itself. Yet at the same time it is the form that gives specific perfection to the composite.[1]

---

1. *Quaestiones de anima* 1. The doctrine is already present in the earliest works of Aquinas. See *Scriptum super libros Sententiarum*, 1.8.5.2; 2.1.2.4; 2.17.3.1; 3.5.3.2. *De ente et essentia* 4, Leonine edition 43 (Rome: Santa Sabina, 1976), 377.185–192, and c. 6, 380.62–64. A list of parallel passages in other works of Aquinas may be found in James H. Robb, *St. Thomas Aquinas, Questiones de anima* (Toronto: Pontifical Institute of Mediaeval Studies, 1968), p. 53. The conclusion is stated succinctly: "Relinquitur igitur quod anima est hoc aliquid ut per se potens subsistere, non quasi habens in se completem speciem, sed quasi perficiens speciem humanam ut est forma corporis; et sic simul est forma et hoc aliquid" (*Quaest. de an.* 1; p. 59). The problem has been discussed by Anton C. Pegis, "St. Thomas and the Unity of Man," in *Progress in Philosophy, Philosophical Essays in Honor of Rev. Doctor Charles A. Hart*, ed. James A. McWilliams (Milwaukee: Bruce, 1955), pp. 153–73.

Clearly, St. Thomas is upholding both the perpetual existence of the human soul after death, as current in medieval Christian tradition, and also the Aristotelian conception of the soul as essentially the form of matter. No mitigation of either stance appears. Rather, there is not even acknowledgment of any incompatibility in the face of the historical and doctrinal problems. What is the reason that engenders this facility in accommodating the Aristotelian texts to Christian needs?

The question has been studied carefully, and the answer has been made incontrovertibly clear.[2] The reason stems from the existential approach that dominates the metaphysical thinking of Aquinas. For him existence is a distinct actuality grasped through judgment. In things that have no activity transcending material conditions, the existence belongs directly to the composite of matter and form. But where there are activities that transcend material conditions, such as human thought and volition do, the existence has to be independent of matter. It belongs immediately to the form, the soul. It is the existence of the soul, shared by the matter and the body. The human soul is accordingly in itself an existent, a singular thing, even though it is essentially the form of a body. This doctrine of existence, not present in Aristotle, enables Aquinas to read without restraint or embarrassment his own notions into the Aristotelian text.

So far, the question has been settled. But, as so often happens, the solution creates new problems. Can reasoning based upon existence demonstrate any *life* of which one is not immediately aware, such as life in the case of the separated soul?[3] In a doctrine where existence as an actuality comes between a thing and its operation, making the operative powers really distinct from the thing's essence, can existence just alone be a cogent guarantee that the thing is exercising vital activities? Yet immortality, both by its etymology and by its use in Greek as well as Christian contexts, means not just perpetual existence but, specifically, unending *life*. Further, does the existential approach distort or falsify the Aristotelian reasoning? Do the Aristotelian premises

2. See A. C. Pegis, "Some Reflections on *Summa Contra Gentiles*, II, 56," in *An Étienne Gilson Tribute*, ed. Charles J. O'Neil (Milwaukee: Marquette University Press, 1959), pp. 169–88; Étienne Gilson, "Autour de Pomponazzi," *Archives d'histoire doctrinale et littéraire du Moyen Age* 28 (1961), 167–68, and "L'affaire de l'immortalité de l'âme à Venise au debut du XVIe siècle," in *Umanesimo europeo e umanismo Veneziano*, ed. Vittore Branca (Florence: Sansoni, 1964), p. 38, n. 12.

3. Cf.: "And may I make the statement, for some perhaps challengeable, that St. Thomas does not attempt to prove the immortality of the human soul? . . . [H]is conclusion is: *Unde relinquitur animam humanam esse incorruptibilem*, which, of course, is not exactly the same thing." John F. McCormick, "Quaestiones Disputandae," *The New Scholasticism* 13 (1939), 369.

necessarily lead to a denial of the soul's immortality?[4] Is their instant adaptation to the Thomistic environment merely a chameleonic change of color, something superficial that does not essentially affect their adverse nature? Or are they expressions of evident truth as far as Aristotle was able to perceive it, yet incomplete and aporematic, neutral in themselves and open equally to an existential thrust that proves the soul imperishable and to a formal approach that has the soul perish with the body?[5] Finally, does the application of existential insights to the problem originate here solely from philosophical considerations, or does it proceed rather from the guidance furnished by Christian revelation?[6]

Aquinas himself is explicit enough in finding an imperishable soul in the statements and doctrine of Aristotle. The Stagirite, he asserts, says that the intellect or intellective part of the soul is a kind of soul that can be separated from the other parts and will continue in existence perpetually.[7] The commentators, whether they think Aquinas is right or wrong in interpreting Aristotle here, are in agreement about his stand. For him Aristotle teaches that the human soul is separable from the body and that it will remain in existence forever. The form of the human body is regarded by Aquinas as meant in the Aristotelian text to be something that can exist apart from matter, and will exist as a thing just in itself after bodily death takes place. There seems no reason to doubt that he understood the text itself as teaching that the human soul is imperishable, even though it is the form of a perishable body.[8]

4. On the two different traditions of Aristotelian interpretation that upheld this stand, namely those of Alexander of Aphrodisias and of Averroes, see Gilson, "Autour de Pomponazzi," pp. 164–65.

5. On the theologian's use of these philosophical premises, see Gilson, "Autour de Pomponazzi," pp. 274–76. The openness of the Aristotelian texts to both sides in the question of the soul's immortality was noted by Cajetan in observing that they offered the opportunity of interpretation in either direction—"facultas in alteram quoque partem verba illius interpretandi." *Commentaria in De anima Aristotelis*, Praefatio; ed. P. I. Coquelle (Rome: Angelicum, 1938–39), 1, 6.

6. The answer to this question may depend upon the way one accepts the notion of Christian philosophy. See infra, n. 9.

7. "[C]oncludit quod hec sola pars anime, scilicet intellectiua, est incorruptibilis et perpetua; et hoc est quod supra posuit in II, quod hoc genus anime separatur ab aliis sicut 'perpetuum a corruptibili.' Dicitur autem perpetua non quia semper fuerit, set quia semper erit." *Sentencia libri De Anima*, 3.4.212–17; Leonine ed. (Rome & Paris: Vrin, 1984), 45 (1), 222. The conclusion was seen drawn of both the active and the passive intellect: "Dicit ergo primo, quod *solus* intellectus *separatus est hoc, quod uere est.* Quod quidem non potest intelligi neque de intellectu agente neque de intellectu possibili tantum, set de utroque, quia de utroque supra dixit quod est separatus; et sic patet quod hic loquitur de tota parte intellectiua." Ibid., no. 202–207. St. Thomas experiences no difficulty in this context in seeing the same referent for "intellectus" and "hoc genus animae"; cf. *Sent. lib. De an.* 2.4; p. 84.111–17.

8. Neither side in the Pomponazzi controversy had any doubt that St. Thomas read

However, there is some reason to think that the situation is not entirely simple. In one of his early articles on the topic, Aquinas distinguishes rather sharply two aspects of the human soul. One is that of form. The other is that of absolute status or independence in regard to matter. To originate motion or to have independent being belongs to the soul not insofar as it is a form, but insofar as it is an image of God. The latter consideration comes obviously from biblical passages (such as Genesis 1.26–27) in which man is described as made to the image and likeness of God. This is a point of revealed doctrine. It is given here by Aquinas as the ground for the independent existence of the human soul, in express contrast to the notion of form as the basis for the tenet (text infra, n. 23).

Does this indicate that the true reason of Aquinas for the imperishable character of the human soul is not philosophical but scriptural? Is his conclusion that the soul is perpetually existent based upon this revealed premise? If so, is not the conclusion theological rather than philosophical? Or is the procedure more finely nuanced? Is it a case of the revealed tenet focusing attention upon a particular aspect of a doctrine seen indeed in Aristotle but hardly noticed and not at all developed by him? If so, the premises for the conclusion would be available to human reason in virtue of its own powers, even though it is led to these naturally knowable premises by the guidance of revealed truth. The case would parallel the notion of God as subsistent existence, presented basically by the traditionally quoted passage of Exodus (3.14) but then seen as a conclusion, deduced from the existence of sensible things, that is grasped in judgment. The reasoning would not be theological, but would remain frankly on the level of Christian philosophy.[9]

The problem accordingly has its complications and invites close study. It has a perennial metaphysical interest, for the nature and survival of the human soul is a topic about which man naturally desires to know, and which calls for philosophic treatment in the domain of metaphysics. It has likewise a special contemporary interest, for in some circles the notion of soul is bypassed in discussions of human existence after death. The superiority of a pre-Hellenic conception of human immortality, it is true, is far from established. But the fact that the issue has been raised suggests the need of careful acquaintance with the most highly developed doctrines of soul in western tradition,

---

Aristotle in this way. The only scruple on the favorable side was: if Aristotle thought the soul immortal why had he never said so? See Gilson, "L'affaire de l'immortalité de l'âme," p. 40.

9. I.e., no matter how much the religious faith calls attention to naturally accessible starting points, it does not at all enter into the reasoning processes.

those of Aristotle and of St. Thomas Aquinas, in their specific application to the soul as a vital agent in some type of independence of its union with matter.

II

The first task, obviously, is to determine as exactly as possible what is meant by soul in this context, and what is meant by the body with which soul is contrasted. The distinction is far from simple and clear-cut. Against the Aristotelian background, the soul has to be a form of something material. But that "something material" should be precisely the body. The body is a physical composite of the matter and the form. It thereby already includes the soul. Unlike the doctrine of Plotinus (*Enneads* 4.3.9.36–38), for whom body lies in the soul that sustains it, the soul is for Aquinas a physical part of the body and is contained in the body.

When the soul is contrasted with the body in this context, then, soul is placed on both sides of the dividing line. Soul considered as apart from matter is opposed to a composite in which it is present and of which it is an essential part. The contrast is like that of a human head or a human heart with the man who possesses each and whose nature makes each of them human. With regard to the contrast between matter and form, on the other hand, the case is quite different. The matter, in the Aristotelian setting, is physically distinct from the form. The soul, since it is a form, is accordingly distinct in a physical sense from the matter. The contrast between soul and matter is sharp and real. But is it at all the same with the distinction between soul and body? If soul is found on both sides of the couplet, how could it be really separable or distinct from the body without thereby being really distinct from itself? To regard body as wholly separate from the physical form, even conceptually, is to destroy the notion of body. A complete distinction is not possible.

The most that can be achieved in this regard is a physical distinction between part and whole. The body is the whole composite, the soul is one of its parts. The contrast would be like that of head or heart or hand with the entire human body. But does not a distinction of this kind run into the difficulties encountered by the meeting of Christian tradition with the Aristotelian thought in the middle ages?[10] If there

---

10. A survey of the controversy on the plurality of forms in the thirteenth century may be found in É. Gilson, *History of Christian Philosophy in the Middle Ages* (New York: Random House, 1955), pp. 416–20. "Forma corporeitatis" is in fact used by Aquinas,

can be only one substantial form in a single thing, as required by strict Aristotelian thought and as emphasized in the existential setting of St. Thomas, how can one speak of a human body once the soul has left it? What meaning can there be for a human body awaiting the resurrection, or for the body of Christ during the days immediately after the crucifixion? Why should not one speak frankly of the separation of soul from its matter, rather than from its body? One may indeed speak of the separation of hand or leg from the body, for neither of these is what primarily constitutes it as a body. But the soul is what formally makes the matter into a body. What meaning can the separation of soul from body have, even in the sense of separation of part from whole, once the philosophical implications of the notion "body" are grasped? Integral parts such as arm and leg may be considered apart from the whole they constitute. But what gives a thing its basic distinguishing feature, as does the substantial form, cannot be separated without destroying the notion of the term with which one would like to contrast it. How can one have even a concept of body apart from that of form, which in this case is the soul?

Aquinas, however, experiences little or no embarrassment in dealing with these issues. He speaks regularly and without hesitation of soul as distinguished from body, in full accord with the tradition of Christian thought.[11] His deep adherence to the Aristotelian notions does

---

Sent. 1.8.5.2.Solut.; ed. Mandonnet, 1, 228–29, and *ST* 1.66.2c and ad 3m. Yet for him it means but an aspect of the specific forms that does not differ in reality from those forms themselves—"cum non sit alia a formis quibis corpora distinguuntur," *ST* 1.66.2.ad 3m.

11. The corpus of medieval Latin and vernacular literature on this topic is enormous, as stressed by Robert W. Ackerman, "The Debate of the Body and the Soul and Parochial Christianity," *Speculum* 37 (1962), 542. The scriptural background is the conflict between flesh and spirit, as at Gal. 5.17. But the whole complex of highly developed Greek philosophical distinctions between soul and body was available in synoptic form to Christian tradition through the influential *Premnon physicon* of Nemesius (fl. 390–400 A.D.), as well as in more scattered ways. The *Premnon physicon* introduces man as constituted "ex anima intellegibili et corpore," 1.1; ed. Carolus Burkhard (Leipzig: Teubner, 1917), p. 5.2. The work was known in Latin translation in the eleventh and twelfth centuries, and was used considerably by Aquinas (cf. *ST* 1.23.3; 1.81.2.sed contra; 1.103.6.arg.1; *Q. de an.*, ed. Robb, pp. 58–59 nn.). On its diffusion, see E. Amann, s.v. Némésius d'Emèse, 3, *Dictionnaire de théologie catholique*.

More precisely, the Greek notions were regarded by Cassiodorus (*De anima*; PL 70, 1279–1307) in a Christian context in which body is subject to soul, soul to itself, and the whole composite to God: "Credo divina miseratione provisum, ut corpus subderet animae, animam sibi, totumque salubriter ad Deums respiceret Creatorum" (c. 9; col.1279D). This treatise of Cassiodorus does not seem to have been very widely read or quoted in earliest times. An instance of its influence on the *Liber de spiritu et anima*, however, is traced through Gundissalinus by Sr. Frances Carmel (Teresa Regan) in an unpublished doctoral dissertation, "A Study of the *Liber de spiritu et anima*," Diss. University of Toronto 1948, p. 267. But the threefold perspective continues in Isaac of

not force him into unusual ways of expression. He does not feel compelled to refer continually to the separation of soul from matter, in the context of Christian problems of body and soul. Nor does his part in the then-current controversies about the plurality of forms, in which he was perhaps even dangerously involved,[12] mitigate his understanding of the accidental character of anything added to a substantial form. The substantial form makes a thing an existent. Anything added, even a spiritual soul, could be only accidental to it. The substantial form had to be one, and one only. In a man, it had to be the spiritual soul. With these tenets Aquinas is able to think through each theological problem at issue, without feeling any need to dilute their thoroughly Aristotelian flavor.[13]

How, then, is Aquinas conceiving the human soul when speaking of it in contrast to body? He is quite evidently representing soul and body as two different things, each of which can be considered apart from the other. He is also dealing with them as though they were integral parts that go together to constitute the one existent, a man. But how can this be done, when the body itself is physically the whole man and in no way in reality an integral part?

The procedure is explained carefully by Aquinas in the chronologically early work De ente et essentia. Elsewhere it seems merely taken for granted. It is definitely an abstractive process. It is the precisive type of abstraction, the type in which the abstracted notion rigorously excludes from itself all the rest of the thing from which it was abstracted. Precisely abstracted, the notion "body" becomes a definite unit that is set up over and against any higher perfection in the Porphyrian tree, be it life or sensation or intellection:

The term "body," therefore, can signify that which has such a form as allows the determination of three dimensions in it, prescinding from everything else, so that from that form no further perfection may follow. If anything else is added, it will be outside the meaning of body thus understood. In this way body will be an integral and material part of a living being, because the soul will be outside what is signified by the term "body" and will be joined to this

---

Stella, De anima, PL 194, 1875C "Tria itaque sunt, corpus, anima et Deus." Further, in the extensively used (see Regan dissertation, pp. 1–3) Liber de spiritu et anima, referred to by Aquinas (De ver. 15.1.ad 1; Quodl. 10.3.1; ST 1.77.8.arg.1; Q. de an. 12.1 and 2, and elsewhere) soul is regarded as spirit, and flesh as body: "Itaque anima quae vere spiritus est, et caro quae vere corpus est"—chap. 14; PL 40, 789. The tendency of the compiler is to use the terms interchangeably throughout. So the Pauline struggle between spirit and flesh takes place between soul and body. See for instance André Wilmart, "Un grand débat de l'âme et du corps en vers élégiaques," Studi Medievali, N.S. 12 (1939), 192–209.

12. See Gilson, History of Christian Philosophy in the Middle Ages, pp. 417–18.
13. E.g., Sent. 4.50.1; ST 1.50.3–5; Q. de an. 19; Compendium theol. 232.

body in such a way that a living being is made up of these two, body and soul, as of two parts.[14]

The expressions in this passage are crystal clear. There is a way in which any visible living thing, be it plant or brute animal or man, can be conceived as made up of two parts, body and soul. The way is by precisive abstraction. You conceive something capable of three dimensions, and from its formal element you exclude any capacity for life or sensation or intellection. You then have the concept of a body, precisively abstracted. The thing with which you are dealing may be an oak tree, a robin, or a man. It makes no difference at all. In every instance you have abstracted the notion of something capable of three dimensions but without a type of form from which higher perfection could follow. You have a notion of body that is contrasted now with any kind of soul, whether vegetative or sentient or rational. You have placed the notion of soul outside this notion of body, as something left in the residue that is excluded by the precisive abstraction. You have conceived it as an integral part. In this way the two integral parts, body and soul, constitute the one living being.

In modern thought it is not customary to speak of a plant body or a plant soul. Yet body is still defined as "the whole physical structure and substance of a man, animal, or plant." The notion "body" is applied to each generically, but in the case of plants the precisive abstraction from the vital principle is not made except in the context of Aristotelian or Scholastic thought. It is still quite permissible to speak of a brute animal's body, though less usual to speak of its soul. For contemporary purposes, then, the contrast of body with soul is in practice restricted to the case of man. Here the distinction is regularly made between the spiritual soul and the living sentient body. This is the way body is understood when its drives and urges are contrasted with those of the soul in Christian ascetical literature. The body is not represented as devoid of life and passion, though it was in that way contrasted with vegetative and sentient soul in the abstraction just described by Aquinas in the passage from the *De ente et essentia* (supra, n. 14).

The same intellectual activity of precisive abstraction is, however, fully capable of setting up a notion of soul that is contrasted with sentient body in just this way. The form of the body can be envisaged as retaining the capabilities of endowing the body with life and sen-

---

14. *On Being and Essence*, 2.6; trans. Armand Maurer, 2nd ed. (Toronto: Pontifical Institute of Mediaeval Studies, 1968), p. 39. On the notion of precisive abstraction, see ibid., p. 39, n. 15.

sation, while definitely excluding from its concept the further capability of thinking and willing. This procedure is described in the *De ente et essentia* in terms of the contrast between the animal part and the higher part in man:

If "animal" designated only a certain reality endowed with a perfection such that it would sense and be moved through an internal principle, prescinding from any other perfection, then any further perfection would be related to animal as a part.[15]

By precisive abstraction, "animal" in this text is represented as something living and sentient, by way of a part that combines with a further part, a part that exercises the intellective activities, to form the composite that is a man. It is exactly what is required by the notion "body" when Christian asceticism speaks of the struggle of body against soul. It is likewise the exact notion that is at work in the arguments for the spirituality of the soul that proceed from human activities exercised in independence of matter. Vegetative and sentient activities are in this context recognized as proceeding from the composite of soul and body, while activities of intellection and free choice are traced to soul acting alone.[16] The spiritual soul is accordingly regarded as one agent, the sentient body as another.

At any rate, in the context, the *De ente et essentia* parallels the precisive distinction between soul and body with the non-precisive one between the grades of rational and animal:

That is why we say that man is a rational animal, and not that he is composed of animal and rational, as we say that he is composed of soul and body. We say that man is a being composed of soul and body as from two things there is constituted a third entity which is neither one of them: man indeed is neither soul nor body.[17]

These texts leave no doubt about the way Aquinas is conceiving the spiritual soul when he thinks of it in contrast to the body. They show that he is representing both as separate things in the sense of integral

15. *On Being and Essence*, 2.7; pp. 39–40.
16. "Et ideo patet quomodo operationes anime vegetabilis et sensitiue, non sunt motus anime, set coniuncti; operationes autem intellectus non dicuntur motus nisi metaphorice et sunt solum anime intellectiue absque aliquo determinato organo"—Aquinas, *Sent. lib. de an.* 1.10; 45, 51.210–15. In Aristotle, *De an.* 1.4.408b24–30, thinking and also loving and hating are presented as actions of the individual who possess the mind, rather than of the mind itself. Yet even in this context, memory and love are described as activities of a common agent that perishes, while mind should be impassive. The impassive and separate character is definitely established later, at *De an.* 3.4.429a18–b10. In man, free activity requires the universal cognition and the full reflexiveness that belong only to the rational faculty—Aquinas, *De ver.* 24.2
17. *On Being and Essence* 2.9; p. 41.

parts (texts supra, n. 14) out of which a third thing (*tertia vero res*) is constituted. Precisive abstraction allows this mental separation to be made at any of the stages in the Porphyrian tree. It can be made at the level of three-dimensional substance. You then have the soul as vital principle represented in one concept, and the soul as merely bodily form (*forma corporeitatis*)[18] included in the other concept. Abstracted precisively at the animality cutoff, you have on the one side the soul as the source of intellectual and voluntary activities, and on the other the soul included in the concept of the substantial source of man's lower activities and three-dimensional figure. In both cases the mental separation is possible because of the different groupings of activities or accidents that allow conceptual distinction in their substantial source. With Aquinas, moreover, the real distinction between substance and powers in everything created[19] renders the mental separation more vivid and easier to grasp in the basic source of these activities and accidents.

Does this mean that the soul as the source of spiritual activities is merely an abstraction and not a real agent? Hardly. Abstraction is fundamentally a way of conceptualizing a real thing. The soul is the real form that is known as functioning under all these abstractions, whether as agent or as formal cause. Just as an existent man, when known under the non-precisive abstractions of man, animal, living thing, or corporeal substance, does not become any less real, so the precisive abstraction has for its content the real soul that informs matter and exercises the vital, sentient, or intellectual activities.

The background of this whole problematic undoubtedly lies in the *De anima* of Aristotle. There the soul is defined as the first actuality of a physical organic body (*De an.* 2.1.412a19–b6). Yet this organic body with capacity for life, as placed in the definition, already includes the soul—a dead body would not satisfy the definition (412b11–413a3). The problem of soul lying on both sides of the couplet is already present in Aristotle and arises from the very nature of soul as form of a physical body. Likewise, the problem of the soul as agent in one of its parts has its ground in the Aristotelian text (413a4–9), where the possibility of a part that is in no way the form actuality of a body is broached. The question whether the part by which the soul

18. On "forma corporeitatis" in Aquinas, see supra, n. 10.

19. On this distinction see *Sent.* 1.3.4.2; *Quodl.* 10.3.1; *ST* 1.54.3 and 1.77.1; *De spirit. creat.* 11; and *Q. de an.* 12. It requires the distinction between essence and being. It expressly is described as real: "[I]nter essentiam et talem operationem cadit virtus media differens ab utroque, in creaturis etiam realiter, in Deo ratione tantum"—*Sent.* 1.7. 1.1.ad 2m; 1, 177.

knows and understands is something really separate is faced (*De an.* 3.4.429a10–13), and the answer is given. There is one intellect that is cause and agent, an intellect that exercises activity independently of the body, that has separate status, and is immortal and imperishable. (3.5.430a10–23). The requirement of a soul that in one or the other of its parts has somehow the role of an independent agent is in this way indicated clearly enough in the problem side of the *De anima.*[20]

III

Against this articulation of the Aristotelian background, Aquinas meets the problem how the human soul can be the form of a body and nevertheless be an agent in itself. The problem is coupled with the independent existence of the human soul, that is, how the soul can exist in itself apart from the body instead of merely sharing in the existence of the composite man. Philosophically the two problems are intimately connected, and in the Aristotelian setting the separate status of an intellectual part of the soul is reasoned to from the reflexively experienced intellectual activities.[21] If the soul can act independently of the body, it accordingly has being that is independent of matter. But the soul is the mover of the body (*motor corporis*), contrary to the teaching of the Aristotelian *Physics* (8.5.257b9–10) that the form

20. Klaus Bernath, *Anima Forma Corporis* (Bonn: H. Bouvier, 1969), p. 200, remarks that Aquinas is compelled by theological presuppositions to make appear ambiguous what in Aristotle is unequivocal: "[D]ass er unter diesem Druck die eindeutige aristotelische Lehre von der Seele als der substantialen Wesensform des Leibes zweideutig erscheinen lässt." A close study of the *De anima*, however, shows that the question is more complicated. In the Aristotelian problematic the requirement of a part that is separate and unmixed with matter is explicit. "Part" may be understood in different ways, but the necessity of seeking a part of the soul that is immaterial and subsistent lies in the Aristotelian problematic itself, regardless of sacred theology.

On the notions of immortality in the Greek background against which Aristotle developed his own thought, see Giacomo Soleri, *L'immortalità dell'anima in Aristotele* (Turin: Società Edit. Internazionale, 1952), pp. 5–44. On Plotinus's critique of the Aristotelian views, see G. Verbeke, "Les critiques de Plotin contre l'entéléchisme d'Aristote," in *Philomathes*, ed. Robert B. Palmer and Robert Hamerton-Kelly (The Hague: Martinus Nijhoff, 1971), pp. 194–222. For a study of the Neoplatonic influence in early patristic tradition, see Ernest L. Fortin, *Christianisme et culture philosophique au cinquième siècle: la querelle de l'âme en Occident* (Paris: Etudes Augustiennes, 1959).

21. See Aristotle, *De an.* 3.4.429a10–b10. Cf. Aquinas, *Sent. lib. de an.* 3.1; 45, 201–209. *Q. de an.* 1; ed. Robb, pp. 58–60. Also numerous other passages in which Aquinas approaches the soul's spiritual character bring out the same point. The procedure is summed up succinctly in the text from the *Q. de an.* quoted infra, n. 29. No matter how the text of Aristotle is explained, it requires that the separate as well as the passive intellect has to *know*—see Karl Bärthlein, *Die Transzendentalienlehre der alten Ontologie* (Berlin: Walter de Gruyter, 1972), 1, 67–69. On Aquinas in this regard, see infra, n. 27.

of fire is not a mover, and to the general tenet that a form, though a principle of motion, is not in itself a movent:

But that which has being only because it is in something else is not able to outlast it. Also it cannot be a mover, although it may be a principle of motion, because a movent is a completed being in itself. Hence the form of fire is not a mover, as is stated in the eighth book of the *Physics*. But the soul outlasts the body, and is the mover of the body.[22]

In this early text of Aquinas the soul is represented as an agent that imparts motion to the whole body. The situation envisaged is easy enough to grasp. Through intellection and decision the soul controls and guides the body, as in walking, eating, painting, building. The soul as intellective is regarded as causing motion in the composite of which it itself as form is but a part. This way of understanding the soul on both sides of the division is possible through the precisive abstraction already discussed. But to function as a movent the soul has to be, just in itself, an existent. As in Aristotle, the existence of the soul in itself, or, in the Greek mode of expression, its separate status, is reasoned to from activities on the intellectual plane. The independent existence is a conclusion from the imparting of motion: "because a movent is a completed being in itself."

In the answer to the above argument, that a form cannot exist in itself or be a movent, the activity of intellection is inserted ahead of the imparting of motion. The solution of the difficulty is found not

---

22. "Sed illud quod non habet esse nisi per hoc quod est in altero, non potest remanere post illud, nec etiam potest esse motor, quamvis possit esse principium motus, quia movens est ens perfectum in se; unde forma ignis non est motor, ut dicitur VIII *Physic.* Anima autem manet post corpus, et est motor corporis"—*Sent.* 1.8.5.2.arg.5; 1, 228. Cf. *De unitate intellectus*, 1.37.Spiazzi no. 198. With Aristotle all natural things have a source of motion within themselves—*Ph.* 2.1.192b13–23; 8.4.254b15–17. Accordingly, any natural form is a source of motion. But in ordinary sensible composites, such as fire, the movent is the thing that possesses the form: "The movent on the other hand is already in activity: e.g., that which is hot that produces heat: in fact, that which produces the form is always something that possesses it"—*Ph.* 8.5.257b9–10; Oxford trans. This is the Aristotelian doctrine to which Aquinas is referring. The doctrine is authentic enough. The terminology, however, can become confusing. Aristotle regularly in the eighth book of the *Physics* speaks of soul in general as that which moves the self-movent, e.g.: "Therefore when a thing moves itself it is one part of it that is the movent and another part that is moved"—*Ph.* 8.5.257b12–13; Oxford trans. The background of this twofold way of regarding soul is Plato's (*Phaedrus* 245CE; *Lg.*, 10.894B–897C) notion of the soul as the self-moved and the cause of all other movement. Carried into the Aristotelian setting—see *Ph.* 8.9.265b32–34—this occasions the style of referring to the soul as the movent, or the movent part of the self-movent, even where it is not separate in reality—see *Ph.* 8.6.258b10–259a6 and 259b14–22. Hence the formulation of the question by Nemesius: "Unde igitur corpori moveri, nisi ab anima?"—*Premnon physicon*, 2.65; p. 39.16.

in the Aristotelian notion of form but in the likeness of the soul to God:

> Every form is some likeness of the first principle, which is pure actuality. Hence to the extent a form more closely approaches the likeness of that actuality, the more of its perfections does it share. But among the forms of bodies the rational soul approaches more closely the likeness of God; and therefore it shares in the excellences of God, namely that it understands, and can impart motion, and has existence in itself. The sentient soul approaches less closely, and the vegetative soul still less, and so on. I say therefore that it does not belong to the soul to impart motion, or to have independent being, insofar as it is a form, but insofar as it is a likeness of God.[23]

The measuring rod used in this solution is actuality.[24] Actuality is a typical Aristotelian notion, arising epistemologically from its imperfect manifestation in movement, then located firmly in the corporeal forms, and reaching its fullness in the separate forms where the entire substance is actuality. In Aquinas the notion is envisaged as going beyond the order of form that is attained through conceptualization and as finding its apex in the pure actuality reasoned to from the existence originally grasped through judgment. This pure actuality, God, is existent in virtue of itself, is omniscient, and is the primary efficient cause of all motion. Among all corporeal forms the human soul shows the closest resemblance, by the measuring rod of actuality, to God. Accordingly, it shares in more perfections of God than do the sentient, vegetative, and non-vital forms. In particular, it shares in the higher perfections of God insofar as it understands, imparts motion,

23. "[O]mnis forma est aliqua similitudo primi principii, qui est actus purus: unde quanto forma magis accedit as similitudinem ipsius, plures participat de perfectionibus ejus. Inter formas autem corporum magis appropinquat ad similitudinem Dei, anima rationalis; et ideo participat de nobilitatibus Dei, scilicet quod intelligit, et quod potest movere, et quod habet esse per se; et anima sensibilis minus, et vegetabilis adhuc minus, et sic deinceps. Dico igitur, quod animae non convenit movere, vel habere esse absolutum, inquantum est forma; sed inquantum est similitudo Dei." *Sent.* 1.8.5.2.ad 5m; 1, 231. "Esse absolutum" in this context means being that is "freed from dependence on matter." Cf. "quia anima est forma absoluta, non dependens a materia, quod convenit sibi propter assimilationem et propinquitatem ad Deum, ipsa habet esse per se quod non habent aliae formae corporales"—ibid., ad 1m; p. 230. Freedom from dependence is best expressed in English as "independence." "Absolute being" would hardly convey the meaning in this context of the Latin "esse absolutum."

24. Cf.: "These substances, moreover, are distinct from one another according to their degree of potentiality and actuality, a superior intelligence being closer to the primary being, having more actuality and less potentiality, and so with the others. This gradation ends with the human soul, which holds the lowest place among intellectual substances." Aquinas, *On Being and Essence* 4.10; trans. Maurer (1968), pp. 58–59. On Cajetan's accommodation of these possible grades into a proof, and the sole proof, for human immortality, see Gilson, "Autour de Pomponazzi," pp. 181–82, and "L'affaire de l'immortalité," p. 42.

and exists in itself. Not in virtue of informing matter, but rather in virtue of resembling God, is the human soul an agent and in itself an existent.

What is to be thought of this quite extraordinary way of reasoning? To what extent is it conclusive, and to what extent merely exploratory? Certainly it makes no attempt to deny or even to minimize the nature of the soul as form. The human soul remains through and through a form of a material body, in the full sense of the Aristotelian definition in the *De anima* (2.1.412a19–b6). It is not made anything else. But within that notion of form the parameter of actuality is allowed to function. Soul, just as any other form, is a likeness of God in virtue of being actual.

This view of likeness or resemblance fits readily enough into the framework of graded community that had been developed earlier in the commentary on the *Sentences* under the caption of "analogy." A creature has an aspect such as being or wisdom or any other perfection predicated of it, insofar as it imitates the primary instance from which the perfection comes. By another type of "analogy" the perfection is shared in further graded ways within the various categories of beings (*Sent.* Prol, 1.2.ad 2m; ed. Mandonnet, 1, 10). All the excellences of all creatures are found in God in the most perfect way. In different degrees he causes effects like to himself and is in this way the exemplar form of things: "[C]um secundum formam suam producat effectus similes, non univoce sed analogice; . . . unde ipse est exemplaris forma rerum" (*Sent.* 1.2.1.2.Solut., 1, 62–63). Later (1.24.1.1.ad 4m; 1, 577) the graded community between God and creature is described as one in which creatures imitate God as far as they are able (*prout possunt*).

The problem of the special status of the human soul has accordingly been placed in the framework of the "analogy" of creatures to God. In later Scholastic classification it would come under "analogy of simple proportion" or "analogy of intrinsic attribution." The one aspect or notion is found in the most perfect degree in the highest instance, and in the other instances in degrees that vary according to their greater or lesser approximation to the primary instance. In this fashion likeness or resemblance is present in the secondary instances. In regard to the special status of the human soul the one aspect or notion signalized is that of actuality. Here the grade of actuality reveals an agent and an existent.

Does the locating of the problem in the definite framework of "analogy" have any genuine probative force in regard to the last conclusion? Obviously not. The framework itself is a second intention structure worked out after the first intention relations had been established.

Sensible things are directly studied. They are shown through cogent demonstration to have their being and all their perfections from a unique primary cause, God. This production is similarly shown to take place through intelligent action and, in consequence, to require exemplar forms in God. The things modeled after those forms will therefore resemble their maker in the varying degrees in which the forms manifest his perfection. Only afterwards, in a second look over the whole procedure, is the "analogy" framework seen and formulated. It itself does not demonstrate anything in the order of first intention. Rather, it provides a setting in which a demonstration based directly on real things may be conveniently located.

What is the demonstration concerned in the present case of the human soul? One may expect that it is that of Aristotle, since the argument faced by Aquinas (*Sent.* 1.8.5.2.arg.5; 1, 228) is explicitly based on the Aristotelian *Physics*. In the *De anima* (3.4.429a18–b22), Aristotle had shown that intellectual activity transcends material conditions and thus involves the activity of an agent that is unmixed with, or separate from, matter. Aquinas (*Sent.* 1.8.5.2.ad 5m; 1, 231) in reply to the argument has only to mention that the human soul has intellectual activity. In this context the two considerations at stake, namely that the soul is a movent and has being in itself, follow at once in the light of the Aristotelian demonstration.

The tenet that the human soul has these perfections that are not possessed by merely sentient and vegetative souls and the forms of inorganic bodies is accordingly a conclusion that has been established independently of and in priority to the "analogy" structure. The superiority of these perfections is considered evident. The one outstanding question is how they can be possessed by the form of a material thing. Aristotle's answer had proven difficult and unsatisfactory.[25] It

---

25. *De an.* 3.5.430a10–25. Alexander of Aphrodisias (*De an.* p. 88.23–24) called the Aristotelian passive intellect the "material intellect," in accord with the equation of the passive with matter and subject (89.15–16). The agent intellect he called "the first cause" (89.18). The material intellect perishes with the soul of which it is a power, along with its habitual and completed perfection (90.14–16). The way was thereby left open for the unicity of the whole intellect for all men. Philoponus (*In De an.* p. 535.20–29) regarded Alexander as mistaken in saying that the intellect in actuality is the first cause, God. Since for Aristotle a part of the soul is immortal, and the intellect from outside is not a part, Philoponus (541.6–17; 542.1–5) asserted immortality for the intellect within us. Against Alexander, then, Philoponus seemed able to read Aristotle in a way that would be acceptable to Christian faith. On the problems in this regard, see Gerard Verbeke, *Jean Philopon: Commentaire sur le De anima d'Aristote* (Louvain: Publications universitaires, 1966), pp. xi–cvi, and *Thémistius: Commentaire sur le traité De l'âme d'Aristote* (Louvain: Publications universitaires, 1957), pp. lxiii–lxxv. Gilson, "Autour de Pomponazzi," p. 170, n. 5, remarks that St. Thomas felt free from all scruple when he could

had been interpreted in the sense of a single intellect for all men, in conflict with the personal responsibility and the personal immortality required by the Christian faith. But does Christian faith point the way to any other answer to the question?

The text indicates quite strongly that the doctrine in Genesis (1.26–27) describing the creation of man is playing a guiding role with Aquinas. After the other things had been created, man was made to God's image and likeness. In the reply to the first argument in the article under consideration, Aquinas reasons that the soul has existence in itself because it is independent of matter, and adds that this feature belongs to it "on account of its likeness and proximity to God."[26] There is as yet no mention of degrees in likeness to God that animals and plants and inorganic bodies may possess. But shortly after, in the reply to the fifth argument in the article, the problem of likeness to God is faced in terms of the Aristotelian notion of actuality. Approached from this Aristotelian viewpoint, the likeness of man to God as described in Genesis has to be understood in terms of form, since matter has in itself no distinguishing characteristics upon which resemblance could be based. No explicit mention is made of this reason for restricting the gradations to terms of form. In the context, no need of any could be felt. But form is actuality, whether in man, brute, plant, or inanimate things. The likeness to pure actuality is accordingly present in greatly varying degrees in all created existents. In man, however, the actuality in which the likeness is found is the rational soul.

---

support his own interpretation by that of Philoponus. Against the fact of this use of Philoponus by Aquinas, see Verbeke, *Jean Philopon*, pp. lxxii–lxxiii, nn. 4–8. For Aquinas's critique of Alexander, see *Summa contra gent.* 2.62, and *De unitate intellectus* 2, Spiazzi no. 211. A short survey of the Aristotelianism in the immediate background of Pomponazzi may be found in Bruno Nardi, *Studi su Pietro Pomponazzi* (Florence: Felice le Monier, 1965), pp. 371–76.

26. "quod convenit sibi propter assimilationem et propinquitatem ad Deum." *Sent.* 1.8.5.2.ad 1; 1, 230. In the *Q. de an.* 14, sed contra 1 (Robb, p. 300) the notion is taken from Wisdom 2.23: "Deus fecit hominem inexterminabilem et ad imaginem suae similitudinis fecit illum." Here the interest is in the notion expressed by "inexterminabilis": "id est incorruptibilis, secundum quod est ad imaginem Dei" (ibid.). The consequence that man is imperishable is regarded as expressly drawn in this scriptural passage. The application to the soul is seen without difficulty in the wake of the teaching on mind and soul in Augustine: "Est autem ad imaginem Dei secundum animam, ut Augustinus dicit in libro *De Trinitate*" (Aquinas, *Q. de an.* 14, sed contra 1; Robb, p. 300). See Augustine, *De Trin.* 10.12.19 (PL 42, 984), and cf. Gen. 2.7. At *De ver.* 24.2.sed contra, moreover, Damascene and Bernard are cited by Aquinas for the assertion that man is "ad imaginem Dei" because he has free will. The Vulgate text of Gen. 1.26–27 reads: "Faciamus hominem ad imaginem et similitudinem nostram. . . . Et creavit Deus hominem ad imaginem suam: ad imaginem Dei creavit illum." Cf. Gen. 5.1; Eccli. 17.1. The "propinquitatem" in the text of Aquinas comes obviously enough from the philosophical tenet of grades of actuality—see supra, n. 24.

If man is singled out in Scripture as manifesting the likeness of God, the reason should be that his soul possesses higher excellences by which he resembles the divine perfection more than do other things. The activity of intellection and the separate existence it involves are excellences of this kind that on Aristotelian grounds the human soul does possess. In virtue of this special likeness, then, and not by reason of informing the body, is the soul an agent that has its own existence.

Does this guiding function of the revealed doctrine lead to anything pertinent that could not be reached from purely Aristotelian premises? Certainly the tenet that the soul is an agent and is separate in an intellectual part is a thoroughly Aristotelian conclusion. But that is still a long way from the Thomistic conclusion that the entire physical soul continues in existence after bodily death. For Aristotle, expressly, the passive intellect and presumably the lower parts of the soul perish with the body. Only the intellect that acts is eternal. For Aquinas, on the other hand, the agent intellect is but a faculty of the one existent soul along with the other faculties. For him it is this soul, which subsists under all those faculties, that continues to exist.[27] Does the scriptural setting, in which the Aristotelian reasoning is now placed, point out facets in the naturally known premises that would allow these new conclusions?

For Aristotle, the manifest nature of human thought shows that the part of the soul causing the intellection has to be unmixed with matter, impassive, limited to itself alone in its separate existence, immortal and eternal.[28] The intellect so described becomes practically impossible to distinguish from the separate substances reached as pure actuality in the *Metaphysics* (12.6.1071b19–22; 7.1072b20 –28; 8.1074b33–35), though the problems how it can be a part of the human soul and how it can exercise efficient causality on the passive intellect are not even raised in the text. The intellect reasoned to in this way was criticized by Plotinus (*Enneads* 4.7.85.15–16) as another soul, brought in over and above the first soul in order to account for

27. On the agent intellect as a principle "formally inherent" in the soul and a power within the soul, and the attribution of this doctrine to Aristotle by Aquinas, see *ST* 1.79.4. Nevertheless Aquinas can speak of intellect as synonymous with intellective soul: "necesse est dicere, secundum opinionem Aristotelis, intellectum secundum suam substantiam alicui corpori uniri ut formam"—*CG* 2.70, Et quia. Cf. supra, n. 7. The only separate intellect, in this context, is God: "Sed intellectus separatus, secundum nostrae fidei documenta, est ipse Deus"—*ST* 1.79.4.

28. On the interpretation of "as separated" at *De an.* 3.5.430a22, in a causal rather than a temporal sense, see Gerard Verbeke, "Comment Aristote conçoit-il l'immatériel?" *Revue philosophique de Louvain* 44 (1946), 227–28.

intellection. But though this further type of intellect may resemble the Platonic type of soul accepted by Plotinus (1.1.3; 4.2.1), it can hardly be regarded by any stretch of the concept as immediately and in itself the form of body. It is a "part of the soul" only through its function of agent in relation to the passive intellect, and not through any direct function of informing matter.

Approached in the light of the Genesis text, however, the human soul appears not as divine and as pure actuality, but as, in a specially significant way, a created likeness of pure actuality. With pure actuality now understood as subsistent existence, the specially significant likeness should be approximation in the line of existence, and of bestowal of existence as agent. Because it is a creature, the human soul cannot be existence nor can it create. But with this guidance the data presented by Aristotle take on a new direction, entirely on the philosophical level. The activity exercised in independence of matter, namely intellection, requires indeed an agent that in itself is independent of matter. Yet in the existential framework, this requirement can be filled by something that exists independently of matter even though by nature it is the form of material body. The human soul does not have to be a nature separate from matter in order to function as an existent in independence of matter.

The immediately knowable data described in the *De anima* are in consequence open to two different processes of reasoning on the purely philosophical plane. They can be interpreted solely in terms of form, as with Aristotle himself, and thereby lead to an agent that is in its nature separate from matter. Or, as with Aquinas, they can be gauged in terms of existence, and lead to an agent that exists independently of matter even while informing matter. Each of these two conclusions satisfies in its own setting the data advanced. Each presents the agent for intellection as a part of the soul only, and not as the composite nature. For Aquinas, however, the part is isolated by precisive abstraction. For Aristotle, it is really unmixed with matter but is a part through its relation to the passive intellect. Further, one may even say that for Aristotle the intellectual part is an agent, not as a form of a body, but as a separate entity, paralleling, though in a radically different way, the stand of Aquinas that the soul is an agent not as form but as made to the likeness of God. Yet in Aquinas the soul does its thinking through the passive intellect, while in Aristotle the passive intellect is perishable and in consequence could not possess the independent type of existence required for all intellect by the medieval thinker.

IV

The demonstration in Aquinas that the human soul is in itself an agent is therefore the basis for the conclusion that it is in itself an existent. The starting point of the argument is the nature of reflexively observed intellectual activity. This activity requires an agent acting independently of matter and thereby an agent that exists independently of matter. The human soul, then, possesses its existence in independence of the matter it informs.[29]

This means that the human soul, once it has received being, exists necessarily and perpetually. It can no more be separated from its existence than from itself.[30] It has in itself no principle of dissolution, such as the matter in a composite. As form only, it is the cause of being and has no orientation to non-being. There is consequently nothing in the nature of things or in ordinate power of God that could destroy it. It is imperishable.

But does this conclusion entail immortality, in the sense in which life is the opposite of death? Does it demonstrate that the soul will live after the separation from the body? This is quite another question. Intellectual activity while soul informs body is sufficient for the demonstration that the soul will continue to exist perpetually. But can it conclude that the soul will continue to *live* perpetually? Does a separate existent mean a separate agent?

In a separated soul, life will consist in intellection and what follows upon intellection. Without intellection, then, there will be no life. But human intellection, as naturally knowable, requires the sensible images of the imagination. It cannot take place outside them. Separated from the body, however, the soul does not have any merely natural means of thinking in these images.[31] The independence in regard to

29. "Sic igitur ex operatione animae humanae modus esse ipsius cognosci potest. In quantum enim habet operationem, materialia transcendentem, esse suum est supra corpus elevatum, non dependens ex ipso." *Q. de an.* 1c; ed. Robb, p. 60.

30. *ST* 1.75.6. Cf. *De pot.* 5.3; *Q. de an.* 14.

31. Preternatural means of obtaining and using species cannot, of course, be ruled out, but the evidence naturally available does not seem to provide grounds for proving that as a fact the separated soul will enjoy knowledge of this kind. On the seeming evolution of Aquinas's views on knowledge in the separated soul, and the chronological indications this development provides, see A. C. Pegis, "The Separated Soul and its Nature in St. Thomas," *St. Thomas Aquinas 1274–1974 Commemorative Studies* (Toronto: Pontifical Institute of Mediaeval Studies, 1974), 1, 131–58. But the immediate data of awareness, as assessed by Aristotle in *De anima* 3.4.429b4–10, and *Metaph.* 12.9. 1074b35–36, ground the conclusion that, as far as unaided natural reason is concerned, even self-knowledge on the part of the soul takes place objectively through material images. For Aquinas (*De ver.* 19.1; cf. *Summa contra gent.* 2.81, Sciendum and Reminisci) the intellectual species corresponding to the images are conserved in the separated soul, but use of them by it is preternatural or supernatural.

matter, found in reflexively observable intellection, is the basis for demonstrating that the soul will continue to exist perpetually even apart from matter. It is not a basis for demonstrating that the soul will think apart from images, at least in an Aristotelian context.

Nor does the purposelessness of perpetual existence without activity provide a convincing demonstration in this case. The human faculties are naturally directed towards infinite truth and infinite good, yet on the level of nature man has no means of attaining an object of that kind. In consequence, human existence has factually no ultimate purpose that is demonstrable by natural reason.[32] As intermediate goals function only in virtue of the ultimate purpose, an intermediate end cannot be required where a final end cannot be established. A teleological argument, then, does not seem applicable here. If on the other hand one would care to accept the achievements of human life on earth as a sufficient reason for a perpetually existent soul in each transient body, one might possibly tolerate the utterly useless existence of the soul after death as one more instance of nature's prodigious waste in attaining a comparatively limited number of good effects. A Christian philosophy, however, could hardly be expected to acquiesce in this estimate of the intrinsic worth of a human soul. But at the same time does it not hesitate to accept the natural demonstrability of the soul's perpetual existence while declining to allow cogency to the purely rational arguments for its *life* after bodily death? Can it tolerate the notion of an inert soul? As Plato (*Phaedo*, 105DE) had insisted, does not the very nature of soul mean life? Will not the nature of the soul require that its perpetual existence involve unending life?

Yet in a Thomistic context the demonstration of disembodied life has to be based upon the existence, not the nature, of the soul. Life, as the term is commonly understood today, means vital activity. It means operation, as contradistinguished from existence. But vital activity apart from the body is for St. Thomas something beyond the nature (*praeter naturam*—*Summa theol.* 1.89.1) of the soul. It takes place in a state that is against the soul's nature (*contra naturam animae*—*Summa contra gent.* 4.79.Ad ostendendum). It is illustrated by the notion of a light body as taken from ancient physics. The nature of a light body was supposed to show that it tended upwards. Downward movement, or rest for it in a low place, could not be explained by its nature but only by external influence. Correspondingly, nothing in the nature of

32. On the "naturally endless" character of man, see the papers by A. C. Pegis, "Nature and Spirit: Some Reflections on the Problem of the End of Man," and G. Smith, "The Natural End of Man," *Proceedings of the American Catholic Philosophical Association* 23 (1949), 62–79 and 47–61.

the soul provides a ground for demonstrating the occurrence of an activity beyond the scope of its dependence upon material images.

The demonstration, then, will have to be based upon the soul's perpetual existence. In its most general form it readily takes for granted that no substance can exist without having its own corresponding operation. Accordingly, "since no substance is bereft of its proper operation, it must be asserted that the intellective soul, since it remains after death, does understand in some way" (*Quodlibeta* 3.9.1c). In fact, in both his earlier and his later works Aquinas affirms unhesitatingly that the human soul is immortal in the sense that it will exercise vital activity forever after bodily death, and he outlines the possible ways. He shows that its mode of operation will then correspond to its new mode of being (*De veritate* 19.1; *Summa contra gent.* 2.81.Sciendum tamen; *Summa theol.* 1.89.1), and in his later works that it will be naturally proportioned to an indistinct type of universal cognition instead of attaining the clear types proper to pure spirits (*Summa theol.* 1.89.1; 3–4; *Quaest. de anima* 15; 20).

There is not the least doubt, then, that for Aquinas unending life follows upon the soul's perpetual existence. The only question is whether the sequence of thought rests on purely philosophical grounds. Rather, is it not theological in character, based on the tenet that in the present order of divine providence every existent, including the separated soul, is exercising its appropriate operation? The problem in that case would be merely to determine what types of operation are appropriate to a disembodied soul.

In a Cartesian setting, of course, there would be little difficulty. For Descartes (*Ad Hyperaspistem*, Aug., 1641; A–T, 3, 423.16–27), the mind could not exist without thereby actually thinking. It always thinks, even in the womb or in sleep (*Quintae resp.*; A–T, 7, 356.24–357.6). Today, moreover, even the fundamental particles are conceived with wavelike activities. A totally inert substance seems incapable of existence.

Yet for Aquinas no finite substance is immediately operative. One starting point for the demonstration of this conclusion is that "what has a soul is not always in the act of vital operations" (*Summa theol.* 1.77.1c). The existence of a soul, accordingly, does not immediately entail the exercise of vital activity. Its perpetual existence after death should not guarantee metaphysically, in the Thomistic framework, any type of operation on its part.

On the other hand, there is the difficulty of conceiving a spiritual substance, or any kind of substance, as inert. No way of obviating this objection is apparent. It gives rise to a situation that remains in the state of an Aristotelian aporia. On the one hand, the separately existent soul is not immediately operative, yet in this case the existence is the only basis for arguing metaphysically to its operation. On the other, the notion of a separate form that is not in operation is unacceptable in the Aristotelian setting, since for the Stagirite a separate form is the immediate actual and unimpeded knowing of itself. The situation remains unsatisfactory, but it is enough to cause hesitation in regarding as metaphysical demonstration the reasoning of Aquinas to disembodied life in the soul. On his theological premises, of course, the disembodied soul does have life in the sense of operation. From this viewpoint its vital activity is a fact and a mystery rather than the subject of a philosophical aporia.

It was easier, too, for Aquinas to say that he had demonstrated the immortality of the soul than it is for people today. In using Aristotle's much-quoted assertion that to live is the being of living things, he emphatically restricts the meaning of "to live" in this context to existence as distinguished from operation: "[V]ivere, quod est esse viventibus, est animae actus; non actus secundus, qui est operatio, sed actus primus" (*Sent.* 1.33.1.1.ad 1m; 1, 766). In fact, "life" in this context has for Aquinas (*Summa theol.* 1.18.2) as its primary meaning the substantial source instead of the operation. Today, on the other hand, the notion of life is primarily located in vital activity. In having proved the soul's perpetual existence Aquinas could therefore without further thought speak of having proved its immortality. But in the modern setting where life means first and foremost vital operation, words like "immortality" and "survival" carry a meaning that is not satisfied by mere existence. Demonstration of the soul's perpetual existence may still leave open the question of its immortality in the sense of an agent that is exercising vital activity. The Thomistic tenet that no created substance is immediately operative intervenes. It makes one hesitate to conclude on the merely metaphysical level that the perpetually existent soul exercises vital activity after bodily death.

V

In two interesting and illuminative papers mentioned earlier (supra, n. 2), Étienne Gilson has shown how the Pomponazzi controversy on the soul's immortality brought to the fore a notable consequence for the Thomistic tradition. It emphasized that Aristotelian philosophy has to be kept carefully distinguished from philosophy itself when one is interpreting the philosophical thinking of Aquinas.[33] This obser-

33. See Gilson, "L'affaire de l'immortalité," pp. 52; 56.

vation, strangely perhaps, is still relevant today—for instance, when one reads the statement that if Aristotle did not arrive at knowledge of the true God, then nobody can by natural reason grasp God's existence.

But perhaps another consequence might be drawn. It was not drawn in the sixteenth century. In the circumstances then it hardly could have been drawn. The consequence is that in speaking about the soul after bodily death, the demonstration of its perpetual existence should be kept carefully distinct from the question of its immortality or survival. On account of their etymologies these two words place the discussion in terms of *life* after bodily dissolution. Today "life" means vital activity. Yet in the metaphysical reasoning developed by St. Thomas the purely philosophical demonstration of disembodid life in this sense is questionable, even though the demonstration of the soul's perpetual existence is fully cogent. On the philosophical level the soul is shown to be indestructible and forever existent. But to show how it can be an agent apart from the body, in the sense of actually thinking and willing, seems beyond the reach of cogent metaphysical reasoning. The problem is left in a state of philosophical aporia, and handed over to religion and sacred theology.

The Thomistic reasoning for the perpetual existence of the soul played but little part, as Gilson noted,[34] in the controversy initiated by Pomponazzi's treatise. One would be hard put to show that it has played any serious role in the major controversies on the subject before or since. Perhaps people prefer it that way. Those who wish to have no demonstrative force in the proofs for immortality will for the most part hardly be impressed by reasoning in terms of existential actuality.[35] They may not even be interested in the tenet of perpetual existence apart from life. Certainly Cajetan has been able to maintain

34. "à peu près aucun rôle"—Gilson, "Autour de Pomponazzi," p. 167. Cf. p. 173. It is hard to see, however, that in its really pertinent bearing on the topic it played any role at all. Cf. Gilson, "L'affaire de l'immortalité," p. 38, n. 12.

35. E.g., Paul Tillich, *The Courage to Be* (New Haven: Yale University Press, 1952), p. 124. For an instance of the attitude on immortality "I want to keep my faith in it and not have it proved," see Robert Speaight, *Vanier* (Toronto: Collins, 1970), p. 124. Cf. "Nobis autem sufficit ad demonstrationem immortalitatis eius divinorum verborum doctrina de ea continens, quod verum est, quia divinitus est inspirata. Contra eos autem, qui non recipiunt Christianorum scripturas, sufficiat ostendere animam nullum esse corruptibilium"—Nemesius, *Premnon physicum* 2, 117–118; p. 51.18–23. On the other hand, for a defense of the tenet that knowledge of the soul's perpetual existence means knowledge of its future life, see George St. Hilaire, "Does St. Thomas Really Prove the Soul's Immortality?" *The New Scholasticism* 34 (1960), 340–56. The reason alleged is "the soul of man is even here and now exercising a life which goes beyond the entire material and historical world. This is the soul's immortality, a here-and-now actuality known confusedly to every man"—ibid., p. 350.

through the centuries his high reputation as a leading Thomistic commentator in spite of his denial of philosophical demonstration for the soul's immortality. As Cajetan noted, independence of matter on the part of the soul as agent does not in any philosophically demonstrable way entail independence of a material image from the standpoint of object.[36] What it does entail, though not brought to the fore by Cajetan, is that the agent so established possesses existence in a manner that will never allow it to perish in the whole course of nature or in the ordinate power of God.

Returning to the question proposed at the beginning of this paper,[37] one may stress the difficulty in seeing how perpetual existence can be a premise for demonstrating *life* in the separated soul. Radical possibility of that life it certainly does prove, for a soul is always just in itself a substantial principle of life. But it does not seem to demand necessarily the further conclusion that the soul does so live in its separated state, by way of natural consequence. That conclusion, as actually drawn by Thomas, seems based rather on a theological premise of congruence and divine providence. Yet is not perpetual existence for a soul a sufficient philosophical underpinning for the concerns of Christian faith? What more is necessary in this regard for a Christian philosophy?

Second, from the viewpoint of Aquinas, perpetual existence does follow with cogency from the Aristotelian premises of observed activities that transcend material conditions.[38] Aristotle's texts may be regarded as leading in their own historical setting to the conclusions of a perishable soul, without infringing on their capability of leading to the opposite cogent conclusion when they function in the existential framework of Aquinas. Their intrinsic openness to both conclusions is thereby guaranteed. Not only philosophy itself, then, but also the Aristotelian premises will be found contributing to conclusions that accord with and support Christian dogma.

Finally, the biblical notion of man's creation in the image and likeness of God seems to have been the guide of Aquinas in seeking a ground other than the Aristotelian concept of form in order to demonstrate that the soul is an existent in its own right.[39] This appears to have been the consideration that focused his attention upon the nat-

36. On the role played in the Pomponazzi controversy by the distinction between dependence on a material *organ* and dependence on a material *object*, see Gilson, "Autour de Pomponazzi," pp. 177–79.
37. Supra, nn. 3–6. Cf. supra, n. 35.
38. See supra, n. 4.
39. See supra, nn. 6 and 21–26.

urally knowable facet of existence in its bearing upon the human soul. It pointed the way to a ground other than the function of form in the human soul for its role as existent and agent. The intellective soul in its entirety, and not just in a separate part, was thereby established as perpetually existent, with at least the radical capacity of exercising activity apart from union with the body. But the fact that it does exercise this activity seems difficult to demonstrate cogently on the purely metaphysical level when one is following the reasoning of St. Thomas Aquinas.[40]

40. In this regard, one might compare the reasoning of Aquinas on the resurrection of the body at *Summa contra gentiles* 4.79.Ad ostendendum: "Nihil autem quod est contra naturam, potest esse perpetuum. . . . Immortalitas igitur animarum exigere videtur resurrectionem corporum futuram." The state of the separated soul is against nature, and accordingly the soul naturally requires union with the body. But the fact that the union will actually take place does not seem to follow with cogency, except in the theological context of congruence or present providence.

13

AQUINAS ON THE INSEPARABILITY OF SOUL FROM EXISTENCE

I

A distinctive and intriguing tenet in Aquinas's demonstration of indestructibility for the human soul is that the soul can no more be separated from its existence than from itself. Though worded in varying ways and from different angles, that conclusion always has the same probative force. Separation of the soul from its existence, or of the existence from the soul, is just as impossible as the separation of either of the two from its own self. Each is regarded as embracing the other with all the tenacity that identity of self with self can involve.

Is not this an unusual and at first sight seemingly unacceptable tenet? Obviously enough it reflects in some tantalizing fashion the problem of the way a thing and its existence are distinguished in reality from each other for Aquinas. The one is not the other. They can be contrasted with each other as two different terms. By that very token they are not identical with each other. How then can their union be looked upon as having the full binding force of self-identity? No lesser force seems able, however, to satisfy the requirements for cogency in this reasoning of Aquinas.

A close look at the different versions or formulations of the argument in Aquinas is accordingly in order. These have interest from several viewpoints. Their respective phraseology and chronological order will need to be probed. Likewise, the occasion for the introduction of the theme and its relation to the general problem of the distinction between thing and being call for some attention. Finally, careful scrutiny needs to be given to the bearing that the indestructibility so demonstrated has on the soul's immortality.

II

In the very early period of Aquinas's academic career the motif of inseparability does not seem present in the discussions on the indestructibility of the human soul. The reasoning stays quite strictly within the framework of the Aristotelian and Neoplatonic traditions. There the immaterial status of the human soul was shown from the nature of its intellectual activity:

[T]his is clear especially from three considerations. First, because this activity has all corporeal forms as its objects; hence the principle to which this activity belongs has to be free from all corporeal form. Secondly, because intellection is of universals; in a corporeal organ, just individuated notions can be received. Thirdly, because the intellect understands itself . . . This proof is touched upon in the *Liber de causis*, in the fifteenth proposition: "Every knower who knows his essence is one who bends back upon his own essence in a complete way."[1]

The reasoning is that the intellection, which is immediately evident through reflexion upon our cognition, transcends material conditions. The agent that performs this activity transcends them correspondingly. To act above the material order one must *be* above it. Independence of material conditions in acting, that means, requires independence of them in being. This was the way that Aristotle (*De an.* 3.4.429a18–b22) had reasoned. To the extent that its objects are separate from matter, so also are the corresponding features of mind. Mind, accordingly, cannot have any corporeal characteristic. It knows the essence, as contrasted with the singular, thereby knowing things universally in the way mentioned by Aquinas in the above text. The reason is that the sensible thing's nature is a universal object through abstraction from the individuating material principles.[2] The argument from the knowledge of things through their essence, as in the *De anima* (429b14–22), in that way coincides for the present purpose with the argument from universality. The other argument, from the complete reflexion or self-reversion in the mind's self-knowledge, had received its development in Proclus.[3]

1. "[P]atet praecipue ex tribus. Primo, quia haec operatio est omnium formarum corporalium sicut objectorum: unde oportet illud principium cujus est haec operatio ab omni forma corporali absolutum esse. Secundo, quia intelligere est universalium; in organo corporali recipi non possunt nisi intentiones individuatae. Tertio, quia intellectus intelligit se; . . . haec probatio tangitur in libro *De causis*, in illa propositione 15: 'Omnis sciens qui scit essentiam suam, est rediens ad essentiam suam reditione completa.'" *Scriptum supra libros Sententiarum* 2.19.1.1.Solut.; ed. Mandonnet, 2, 481–82.

2. On the way Aquinas views knowledge of a thing's nature as universal, see text cited infra, n. 14. Cf. text in n. 6.

3. *The Elements of Theology*, Props. 15–17, ed. E. R. Dodds, 2nd ed. (Oxford: Clarendon Press, 1963), pp. 17–21.

In this context destruction is looked upon as the separating of the form from the matter, with the resultant cessation of the composite's existence. Where an existent is not dependent in that way upon its matter, it is not subject to the process of destruction:

For, since destruction is properly a change from existence to nonexistence, it pertains essentially to destruction that a composite cease to exist; and since a composite has existence from the joining of form with matter, the dividing of form from that matter is therefore found in every instance of destruction. . . . For if the form be of a kind whose existence is absolute and not dependent . . . the form itself remains in its existence, and in that way the destruction is of the composite, with the form remaining.[4]

The force of the reasoning is accordingly rather negative in character. Destruction means cessation of existence because of the separation of the matter from the form. Where the form is independent of matter for its existence, the notion of destruction cannot be applied to it. It cannot cease to exist through destruction. But no positive reason is sought for its continuation perpetually in existence. In the Aristotelian setting, where passage of matter from one form to another was an eternal process, the negative account seemed all that was required. The only way a thing could cease to exist was by being destroyed. One had merely to show negatively that the human soul, having no matter in its constitution, did not have any intrinsic means for undergoing destruction. No more positive reason for its perpetual retention of existence needed to be given. More sharply, in the context of the argument in the commentary on the fourth Book of the *Sentences*, matter is called the *cause* of destruction insofar as it is the subject both of the actually inherent form and of the privation of a form yet to be acquired:

Now every substance of this kind has to be indestructible; for matter, insofar as it can be the subject both of the privation and of the form, is the cause of destruction in material things.[5]

Earlier, in the commentary on the first Book of the *Sentences*, Aqui-

---

4. "Cum enim corruptio sit proprie transmutatio de esse in non esse, hoc per se ad corruptionem pertinet ut compositum esse desistat; et quia compositum habet esse ex conjunctione formae ad materiam, ideo divisio formae a tali materia invenitur in qualibet corruptione; . . . Si enim sit forma talis cujus esse sit absolutum et non dependens, . . . ipsa forma remanet in suo esse, et sic est destructio compositi, forma remanente." *Sent.* 2.19.1.1.ad 2m; 2, 483. For "transcendent" in this sense, cf.: "In quantum enim habet operationem, materialia transcendentem, esse suum est supra corpus elevatum, non dependens ex ipso." *Q. de an.* 1c; ed. Robb, p. 60.

5. "Omnem autem hujusmodi substantiam oportet incorruptibilem esse; quia materia, inquantam potest esse subjectum privationis et formae, est corruptionis causa in rebus materialibus." *Sent.* 4.50.1.1.Solut.; ed. Vivès, 11, 554b.

nas had used the Aristotelian reasoning to support Augustine's proof for the immortality of the soul. The indestructibility of the human soul follows merely from its lack of dependence on the body, as shown by its intellectual activity. The sense powers

do not grasp the meaning of a notion, for instance the notion of man or of color, but grasp them only insofar as they are particularized. Now a power that does not depend on the body is indestructible; and in that way runs the proof that the intellective soul is immortal from the fact that it grasps truth.[6]

Likewise in the tenth of the *Quodlibetal questions*, dated early (1258),[7] the reasoning seems kept strictly within the Aristotelian context:

Only if it were composed of matter and form that allowed contrariety could it be destroyed in virtue of itself. . . . But the rational soul has activity in virtue of itself, which it exercises without the mediation of any corporeal organ, namely understanding, as the Philosopher proves in the third book of *De anima*. . . . It remains, therefore, that the human soul itself, which is the form of the body, is indestructible.[8]

The one argument taken from the *De anima* in this article to show that the soul has an activity transcending the material order is the lack of all corporeal characteristics in a soul able to understand all sensible forms.[9] The use of the verb "to understand," when taken strictly, includes implicitly the second Aristotelian argument noted above (n. 1). So the reasoning remains squarely within the Aristotelian setting. In that early period of his writing no need seems to have been felt by Aquinas to face in this context the accidental aspect of every creature's existence. Real difference between a creature and its existence had been emphasized from the start, but it did not seem to bring out any problem in regard to the unending possession of existence by the human soul.[10] All goes as though the negative consideration of lack of matter in the soul's constitution is sufficient in Aristotelian fashion to guarantee its perpetual duration.

6. "[N]on apprehendunt intentionem rationis, ut rationem hominis vel coloris, sed tantum apprehendunt hujusmodi, secundum quod sunt particulata. Virtus autem, quae non dependet a corpore, est incorruptibilis; et ita probatur quod anima intellectiva est immortalis ex eo quod apprehendit veritatem." *Sent.* 1.19.5.3.ad 3m; ed. Mandonnet, 1, 497.

7. On the chronology, see *Quaestiones quodlibetales*, ed. R. Spiazzi, Introductio, p. IX, and J. Weisheipl, *Friar Thomas d'Aquino* (Garden City, N.Y.: Doubleday, 1974), p. 367.

8. "*Per se* quidem corrumpi non posset nisi esset composita ex materia et forma contrarietatem habente: . . . Anima autem rationalis habet *per se operationem,* quam exercet nullo organo corporeo mediante, scilicet *intelligere,* ut probat Philosophus III *De anima*. . . . Restat ergo quod ipsa anima humana, quae est forma corporis, sit incorruptibilis." *Quaest. quod.* 10.3.2c; ed. Spiazzi, p. 202a.

9. See *De an.* 3.4.429a18–27, where the argument leans heavily on Anaxagoras's requirement that mind be "unmixed." Aristotle is interested rather in showing that its nature is entirely potential.

10. See *De ente et essentia*, ed. Leonine 43, 378–79.59–71, where concern is shown

III

With the middle period of Aquinas's academic career, however, the motif of inseparability in soul and its existence begins to appear. In the short work *On the Immortality of the Soul,* dated not too long after 1261 and edited for the first time in the present century,[11] the *Solutio* takes its start from the Platonic theme (*Phaedo,* 105C–106E) that the soul as cause of life cannot admit the opposite, death. Aquinas expresses this as the inseparability of soul from the cause of its own life, on the ground that nothing can be separated from itself:

Therefore, since the soul is the first self-movent, it cannot be separated from its mover, since nothing is separated from its own self. Hence the motion of life cannot fade out in it. And for this reason Plato concluded that the soul is immortal.[12]

This argument is rejected by Aquinas on the requirement that "the reasons for immortality be taken from what is proper to the human soul in comparison with other souls, that is, intellection" (ibid.). He wants a proof not just from "the fact," but rather from "the reason why."[13] Of the latter type there is only one. It is the familiar Aristotelian demonstration, with the two reasons given above (n. 1) now condensed into one:

If therefore we are in potentiality through the intellect to know the natures of all sensible things, it is necessary that the power by which intellective cognition is completed in us be stripped of every feature characteristic of sensible things. . . . Now everything is found to act in the same way in which it exists. . . . It remains therefore that the power by which a man understands is entirely indestructible.[14]

In this *Solutio* there is still no application of the inseparability ar-

---

for the perpetual individuality of the human soul after death, but no problem seems felt regarding its perpetual existence in face of the composition that had just been maintained between essence and existence in every created thing.

11. See *De immortalitate animae,* ed. L. A. Kennedy, in *Archives d'histoire doctrinale et littéraire du moyen âge* 45 (1978), 206.

12. "Cum igitur anima sit primum movens seipsum, non potest a suo motore separari, cum nihil a seipso separetur. Unde nec in ipsa potest motus vite deficere. Et ex hoc concludebat Plato animam esse immortalem." *De immort. an.,* Solut.; pp. 213–14. In regard to Plato's proof: "Oportet quod rationes immortalitatis sumantur ex eo quod est proprium anime humane inter ceteras animas, quod est intelligere." Ibid., p. 214.

13. These are the revised Oxford (Barnes) renditions of the original Aristotelian *hoti* (*quia*) and *dioti* (*propter quid*) at *Post. Analyt.* 1.13.78a22–79a16. Ross had translated "reason why" at 79a16, but elsewhere "reasoned fact."

14. "Si igitur per intellectum sumus in potentia ad cognoscendas naturas omnium sensibilium rerum, necessarium est id per quod completur intellectiva cognitio in nobis denudatum esse ab omni natura sensibilium rerum. . . . Unumquodque autem invenitur eo modo agere quo modo est. . . . Relinquitur ergo, id quo homo intelligit omnino incorruptibile esse." *De immort. an.,* Solut.; p. 217.

gument to the demonstration "from the reason why." But in the preliminary arguments an objection had been brought forward from the composition of being and thing in creatures, phrased in the terms used to describe it by Aquinas in the *De ente et essentia* and in the commentary on the *Sentences*:

> Wherever there is any composition there is possibility of dissolution. In the soul there is some composition, at least of "that by which" it is, and "what" it is. Therefore it is dissoluble and not indestructible.[15]

In the reply Aquinas maintains that the existence is a component other than the thing's substance, yet insists that it follows upon the form in virtue of the form itself. The form accordingly cannot be separated from this causation of existence:

> But in immaterial yet created substances the existence and the substance of the thing are other. . . . [N]ow the existence is consequent upon the form in virtue of the form itself. Hence a material substance loses existence only through separation of the matter from the form. This separation cannot even be understood in a substance that is form only, for nothing can be separated from itself. Hence it is impossible for a substance that is only form to be destructible.[16]

Here the dictum that "nothing can be separated from itself" is applied to one of the components only, the subsistent form, just as it had been applied immediately to soul alone in the *Solutio* (supra, n. 12). Soul as the cause of life cannot be separated from soul. Form likewise as the cause of being cannot be separated from form. Does that come to grips at all with the objection? The objection was that the composite of being and thing should be dissoluble. It meant that the two components should be separable from each other. How can it be met by showing that one of the two is not separable from itself? The subsistent form is something other than its own existence. How then can identity with itself be the reason why it cannot be separated from its existence? What would seem to be required for the cogency of the argument is that separation from its existence would mean separation from itself, and is therefore just as impossible.

15. "Ubicumque est aliqua compositio, ibi est possibilitas ad dissolutionem. In anima est aliqua compositio, saltem ex quo est et quod est. Ergo est dissolubilis et non incorruptibilis." *De immort. an.,* arg. 5; p. 209. Cf. *Sent.* 1.8.5.1.Solut.; 1, 127. Also, *De ente et essentia* 4.90–166; 43, 376–77.

16. "In substantiis autem immaterialibus sed increatis, aliud est esse et substantia rei. . . . esse autem est per se consequens formam. Unde substantia materialis non amittit esse nisi per hoc quod materia separatur a forma. Que quidem separatio nec intelligi potest in substantia que est forma tantum. Nihil enim potest a seipso separari. Unde impossibile est quod substantia que est forma tantum sit corruptibilis." *De immort. an.,* Solut.; p. 219.

This way of reasoning, applied to one or the other of the two components, is in fact the way the demonstration is presented in the other works throughout the middle and later periods of Aquinas's literary activity:

Substances that themselves are forms, can never be deprived of existence; just as, if a substance were a circle, it could never become not-round.[17]

Nothing is destroyed except by separation of form from it, for existence always follows upon form. Forms of this kind, since they are subsistent forms, cannot be separated from their own forms, and thus cannot lose existence. Therefore they are indestructible.[18]

Where the form itself subsists in its own existence it will in no way be able not to exist; just as existence also cannot be separated from itself.[19]

For it is clear that what belongs to something in virtue of itself is inseparable from it. Now in virtue of form itself existence belongs to a form that is an actuality. Hence matter acquires existence in actuality insofar as it acquires form; but destruction occurs in it insofar as form is separated from it. But it is impossible that the form should be separated from itself. Hence it is impossible that a subsistent form cease to exist.[20]

If therefore there be a form possessing existence, it is necessary that that form be indestructible. For existence is not separated from any possessor of existence except through separation of the form from it. Hence if what possesses existence is the form itself, it is impossible that existence be separated from it.[21]

If therefore a substance subsistent through its own essence were destroyed, it

17. "Substantiae vero quae sunt ipsae formae, nunquam possunt privari esse: sicut, si aliqua substantia esset circulus, nunquam posset fieri non rotunda." *Summa contra gent.* 2.55.Amplius. Cf. 2.79.Ostensum.

18. "Nihil corrumpitur nisi per separationem formae ab ipso, nam esse semper consequitur formam. Huiusmodi formae, cum sint formae subsistentes, non possunt separari a suis formis, et ita esse amittere non possunt. Ergo sunt incorruptibiles." *Comp. theol.* 74; Verardo no. 129. Cf. ibid., no. 128, and c. 84, nos. 146–47, where the argument is neatly summarized: "Intellectus autem omnino secundum suam naturam supra materiam elevatur, quod eius operatio ostendit: non enim intelligimus aliqua nisi per hoc quod ipsa a materia separamus."

19. "Ubi ipsa forma in esse suo subsistit nullo modo poterit non esse; sicut nec esse potest a seipso separari." *De pot.* 5.3c.

20. "Manifestum est enim quod id quod secundum se convenit alicui, est inseparabile ab ipso. Esse autem per se convenit formae, quae est actus. Unde materia secundum hoc acquirit esse in actu, quod acquirit formam; secundum hoc autem accidit in ea corruptio, quod separatur forma ab ea. Impossibile est autem quod forma separetur a seipsa. Unde impossibile est quod forma subsistens desinat esse." *ST* 1.75.6c. "Per se" is meant in contrast to causing existence through the composite. See also texts supra, nn. 4, 8, and 16.

21. "Si igitur sit aliqua forma quae sit habens esse, necesse est illam formam incorruptibilem esse. Non enim separatur esse ab aliquo habente esse nisi per hoc quod separatur forma ab eo. Unde si id quod habet esse sit ipsa forma, impossibile est quod esse separetur ab eo." *Q. de an.* 14; ed. Robb, p. 201.

would have to be separated from its formal cause. But its form is its essence. Therefore it would be separated from its own essence, which is impossible. Therefore it is not possible that a self-subsistent substance be destroyed.[22]

These passages, from the *Contra gentiles*, the *Compendium theologiae*, the *De potentia*, the *Summa theologiae*, the *Quaestio de anima* and the commentary on the *Liber de causis* respectively, present a consistent doctrinal picture. Perhaps the most enlightening in regard to the problem posed by the passage from the *De immortalitate animae* (supra, n. 15) is the text listed last and chronologically the latest (1272), the one from the commentary on the *Liber de causis*. After calling attention to "the twofold cause of being, namely the form through which something exists actually and the agent that makes it exist actually," the text goes on to show that self-subsistence can belong only to immaterial substance: "For it is clear that in destructible things destruction occurs through separation of something from its formal cause, through which it has existence in actuality. For just as generation which is a way to existence takes place through the acquiring of a form, so destruction which is a way to non-existence takes place through the losing of a form."[23] It then goes on to draw the conclusion given in the passage just cited (supra, n. 22).

This text recalls succinctly that a thing's matter is made actual by the form, while through that same form the thing has existence in actuality. As long as the form is exercising its causality the thing continues to exist. There is no way of separating the actual functioning of the form and the thing's continuance in existence. But where it is the actuality of matter, the form requires the matter to sustain it. It cannot be actual without the matter. Accordingly, loss of the matter means loss of the actuality, and in consequence loss of existence for the material thing. Where on the other hand the form is subsistent in itself, there is no matter to be lost. So there is no intrinsic possibility for it to lose existence.

22. "Si igitur substantia stans per essentiam suam corrumperetur, oporteret quod separaretur a sua causa formali, sed sua forma est eius essentia, ergo separaretur a sua essentia, quod est impossibile. Non ergo est possibile quod substantia stans per seipsam corrumpatur." *In lib. de causis*, Prop. 26; ed. Saffrey, p. 128.23–27. "Stans per se" had just been explained as meaning "subsistens"—"cum praepositio 'per' denotet causam, illud dicere *per se stare* sive subsistere quod non habet aliam causam essendi nisi seipsum." Ibid., lines 2–3. On the requirement of accompanying efficient causality, cf.: "Est autem duplex causa essendi, scilicet forma per quam aliquid actu est et agens quod facit actu esse." Ibid., lines 3–5.

23. "Manifestum est enim in rebus corruptibilibus quod corruptio accidit per hoc quod aliquid separatur a sua causa formali per quam aliquid habet esse in actu; sicut enim generatio quae est via ad esse, est per acquisitionem formae, ita corruptio quae est via ad non esse, est per amissionem formae." *In lib. de causis*, Prop. 26; p. 128.18–23.

In that way the meaning of the text from *De immortalitate animae* meets the objection it was meant to answer. Separation of the form's causation of existence from the form itself "cannot even be understood in a substance that is form only, for nothing can be separated from itself " (supra, n. 16). Even though the thing and its existence are really distinct, the impossibility of separating existence from the actually subsistent form has the same cogency as the form's necessary identity with itself. Accordingly, separation of form and existence in an already existent immaterial form would be as impossible as the separation of roundness from circle (supra, n. 17), or of form from itself (nn. 16, 18, 20, 21, 22), or of existence from itself (n. 19). Actual subsistent form allows no exit from existence. In that regard it sets up in sharply positive fashion a permanent *Huis Clos*.

IV

The tenet, then, is consistent in content throughout these passages, in spite of different ways of expression. But is it acceptable metaphysically, within the framework of its own starting points?

For Aquinas, the form exercises its proper causality in a twofold manner. On the one hand, form specifies matter in actualizing it. On the other hand, form specifies existence by way of potentiality in regard to it.[24] Form is never found in the real sensible world unless it is exercising this twofold causality. That is its function as form. If it is actuating the matter it has to be making the thing exist, and, correspondingly, it cannot cause existence except as actuating matter. The result is that it causes existence not just by reason of itself, but by reason of actuating the composite. Here the composite is what exists. But form can be separated from matter through destruction.[25] In this way the form ceases to cause existence.

With a subsistent form, however, the case is different. As with any form, its potentiality is for existence. But unlike the form of a merely material thing, it rises above dependence on matter that would allow destruction because of potentiality to another form. In causing existence it is not dependent upon an element that can be separated from it. It itself is what exists. It cannot be separated from itself in the way a material form can be separated from the matter on which it is de-

---

24. "Unde non sic determinatur *esse* per aliud sicut potentia per actum, sed magis sicut actus per potentiam." *De pot.* 7.2.ad 9m.

25. "Si enim forma ex hoc quod inest materiae, est principium essendi in rebus materialibus, nec res materialis potest non esse nisi per separationem formae." *De pot.* 5.3c. Cf. supra, nn. 20 and 23.

pendent for causing existence. As a consequence its causation of existence continues perpetually. It can no more be separated from its causation of existence than from itself. The meaning is that since it cannot be separated from itself it cannot cease making itself exist. A positive reason, the formal causality exercised by the soul, has infused new probative vigor into the negative consideration of immateriality.

The separation referred to, in consequence, is basically separation in what goes to make up a thing's essence. The form can be separated from the matter, but not the form from itself. This appears clearly enough in most of the passages listed above. One need only compare their wording: "[A] material substance loses existence only through separation of the matter from the form. This separation cannot even be understood in a substance that is form only, for nothing can be separated from itself " (supra, n. 16). "Forms of this kind, since they are subsistent forms, cannot be separated from their own forms" (n. 13). "Hence matter acquires existence in actuality insofar as it acquires form; but destruction occurs in it insofar as form is separated from it. But it is impossible that form should be separated from itself " (n. 20). "But its form is its essence. Therefore it would be separated from its own essence, which is impossible" (n. 22). In all these passages the separation referred to is the same. It is the separation of parts within in an essence, possible in material things, impossible in a subsistent form.

In the passage cited from the *Quaestio de anima*, however, the notion of separation is applied also to existence: "For existence is not separated from any possessor of existence except through separation of the form from it. Hence if what possesses existence is the form itself, it is impossible that existence be separated from it" (supra, n. 21). But the separation of existence from the existent is made consequent upon the separation of form from that same existent. If separation of form is impossible, likewise separation of existence is. This is also understood in the passage from the *Contra gentiles*: "Substances that are themselves forms, can never be deprived of existence" (supra, n. 17), just as a circle cannot be deprived of roundness, which is consequent upon the circle by reason of the circle itself. The text there states: "So substances that are not the forms themselves, can be deprived of existence insofar as they lose the form."[26] The basic separation is loss of form by substance, upon which loss of existence is consequent. Where a substance cannot lose form, loss of existence is impossible. Separa-

---

26. "Substantiae igitur quae non sunt ipsae formae, possunt privari esse, secundum quod amittunt formam." *CG* 2.55.Amplius quod.

tion of existence from the existent is in this way described as loss of it, and is shown to be impossible where the formal cause of existence cannot be lost. Even though the existence is spoken of as separated, then, it is understood merely as lost by the substance.

Different at first sight, however, is the more daring formulation in the passage from the *De potentia*: "Where the form itself subsists in its own existence it will in no way be able not to exist; just as existence also cannot be separated from itself " (supra, n. 19). Here the existence itself is represented as inseparable from itself, and not just from an existent. What does that mean? If separation from itself merely means ceasing, the assertion does not hold universally. The existence of material things can come to an end. The parallelism of the two members of the passage would, however, indicate that subsistent existent is meant. Where form subsists, its existence cannot cease; correspondingly, where existence subsists, it exists eternally. But there is another consideration involved. Existence taken just in itself does not allow any diversification. It can be diversified only by something other than itself, in the way the existence of a stone is not the existence of a man.[27] It itself provides no means for distinction within itself, let alone for separation. The cause for its cessation, then, will have to be found in the thing it actuates. This in turn will have to be a composite, bringing the cause of separation back to matter. Separation of matter from the form actuating it continues to be the ultimate explanation. In fact, in the *De immortalitate animae*, where the composition of existence and existent was introduced in one of the opening arguments (arg. 5; p. 209), the *Solutio* (p. 218) in offering a "reason why" (*propter quid*) demonstration gives only the Aristotelian proof without adding the inseparability motif.

Does this mean that the inseparability is only an afterthought, introduced just to meet a possible objection arising from the doctrine of the *De ente et essentia*, but with no essential role in the "reason why" explanation? The consistent use of the inseparability theme through the subsequent presentations of the argument militates against this view. The Aristotelian background had not been meant for subsistent forms that are created, that begin in time, that inform matter. Of that class, however, was the human soul whose indestructibility Aquinas wished to demonstrate by way of the "reason why." Its own essence had to provide the reason, in contrast to arguments merely from "fact"

27. "Esse autem, inquantum est esse, non potest esse diversum: potest autem diversificari per aliquid quod est praeter esse; sicut esse lapidis est aliud ab esse hominis. Illud ergo quod est esse subsistens, non potest esse nisi unum tantum." *CG* 2.52.Si enim.

(*quia*). The soul had to be regarded as a potentiality for existence other than itself, existence received from God but not separable from the soul in God's ordinate power.[28] For this the negative Aristotelian argument that one part of the soul lacked matter did not suffice. The function of the soul as simultaneously the formal cause of the body and the formal cause of existence had to be added to its functioning in independence of material restrictions. In this way the nature of a soul that is in actuality the form of matter was shown in positive fashion to require unending existence. As a subsistent form it was exercising a formal causality that made its existence naturally inseparable from itself even though different from itself, and that was illustrated by the way subsistent existence could be understood as causing its own eternity which was identical with itself.[29]

This illustration, however, serves only to point up the cogency of the reasoning. It does not serve as model for the union. The union of subsistent form with existence is not the same as the identity of self with self. The form and the existence still remain really distinct in really existent things. What it does mean is that in the natural order of things the separation of a subsistent form from its existence would entail the separation of the form from itself, since that would be the only way to break up its essence and bring on its destruction. In that way it is no more separable from its existence than from itself. Similarly, since it entails its own existence by formal causality once it is actual, it would carry its own existence along with it in the case of the alleged separation. The separation would thereby entail the separation of the existence from the existence itself. All this lies in the nature of the human soul.

There is accordingly nothing mysterious in the assertions that the subsistent soul can no more be separated from existence than from itself, nor than the existence from its own self. For the separation, matter would be required as a component of the thing's essence. The basic ground for the "reason why" demonstration remains in consequence the absence of matter in the substantial principle of intellective activity, as shown by Aristotle and Proclus. In the framework of Aquinas's starting points, however, this basic ground has to be developed in terms of a subsistent soul that is the form of the human body, as

28. "Relinquitur ergo quod non est impossibile Deum res ad non esse reducere; cum non sit necessarium eum rebus esse praebere, nisi ex suppositione suae ordinationis et praescientiae, . . ." *De pot.* 5.3c.

29. "Posset enim dici, quamvis non ita bene . . . dicetur ipse Deus esse causa suae aeternitatis secundum modum intelligendi, quamvis ipse sit sua aeternitas secundum rem." *Sent.* 1.19.2.1.ad 1m; 1, 468.

well as of existence that is really other than essence, and of an omnipotent God whose absolute power extends to annihilation. Within that metaphysical world, the immateriality of the human soul provides the basis for the only "reason why" demonstration of its perpetual existence.[30] The positive nature of the soul, in its exercise of formal causality, rather than just its lack of matter, becomes the emphatic feature in the proof. But what triggers the reasoning is the immateriality.

V

Finally, one may ask if this "reason why" demonstration extends to the soul's immortality. In the *De immortalitate animae* Aquinas proposed to seek the sole "reason why" demonstration of it. But both in the *Solutio* and in the answer to the argument (arg. 5; p. 209) that the soul should be dissoluble on account of its composition, he concludes only to its indestructibility. Likewise in *Q. de an.* 14, the question phrased in terms of immortality is answered (pp. 201–202) through demonstration of indestructibility. In the other presentations of the argument in his own name the conclusion is consistently the same. Only when speaking of Augustine's proof for the immortality of the soul on the ground that it knows truth does he offer the support of the Aristotelian argument for indestructibility and explain that in this way "it is proven that the intellective soul is immortal on the ground that it knows truth."[31] The meaning seems clearly enough that Augustine's argument can reach its conclusion in that way. In the background of the argument in Plato (*Phaedo*, 106) the indestructibility followed upon the immortality. Aquinas seems to be implying that even though in

30. "[U]na est tamen via demonstrans immortalitatem ipsius, et propter quid immortalis sit hostendens." *De immort. an.*, Solut.; p. 213. Cf.: "Sed ratio ostendens propter quid anima sit immortalis oportet quod sumatur ex modo substantie ipsius. Substantia autem anime non cognoscitur nisi ex eius operatione." Ibid., p. 215. The other arguments *ex signis*, ibid. Cf.: "in syllogismis, qui fiunt per signa, in quibus conclusionem, quae est *per se*, non scit aliquis *per se*, neque *propter quid*." *Post. analyt.* 1.14.Leonine no. 7. Similarly, "[D]e genere demonstrationum quae dicuntur demonstrationes *signi*, vel demonstrationes *quia*." *In Phys.* 7.1.Leonine no. 6. The background is in Averroes: "Declaratum est igitur ex hoc sermone quod ista demonstratio est vera, et quod est de genere signorum certorum: licet non sit de genere demonstrationum simplicium." Averroes, *In VII Phys.*, comm. 2 (Venice: apud Junctas, 1562), fol. 307v2.

31. See supra, n. 6. George St. Hilaire, "Does St. Thomas Really Prove the Soul's Immortality?" *The New Scholasticism* 34 (1960), p. 341, n. 6, cites this text as meaning that "St. Thomas does conclude a philosophical argument in favor of the soul's incorruptibility with the word *immortalis*." For Aquinas, Plato has the soul "immortalem et per se subsistentem ex eo quod movet seipsam," in contrast to Aristotle's "non corrumpitur"—*Q. de an.* 1; Robb, p. 59.

Platonic fashion the soul is regarded as something essentially alive, its substantial indestructibility has to be proven before the conclusion of perpetual life may be drawn. In any case, he is concerned here with an Augustinian proof rather than with one of his own.

Aquinas of course was aware that the notions of immortality and incorruptibility had been coupled in Lombard's work, upon which he had been commenting.[32] The coupling of the two is found as far back as Plato (*Phaedo*, 106BE) and St. Paul (I Cor. 15.53), and in the influential treatise of Nemesius.[33] In a theological context probably nobody will be inclined to contest the inference of the soul's immortality from its indestructibility. For Aquinas, moreover, any real existence of the soul carries with it in fact the accompaniment of vital activity, since no substance lacks activity.[34] Nevertheless, the two notions remained formally distinct. The one referred to existence, the other to vital action.[35] Since for him no created substance was immediately active, potentiality for existence was really different in the human soul from potentiality for acting.[36] The soul's perpetual life could hardly be expected to follow with metaphysical cogency from its perpetual existence. On one occasion, in fact, he had asserted firmly the incorruptibility of the soul on the strength of the Aristotelian argument: "Now the intellective power is not the actuality of a corporeal organ, as is proved in the third book of the *De anima*; therefore it must remain after the destruction of the body." Yet later in the same work he can say: "If the resurrection of the body be denied it is not easy, in fact it is difficult, to maintain the immortality of the soul" and add with backward reference to this stand: "Nor against this may one say that the separated soul is rewarded, because, as has been proved above, it is not possible to prove that the soul is immortal."[37]

32. Peter Lombard, *Sententiae* 2.19.6.2; 3rd Quaracchi ed. (Rome: Coll. S. Bonaventurae, 1971), p. 426.3.

33. Cf. sequence "est autem incorruptibilis, est ergo et immortalis," Nemesius, *De Natura Hominis*, ed. G. Verbeke and J. R. Moncho (Leiden: Brill, 1975), p. 50.00–1.

34. See *Quodl.* 3, 9, 1, c. In practical use, following the long tradition before him, Aquinas readily couples the two notions, as may be seen by glancing through the instances of *immortalis* and *immortalitas* in Busa's *Index thomisticus*, Sect. 2, Concord. 1, vol. 11, pp. 57–62.

35. "[I]mmortalitas signat vitam indeficientem; vivere autem non solum nominat ipsum esse viventis, sed etiam operationem vitae. . . . non dicit quod Dei operatio sit incorruptibilitas, quae importat solum sempiternitatem ipsius esse, sed dicit *immortalitas*, ut includat sempiternitatem operationis." *In De caelo et mundo* 2.4.5. Cf. the distinction at *De immort. an.*, arg. 7; p. 210.

36. "[I]nter essentiam et talem operationem cadit virtus media differens ab utroque, in creaturis etiam realiter, in Deo ratione tantum." *Sent.* 1.7.1.1.ad 2m; 1, 177.

37. "[V]is autem intellectiva non est actus organi corporei, ut probatur in III *De anima*; ideo necesse est quod maneat corpore corrupto." *In I Cor.* 13.3; ed. Vivès. 21,

The difficulty in this particular context arises from Aristotle's (*De an.* 3.8.432a8–9) requirement of a sensible image, a phantasm, for any human thinking. Separated from the body, the soul has naturally no means of having phantasms, and accordingly no means of exercising its radical power to think. The soul, this implies, can have no cognition, at least in any natural way, apart from the body. With the separated soul, however, "the first activity and the root of all the others is cognition."[38] Lacking actual cognition, the soul can have no appetitive activity. There is no natural means for the soul to exercise vital activity after death. Consequently, life after death, or immortality for the soul, cannot be demonstrated philosophically. Preternaturally the separated soul may be able to receive cognitional forms that are not dependent on phantasms, but it cannot be demonstrated metaphysically that this will take place.

Cajetan, in his comment II upon the passage cited above from the *Summa theologiae* (1.75.6c; supra, n. 20) did not question the conclusion of indestructibility for the human soul, even though in comment XV he had occasion to mention the difficulty caused by the Aristotelian requirement of a phantasm. The difficulty was the center of a vivid controversy at the time.[39] At any rate, Cajetan came to deny in unmistakable terms the possibility of proof on the philosophical level for the immortality of the soul.[40] Yet he has maintained his position as the leading Thomistic commentator. This should be enough to alert one to the danger of a too-hasty acceptance of the extension of Aquinas's demonstration to a further conclusion of immortality. The apparently studied avoidance of "immortality" in the conclusion of the demonstration in its various forms increases this hesitation. What the argument demonstrates with metaphysical cogency is only the soul's indestructibility.

The motif of inseparability, then, may well have taken its rise from

---

7b. "Si negetur resurrectio corporis, non de facili, imo difficile est sustinere immortalitatem animae" (ibid., 15.2; p. 33b). "Nec obstat si dicatur quod anima separata praemiatur, quia, ut probatum est supra, non posset probari quod anima esset immortalis" (lect. 4; p. 39b). The indirect discourse imperfects in the last sentence occur through attraction to the "probatum est," and accordingly do not imply any doubt in the original assertion.

38. "[P]rima operatio et radix aliarum est cognitio." *De immort. an.*, Solut.; p. 215.

39. On the topic, see É. Gilson, "Autour de Pomponazzi. Problématique de l'immortalité de l'âme en Italie au début du XVIe siècle," *Archives d'histoire doctrinale et littéraire du moyen âge* 28 (1961), 163–279.

40. For references, see John P. Reilly, *Cajetan's Notion of Existence* (The Hague and Paris: Mouton, 1971), pp. 95–102, esp. pp. 99–100. On Cajetan's negative vote in this regard at the eighth session of the Fifth Lateran Council, see Mansi, *Sacrorum Conciliorum nova et amplissima collectio* 32, col. 843D.

reflection on the Platonic notion of the soul as self-movent (supra, n. 12). There it meant that the soul could not be separated from the cause of its *life,* since it itself was that cause. Aquinas required the transference of this motif to the level of *substance,* where form was the cause of existence. Here likewise the cause could not be separated from itself, and where the resultant existence was by virtue of the form alone there was no possibility of its separation from the actualized form.[41] But Aquinas seems to have kept this demonstration strictly in the order of substance. He gives no satisfactory indication of extending it to vital activity in his own reasoning.

41. By the same token the existence always remains human. Yet for Anthony Kenny, *Aquinas* (New York: Hill and Wang, 1980), p. 49, Aquinas "denied that a disembodied soul was a human being." This assertion seems incompatible with the doctrine that being is specified by the kind of thing it actuates (supra, n. 27). The *esse hominis* is the existence of the soul, inseparable from the soul in all its states. The disembodied soul accordingly is a human being. For Aquinas, however, the separated soul is not a person, on account of the natural completeness required by Boethius's definition of "person": "[A]nima separata est pars rationalis naturae, scilicet humanae, et non tota natura rationalis humana, et ideo non est persona"—Aquinas, *Pot.* 9.2.ad 14m. Cf. 29.1.ad 5m; 75.4.ad 2m. See Boethius, *De duabus naturis* 3; PL 64, 1343–1345. Aquinas (*ST* 3.16.12.ad 2m) sees the Boethian definition as implying a complete substance—"importat substantiam completam." See also *Sent.* 3.5.3.2.Moos nos. 106–111; 3, 206–207. A recent survey of the problematic may be found in Richard Heinzmann, "Anima unica forma corporis. Thomas van Aquin als Überwinder des platonischen-neuplatonischen Dualismus," *Philosophisches Jahrbuch* 93 (1986), 236–59. Heinzmann (p. 253) stresses the forceful assertion of Aquinas (*De pot.* 5.10.ad 5m) that the soul has greater likeness to God when united with the body than when separated from it, because it has its own nature more perfectly in the state of union. But the text does not justify the conclusion suggested by Heinzmann (p. 258, n. 86) that the separated soul can for Aquinas be regarded as "quasi nihil" in comparison. Aquinas reasons: "Impossibile autem est quod illud quod est naturale et per se, sit finitum et quasi nihil, et illud quod est contra naturam et per accidens, sit infinitum, si anima semper duret sine corpore" (*In I Cor.* 15.2; ed. Vivès, 21, 33b). Here the contrast is between the infinite duration allowed the separated soul and the finite duration alleged for the composite, a duration that would be "quasi nihil" in comparison. That reasoning does not permit the application of "quasi nihil" to the separated soul, which is being represented for the moment as something that would have eternal duration. Yet Heinzmann (p. 258) understands it to mean "verglichen mit dem Menschen ist die anima separata quasi nihil." But this need not hinder agreement with Heinzmann's ultimate conclusion that for Aquinas the separate soul "ist etwas völlig anderes als die unsterbliche Seele der Platoniker" (p. 258).

Epilogue

In retrospect, two questions perhaps need to be asked. First, even if practical agreement could be achieved on the notion and viability of Christian philosophy, is there today sufficient incentive for work towards its development? If so, one may further inquire, exactly how should that enterprise be pursued in the contemporary philosophical world?

Just at present, the prospect of a Christian philosophy may not appear any too exciting. Interest in it stays by and large at a rather low ebb, despite intermittent efforts of dedicated and deeply concerned writers. With the situation that discouraging, why should anyone be prompted to devote time and energy to so questionable an undertaking? Moreover, is not supernatural faith, quite as it stands in itself, amply sufficient for the guidance of one's personal life? If further elucidation of the revealed tenets is required, is not sacred theology at hand to provide it? How then can a Christian philosophy today play any significant role in our contemporary culture? Why bother at all about a lame-duck procedure that methodologically excludes the use of revealed premises as a means for throwing light on revealed truths?

Very briefly, one may answer that, as far as the individual's spiritual life is concerned, Christian truth has been and still can be given marvelous intellectual appeal under floodlighting by Christian philosophy. For instance, faith gives assurance that the ultimate purpose of every thought and every action of one's life is to see God face to face for all eternity. That is human destiny as proclaimed by the Christian kerygma. But how can eternally changeless contemplation come to appear attractive for people trained to place their goals in the dazzling worldly success and prosperity that are idolized in our technocratic age? Facing that background, can anything bring out the supremacy of the eternal contemplative life so clearly and so impressively as the Aristotelian insights on cognition, with their subsequent development in Thomistic thought? Cognition is the closest possible of unions. Intellection is the highest kind of cognition. All things have their first and best mode of existence in the divine creative essence. When faith provides the assurance that God is possessed face to face in the beatific vision, the clarification given by those three philosophical tenets can make the outlook glow with warm brilliance. It dissipates the chilling mists of unreflective opposition to the revealed doctrine. The contemplative union with God in the eternal vision of his essence comes to mean the closest and most intense possession of all the things one desires or could possibly wish for. The beatific vision is seen to involve the fullest and unending enjoyment of all desired activities in their primary mode of being, insofar as their existence in the divine creative essence is now understood as infinitely superior to the real finite existence the things and the activities have in their own selves.

In corresponding fashion the notions of creator and father, when contemplated in the union they are given in the creed, take on a profoundly rich meaning that neither of them could have in separation. Likewise the notion of sanctifying grace as a real habituation of the soul illumines the import of the new spiritual life to which one is reborn in baptism. Also, the philosophical tenet of the soul's immediate possession of existence shows how one and the same individual may continue on in a different way of being after bodily death. Similar elucidation on the philosophical level can be given to numerous other tenets of Christian belief, such as the ubiquitous presence and power of God, the inviolability of human life, and the Christian tradition on sexual morality. Of most practical importance at the present moment of ecumenical concern is perhaps the Aristotelian (*Metaphysics* 2.1. 993b24–31) notion of focal reference, in which a nature is located in its fullness in a primary instance only, but is found in all other instances in varying degrees and in various manners, through focal reference to what is primary for its meaning. This philosophical tenet furnishes the rational underpinning for adherence to the belief that the deposit of divine revelation is to be found in its fullness in one church only, and in all other churches and world religions in varying degrees but always in focal relation. In this perspective there is no incoherence in the beliefs that "the Word was the real light that gives light to everyone" (John 1.9; trans. *The New Jerusalem Bible*), and that "at many moments in the past and by many means, God spoke to our ancestors through the prophets: but in our time, the final days, he has spoken to us in the person of his Son" (Hebrews 1.1–2), and that according to the divine intention "there will be only one flock and one shepherd" (John 10.16). These considerations allow the divine truth to be seen and respected in all people, with courteous understanding of others but without detriment to the firmness of one's own belief.

True, philosophical elucidation of those beliefs is not essential to the workings of faith. It remains accidental to them. But that does not imply that it is expendable. The beauty of the Christian message is brought out vividly by the majesty of the Gothic cathedrals, by the splendor of Renaissance painting, and by the deep appeal of Gregorian and other religious music. Correspondingly, the sublimity and solidity of the truth in that Christian message come to glow brilliantly under the intellectual sweep of a clarifying Christian philosophy. The philosophical elucidation, though accidental to faith and based on sources external to faith, has its place in the integral conception of Christian life, just as has the accidentally connected but highly desirable functioning of Christian architecture, art, and music. In the absence of mystical or charismatic vision, philosophy is the natural means for appreciation of the intelligible depths of revealed Christian doctrine.

But can these insights not be achieved by sacred theology itself, apart from the cultivation of a separate philosophical discipline? Hardly. History speaks against that possibility. The church fathers went to the pagan Greeks for their philosophical tools. Aquinas and Suarez, both lifelong theologians, were impelled to take time away from their strictly theological writing to devote attention to straight philosophy for the needed help. Philosophy as a prerequisite for scientifically developed theology was emphasized by Leo XIII's *Aeterni Patris*.[1] Much philosophy, one will find, has been engendered in the course of theological study. But that concomitant encounter never seems to have sufficed for the formation of a satisfactory philosophical *habitus*. To be effective, philosophy had first to be developed as phi-

1. [A] perpetual and varied service is further required of philosophy, in order that sacred theology may receive and assume the nature, form, and genius of a true science." *Aet. Patr.* 6; in *The Papal Encyclicals*, ed. C. Carlen (Wilmington, NC: McGrath, 1981), 2, 19. One modern writer would see metaphysical structure already present in the biblical accounts, with doubts that a theology without metaphysical structure could have any meaning: "This metaphysical structure of Christianity is, fundamentally, the metaphysical structure of biblical theology." Claude Tresmontant, *Christian Metaphysics*, trans. Gerard Slevin (New York: Sheed and Ward, 1965), p. 144. In any case, though, this should not be taken to mean that philosophy's ancillary function in regard to theology is essential to Christian philosophy. Rather, it is accidental to it, in spite of the fact that the philosophy was engendered within sacred theology in patristic and medieval times, and exercised so extensive a role in medieval theology. Today Christian philosophy is an independent discipline in its own right. Yet the contrary view may be found advocated: "I consider the idea of a Christian philosophy, as an exercise of natural reasoning distinct from revealed theology, to be a self-destructive (indeed contradictory) notion." Peter Redpath, "Romance of Wisdom: The Friendship between Maritain and Saint Thomas Aquinas," in *Understanding Maritain: Philosopher and Friend*, ed. Deal W. Hudson and Matthew J. Mancini (Macon, GA: Mercer University Press, 1987), p. 99.

losophy. Occasional work at it in the course of theological writing was not enough. It needed to be worked out on its own plane and in the sequence of its own order. It demanded penetration right to its basic principles, and then reflexive consciousness in regard to the way its conclusions were gradually developed from those starting points, in its own proper setting. The former seminary tradition of two or even three years of philosophical training *before* entering into theology seems to have been sound.

Today's theological grappling with many important religious problems tellingly illustrates the need for already-prepared philosophical tools. The union of the two natures in the one person in the Incarnation, for instance, calls for painstaking application of the philosophical notions of existence, nature, faculties, and personality. Without a sound philosophical notion of substance, the traditional doctrine of the Eucharistic presence has been difficult to defend, when notions of transignification and transfinalization have striven to substitute for transubstantiation. The efficacy of divine providence in the face of human free will, and the certainty of the divine foreknowledge in regard to free future contingents, have posed problems that demand profound philosophical knowledge.[2] Likewise, the tradition of offering prayers and Masses for the departed is rendered bewildering when no possible conception of an individual's status between bodily death and the general resurrection can be offered. Difficulties about ignorance and doubt on the part of the human knowledge in Christ, or on the transmission of original sin, or on the *ex opere operato* efficacy of the sacraments, or on the use of Marxist categories in Christian exegesis, and so on, all require elucidation in philosophical terms and by a philosophy already worked out independently in its general contours. But in regard to problems of this kind, contemporary theology has quite regularly, to judge from today's journalistic writings, preferred to bypass the Greek and medieval achievements. Vacant of those glorious gains, some writers have even made attempts to get back, through dehellenization, to a primitive Christianity uncontam-

2. A single word for the expression "free future contingent" is not easy to find in English. "Futurable," specially coined for it, is considered obsolete by the *O.E.D.*, s.v. *The New Catholic Encyclopedia*, s.v., uses "futurible," rendering the very late Latin *futuribile*. The notion to be conveyed is that of a free decision never made or to be made but which would be made had circumstances been different. For Aquinas (*In periher- meneias* 1.14.Leonine n. 22) the efficacious causality of God upon the free act of a creature was above the order of necessity and contingence. Above limitation in those ways, it had to be of infinite efficacy, quite as does creation. In that setting it poses exactly the same problem for futuribles as for any free act of a creature. In consequence the late sixteenth-century controversy between "physical premotion" and freedom was not a special problem for Aquinas.

inated by philosophical intrusion. From the viewpoint of traditional philosophy, this would suggest a tinge of dinosaur mentality hardly boding well for expectations that solid and durable philosophy will be produced within the ambit of today's theological activities. The internal organization of theology, of course, is an affair for its own experts. It is not within the competence of an outsider to offer any critique of its internal status. But viewed solely from the standpoint of capacity to produce acceptable philosophy, today's theology seems to illustrate more than ever the tenet that philosophy has to be learned from philosophers, through independent study and in primary sources. Dabbling in philosophy for the occasion has not sufficed.

That is what history has to say. The inherent reason is not difficult to fathom. The starting points of philosophy are naturally evident truths. Their intrinsic certainty is absolutely guaranteed by the unshakable principle of contradiction, in regard to both the nature and the existence of things. The philosophical tenets do not look elsewhere for that guarantee. Each step in the philosophical reasoning processes, moreover, has to be seen as following from the premises with corresponding intrinsic evidence. Philosophy does not seek authority to guarantee its truth. The philosopher as philosopher is trained to proceed on intrinsic evidence only. On the other hand, the starting points of theology are revealed truths accepted on faith without intrinsic guarantee. The theologian investigates how they are found in the sacred scriptures and in religious tradition—for instance, how the doctrine of the Trinity is presumed in the New Testament and given its details in the church fathers and the early councils. To that extent the theologian enters into the sublime recesses of divine doctrine. But the evidence for the dogmas is not intrinsic to them. The guarantee of their certainty lies outside the particular truths themselves. Sacred theology depends for its certainty upon the authority of its sources, while authority, if appealed to at all in philosophy, is looked upon as the weakest of arguments. The result is a basic difference in type of habituation between the two disciplines. In consequence, philosophy as a procedure on the strength of intrinsic evidence alone has to be learned from philosophers as regards its practice, and not from sacred theology. Barred from revealed premises, it gazes on the faith from the outside.

But even if today a philosophy could be developed within the activities of sacred theology, the need for an independent Christian philosophy would still be felt in general Christian culture. The crucial difference between Christian philosophy and theology in function of cultural role lies in the respective ways in which each regards the content of Christian faith. For Christian philosophy the content of that belief is accepted as handed down through the centuries in Christian tradition and life. With the Christian philosopher, its face is clearly recognizable for his purposes as it stands. As a philosopher he feels no call to probe its subtle theological difficulties. He has no other ambition than to understand it as it is present in his belief. Like the St. Anselm of the *Proslogion,* he does not ask to enter into the divine sublimity of the revealed truth. Nor is he asking to understand it through theological starting points. He is looking at his belief definitely from without. He is always conscious of the difference between belief and knowledge, and as a philosopher he has no inclination to treat his beliefs as though they were something he knew by way of intrinsic penetration. He is likewise conscious of the differences between speculative and practical philosophy on the one hand, and productive (*poiētikē*—Aristotle, *Metaphysics* 6.1.1025b18–24) knowledge on the other hand. He claims no mission to suppress or alter or invent religious doctrines themselves, or to direct the course of their development. He attributes his own firm belief in the Christian doctrines to supernatural grace. Accepting through that belief the overall tenet of infallibility in the teaching church, he confidently goes about his own work of philosophical understanding both in the speculative and in the practical orders. But he does not enter the productive area. He has no temptation to regard his discipline as an art. He leaves the structure of his object to divine providence under the guidance of the ecclesiastical magisterium.

To a contemporary theologian this approach may conjure up the features of a "think tank" mentality, hopelessly speculative in its abstention from active part in the fray, Neoscholastic in its general outlines and Protestant rather than Catholic in the way it relates nature to grace. It may even prompt the question about how pope and bishops can know more about the mysteries of the faith than theologians who devote their entire lives to the scholarly study of those beliefs.[3] For the Christian philosopher, in sharp contrast, a question of that type does not arise. As a Christian he believes, in virtue of what he regards as supernaturally given faith, that the magisterium is divinely guided in its authoritative interpretation of the content of Christian revelation. He is not looking for superior knowledge in pope or bishops, but only for decision on what the church *believes.* He recognizes the

3. "How, *precisely,* do bishops (including the Pope) come to know more about the mysteries of faith than do those who study those mysteries in a sustained and scholarly way?" Richard P. O'Brien, "Academic Freedom in Catholic Universities: The Emergence of a Party Line," *America* 159 (Dec. 3, 1988), 457a.

various and intricate workings of this guaranteed infallibility in the ecclesiastical teaching. He does not homogenize it. But he has no hesitation in accepting the general picture of the faith and then proceeding straightway to elucidate its teachings in strictly philosophical fashion. He wants to deal with what is true in the real world, in both its natural and supernatural facets. He sees his philosophical starting points as absolutely certain. In consequence he has no general tendency to think that the fear of infallibility is now to be regarded as the beginning of wisdom. He expects appropriately graded certitude in the supernatural order fully as much as he finds it in the natural sphere. He does not look to any special ecclesiology to justify his acceptance of the church's infallible teaching authority. Rather, he expects any ecclesiology to develop in conformity with the already-accepted magisterial decisions. In a word, he knows that theologians are fallible, while he firmly believes that the magisterium is endowed with infallibility. He sees in himself no calling to become part of the magisterium, no power to decide what is or what is not revealed doctrine, no ability to change existing doctrine or to work towards a meta-Christianity. He is not producing religion. Rather, he is probing the present intelligibility of the revealed doctrines, with their capacities for development along the lines naturally apparent in their own content. He is always looking at Christian truth from the outside. Philosophy, as the term is understood in the academic division of the disciplines today, remains in this way accidental and external to Christianity. It does not penetrate into the sublimity of Christian doctrine, not even in the limited extent to which sacred theology is able to investigate it from the viewpoint of the Scriptures, conciliar decisions, and religious traditions. Christian philosophy bases its inquiry solely upon naturally known principles, with the believed doctrine having the status of an object that is viewed from the outside.

These considerations show sufficiently that even if Christian philosophy could be engendered today within theological activity it would still have to lead its own independent life and do its own independent work. It is neither a rival nor a substitute for theology. It feels sadness at attacks on magisterial authority.[4] But it does not experience any Luddite urge to destroy the instruments of theological progress. It leaves the gins intact. Yet from its own working standpoint as an ac-

4. Ralph McInerny, "Reflections on Christian Philosophy," in *One Hundred Years of Thomism,* ed. Victor B. Brezik (Houston: Center for Thomistic Studies, 1981), pp. 68–69, notes how the Catholic philosopher takes the magisterial documents "with the utmost seriousness," in contrast to the seemingly eager tendency of theologians in the opposite direction. This gives rise, McInerny notes, to incredulity towards their work.

ademic discipline it requires that interpretations made through use of the scholarly tools be kept under the pastoral surveillance of the authoritatively designated "overseers" (ἐπισκόπους—Acts 20.28, trans. *The New Jerusalem Bible*) of the church of God. Theological conclusions not in accord with the magisterium do not come under the thematic object of Christian philosophy.

To sum up, Christian philosophy bears on the world as it really is, both as known through natural cognition and as believed in through faith. Where the supernatural side is guaranteed by the magisterium as definitely factual (for instance, in regard to heaven and hell and purgatory), Christian philosophy has the task of elucidating the doctrines on the philosophical level. Where factual status is gauged as minimal or entirely lacking (as in the case of limbo), Christian philosophy has no positive concern. In the case of limbo it can make only the negative comment that the soul has no natural means for, or natural right to, any actual life after bodily death. A soul's perpetual existence without life poses no greater problem for it than the natural indestructibility of matter after the end of the biologically active universe. But the point here is only that in regard to limbo, Christian philosophy has either absolutely, or at least for practical purposes, no object to work upon. It is of course sensitive to Aristotle's (*Metaphysics* 1.2.982b18–19) profound comment that the lover of wisdom is in a way a lover of myths, on account of the wonder both excite. But for Christian philosophy this has to be understood strictly in the focal reference framework signalized by Chesterton's observation about the paradox of Christianity, namely, that we can really understand all myths only when we know that one of them is true.[5]

Christian philosophy, then, aims to enlighten revealed beliefs through philosophical study. In that perspective, when it is taken reduplicatively as Christian philosophy, it itself does the enlightening. But at the same time there is a sense in which one may say that here Christianity gives enlightenment to philosophy taken just as philosophy. By offering to philosophy an object containing the revealed truths about the real world's actual constitution, it provides philosophy with factual connections in that object that philosophy would otherwise miss. If assurance of existential connection without evident interconceptual involvement may be called enlightenment, there seems to be no cogent reason for rejecting the claim that in Christian philosophy one finds philosophy itself enlightened by faith. But it is light of belief, not of evidence.

5. G. K. Chesterton, *George Bernard Shaw* (New York: John Lane Company, 1909), p. 176. Text supra, chap. 4, n. 19.

In regard to the first question faced in this epilogue, therefore, an affirmative answer should be sufficiently apparent from the work that Christian philosophy can do. As in the case of the arts, mentioned at the beginning of this discussion, it can help very effectively to drive home the appeal of Christian teaching. In the twenties and thirties of the present century the writings of Chesterton and Belloc and Gilson and Maritain flashed into public view the eminent intelligibility of Christian truth, in face of a self-labeled "rationalism" that had dominated western thought during the preceding two hundred years. In this regard their writings were a stirring challenge, especially to the Catholic youth of that period. In corresponding fashion, a solid Christian philosophy is able at any time to provide the intellectual assurance and stamina that enable believers to hold their heads high in the forum of world debate. Today, especially after the unsettling theological turmoil of the last three decades, the quiet and deep and firm assurance to be expected from this type of thinking should play a stabilizing role that is more than welcome. The work is clear and important, and is a task for philosophers. Surely a vigorous Christian philosophy is something well worth striving towards.

The second question posed in this epilogue bore upon the manner in which Christian philosophy may be pursued today. In that regard the lessons of the Bréhier debate are truly fundamental. Well along in the further progress of the controversy a participant observed that Bréhier himself had soon been forgotten and that the discussion about the nature of Christian philosophy had been carried on by Catholic writers in terms of their own principles and positions.[6] The wisdom of this tactic may be questioned. No matter how the future development of Christian philosophy in itself is to proceed, the basic manner in which its nature or possibility was originally challenged can ill afford to let itself be forgotten. In initiating a debate that has lasted so long, Bréhier may be expected to have reasoned on deep foundations and to have laid down clearly the outlines within which the

---

6. "In the controversies which followed, M. Bréhier was forgotten and Catholic philosophers directed their efforts to resolving the problem from principles of their own philosophy and defending their own positions." David A. Dillon, "The Nature of Christian Philosophy," *Proceedings of the American Catholic Philosophical Association* 27 (1953), 156. But the topic has not suffered from overexposure at the ACPA meetings. There were two group discussions, *Proceedings* 12 (1936), 17–45, and 27 (1953), 156–68. The *Index 1926–65* lists 17 entries s.v. "Christian Philosophy." Since then there have been papers in 41 (1967), 221–29 (Cudahy); 53 (1979), 5–15 (Bourke) and 36–44 (Morkovsky); and 54 (1980), 126–34 (McCool). There are also a note in 53 (1979), 3–4 (Wojtyla) and an "Abstract" in 55 (1981), 171 (Dinan).

continuation of the discussion would be predetermined. A comprehensive grasp of what his positions involved has, in consequence, a role that can be considered indispensable for mapping out the way in which the pursuit of Christian philosophy may best be undertaken at the present time. The basic issues are thereby brought into focus.

Striking in themselves, and far-reaching from the viewpoint of method, are the stark contrasts set out by Bréhier in lucidly penetrating terms for his two conceptions of Christian philosophy. In the first conception, Christian philosophy is an assemblage of dogmatic assertions that has been accepted by a magisterium, the formal magisterium in the Catholic church and whatever corresponds to it in the other Christian churches.[7] For him this was the only Christian philosophy that has ever existed in historical fact. As a collection it was considered by him to be entirely arbitrary. It had no genuinely philosophic character or binding links. The conclusion follows that this sole historical type of Christian philosophy exhibits nothing whatsoever of authentically philosophic interest. In Bréhier the contrast with the Christian perspective was that stark. No place at all was allowed for consistency or adhesion based on the firm and definite belief with which the Christian philosopher approaches his subject matter, a deeply inherent belief that, according to the faith, springs from supernaturally infused grace. This virtue of faith gives full assurance, though without intrinsic evidence, that the revealed doctrines are factually true. They have the infinite divine wisdom and truth as their source, their measure and their guarantee. They are strictly regulated by that norm. There is nothing arbitrary about the way they are included and grouped in the deposit of the faith. They have always constituted for Christian tradition a wisdom that from start to finish could stand up face to face with any wisdom of human origin and come out on top in comparison. In spite of their apparently barbarous character at first sight, they shone out as eminently superior wisdom for the believing Christian. St. Paul (Colossians 2.8; I Corinthians 1.22–25) contrasted them with what the Greeks praised as philosophy. Though foolishness from the Greek viewpoint, they offered a wisdom wiser than any human achievement. In similar vein they were seen by Tatian as "our philosophy," even though, insofar as this wisdom was non-Greek, it was open to the label "barbarian." In that spirit he saw

7. "Autant dans le catholicisme que dans toute confession chrétienne, il y a, je crois, ce qu'on appelle un magistère, qui dit ce qui est chrétien et ce qui ne l'est pas." Émile Bréhier, "La notion de philosophie chrétienne," *Bulletin de la Société française de Philosophie* 31 (1931), 50.

it originating in Moses, thereby ranking it in seniority with Homer.[8] The divinely revealed truths were given the prestige and dignity that the honored notion of philosophy had enjoyed in Greek tradition. In spite of their drastic deviation from the spirit of Greek thought, they were regarded from the earliest days of Christianity as bearing the stamp of true wisdom. In Bréhier's outline of the problem the same contrast, with reversed empathy, is brought to bear upon the issue in its sheerest form. In his perspective this Christian philosophy, the only kind of Christian philosophy that has ever existed in reality, cannot be philosophy at all. The reason is that it bears upon an object entirely arbitrary, an object without any philosophical consistency or any intrinsic evidence for its assertions.[9] The basic contrast is made fully that stark.

The stand that what was originally known as "Christian philosophy" was in fact the Christian kerygma is not subject to question. But what the Christian philosopher does reject is the claim that this kerygma is characterized by arbitrariness or uncertainty. For a Christian, the kerygma is solid truth, even though without intrinsic evidence. The kerygma, moreover, is not something abstract. It proclaims a way of life, a life of grace to be lived in the visible and tangible world. What it involves is a natural world raised to the supernatural level by grace. From the professedly Christian viewpoint, Christian philosophy faces an object that has both natural and supernatural facets. The natural facets are knowable with certainty by unaided reason. The supernatural facets are firmly believed to have factual truth and to be definitely determined by an infinite and infallible divine wisdom. Precisive abstraction of the supernatural aspect from the natural world would be regarding grace as though it were a substance in itself rather than as a qualification of the natural substance it elevates to the higher order. To be understood as the subject matter of Christian philosophy, the kerygma has to be taken as presenting one and the same object that has both natural and supernatural facets. Against the background sketched in Bréhier's outline, the contrasts of certainty, arbitrariness, knowledge, and faith become manifest in their sheerest opposition to each other. The challenge of putting them into their correct interrelation in the problem of Christian philosophy is highlighted. Could the issues be more graphically set?

8. Tatian, *Oratio ad graecos* 31.5–8; trans. Molly Whittaker (Oxford: Clarendon Press, 1982), p. 57. Cf. "the only sure and useful philosophy. Thus it is that I am now a philosopher." Justin Martyr, *Dialogue with Trypho* 8; trans. Thomas B. Falls, *Saint Justin Martyr* (New York: Christian Heritage, Inc., 1948), p. 160.

9. "quelque chose de tout à fait arbitraire." Bréhier, *Bulletin*, p. 50. Cf. supra, "Introduction," n. 11.

The lessons to be gleaned from reflection on Bréhier's first conception of Christian philosophy are surely clear enough from these considerations. First, the kerygma is what grounds the designation "Christian" in the phrase "Christian philosophy." Second, the kerygma is something that is believed. Abstracted precisely as such, it cannot at all be philosophy in today's academic acceptation of the term, for as believed it is not based on intrinsically evident premises. Third, the kerygma presents a way of life in which nature is elevated by grace. It requires that both the natural and supernatural facets receive appropriate consideration. The unitary object may be studied basically in the light of its supernatural aspects by sacred theology. It may also be studied in the light of its natural aspects by philosophy. Christian philosophy, in examining it under the natural facets, will look for the way naturally known aspects such as being, unity, truth, goodness, person, relation, and so on, can elucidate the truths that are believed. It will have to make plain that it is reasoning solely on the basis of those naturally known principles, principles that are intrinsically evident to the unaided mind. Use of revealed premises would make it sacred theology. In no way, however, can Christian philosophy regard itself as working on an object that is basically arbitrary and uncertain, à la Bréhier. Gilson was quick to point out, trenchantly, that Christian philosophy in Bréhier's first sense had never existed in fact.

The second of Bréhier's two ways of conceiving a Christian philosophy is as sharply etched as the first. It is the hypothetical case of a philosophy that would draw philosophic inspiration and truth from revealed sources. Bréhier showed that, in its alleged instances, the sources had been in fact attained in purely philosophical fashion. The implication was that philosophy by its very essence excluded Christian influence. In consequence no philosophy could ever be Christian in character. The indispensable requirement of naturally known premises only was thereby emphasized. It is a requirement that was unhesitatingly insisted upon by both Gilson and Maritain in the original debate.[10] Nevertheless, for them it did not prevent a philosophy from

10. Texts supra, "Introduction," nn. 15 and 18; also chap. 4, n. 9. See *Bulletin*, pp. 39 (Gilson) and 59 (Maritain). From Bréhier's (*Bulletin*, pp. 50–52) viewpoint, whatever was rational in the Christian doctrine of the *Logos* belonged to philosophy only. It did not belong to the "histoire mystérieuse" in which revelation consisted. This simplified the question magnificently for his second and hypothetical conception of Christian philosophy. By the very fact that something was rational it did not belong to the "histoire mystérieuse" and in consequence had a purely rational origin. It could not be part of an "inspiration positive" (p. 50) coming from revelation, as would be required for that hypothetical type of the philosophy. Bréhier's (p. 52) "séparation" of the two means that the notion of Christianity excludes philosophy, and that of philosophy excludes Christianity.

being essentially Christian in character when the selection of the starting points had been occasioned by Christian interests.

Here emerges a contrast as sheer as in the case of the kerygma. Bréhier, as noted above ("Introduction," nn. 35–37), was taking the essence of philosophy in precisive abstraction from its real existence, thereby excluding something very essential to it in actual fact. Excluded from consideration was the accidental character of the selection of its principles, together with the essential role played by those starting points in the specification of a philosophy. Just as for Aquinas nothing is more essential to a thing than its existence, which at least in material things is accidental, so for a philosophy the accidentally acquired starting points are utterly essential to it in its real existence.[11] From the viewpoint of real existence the dichotomy "accidental, therefore not essential" does not necessarily hold. Rather, the Christian philosopher selects in naturally known things a set of starting points that essentially distinguishes a Christian philosophy from any other kind. For purposes of the debate, this disagreement in the way philosophy itself is to be taken is fundamental. It gives rise to diametrically opposed views on the possibility of a genuinely Christian philosophy. Moreover, since the selection of the starting points is accidental and varies with the individual, an essentially pluralistic conception of the entire philosophical enterprise is thereby rendered necessary. Christian philosophy, because it is philosophy, cannot be an exception. It will have to be pluralistic in character. What is essential to any philosophy is determined in one way by its precisively abstracted essence and also in another way by the accidental circumstances that determine the individual's starting points. These are different in every case.

From Bréhier's second, though hypothetical, conception in regard to a Christian philosophy, two really crucial considerations for the future course of the enterprise may be educed. First, what makes a philosophy essentially Christian does not consist in premises or inspiration derived from revealed doctrine. It consists in the set of naturally knowable starting points to which the interest of the kerygma leads. This guidance is accidental and extrinsic to philosophy as such, and is profoundly personal and existential. But it is a necessary requirement for any Christian philosophy that may be projected. Sec-

---

11. "[C]um nihil sit essentialius rei quam suum esse." Aquinas, *Scriptum super libros Sententiarum* 1.8.exp. 1ae partis textus; ed. Mandonnet, 1, 209. As a human *habitus*, a philosophy essentially requires starting points from which it is developed. These starting points are accidentally acquired, in accordance with the teaching and the reading to which the student happens to have been exposed.

ondly, and by the same token, Christian philosophy will have to be essentially pluralistic. There can be innumerably different groupings of starting points that can give rise to just as many different types of Christian philosophy. Christian philosophy can be Augustinian, Thomistic, Scotistic, Cartesian, Kantian (in the Maréchal sense, as in followers of Rahner and Lonergan), phenomenological, existentialist, analytic, and so on.[12] In a word, alongside the Christian source for specification, other determining characteristics arising from the individual philosopher's environment and education have to be allowed to play their role in the formation of his or her Christian philosophy.

These reflections, prompted by the original Bréhier debate, should make clear the framework for future progress in Christian philosophy. It will have to be a philosophy that bears upon a unitary integrated world. On the supernatural side, the deposit of faith to which a Christian gives credence is to be accepted as firm and unshakable, even though completely lacking in intrinsic evidence. Awareness of the all-pervasive leaven that gives supernatural qualification to the unitary object comes from faith only, and elucidation on that level is in the sphere of sacred theology. The philosophical reasoning is kept based on naturally known premises from start to finish. With that understanding, the foregoing discussions in this volume pursued their entire course. The type of intellectual treatment thereby involved is obviously different from sacred theology. It does not use revealed starting points for any demonstrations.

This framework indicates, moreover, that Christian philosophy should be carried on in solidarity with the way it has kept unfolding through the centuries, though with special emphasis today on a frankly overt pluralism. It may be pursued in the form of monographs and articles, conferences and oral instruction, in direct continuation

12. "Russian Christian Philosophy" has been used, without causing surprise by the double qualification, in Elias Denissoff, "The Russian Christian Philosophy of Man," *Proceedings, ACPA* 37 (1963), 228–32. On the Thomistic varieties, see Gerald A. McCool, "The Tradition of Saint Thomas in North America: At 50 Years," *The Modern Schoolman* 65 (1988), 185–206. "Although unrecognized, pluralism was in it from the start" (p. 189). Pascal and Gabriel Marcel may be regarded as existential in attitude. Analytic influence may be seen in David B. Burrell, *Knowing the Unknowable God: Ibn-Sina, Maimonides, Aquinas* (Notre Dame, IN: University of Notre Dame Press, 1986), presented as a work in "conceptual clarification" (pp. 1–18; 37) and in "grammar of divinity" (p. 2), though it is fully alert to the role played by "attitudes" (pp. 22–23). On possibilities for phenomenological approach, see Henry Duméry, *Phenomenology and Religion*, trans. Paul Barret (Berkeley and Los Angeles, 1975). "The only harm that could be done to the faith by this philosophic method would be if it proved that religious values were illusory and deluding." Duméry, p. 107. On the starting points for liberation philosophy, see Enrique Dussel, "Philosophy and Praxis," *Proceedings, ACPA* 54 (1980), 108–118; cf. supra, "Introduction," n. 29.

with the way it has developed from its patristic, medieval, and earlier modern sources. Overall coverages in the manner of the abundant tradition, from Sanseverino's *Elementa philosophiae christianae* to Gredt's *Elementa philosophiae aristotelico-thomisticae,* are still theoretically possible. But today's pluralism would render the preparation of newer ones difficult and their value questionable. The Christian philosophy itself, however, is there for all to see in its progress down the centuries. Whether the name "Christian" should be kept as the ordinary way of referring to it is relatively immaterial. *Aeterni Patris* could cover the whole topic without once using "Christian philosophy" in its text. In the past, "Christian philosophy" has not been the predominantly used designation. But a more apt one would be hard to find.

There is no danger whatever that this Christian philosophy will be confused today with theology, regardless of what its opponents may claim. No contemporary theologian would recognize it as theology as it is found, for instance, in Del Prado's *De veritate fundamentali philosophiae christianae* or in Gilson's *The Christian Philosophy of the Middle Ages* and *Elements of Christian Philosophy.* Works of this type lie manifestly outside today's theological field. The manner of treatment is too different even at first sight to allow any confusion. Though immersed in the wine of sacred theology during the patristic and medieval periods, the philosophical reasoning was kept firmly based upon naturally evident premises. This is what has allowed it to be detached from the theological matrix in later times and to be used independently for teaching philosophy. Today, however, the development upon the philosophical starting points is independent of theology from the start. In the middle ages the theological connection was an accident of the times. It led to the starting points, but did not affect the reasoning itself. The contrast is not thematically concerned with Christian philosophy going from what is under to what is above, while sacred theology proceeds from what is above to what is below. Still less is Christian philosophy trying to go in both directions at the same time. Rather, this philosophy is work of a markedly different character from theology. Christian philosophy does not try to prove or establish any dogmas. Taking the dogmas in the way they have been believed and handed down in the church, it merely seeks to elucidate them on the purely rational level, as far as that is possible. It does not reason to them.

Excluded by the framework that emerges in the Bréhier debate, therefore, are all attempts to use theological premises in Christian philosophy. In his coverage of those attempts, Nédoncelle asked how that type of thinking can "fail to be confused with theology pure and simple."[13] To the extent that it uses revealed premises, the reasoning is theological, not philosophical, in character. Likewise, the attempts to demonstrate on natural evidence the fallen state of human nature unwittingly rely on theology, as the analysis of the situation by Duns Scotus in his day showed.[14] A strict demonstration of fallen nature requires comparison with the state of grace, and accordingly has to take the premises for this from revelation. Further, attempts to reduce

13. Maurice Nédoncelle, *Is There a Christian Philosophy?* trans. Illtyd Trethowan (New York: Hawthorn Books, 1960), p. 103. Nédoncelle (p. 103) ranges Gilson in this grouping. Gilson (*Bulletin,* p. 39) insisted uncompromisingly that only naturally known premises were used by Christian philosophy and that the aspect of revelation belonged only to the object under consideration. The discourse itself is entirely philosophical, even though the motivation, like Anselm's desire to understand, is Christian. Nédoncelle (p. 149) distinguishes the type under which he classes Gilson from one that "is constituted under the indirect but avowed influence of Christianity." This latter presumably refers to a type that *"inherits from Christianity"* (p. 104) in residual fashion after the faith has been lost, quite like the painter who insists that his work is still Catholic even though he has ceased to believe in God. Be that as it may, the "avowed influence of Christianity" on Christian philosophy is certainly direct for Gilson, since Christian interest determines the selection of its starting points. Surely nothing could influence a philosophy more directly than that. Nédoncelle's basic notion of philosophy as "always more or less detached from events and from the subject considered simply as such" (p. 151) does not allow him to see that the accidental interest occasions the intrinsic specification of the philosophy itself. Similarly this failure to allow for the role of interest makes "a Christian philosophy" sound "as shocking as a Catholic geometry" (p. 55), in line with Bréhier's comparison to a Christian mathematics or a Christian physics, in "Y a-t-il une philosophie chrétienne?" *Revue de métaphysique et de morale* 38 (1931), 162, or Christian medicine (Brunschvicq, *Bulletin,* p. 76) or chemistry. There is no direct Christian interest for special sets of starting points in them. But philosophy has notions and principles that are transcendental in the sense of ranging through and above all the categories. These notions have keen interest for the Christian philosopher as a means of elucidating what he believes. But the concepts and principles of mathematics and of the sciences subalternated to it, as well as those of medicine and of the crafts that bear on material things, are restricted to the natural order. They do not offer direct interest in regard to what is specifically Christian. Fine arts do. Poetry, painting, architecture, and music find vivid themes in Christian life and doctrine. They readily allow the adjective "Christian." Also, history is an area where, as in philosophy, selection of starting points radically influences interpretation. This would indicate that Catholic university teaching in history and philosophy is open to doctrinal vigilance. Accordingly, where Christian interest directly occasions the selection of a distinct set of starting points, and in those areas only, is there question of a specifically Christian discipline. The answer to the query made classic by Bréhier is in that way factually clearcut and theoretically definite.

14. See supra, chap. 2. Avicenna, Scotus insisted, knew only as a theologian, and not as a philosopher, what the true object of the human intellect is. He mixed this revealed tenet with his philosophy, as Scotus saw the situation. Cf. today: "Philosophy is fully realized *only* when it has made contact with theology; only then is its project complete," Patrick Madigan, *Christian Revelation and the Completion of the Aristotelian Revolution* (Lanham, MD: University Press of America, 1988), p. 117. This *culmination* in theology is not the same as Gilson's requirement of Christianity's active role in selecting the *starting points* for Christian philosophy: "[I]l faut que le christianisme ait joué un rôle actif dans la constitution même de cette philosophie," *Bulletin,* p. 48.

Christian philosophy to a single monochromatic type are excluded by the innate pluralistic character of Christian philosophy.[15] Finally, the suggestion that Christian philosophy should be integrated with theology into a one inclusive Christian wisdom would seem to be setting the clock back to the epoch before philosophy was solidly reestablished as an independent academic discipline.[16]

15. Pluralism in Christian philosophy will usually follow one's concept of pluralism in philosophy as such. E.g.: "Non vi sono molte filosofie cristiane. Vi è una sola autentica filosofia cristiana come vi è una sola autentica filosofia umana." Luigi Bogliolo, *Il problema della filosofia cristiana* (Brescia: Morcelliana, 1959), p. 250. Bogliolo (pp. 252–55) recognizes a relative and factual plurality, with the multiplicity consisting in accentuation. Claude Tresmontant, *Christian Metaphysics,* p. 19, maintains "that there is *one* Christian philosophy and one only." On the import of this assertion, especially as not leading to a "single philosophical system," see Brian J. Cudahy, "Claude Tresmontant and 'Biblical Metaphysics,'" *Proceedings, ACPA* 41 (1967), 222. Cf.: "There will only be one philosophy when all men are agreed about truth. Meanwhile there are many philosophies." Tresmontant, *The Origins of Christian Philosophy,* trans. Mark Pontifex (New York: Hawthorn Books, 1963), p. 15. Where the thought proceeds from the one starting point of subsistent existence, as in the beatific vision, it may be expected to be thoroughly unitary. But where it proceeds from a number of different sets of starting points, as in philosophy, it will be radically different in different philosophers in accordance with the difference in those principles. Christian philosophy can hardly expect to be an exception, as long as it remains genuinely philosophy. Yet Tresmontant speaks of "a Christian philosophy, which has its own structure principles and theories forming an harmonious and original system" (p. 15), "radically and fundamentally different" and "utterly opposed" to the secular philosophies. The fact is, however, that people are built differently. What appeals to one may not appeal to another, and the philosophy best in itself is not necessarily best for a particular individual. But the opposite view has been strongly upheld: "the affirmation of a specifically Catholic philosophy, which is the only true philosophy" Robert F. Harvanek, "The Church and Scholasticism," *Proceedings, ACPA* 32 (1958), 221. "[P]hilosophical pluralism is fine for teachers of philosophy but not for students." Rocco E. Porreco, "Philosophical Pluralism and the Teaching of Philosophy," *Proceedings, ACPA* 37 (1963), 158. A detailed discussion of the pluralism in Christian philosophy may be found in Duilio Bonifazi, *Filosofia e cristianesimo* (Rome: Università Lateranense, 1968), 76–148.

16. "Let us put the question of Christian philosophy back into place as part of the question of Christian wisdom." Mark D. Jordan, "The Terms of the Debate over 'Christian Philosophy,'" *Communio* (Notre Dame), 12 (1985), 310. The specter that hangs over this suggestion, however, is the Neoscholastic experience of a theological order imposed upon philosophy. Cf. "Let us admit that a theologically managed philosophy—philosophy used and shaped by the theologian in his world and for his purposes—is not philosophy." Anton Pegis, *St. Thomas and Philosophy* (Milwaukee: Marquette University Press, 1964), p. 39. From what has been seen in the foregoing pages, rational thinking done in theological work is theology. Its nature as philosophical will be enervated by attempts to reproduce it independently in the same theological order. To be genuinely philosophy, it has to be presented as developed from its philosophical starting points in the order and method they demand when considered in themselves. But in that context it will have to be recognized as one's own thought, and not that of the theologian. See Pegis, pp. 85–89. Only in keeping carefully separate the two ways of developing the thought can there be agreement with the stand that "the philosophy of St. Thomas, like that of all great Christian theologians, lives simultaneously in its own house and in that of sacred theology." James F. Anderson, "Was St. Thomas a Philosopher?" *The New*

Still far from proven is the allegation that Leo XIII's *Aeterni Patris* was wrong in gauging the temper of its era or the needs for the future. After the triumphalistic sweep of Thomism from the twenties through the fifties of the present century, the *Aggiornamento* under Pope John XXIII seemed to reduce the role of philosophy in the church to almost negligible proportions. Yet good work in Christian philosophy has continued to appear, though with a notably more modest mien. Much confusion has followed in the wake of the *Aggiornamento*, with increasing consciousness of the need for more control. Solid Christian philosophy here provides the desired order on the intellectual level. Today it will be frankly pluralistic in action. But even Leo's encyclical recognized the roles of Augustine, Bonaventure, and Albert along with Thomas Aquinas. However, the intent of the encyclical was deliberately to give the primacy to Aquinas.

Yet what is best in itself need not be best for every individual. Wide choice is accordingly in order. But even on Thomism's place there is still no final proof that *Aeterni Patris* was not feeling the pulse of the times correctly. The philosophic pluralism does not rule out the possibility that one philosophy may on the whole serve the desired purposes better than any other. Rather, in full accord with the spirit of Aristotelian focal meaning, a primary instance is required for giving the pluralism its overall unity. This does not deprive the other instances of their own intrinsic worth, nor does it keep each from seeing itself as the primary instance on the basis of its own starting points. For some people Thomism has little or no appeal, while other philosophies attract them. In consequence, the top place given Thomism in the encyclical need not keep the other philosophies from being notably helpful and sincerely welcome. At the far end of the spectrum, of course, will lie types of extreme materialism and monism that do not lend themselves in any general way to the elucidation of revealed Christian truth. In particular insights, though, they may have appreciated help to offer, for no general philosophy is without its own indigenous merits.

By careful study of the Bréhier debate, then, the guidelines for work towards a Christian philosophy become reasonably clear. First, in order to remain genuinely *philosophy*, Christian philosophy can use only naturally knowable premises in its reasoning. Both sides in the original Bréhier debate were in solid agreement on that. Otherwise you would have theology, not philosophy. Second, Christian philosophy has to be

---

Scholasticism 38 (1964), 441. Jordan, though, cannot be too adverse to a factual pluralism of the philosophy as philosophy, for he is keenly sensitive (p. 299) to the fact that the opponents in the Christian philosophy debate do not agree about philosophy itself.

positively and intrinsically shaped by direct influence of the Christian kerygma. Otherwise it would not be specifically *Christian* philosophy. Anything less than positive and direct influence will not suffice. The negative condition of not being against Christian doctrine, and the indirect influence through previous formation of the Christian thinker's mind, are not enough. Both of those conditions leave the philosophy specifically what it was in its original sources, as Bréhier showed in examining the cases of Neoplatonic influence on Christian thinkers. Taken just that way, the philosophy used remained specifically Neoplatonic and did not become Christian. Only the direct influence of the kerygma in the selection of a radically new set of starting points in naturally knowable things can explain the coming into being of Christian philosophy as an authentically new type of philosophical thinking.

Finally, and by way of a parting note, any hostility complex should be banned from work towards a Christian philosophy. The real situation need not be regarded as one in which a pinched nerve is continually causing pain in an otherwise normal philosophic undertaking. Yet Christianity and philosophy have been called a reciprocal purgatory for each other. Discomfort and suffering have been marked as the lot of those who seek cooperation of the two in a Christian philosophy. The situation faced by the Christian philosopher has been labeled paradoxical and "difficult."[17] Yet, functioning strictly on the

17. "Philosophy and Christianity are each a sort of purgatory for the other;" Nédoncelle, p. 116. Christian philosophy has to pass through a purgatory that is "first proposed to it from outside" (p. 117). Maritain suggested, good-humoredly, that "the christian philosopher is in an uncomfortable position" and "he suffers for it." *Science and Wisdom*, trans. Bernard Wall (London: G. Bles, Centenary Press, 1940), p. 94. History does in fact record conflicts, as surveyed by Gilson, *Bulletin*, pp. 41–43, or by Roger Mehl, *The Condition of the Christian Philosopher*, trans. Eva Kushner (London: J. Clarke, 1963), pp. 9–32. But the joys of cooperation throughout the centuries as seen in Augustine, Aquinas and so many others, far outweigh any pains of disagreement. If eschatological symbolism is to be used, complacency from a triumphalism in the presentation of Christian philosophy is more to be dreaded than the prospect of penitential encounter between revealed truth and philosophical integrity. Mehl (p. 208) finds the Christian philosopher in a "difficult condition," because he moves in a universe with dimensions of both eternity and time, "where being is given while becoming is not yet abolished" (p. 210). In regard to these difficulties and fears one may remark that today's pluralistic atmosphere in philosophy is amenable to wide variety in notions and attitudes, and calls for humility and tolerance in recognizing how differently people are constituted. In contradistinction to relativism, this pluralistic conception allows Christian philosophy to assert truth definitely, but with the reason why in each case. It thereby avoids the pejorative and derogatory stigmas associated with the notion of dogmatism. Worth noting is the fact that the autonomy and specific distinction of Christian philosophy arise from the same source as its pluralism. The source is the radical involvement of Christian interest, which is highly personal. The unity so given pervades its pluralism. In this very precise sense, Mehl's (p. 209) penetrating comment is acceptable: "Thus,

philosophical level, Christian philosophy is neither polemical nor apologetic. Its purpose is to understand. The strengthening and stabilizing influence it exercises follows upon that understanding. But, as in the case of any understanding, this requires a tranquil mind.[18] With goodwill on both sides, the cooperation of Christianity with philosophy turns out to be exceptionally friendly and thoroughly pleasant, in the natural exercise of the highest human faculty upon its highest object in the widest range. The task and the privilege of Christian philosophy is to impart natural understanding at its best.

At the beginning of the *Cur deus homo* (1.1; ed. Schmitt, *Op. Om.* 2, 48.16–18) Anselm, in accord with the scriptural admonition (I Peter 3–5) about the readiness to give a reason for the hope that faith grounds, set out on an effort to understand what he believed. In that work he proceeded from the viewpoint of the revealed doctrines themselves in their harmonious interrelation. In the *Proslogion* (2; 1, 100.15–18), instead of entering into the doctrines through believed tenets, he wished to reason solely from premises open to the unbeliever. These aimed at conviction on the strength of their own innate evidence, by showing an irreconcilable contradiction in their opposites. In quite similar fashion Christian philosophy, in all its centuries-long development, endeavors to understand to the limited extent of its ability, and as it were from the outside, the sublime truths that the Christian heart believes and loves.

---

the nature of Christian philosophy will be grasped, not by examining doctrines and systems, but by visualizing the Christian philosopher's spiritual condition." Shortly after (p. 210) "the nature" is sharpened by "the specific character" as the translation for the French spécificité, *La condition de la philosophie chrétienne* (Paris: Delachaux & Niestlé, 1947), p. 198, while "spiritual condition" is explained by "existential situation." The importance of "existential" in this context should be apparent from what has been seen supra, "Introduction," nn. 17–22.

18. "[D]octrina debet esse in tranquillitate." Aquinas, *Lectura super evangelium S. Joannis* 13.3.1; ed. Vivès, *Op. om.* 20, 209 (Marietti no. 1770). Cf. "in tranquillitate quadam mentis," *Quaestiones disputatae de malo* 12.1.210–212; ed. Leonine, *Op. om.* 23, 235b.

Index